Adrienne Rich

Recent Titles in
Contributions in Women's Studies

The Dress of Women: A Critical Introduction to the Symbolism and Sociology of Clothing
Charlotte Perkins Gilman, Michael R. Hill, and Mary Jo Deegan

Frances Trollope and the Novel of Social Change
Brenda Ayres, editor

Women among the Inklings: Gender, C.S. Lewis, J.R.R. Tolkien, and Charles Williams
Candice Fredrick and Sam McBride

The Female Body: Perspectives of Latin American Artists
Raysa E. Amador Gómez-Quintero and Mireya Pérez Bustillo

Women of Color: Defining the Issues, Hearing the Voices
Diane Long Hoeveler and Janet K. Boles, editors

The Poverty of Life-Affirming Work: Motherwork, Education, and Social Change
Mechthild U. Hart

The Bleeding of America: Menstruation as Symbolic Economy in Pynchon, Faulkner, and Morrison
Dana Medoro

Negotiating Identities in Women's Lives: English Postcolonial and Contemporary British Novels
Christine Wick Sizemore

Women in Iran: Gender Politics in the Islamic Republic
Hammed Shahidian

Women in Iran: Emerging Voices in the Women's Movement
Hammed Shahidian

Rebecca West: Heroism, Rebellion, and the Female Epic
Bernard Schweizer

Adventures Abroad: North American Women at German-Speaking Universities, 1868–1915
Sandra L. Singer

Adrienne Rich

The Moment of Change

CHERI COLBY LANGDELL

Contributions in Women's Studies, Number 198

Westport, Connecticut
London

Library of Congress Cataloging-in-Publication Data

Langdell, Cheri Colby.
Adrienne Rich : the moment of change / Cheri Colby Langdell.
p. cm.—(Contributions in women's studies, ISSN 0147–104X ; no. 198)
Includes bibliographical references and index.
1. Rich, Adrienne Cecile—Criticism and interpretation. 2. Women and literature—United States—History—20th century. I. Title. II. Series.
PS3535.I233Z75 2004
811'.54—dc22 2003026476

British Library Cataloguing in Publication Data is available.

Library of Congress Catalog Card Number: 2003026476
ISBN: 0–313–31605–8
ISSN: 0147–104X

First published in 2004

Praeger Publishers, 88 Post Road West, Westport, CT 06881
An imprint of Greenwood Publishing Group, Inc.
www.praeger.com

Printed in the United States of America

The paper used in this book complies with the Permanent Paper Standard issued by the National Information Standards Organization (Z39.48–1984).

10 9 8 7 6 5 4 3 2 1

Copyright Acknowledgments

Unless otherwise noted all translations are the author's.

For Mary, Tim, Melissa, Sebastian

The moment of change is the only poem.

—Adrienne Rich

What would it mean to stand on the first page of the end of despair?

—Adrienne Rich

[D]o not think that when I speak as one who knows with certainty that I do not also doubt.

—Cžeslaw Milosž

We therefore have a primary obligation to each other: not to undermine each others' sense of reality for the sake of expediency.

—Adrienne Rich

What we see, we see, and seeing is changing.

—Adrienne Rich

Contents

Acknowledgments

I wish to acknowledge and thank a number of colleagues and mentors whose work has served both as help and beacon to me in preparing this book, especially Camille Roman, Cynthia Hogue, Cristanne Miller, Rachel Blau DuPlessis, Sandra Gilbert, Susan Gubar, and Sabine Sielke. I acknowledge the untiring efforts of the archival and research librarians at Stanford University, California Baptist University, the Young Research Library at the University of California at Los Angeles, particularly Miki Girol and Norma Corral, and the New York Public Library.

I am also grateful for the assistance of Barbara Charlesworth Gelpi and Albert Gelpi, Cecelia Moore, who was kind enough to read drafts of the manuscript and offer constructive suggestions for improvement along with encouragement, and especially to Steve Axelrod, Professor of English and of Teaching Excellence at the University of California, Riverside, who has generously offered invaluable advice and persistent encouragement and has read it all. Great gratitude goes out as well to the Occidental College Writers' Group, especially to Professors Mary Elizabeth Perry, who read it all, and Deborah Martinson. I also thank the Occidental College Reference Librarians Michelle Jacobs and Mike Sutherland for their swift, kind help. Certainly, too, the very helpful team at Impressions Book and Journal Services, Inc., deserves praise for their careful, sustained attention to every detail of the manuscript.

In addition, this book would not have been completed without the able assistance beyond the call of duty of Barbara Holohan, former head librarian, and Barry Parker, Karen Davidson, Erica McLaughlin, and Charlotte Sandoval, librarians at California Baptist University, and Victoria Bauer-Koch, formerly a librarian there; nor could I have completed the manuscript without the attentive reading and editorial help of my academic colleagues in the English Department there and the encouragement of Drs. Dawn Ellen Jacobs and James Lu. I also thank Eileen Mobley and others who wish to remain anonymous but who have helped immeasurably; I acknowledge the ways they have shaped my life through their integrity, passion, and character. My gratitude goes out to others—like Eva, Sammie, Maggie, and Carmen—who have always been there for me. Without the invaluable help of my husband, Tim, this book might never have been written. Finally, I dedicate this book to my intelligent, insightful children, Melissa and Sebastian, engaged, careful scholars of the twenty-first century.

A Note to the Reader

This book is designed to be read in accompaniment with volumes of Adrienne Rich's poetry and prose: the commentary is best understood when readers read the poetry for themselves along with this analysis.

Abbreviations

Citations for all primary sources appear directly in the text together with page numbers. The following abbreviations have been used:

A	*An Atlas of the Difficult World*
AR	*Arts of the Possible*
ARP	*Adrienne Rich's Poetry and Prose* (Norton Critical Edition, 1993)
ARP1	*Adrienne Rich's Poetry* (Norton Critical Edition, 1975)
B	*Blood, Bread, and Poetry*
CEP	*Collected Early Poems*
CW	*A Change of World*
D	*Dark Fields of the Republic*
DC	*The Dream of a Common Language*
DI	*The Diamond Cutters and Other Poems*
DW	*Diving into the Wreck*
F	*Fox*
FD	*The Fact of a Doorframe*
L	*Leaflets*
LS	*On Lies, Secrets, and Silence*
MS	*Midnight Salvage*
N	*Necessities of Life*
OWB	*Of Woman Born*
PS	*Poems: Selected and New, 1950–1974*
S	*Snapshots of a Daughter-in-Law*
SO	*Sources*
T	*Time's Power*

WC	*The Will to Change*
WF	*What Is Found There*
WH	*Women and Honor: Some Notes on Lying*
WP	*A Wild Patience Has Taken Me This Far*
YNL	*Your Native Land, Your Life*

Chronology

1929 Born in Baltimore, Maryland, May 16. Began writing poetry as a child with the encouragement and under the supervision of her father, Arnold Rich, in whose "very Victorian, pre-Raphaelite" library, Rich recalls, she read Tennyson, Keats, Arnold, Blake, Rossetti, Swinburne, Carlyle, and Pater, among others.

1951 A. B., Radcliffe College. *A Change of World,* chosen by W. H. Auden for the Yale Younger Poets Award.

1952–53 Guggenheim Fellowship to travel in Europe and England and write poetry. Onset of rheumatoid arthritis.

1953 Marriage to Alfred H. Conrad, an economist teaching at Harvard. Residence in Cambridge, Massachusetts, 1953–1966.

1955 Birth of David Conrad. *The Diamond Cutters and Other Poems.* Ridgley Torrence Memorial Award of the Poetry Society of America.

1957 Birth of Paul Conrad.

1959 Birth of Jacob Conrad.

1960 National Institute of Arts and Letters Award for poetry.

1961–62 Guggenheim Fellowship; resides with family in the Netherlands.

1962 Bollingen Foundation grant for translation of Dutch poetry.

1962–63 Amy Lowell Traveling Fellowship. Member of the Academy of American Poets.

1963 *Snapshots of a Daughter-in-Law: Poems 1954–1962.* Bess Hokin Prize of *Poetry Magazine.*

1966 *Necessities of Life: Poems 1962–1965.* Moves with family to New York City. Active politically in protests against the Viet Nam War.

1967 *Selected Poems* published in Great Britain. Honorary doctorate, Wheaton College. Orthopedic surgery for arthritis.

1967–69 Lecturer, Swarthmore College. Adjunct Professor, Writing Division, Columbia University School of Arts. More involved in protests against the war in Vietnam.

1968 Begins teaching in SEEK program at City College of New York and continues 1968–72 and 1974–75. Eunice Tietjens Memorial Prize, *Poetry Magazine.* Death of Arnold Rich.

1969 *Leaflets: Poems 1965–1968.*

1970 Death of Alfred Conrad.

1971 *The Will to Change: Poems 1968–1970.* Shelley Memorial Award, The Poetry Society of America. Increasingly identifies with the women's liberation movement.

1972–73 Hurst Visiting Professor of Creative Writing, Brandeis University.

1973 *Diving into the Wreck: Poems 1971–1973.*

1974 *Diving into the Wreck* wins the National Book Award, but she declines to accept it individually, preferring to accept it on behalf of all women and in conjunction with the two other women poets nominated, African-American poets Audre Lorde and Alice Walker. Professor of English, City College of New York.

1975 *Adrienne Rich's Poetry*, edited by Barbara Charlesworth Gelpi and Albert Gelpi (Norton Critical Edition). *Poems: Selected and New, 1950–1974.* Lucy Martin Donnelley Fellow, Bryn Mawr College.

1976 *Of Woman Born: Motherhood as Experience and Institution. Twenty-One Love Poems.* Begins lifelong partnership with Michelle Cliff. Delivers the "It Is the Lesbian in Us" speech at a meeting of the Modern Language Association.

1976–79 Professor of English, Douglass College, Rutgers University.

1978 *The Dream of a Common Language: Poems 1974–1977.* Becomes nationally known for her germinal writings in women's studies.

1979 *On Lies, Secrets, and Silence: Selected Prose 1966–1978.* Honorary doctorate, Smith College. Moves to Montague, Massachusetts.

1980 Orthopedic surgery for rheumatoid arthritis.

1981 *A Wild Patience Has Taken Me This Far: Poems 1978–1981.* Fund for Human Dignity Award, National Gay Task Force.

1981–83 Co-edits *Sinister Wisdom,* a lesbian/feminist journal.

1981–87 A. D. White Professor-at-Large, Cornell University.

1982 Orthopedic surgery for arthritis.

1983 *Sources.*

1983–84 Visiting Professor, Scripps College, Claremont, California.

1984 *The Fact of a Doorframe: Poems Selected and New 1950–1984.* Moves to Santa Cruz, California, a vibrant liberal artistic community.

1984–86 Distinguished Visiting Professor, San Jose State University.

1986 *Your Native Land, Your Life: Poems. Blood, Bread, and Poetry: Selected Prose 1979–1985. Of Woman Born,* 10th Anniversary Edition. Ruth Lilly Poetry Prize.

1986–93 Professor of English, Stanford University.

1987 Honorary doctorate, College of Wooster, Ohio. Honorary doctorate, Brandeis University, Brandeis Creative Arts Medal in Poetry.

1989 *Time's Power: Poems 1985–1988.* Marjorie Kovler Fellow, University of Chicago. National Poetry Association Award for Distinguished Service to the Art of Poetry. Elmer Holmes Bobst Award in Arts and Letters, New York University.

1990 Honorary doctorate, City College of New York. Honorary doctorate, Harvard University. Bay Area Book Reviewers Award in Poetry. Member, Department of Literature, American Academy and Institute of Arts and Letters. Member of the founding editorial group of *Bridges: A Journal for Jewish Feminists and Our Friends.*

1991 *An Atlas of the Difficult World: Poems 1988–1991.* The Commonwealth Award in Literature.

1991–92 Honorary doctorate, Swarthmore College. Robert Frost Silver Medal Award of the Poetry Society of America. William Whitehead Award of the Publishing Triangle for lifetime achievement in letters. *An Atlas of the Difficult World* receives the *Los Angeles Times* Book Award in Poetry and the Lenore Marshall/*Nation* Award. Julia Arden Conrad, grandchild, born. Charles Reddington Conrad, grandchild, born.

1992 Spinal surgery.

1993 *Collected Early Poems, 1950–1970. What Is Found There: Notebooks on Poetry and Politics. An Atlas of the Difficult World* awarded the Poet's Prize.

1994 MacArthur Fellowship and Award, "Genius Grant."

1995 *Dark Fields of the Republic: Poems 1991–1995.* Lammy Award for Lesbian Poetry for *Dark Fields of the Republic.*

1996 Edits controversial *The Best American Poetry, 1996.* Awarded Tanning Prize for Mastery of Poetry by Academy of American Poets. Appointed a Chancellor of the Academy of American Poets.

1997 Wins the National Medal for the Arts, but declines it, protesting against the House of Representatives' vote to end the National Endowment for the Arts and other policies of the Clinton administration regarding the arts generally and literature in particular. She criticizes the Clinton administration's attitudes toward the poor, the welfare system, people of divergent lifestyles, and toward federal funding of the arts and literature.

1999 *Midnight Salvage: Poems 1995–1998.*

2001 *The Art of the Possible.* Supports the Clark Kissinger international campaign to free Mumia Abu-Jamal, signing a letter, along with Michelle Cliff, Barbara Kingsolver, Grace Paley, and Susan Brownmiller, to protest his and Mumia's imprisonment. Is a judge for numerous book and poetry awards. *Fox, Poems 1998–2000.*

2002 Anti-war activities, protests against threat of war in Iraq. Reads at the Hayden Carreuth Memorial Reading in New York City and elsewhere throughout the United States as well as serving as a judge for literary awards and prizes. Appointed a chancellor of the newly augmented board of the Academy of American Poets, along with Yusef Komunyakaa, Lucille Clifton, Jay Wright (who declined the honor, refusing to serve), Louise Gluck, Heather McHugh, Rosanna Warren, Charles Wright, Robert Creeley, and Michael Palmer.

2003 Anti-war protests and poetry readings. Reads in northern and southern California and elsewhere. Winner of the 2003 Yale Bollingen Prize for American Poetry and applauded by the panel of judges for her "honesty at once ferocious, humane, her deep learning, and her continuous poetic exploration and awareness of multiple selves." Participates on February 12 with W. S. Merwin, Lawrence Ferlinghetti, and Stanley Kunitz in the National Day of Poetry against the War, the same day on which Laura Bush's now-cancelled literary symposium on "Poetry and the American Voice" was to have occurred. Reads in April at Barnard College and Columbia University, drawing a large loyal crowd and praise from students and the president of Barnard. *What is Found There,* 2nd ed. Teaches in summer poetry program at Connecticut College. Has poems included in *Christmas at the New Yorker,* a compendium of wit, poetry, and fiction.

2004 *The School among the Ruins, Poems 2000–2004,* due to be published in the autumn.

Chapter 1

Introduction: A Woman Sworn to Lucidity

The one constant in Adrienne Rich's poetry has been change and successive self-transformation. Her poetry refreshes and renews itself constantly. Rich crafts poems for those who are reading, writing, thinking, and desiring social change. The poem "And Now," called her own *Ars Poetica,* clearly says that the reader is not to think that she is trying to state a case or construct a scenery[1] in her poetry. Instead she says she has tried to hear the country's public voice and to record in poetry and prose what is real in our culture and politics. The poetry attempts to survey our public space. Rich is a poet whose work reflects the public voice of America while surveying our public space (*D* 31), recording American public consciousness and the zeitgeist. Exactly how she has accomplished this representation of the public voice is the focus of this book. Rich affirms that we should bear in mind that she has always attempted to record everything accurately, and her poetry marks, metaphorically speaking, what time it is in America, and who coined and who received the definitions, as well as—assessing the political tempo of her time, those who defined what is true and what is not for the time, and Americans' collective identity (*D* 31)—embodies the American zeitgeist, particularly as it impacts American women and political culture. This critical study of Rich's poetry and prose seeks to clarify and comment on the poetry; it is for those who wish to understand her poetry as a provocation to think more clearly about life, poetry, gender, and the body as they relate to the American body politic—and possibly to *act* as a result of what is read, since "The moment of change is the only poem" (*WC* 49).

Although Rich's primary mission is poetic, she is an original critic and gifted writer of nonfiction and critical theory; her reputation may be based ultimately as much on her prose as on her excellence in poetry. Naming her one of America's most original contemporary poets, Fred Moramarco claims she is "surely the most engaged, politically oriented poet writing today."[2] One of America's most outspoken poets, she writes an acutely conscious poetry and is celebrated in America and internationally, both for her extraordinary range and verbal dexterity as a theorist and critic, and also for her courage in speaking out against injustice in the United States and worldwide. These qualities have earned her the kind of international political following few American poets enjoy.

Throughout her poetic career, Adrienne Rich has explored her ideas and feelings about womanhood and female roles, about the use of the will and creative intelligence to accomplish global change by re-visioning the world from a new perspective, and about the need for struggle to accomplish social change at every level. Rich has been critical of traditional concepts of sex, gender stereotyping, and the body; she has contributed to an alteration in global consciousness.

For too long, she feels, women have been estranged from their creative female selfhood. At the beginning of her transformation into a radical poet, she refers to herself as a member of a new generation of women writers creating new work from the "psychic" energy being generated by women's movement toward what was being called the "'new space' on the boundaries of patriarchy" (*FD* 176). Along with other poets of her generation, she has reformed her poetry and now writes as a poet and political activist. Through the lens of her poetry, one sees reality as having a constant potential for transformation. Even if one feels stuck as a boat in winter ice, one can change one's attitude: the mind transforms reality just as wood can in seconds burst into flames. Changing by reconstructing the mind and reforming the self to craft an original poetry of witness, transformation, and excavation of feminine identity are chief goals of Rich's poetry: she shows readers that, among other things, poetry can and must be a force for social, even political, change.

Sometimes writing in the oracular tradition of the visionary poets Walt Whitman and Emily Dickinson, Rich affirms the will to change as a lifelong commitment in her life and poetry, where "[s]*elf-consciousness becomes the dramatic vehicle for self-definition*" (*ARP* 343). Resisting the traditional feminine refuges of passivity, conformity, resignation to conventional societal or sex roles in life, Rich strives to awaken her readers, to challenge threadbare conformist assumptions, and to offer them creative new perspectives on subjectivities and identities they had previously not considered. Although her focus has changed in recent years from radical feminism to a more moderate Marxism, questioning every assumption, she shows her readers how women can achieve success as thinkers and leaders in all professions.

Until now we have had no up-to-date, comprehensive study of Adrienne Rich's strikingly original work, although she is a poet whom the distinguished scholar Camille Roman has recently called "one of this century's major canonical poets."[3] "Arguably one of America's finest and most important contemporary writers of any genre, Adrienne Rich has been a figure of excellence and political integrity for her entire long career."[4] Her career, Charles Altieri reminds us, has displayed "exemplary acts of self-definition" (*ARP* 343) and reveals new possibilities for poetic growth and evolution in the succession of poetic transformations in her poetry. This book covers the entire progression of her poetry and prose from the beginning through her most recent books; it aims to clarify all Rich's poetry, her various subject positions and self-fashionings, her concepts of nationhood, the female body, power, and women's sexuality. She writes analytical, consciously political poetry for a range of readers of all races, genders, nationalities, and political persuasions. I have pulled together the best literary, theoretical, and cultural scholarship on her work, reconciling the best criticism with my own insights into the poetry.

This book explores the ways she integrates women poets' call for integrity and full citizenship in the American canon, giving women's experience and oppression materiality in the text. Altieri says that "her explicit themes" must be read "on two levels: as particular responses to woman's plight in our time and as instances of general human concerns for identity and community" (*ARP* 344). Thus, whatever she writes about can be read as pertaining to all humanity as well as to the female audience assumed; she intends the reader to grasp the universal meanings in her work as well as the specifics. Her poetry *is* her politics, so she establishes an intimate "I/you" relationship with her reader, speaking calmly yet inquiringly so he or she will listen—and think about the questions the poetry asks.

Moreover, unlike other studies that do not cover the entire body of her work, this book treats all periods—if not equally, then at least significantly. Another aim has been to lay a strong foundation for interpreting the intertextual evolution of the poet's cultural consciousness, tracing that development in Rich. The work and theories of Judith Butler, Lillian Faderman, Allen Berube, and many others, partially inspired by Rich's seminal theoretical writings, have contributed to her dialogue between the poet, the reader, and the world. Lately this dialogue has become increasingly intricate and complex with the publication of another volume of essays. My purpose is to investigate Rich's diverse and contradictory relationships with female, feminist, and lesbian subjectivities at various historical moments, a major concern for Rich, as well as her other positioning concerns about nation, state, nationality, and sexuality. Hence the book moves away from a purely male/female binary opposition in the poetry and criticism toward a more complex investigation of her textual strategies and aesthetic, sexual, and political positionings. In short, this study attempts to map out a more complex Rich than we have ever seen before, a poet whose very career trajectory is paradigmatic of the changes undergone by many contemporary American women. Adrienne Rich is and always was ahead of her time, encouraging readers to fuller, more thoughtful socially and politically focused lives in tune with poetry that affords a way of "re-visioning" reality, giving all who listen a new way of seeing.

In the latter part of a productive life, Adrienne Rich has entered a new phase of her career. Having explored a thesis and an antithesis in her poetic styles and diverse self-fashionings, she is now exploring a personal synthesis that comes into alignment—though not convergence—with that of another major American poet, Walt Whitman, and probably secures her place in the Western canon. She is one of the most important and influential poets in America, a poetic voice indispensable to contemporary American poetry because her work tracks a deepening cultural and political consciousness and her keen perception of global change as it transpires.

A careful study of her poetry, however, shows that she may be even more concerned with advancing social justice than was Whitman, and her work provides a better framework for diversity and multiculturalism than his. Her poetic agenda of inspiring political change, perhaps along Marxist lines, and a truly multicultural poetry reflecting the actual multiculturalism of America herself motivates her search for a language of liberation to express this passionate moral imperative.[5] Since World War II, Rich has confronted many major cultural and political events, necessitating her own coming to terms with history intellectually, sensually, politically, and theoretically. In the following pages, I shall be tracing Adrienne Rich's process of poetic growth and its implications for women's literature and history; I shall analyze her visceral, intelligent observations of the evolution of female self-fashioning and the lyric "I." Her creative talents and passion for writing politically committed poems lead her occasionally to an establishment of commonality with others in America today in part at least because many can identify with the changing lyric "I" in her poetry.

Adrienne Rich is one of America's most outspoken, brilliant, and accomplished poets, widely known at home and internationally both as a poet of extraordinary range and verbal prolixity, and as a keen theoretical mind at the vanguard of critical theory and women's literature. When, in 1997, President Clinton sought to award the National Medal for the Arts to an outstanding American poet, he chose Adrienne Rich to receive the honor and offered it to her. She refused it partly because of Clinton's political stands on issues of importance to her and partly because of what acceptance might represent. This rejection gave Rich the opportunity to voice her opposition to the cutbacks in the National Endowment for the Arts and her resistance to his welfare reform policy. Since her most valued character traits are honesty, integrity, and consciousness of one's historical moment, as a seasoned political activist, she voiced protests against the Clinton Administration's policies relating to the arts, welfare, and gender, explaining her ideological position on the front pages of *The New York*

Times Book Review and *The Los Angeles Times Book Review.* This event reveals much about Rich's character: the problematic of resistance parallels the theme of control, the need to speak up for the marginalized in society. To speak the unspeakable becomes a personal vocation. Encountering the status quo as oppressive, she revels in the poet's transgressive revolutionary freedom.

A poet sworn to lucidity, honesty, and reformation of the social order, she proudly articulates her opinions and stands up for the rights of those less fortunate than herself, some female, some poor or otherwise disadvantaged. In an America of economic semi-apartheid, we could benefit from listening and responding to what she has to say. Her address to an omniscient audience she calls *you* and her exploration of various modes of selfhood—various selves—in her poetry enables her to speak to and for a varied multicultural audience, a cross-section of the American people. Like Whitman's, hers is a powerful vision of the common (wo)man.

Could Rich be seen as an American Socrates, a gadfly stinging complacent citizens of the Republic from time to time, challenging everyone to think harder, longer, and more creatively about political questions long ignored? She could. A person of strong integrity, ultimately, she sees poetry as eminently *useful* reading. Poetry helps its readers come to know themselves: through reading poetry they can discover American identity, strengthen connections with others, explore values truer to a vision of democratic communities within the state, and come to grips with the social injustices we still need to abolish.

Apart from the National Medal for the Arts and the Nobel Prize, there are few honors, prizes, fellowships, or awards Rich has not already won. In 1994, she received the MacArthur "Genius" Award along with other prestigious awards and prizes. This is not surprising, given her great appeal, the way she distills an aspect of the American conscience and psyche in poetry; her books appear on the shelves of the most serious bookstores and her essays on poetry and critical theory are taught in a variety of university courses and departments across the English-speaking world.

Rich has been called the William Blake of American letters by the Nobel Prize-winning novelist Nadine Gordimer.[6] Nationally, readers of poetry discern her prophetic vision of the direction America will take: like Blake's, Emerson's, and Whitman's, her poetry is often visionary, sometimes mystical, haunting, full of clear visual images. She speaks from the intimate perspective of "I" and "you," inviting the reader into dialogue on crucial philosophical, political, and spiritual issues. Like the longer poems of Blake, Emerson, and Whitman, her latest poetry transgresses the borders between poetry, philosophy, and prose.

This is not to say that she has no querulous critics: she has many. The eminent critic Helen Vendler has criticized Rich's political poetry incisively, as has Charles Altieri; some have criticized her sharply. Academic critics from the 1970s onward have deplored the lack of form and the presence of politics at every level in her poetry; in *The Western Canon,* Harold Bloom calls her an "ideologue" and excludes her from his version of the Western literary canon. But Rich's poetry is not for those adverse to ethical or political self-examination. If one liked her first books of poetry following conventional models, one might be forgiven for being disappointed in the radical protests expressed in the freer, more experimental work of later periods. But the loyalty of her American and international readership remains constant. While a small number of critics attack her for betraying their expectations, or for moving beyond their ability to understand the poetry, most celebrate the originality of her vision and follow her successive poetic transformations and admonitions with a respect accorded few other American poets.

LEARNING TO CRAFT A POEM

Rich first made her mark by mastering the craft of poetry and becoming one of the best poets writing in America in the 1950s and early 1960s; from the mid-1960s on, she was radicalized protesting the Viet Nam War and by her own growing awareness of her sexual identity. A series of political crises she witnessed the nation experiencing throughout the 1960s and early 1970s registered in seismic shocks in her poetry. She saw America as a society that could not be called the Great Society, as President Lyndon Johnson called it. At this time she began to lose her original more conservative academic readership. By the time she came out as a lesbian after her husband's death in 1970, along with her existing readerships she had acquired a readership of progressives, feminists, students, intellectuals, lesbians, theorists, and critics in women's and gender studies nationwide. She became a strong and pivotal voice of protest in American poetry; indeed, she is a prophet speaking to the American people in the main tradition of American poetry, following Emerson, Thoreau, Whitman, and of course Dickinson.

It is a matter of concern among critics—and an issue I shall address later—that Rich's reputation has been based as much on the content of her poetry and criticism as on the style of her poetry. But when she speaks, a varied domestic and international audience—along with a devoted audience of poets and critics of poetry—listens. Our lives as citizens in the twenty-first century resonate with hers.

Her own luck was to be born into a caring, if strict, home and to ascend meteorically to the heights of the profession, publishing her first book almost by accident yet receiving the coveted Yale Younger Poets Award for 1951. Next, resisting the role of dignified mentor and older poet, she has always stretched her poetic sensibility and range, expanding the compass and scope of her work with each successive pivotally transforming book.

Her voice resembles that of an immigrant or pioneer into new territories of the imagination and the national psyche; the subject is the roof walker, the daring voyager into new spaces.

Rich has taken her place as one of the most powerful, intelligent poets now writing in America, an original poet whose word and reputation have substance and import. She has become a respected elder in American poetry, a judge and keen commentator on poetry and poetics. Her work combines a continuing desire to communicate with the ordinary person, the suffering, and the oppressed, with a need to reach those who need to "get the news from poetry," as William Carlos Williams phrased it, and a sometimes-unpopular imperative to resist oppression. Because one of her missions may have been to listen to and speak for those who are marginalized in American society, some critics have perceived her more recent work as a reproach to those who see poetry as utterly distinct from raw "real life" and to those who think poetry and politics should be kept separate.

Her work is not yet well enough known at educational levels where she probably has a vast potential audience. Still, her poetry is well known at most American universities, but it could be better known in high schools and community colleges, for instance, or in universities or colleges in Great Britain and the Commonwealth. Another purpose of this book is to bring news of her poetry to high school and college readers of poetry, and to show these readers that Adrienne Rich has much to say that still may be useful, challenging, inspiring, even necessary to them. She encourages those wishing to better themselves or change existing adverse social conditions, and her work has a strength and integrity uncommon in American poetry—men's or women's. This integrity imbues her poems with a street credibility and instills in the reader a faith that what she says is indeed so—at least for this moment in time—and like the daily news, the news we get from her poetry is vital to anyone seeking to live justly and compassionately today.

Consequently my approach presupposes that Adrienne Rich is best studied as a poet of recurrent transformations, each new book marking a new departure in her unique evolution as a poet; but her new poetic habitations are not "more stately mansions" but more honest dwellings of her thoughts on consistent themes of excavation, resurrection, and courage. Motifs of constraint and control imbue her later work, along with the problematic of resistance. She is also profoundly concerned with the negotiation of the relationships among gender, culture, the female body, women's creativity, and social justice. In giving birth to herself as a writer and poet in the course of her poetic evolution, she challenges the existing social order and interrelationships between the sexes, provoking, in so doing, much predictable anger because she "celebrate[s] the female dimension of nature as primary"[7] instead of the female as "The Other," as formulated by Simone de Beauvoir, or as the helpmeet of man. This contentious reaction is exactly what the born rebel desires since the combustion of thought can effect action and social change. Rich calls for not just a transformation of our individual lives but also a transformation within American and global culture.

The critic Jeanne Perrault distinguishes Rich's own mode of writing about the self, called *autography,* from the word *autobiography,* the writing of one's life or biography. Rich usually concerns herself with the former, rather than the latter, tracking a moral record of her soul's and self's progress in her more recent writing. Since to her the individual life may not be so important as the ethical or spiritual accounting one must ultimately give for one's actions on earth, often she crafts an ageless poetry bare of limiting specifics or identifying characteristics. Her poetic voice awakens all that is sacred but drowned in commercial contemporary culture.

CLARIFYING HER VISION

Influenced early on by her poetic mentors Yeats, Stevens, Williams, Moore, Eliot, Auden, and the New Critics, Adrienne Rich jettisoned them in the 1970s, finding a more original voice. Of former Modernist mentors and critics she likely wrote in *Midnight Salvage:* she parted ways with a good many former colleagues and peers (*MS* 67). Through a process of systematic elimination, she increasingly refines her focus and clarifies her vision.

Now the longer cataloguing lines of her radical later poetry evoke those of William Carlos Williams' later poetry. Here she achieves a more visionary, even oracular conception of the role of the poet as akin to that of Walt Whitman, Emerson, and Margaret Fuller. In the charged political climate of the early 1990s, Rich became further radicalized. Aware that slavery still exists in America, that voting rights are not yet fully assured, and aware of other social and cultural ills, she roams "the dark fields of the republic" metaphorically, possibly searching for the one honest person who would vindicate a country she sees as having failed to achieve democratic ideals, hence she engages in midnight salvaging and poetic excavation of women's past. Like the prophet Abraham, who bargained with God to forestall destruction of the people, Rich bargains and negotiates new visions of the social order as she extends her search to embrace the possibility of a just community in her native country as well. She seems to seek both to find and communicate with those from every walk of American life who desire to reunite her country with its moral purpose.

Chapter 2

Beginnings: Deliberate Detachment and Conscious Craft

Brought up in a Jewish tradition of reverence for learning and the cultivation of intellectual development (although as a youngster she did not perceive the spiritual, cultural, or political implications of her father's being Jewish), sent to a Christian church and schools, Adrienne Rich grew up as a poet, obedient to her exacting father, working very hard to master the craft. She was fortunate to be born into the Southern and Jewish traditions of respect for learning and for poetry, literature, and love of European art, history, and music. Gradually gaining strength as a critic and as a poet, she completed her education and discovered in herself the courage to be an independent, intelligent woman in her own right in the 1940s and 1950s, at a time when this was, as Stephanie Coontz has shown, unfashionable and difficult.[1]

Born on May 16, 1929, in Baltimore, to a Jewish father and a Christian mother, Adrienne Cecile Rich joined a traditional, highly educated family; yet by her own admission she was from the start culturally, ethnically, and ideologically split at the root; yet the personal is political. She was the older of two daughters born to this accomplished medical professor whose stern control dominated the household and marked her early life. Adrienne Rich's father, Arnold Rich, was an outstanding medical professor at Johns Hopkins University, later chairman of the Pathology Department after a hard-fought battle to ascend to that post. From childhood on, under his guidance, she sedulously copied verses, composing traditional rhymed poetry for her father, writing in his study, reading through his library.[2]

Clearly Adrienne Rich has become an accomplished poet, an original thinker, critic, and literary theorist, creating her own poetic identity and critical perspective. Her focus from the start has been on transformation, self-transformation, and renaming and comprehending the world from her original perspective; from the mid-1960s onward, she became a revolutionary in poetry and theory, varying her style, language, and adjusting her vision. Sabine Sielke points out that, along with Emily Dickinson and Marianne Moore, in her poetry Rich has shown and "foregrounded that subject positions are culturally assigned, fashioned according to historically grown conventions, 'costumes,' and discursive codes. Yet only Rich has been a major participant," in fact "an instigator, in conceptualizing the female self or subject and...has insisted on autobiography as self-assertion"[3]—or rather *autography,* as self-assertion, hence as a way of comprehending womanhood as a whole as it mediates history and subjectivity. Since Rich recognizes "subjectivity and history as constructs and rhetorical strategies, as ongoing and open-ended processes based on appropriations and transformations of concepts, terms, and 'dress codes' ...fundamental to the culture one is engaged in," her work in poetry is to discern her conscious integrity and moral perspective as a historically evolving woman dreaming of a common language all might share. "Reinscribing the female subject as a process between past and present, she comes to accept the fragmentation of subjectivity in history."[4] It becomes her commitment and vocation, thus, as Sabine Sielke puts it, "she continues striving to 'piece together' the 'still fragmented parts' in [or of?] herself (*B* 176), to achieve identity in time,...[hence] Rich's poetry constitutes a feminist practice that insists upon its ethical responsibility and highly moralistic stance" (*B* 17).

Beginning with a focus on the self-in-progress in her first book of poems, she crafts throughout her poetic career a poetry of transformation. Rich envisions her self-transformation as reinscribing female subjectivity, hence changing society and even history as a whole. She writes in *On Lies, Secrets and Silence:* "the transformation of society and of our relation to all life... goes far beyond any struggle for civil liberties or equal rights—necessary as those struggles continue to be. In its deepest, most inclusive form it is an inevitable process by which women will claim our primary and central vision in shaping the future" (*LS* 226). Or as Rich puts it elsewhere:

> When the woman writer takes pen in hand, she has been in some way,...seizing power— seizing some of that male power, that logos, and saying "I," assuming the subject position, hence in some sense daring to speak the previously unspeakable. Both Anne Bradstreet and Emily Dickinson were extremely conscious of seizing power through poetry and used language to create self-hood.[5]

Using language to forge a new female selfhood is Rich's persistent goal, and that selfhood in turn both reflects changing American womanhood and forecasts the future of the American woman and potential American futures. Albert Gelpi has analyzed "change" cogently: " 'Change' has been a word for Adrienne Rich to conjure with ever since her first volume, *A Change of World,* for the 'will to change' (*ARP* 397) is the key to 'time's power' to re-invent reality." Her new approach in poetry reveals a feminism as committed and resolute but one more conscious of the ways gender, class, religious belief, and ethnic groups intertwine and contribute to one another. Her feminism is "committed to a long and painful process of clarification and transformation,... self-transformation."[6] Creating a new female subjectivity in poetry is linked with Rich's concept of a redeemed future for all women—and *all* people on earth.

Her poetic interest in the limits of language, in the tension between language's potential for containment and for liberation of meaning, has been an abiding focus for Adrienne Rich. She writes in what she has called the "regenerative American"[7] tradition. Her poetry gradually transforms itself from a poetry whose lush verbal "music" and form are artistically arresting into a new poetry that retains a psalmic, incantatory music but seeks new forms to embody its radically liberating words. In her poetry, she builds and explores alternate selfhoods, distanced from her real self, yet nourished by life, the range of her true self's experiences. The poems weave a succession of speakers engaging in poetic dialogues about issues that concern a person of integrity and conscience.

From the start transformation is a primary focus of her process of poetic composition: for a poet to write a poem or create either a person or an action, s/he must be free imaginatively to ride the currents of thought and follow where the mind drifts. In other words, one must be free to create alone, to imagine freely whatever one wishes or to turn anything into its opposite or to find new correspondences between otherwise disparate entities, in order to prime the spirit's "underground aquafiers" and regenerate the American imagination aesthetically and politically: she is the poet of "oppositional imagination."

BEGINNINGS IN POETRY

Rich's first book of poetry, *A Change of World,* published in 1951, employing a neoclassical style, tone, and themes, is impressive. At Radcliffe, Rich further perfected her craft, and *A Change of World* won a Yale Younger Poets Award. *A Change of World* was also graced by a foreword written by the most important living poet—and perhaps the most influential critic of the day—W. H. Auden. No debut could have been more auspicious: she was a hard-working, exceptionally bright and learned 21-year-old college senior who had devoted nearly her entire life up to that point to learning the craft of poetry and acquiring her poet's education.

In "When We Dead Awaken," her poignantly titled autobiographical and critical essay on the development of her own poetry (not to be confused with the poem in *Diving into the Wreck* by the same name), she relates the story of her early years and her "luck" of being born white, middle-class; therefore until she graduated from college, she wrote only for her father, who challenged, provoked, cajoled, and sometimes complimented her, but whose opinion mattered greatly to her. It was of great importance not to "displease" him. Gradually "other men—writers, teachers" assumed the role of mentor in her life: always there was "the Man, who was...a literary master" (*ARP* 170). Though her first mentor was her terrifying tyrannical father, the next mentors were male poets and professors, some mild, some condescending, some brilliant.

Growing up in the South, she was brought up as a son and taught by her professor father "to study...not to pray, taught to hold reading and writing sacred" (*ARP* 104). Her description of her upbringing contains a covert criticism of her father's denial of her femininity: in later years she has examined the impact this upbringing had on her, saying that reading and writing were substituted for knowledge of family heritage and religion during her adolescence. Still, her father instilled in her the intellectual, moral, and personal strength necessary to survive in a climate hostile to women. Her first-class education endowed her not only with knowledge but also with confidence and a powerful imagination; her background provided the psychological and intellectual conditions necessary for the making of a great poet. Conversely, implicit in her description of her first experience of patriarchy is a critique of a system that denies women direct access to what it holds sacred.

Her upbringing in unconscious denial of her religious and cultural heritage leaves her, as she puts it in her essay "Split at the Root," a "middle-class white girl taught to trade obedience for privilege"; here she reveals the paradoxes of her schizoid upbringing: although later she becomes a "Jewish lesbian," her upbringing is that of a "heterosexual gentile." Although the Black civil rights struggle first made her aware of oppression, Rich is the mother of three sons and hates "male violence." Almost as an act of atonement for her ignorant past growing up white in the South, the older poet defines herself as one "trying as part of her resistance, to clean up her act" (*ARP* 239).

The colloquial phrase "clean up her act" and level of daring self-revelation—what some critics have called the "sentimentality" of the foregoing analysis—convey Rich's anger at realizing all that was suppressed and lost, all that was absent from her upbringing. What was lacking forced her into the mode of radical re-vision, a feminist re-vision that "makes a historical, cultural and psychic examination of women's cultural past, and creates a women's history."[8] For Rich, this idea of revision and retrieval of women's history and silenced women's lives approximates "Michel Foucault's notion of [linguistic and cultural] 'archaeology'—the exposure of the moral values encoded in language."[9] She conceives of re-visioning not just as a means of reviewing her own past, "but as a method for all women to share."[10] Hence at this time she deliberately and consciously presents her own personal narrative as a model for other women seeking self-understanding to follow.[11]

An excellent professional administrator and professor, her father, Arnold Rich, presided over every detail of her wide-ranging yet intensive academic scholarship, while her mother gave her music lessons. Much of her early poetry shows a breadth of knowledge, a rigorous intellect; but later as the mature woman reexamines the effect her father and later her husband had on her development as a person and intellect, she comes to resent her over-controlled youth and education. For her, marriage may likely have seemed the only means of escape from parental control; but as it happened, for her the married state came to be perceived as a trap as well, offering its own kind of loneliness and self-fragmentation. "Seven Skins" in *Midnight Salvage* sums up her state surrealistically: "What a girl I was then," with a body "ready for breaking open like a lobster" (*MS* 41). This jarring crustacean image of the body as an object of consumption, a lobster, frighteningly conveys a sense of the girl's self as something precious and rare, offered to be consumed or elegantly sacrificed. Here the female is the object of consumption, a delicacy to be eaten and savored, then tossed out. W. H. Auden, the Modernist poet, however, found other ways to objectify and romanticize the young poet.

CERTIFIED AS A POET

As Rich expresses it, she was "certified" by W. H. Auden in her first book.[12] W. H. Auden, in selecting Rich for the Yale Younger Poets Award in 1951, and writing the foreword to *A Change of World*, envisions her and her poetry modest, skilled, and eminently competent. And although he understands she is only 21, he attributes to her "historical apprehension" and her understanding of the "conflict between faith and doubt" (*CW* 10). His foreword begins, "Reading a poem is an experience analogous to that of encountering a person" (*CW* 7). Having praised her for her "good manners," he concludes, "the poems a reader will encounter in this book are neatly and modestly dressed, speak quietly and do not mumble, respect their elders but are not cowed by them, and do not tell fibs: that, for a first volume, is a good deal" (*CW* 11). In retrospect, she and other poets and critics have found W. H. Auden's praise of her work (unwittingly?) patronizing, condescending, or even sexist. On the other hand, by the traditional cultural standards of the day, it was deemed the highest praise and probably piqued the envy of Sylvia Plath and other serious women poets hoping to achieve such success with their first books. Jeri Johnson explains, "During the 1950's, Rich established herself as a serious poet, serious enough that it was she against whom Sylvia Plath repeatedly (and jealously) measured the success or failure of her own poetic career (a privilege Plath reserved almost exclusively for women poets)."[13] In a journal entry Sylvia Plath recorded:

Adrienne Cecile Rich: little, round and dumpy, all vibrant short black hair, great sparkling black eyes and a tulip-red umbrella; honest, pink, forthright and even opinionated.[14]

Johnson comments on this passage, "That speaks volumes: Rich's poems led even a percipient Plath to mistake decorum for a lack of opinion." But I disagree. Plath clearly saw Rich as strong, "forthright," "opinionated," not lacking an original perspective and voice, hardly just demure and decorous. And to have been Plath's model and the object of her envy is a backhanded compliment.

In his foreword, W. H. Auden personifies Rich's poetic self and subject position as he reads *her* into her poems, seeing an image of a "good young woman" working skillfully and successfully in the Modernist tradition, a young woman poet with individual talent. To be sure, her whole life's experience up to the point where she is validated—some would say "christened," but Rich's word is "certified"[15]—had been that of a dutiful daughter, excellent student, and apprentice in the craft of poetry. The person Auden imagined writing this poetry was the image of a good girl, a decent young lady of 1951, exactly the type of deserving young woman he must have thought every young girl aspired to be.

Central to her self-esteem and growth as a poet is the fact that Adrienne Rich was selected for, in her words, "doing my craft right,"—for exceptional talent and proven ability—early on. As she put it to critic Elly Bulkin, "In one sense, the critic has to deal with me respectfully because I was certified by W. H. Auden when I was 21 years old."[16] Indeed, she had learned all she could from her poetic masters, acknowledged in Auden's foreword as Robert Frost, Wallace Stevens, W. B. Yeats, and W. H. Auden himself. By her own admission she had at first consciously imitated these bearers of the Modernist tradition in poetry, been somewhat influenced by them, and then outgrown them. In *A Change of World* (1951) and *The Diamond Cutters and Other Poems* (1955), her chiseled rhyming verse is highly crafted, bearing the marks of a practiced skill and a vision sophisticated beyond her years. Perhaps it is of this period she is writing when in *Midnight Salvage* she writes wryly, suggesting she had "stolen" the humorous, dry Modernist style: one poem speaks of taking a long look at eternity and not returning it (*MS* 41). Certainly her early poetry, as Albert Gelpi comments, tactfully and elegantly, is far "more interesting than Auden's comments" (*ARP* 83).

In her first volume, she wrote as a poet who truly did command the authority of experience, one who saw and understood the historical moment of post-war America; but is the implication that this gaze was perhaps an assumed pose? Some might say so. An aura of high culture and refinement permeates *A Change of World* in particular. The book displays a broad range and control of rhyme, meters, and ornate stanzas as well as a muted frustration and a quiet searching she later calls being split at the root. We see here what Elaine Showalter calls a consciousness of women constituting at this time:

> a muted group, the boundaries of whose culture and reality overlap, but are not wholly contained by the dominant (male) group. A model of the cultural situation of women is crucial to understanding both how they are perceived by the dominant group and how they perceive themselves and others.[17]

According to Showalter, women poets like Rich in her early poetry speak "a double-voiced discourse containing a 'dominant' and a 'muted story,'"[18] the dominant story relating the acts and events centering on the male characters, of which there are many in *A Change of World,* and the muted story being that of the female characters. The tone is detached and refined; the style is the terse, dry, impersonal style characteristic of formalist poetry. Claire Keyes observes that, in his foreword to the book, W. H. Auden embarrassingly "devotes half of his introduction to Rich's volume to explaining why poems written in 1951 suffer in comparison to poems written by the previous generation of poets, the great moderns."[19] If much of his foreword now seems arrogant or condescending, at that time it helped to launch her career into the stratosphere and certify her as an excellent poet.

RICH'S POETIC TRADITION(S)

One might legitimately inquire, What poetic tradition does Adrienne Rich work in? The *Cambridge History of Literature* groups her with the "postconfessionals." Others have called her postmodern or, more generally, later placed her among feminist poets. But I see her as working in two distinct traditions, first in the "Anglo-European" branch of Modernism and the tradition of Eliot-Tate-Auden, and next, after her political conversion, in an oracular tradition following Emerson and Whitman, one she describes as "regenerative American,"[20] and the female tradition generated by Anne Bradstreet and followed by Emily Dickinson, as Wendy Martin has shown in *An American Triptych.*[21] My book is devoted to clarifying these connections.

Throughout I shall be arguing that ultimately her career trajectory has come in some respects to parallel that of Whitman and in other ways to parallel that of Wallace Stevens. As a young poet, she is inspired by Stevens's preoccupation with the role of the artist in American society, his lush, showy, esoteric vocabulary, the sensuousness of his poetry and its music.

She has also followed Whitman and Emerson in the sense that she writes an oracular poetry and may unconsciously be a prophet of the Republic; like them she conceives of the role of the poet as someone responsible for the soul of the American people. She has echoed the lush music and verbal pyrotechnics of Wallace Stevens's poetry, searching, like Stevens, "for a new version of modernism that could contain a response to the events of the day"[22] and react to current happenings in America's changing culture and society. While feminist critics have dwelt on Rich's literary rapport with Emily Dickinson and others have compared her with Modernists T. S. Eliot and William Carlos Williams, I am more interested in the correspondences with Wallace Stevens and Walt Whitman. I shall demonstrate that these links are stronger than critics have previously acknowledged. Another purpose of this book is to show how Rich's view of herself as the conscience of American poetry and her sense of an ideal American Woman resemble Whitman's ecstatically democratic American Man, tangibly embracing humanity.

What did Rich say about poetic traditions in her first critical writings? In 1964, in a *Poetry* review of Louis Zukofsky's poetry, one of her first substantial published reviews in a major journal, Rich identifies

> two traditions—the Anglo-European mainstream containing Dante, Chaucer, Shakespeare, the Bible, the great formal structure—and the regenerative American breakthrough of the early part of this century, with its demands for a more spontaneous measure, for a closer look at things, for an independent movement belonging to the American inflection and American consciousness. I wish Zukovky might undertake what is the task of all today who...want the best of both worlds: the work of fusion not in separate poems, but in individual lines and whole poems: the coming honestly and uniquely by the "torsion" of grace and ungainliness, casualness and splendor.[23]

This might be seen as indicative of her theory and poetics at the start of her transition from Modernism to the oracular transcendentalist and other traditions, in contrast to her early work, which placed strong emphasis on highly crafted forms, complex rhyme schemes, and on ornate figures of speech. Her early poetry was beautifully crafted, with a concern for skill, artistry, an ironic tone and style, over and above its sophisticated, universal, or sublime locus and focus.

Her first books were full of literary allusions and a classical reserve. Although W. H. Auden in his foreword notes the influence of W. B. Yeats and possibly T. S. Eliot in her poetry, she herself has openly acknowledged the impact of Robert Frost and, more important, Wallace Stevens on her early writing. As she matures as a poet, gradually she aligns herself more and more with the "American regenerative" tradition—the open forms of H. D., William Carlos Williams, Wallace Stevens, Charles

Olson (to mention only four twentieth-century precursors), and Walt Whitman. Some of her poetry resonates with the transcendentalist, idealist tradition of Ralph Waldo Emerson and Walt Whitman in her conviction that the natural and spiritual are intimately connected in poetry. Moving on from Emerson and Whitman, however, she comes to believe that the personal is political and that women share a common cause and a common destiny to redress the sexist balance of civilization. Like Emerson, she sees the poet as the oracle of our civilization—and voice of its discontents. While Emerson's essays were largely encouraging, positive, exhortative, and her poetry later came to be seen as unduly negative, political, or "shrill" by some critics and reasonable, or necessarily corrective by others, essentially their impulse to speak emanates from the same source—the urge to reach out to, help, and even reform their fellow American citizens. And after the events of 9/11/01, many of her poems of the 1990s, beginning with *Dark Fields of the Republic,* seem prophetic of the new world order of the twenty-first century. Like Whitman and Emerson, she desires to communicate with other Americans and to enable them to see her vision as well as to warn them.

A CHANGE OF WORLD

Adrienne Rich began writing in the era which Jane Smiley and other critics have referred to as "the era of High Propaganda," the post-World War II Modernist era, when influential American poets and critics were seeking to define and craft American cultural identities in American literature and to advance in their poetry a certain conception of American art and life. In her early poetry she is trading obedience to the dominant Modernist poetic conventions for acceptance, trading obedience for the privilege of recognition, publication, and awards. It afforded her access to the men who controlled publication on the eastern corridor of the United States and in London and frequently denied access to all but the "best" women and "minority" writers. All that was to change with the impact of the second wave of the women's liberation movement. Many of these token women defected to the ranks of those previously excluded, with Rich leading the charge.

Rich's first book, *A Change of World,* is an investigation into the philosophical problem of mutability and change, an examination of truth and lies, power and powerlessness, social domination as opposed to internalized fear and submissiveness. The effect of external political changes on the thinking individual and the dynamics of personal transformation will continue to engage her for the rest of her poetic career, with politics and wars represented closely and globally in her poems. She fixes "[t]he word 'change'... in the titles of both the first and last books in [the] collection, and in the first and last poems" (*CEP* xix). *Change* is inscribed in every line;

a sense of anxiety born of change imbues the mood or tone of most of the poems, too.

The book's title may refer to a number of types of change—change of inner or outer worlds or a transformation of a personal, internal world or the recent external change of world experienced by all in the aftermath of World War II. Some poems refer to one kind of change and some to another; Rich sees change as the only constant in human life. As a whole, the poetry reflects the impermanence of power, how power of the intellect or other forms of power can and do slip away. Various individual poems adopt the characters and voices of jaded rulers or tyrants in their dotage. And in these impersonal poems, the speaker's high expectations for women may be dashed. Women should know their places, the subjects seem to be saying. The poems' sophisticated, cultured subjects and style reflect Rich's careful, even studious observance of the poetic conventions and the rules of poetic decorum. Everything combines to confirm Rich as a mature, accomplished poet of self-restraint and skill, adept at controlling rhythm, rhyme, meter. Auden praises her "talent for versification . . . [and] ear and . . . intuitive grasp of much subtler and more difficult matters like proportion, consistency of diction and tone" (*CW* 10). He acclaims her consummate control of language for subtle, often sardonic effects. The tone and style largely belie the fact that the book was written by someone under 21 years.

Many poems in *A Change of World* focus on the ruminations of strong-minded people who are threatened by contemporary events and storm warnings, meteorological or political. Indeed, the important initial poem in the book, "Storm Warnings," is written in blank verse. According to Rich, "Storm Warnings" is a poem about powerlessness—about a force so much greater than our human powers that, while it can be measured and even predicted, is beyond human control. All "we" can do in a World War, for instance, is create an interior space of calm as bulwark against the storm, an enclave of peace and self-protection, though the winds of change still penetrate keyholes and unsealed apertures and windows (*CEP* xix). The speaker vacillates between stoic activity and resignation in a ritual of mindful preparation.

The setting and tone of "Storm Warnings" establish an ideological construct for the other poems to follow. The focal points of the first stanza are a neutral, disembodied "I" and the barometric glass, symbolic of incoming war, that "has been falling all the afternoon" (*CW* 17). The lyrical "I" knows better than the instrument exactly where the wind blows as well as what weather system—metaphoric or real—is coming in (*CW* 17). The ungendered "I" leaves a book on a pillowed chair to close all windows, to draw the curtains, and light glass-globed candles as sole protection against the drafts or winds of war (*CW* 18). The storm of war, impossible to resist, moves inevitably toward the "I."

Although there are certainly other critical readings free of such teleology, I see the poem's concluding lines as registering an ominous sensitivity to change, a sensitivity that from a contemporary perspective also seems prophetic of the revolts and student riots throughout the world in the late 1960s. The narrator merely acts defensively in the face of events that, like riotous bad weather, seem about to destroy the snug fastness of the traditional home and family—and their security. One can see how while reading this poem W. H. Auden might imagine the poem's speaker in a traditional woman's passive role and see her in his mind's eye an ideal keeper of the hearth. The final lines tell of a traditional accustomed female powerlessness, familiar to Auden: these feminine ministrations are the speaker's only defense against the incoming storm (*CW* 18). These are necessities of life for inhabitants of dangerous regions, indeed, those who lived through World War II (*CW* 18). The presages of disaster and the storm warnings allude to the recently ended global conflict, with its all-engulfing horror, experienced by so many soldiers, Jews, civilians, and others oppressed or exterminated worldwide. Or they may allude to the psychic chill of inner problems and torment with which the textual "I" wrestles.

In her foreword to the *Collected Early Poems 1950–1970,* Rich advances another reading of "Storm Warnings":

> Nothing in the scene of... ["Storm Warnings"] suggests that it was written in the early days of the Cold War, within a twenty-year-old's earshot of World War II, at the end of the decade of the Warsaw Ghetto and Auschwitz, Hiroshima and Nagasaki, in a climate of public fatalism about World War III. (*CEP* xix–xx)

Characteristically Rich interprets the poem clearly, personally, and logically. Although I see it more as resonating with rumblings of war than Rich does, I share with her the sense that it seems to have been written by an older person; this speaker seems to have witnessed the funerals of many of her friends and family; this is a poem filled with a tone of imminent doom (*ARP* 283). The subject positions here are capable of "historical apprehension"; their perspective is that of persons over 40 commenting on art, literature, and music to intelligent colleagues. These remain the speakers of her poetry in her first two books of poems. Rich, Gelpi explains, consistently "seeks shelter as self-preservation" in a traditionally feminine way. Her fatalism is the sophisticated pose adopted by poets and youth of the post-war era. In "Storm Warnings," the textual "I" fortifies and seals off a "comfortable weather-proof sanctuary" (*ARP* 284).

Poetically embodying America's awareness of her potential vulnerability in the face of global change and a sense of the human cost of World War II, the poem has a tone of guarded fear. A contemporary reader may wonder at the degree of powerlessness and passivity evoked and experienced here, but when the poem is seen as a possible depiction of the efforts of those whose mission was to preserve all of Western civilization, its sentiments and formal decorum are warranted, even plausible and accurate. And Rich is one of an entire generation of poets—Allen Tate, Robert Lowell, W. S. Merwin, and others—who adopted the then-fashionable guise of world-weary sophistication, alternating with panic and angst. One is reminded of the line from Bob Dylan, "Ah, but I was so much older then. I'm younger than that now." Hers might be said to be the generation who never had a chance to enjoy its youth.

RECOVERY OF THE JEWISH HERITAGE

Certainly at Radcliffe College Adrienne Rich discovered the beauty of Judaism and came to identify with other Jews, experiencing her communality with them and a connectedness with her own Jewish heritage. Her parents had never taken her to synagogue or imparted anything of the Jewish cultural or religious traditions. But this was perhaps understandable since they represented two different religions—her mother was Christian and her father, Jewish. "Passing" as white, middle class, and Christian was necessary to the family's continued upward mobility. In her autobiography, Katharine Graham clearly describes how members of her own family successfully "passed" in society although like Rich she, too, had a Jewish father and a gentile mother.[24] Rich's passing was more unconscious and pernicious since she was unaware of it.

But when Rich reached university, she desired to reclaim a more authentic identity and discover more about Jewish traditions and religion, and possibly also to sow her wild oats; this drove her to learn about Judaism and her heritage. What had been suppressed in frustratingly conservative Baltimore was heartily embraced by the college student at Radcliffe, where she was welcomed into a lively community of Jewish intellectuals, students, and faculty, and where being Jewish was becoming increasingly acceptable and better appreciated in the mainstream academic establishment. Rich rejoiced in this newfound freedom to discover her personal roots in Judaism. Her faith—and this acceptance into the culture—gave her a sense of belonging to all Jewish people and to their ancient traditions; it provided her with that sense of identity and roots her upbringing had lacked. What she may have found is best expressed in the lines of a poem of that period, "By No Means Native," a poem that concludes by referring to a sense of belonging to one ancestral plot of local land (*CW* 32). Judaism represented that sense of permanence for her at a time in her life when she was reaching beyond the strained familial sphere to a broader, more life-affirming philosophy and gestalt.

At Ivy League colleges during the 1940s and 1950s, especially in the era of the G. I. Bill, higher education suddenly opened up to everyone, not just the white middle and upper classes to whom it was available formerly. Correspondingly, along with so many others who were not WASPs, Jewish professors were being hired in increasing numbers and were quickly revealing they were excellent professors and often brilliant scholars, too. Among them was Alfred Hilton Conrad, the young Harvard economics professor whom Adrienne Rich married in 1953. Predictably, her parents disapproved of this marriage partly because Conrad was Jewish, and partly because he was from a lower social class and from New York. Of her family she would later write that her family was proud, very concerned about its reputation; they need to have behavior "more impeccable" than others. They trusted neither strangers nor friends since they believed "the world was full of potential slanderers, betrayers, people who could not understand" (*ARP* 232).

An inability to trust others, strangers or friends, has haunted Rich throughout her life and is what ultimately made it impossible for her to continue as a feminist leader. Rich is painfully aware of the irony and arrogance inherent in a phrase like "could not understand," yet to her credit she forces herself to be honest about her family's arrogance, an arrogance she probably was unconscious of as a girl.

In the Riches' eyes, Alfred H. Conrad may have seemed not the right sort—a suitable son-in-law—since he was a "real Jew." Still, after some years and with the birth of two of her sons, eventually the family was reconciled.

Of her own sense of self and sexuality at the time, she says that she lived, as all her classmates lived, "under the then-unquestioned heterosexual imperative" and thus she married partially "in part because I knew no better way to disconnect from my first family." To marry and leave home was her motivation, but since she wedded the very person her father may have wanted most to avoid, a real Jew, a man himself divided between his heritage and a need for "Yankee approval, assimilation" she married someone potentially as conflicted as herself (*ARP* 233). Their marriage lasted until her husband's death in 1970 by suicide, and he remains a silent witness in and audience to her poetry to this day.

POETIC POWER AND CHANGE IN *A CHANGE OF WORLD*

The early poems in *A Change of World* resemble Neoclassical poetry in their absence of descriptors, their stylistic purity and restraint, their aura of cosmopolitan refinement and high culture (they refer to Bach, Baudelaire, Gide, et al.), and their highly reserved and often ironic tone. "By No Means Native" (*CW* 31–32), for example, engages the frequently encountered experience of the traveler who desires to be accepted, to be "native," yet who can never get past the barrier some locals erect to wall the foreigner out. No matter how hard he or she tries to master the language and be comprehensible, in the provinces a foreigner can be treated as someone *who could not understand.* This nonnative person is skilled in the language, a man who has mastered the local accent and manner. How better to describe a desire for assimilation?

In smooth true rhyme, Rich recounts the learner's earnest efforts to be assimilated, only to see in the end that no one would fully accept and receive him. Here the lines convey her *split* sense of being an outsider, which she may have unconsciously felt as an intellectual woman contending for top honors in poetry and in her studies in academe.

In "By No Means Native" the textual "I" determines to persist in living there as if in exile to die as in exile (*CW* 32). Ultimately, he chooses this latter course, an existentialist choice, a choice of being over essence, existentialism having been an influential philosophy in the postwar 1940s. The poem's speaker remains "By No Means Native," (*CW* 32) though he or she is understandably impassioned with local ways, and the sense of being affectionately attached to this place is profound. He/she is conscious of something the natives take for granted and more blissfully grateful than they are for this heritage in that she has had the opportunity to choose it.

The perfect rhythm, meter, and half rhyme of the poem's final couplet counterbalance the odd compromises of the tourist or exile, who may appear to the locals to have overstayed his welcome—indeed, who may have sold out or settled for too little. The Shakespearean elegance of the final couplet in iambic pentameter reveals that her sensibilities would dictate staying on one ancestral patch of local ground. This poem closely resembles Auden's "In Praise of Limestone" in feeling and tone: this love for one's own country might appeal to her American readership and is one of the first indications of her lifelong loyalty to her nation.

An early poem reflecting on passive power or powerlessness is "An Unsaid Word" (*CW* 51), where the protagonist is praised for *not* bothering "her man," presumably a person superior to her in intellect. She remains silent, keeping her peace, leaving him freed to go where his mind *forages* alone (note the interesting use of the term *forages* here, which has the secondary connotation of the hunter-gatherer's securing of food for the family). Ironically, this woman, the poem's subject, is praised for *not* speaking and *not* moving: she "[s]tands where he left her, still his own," with the dual meaning of "still" creating an interesting double play: The woman who could (but doesn't) summon him or distract him, and this is the hardest skill to learn. Yet it is an essential skill of the modest, decent wife. Here Rich's "I" acts the part of Auden's proper young woman (or good Jewish wife), aware of her lesser status vis-à-vis the man; the female subject is a willing helpmeet, well-educated to serve as consort to an intelligent man but alert to the fact that his mind forages alone, not with hers. *He* is the one whose intellectual occupations dominate his waking life: *his* scholarship must not be disturbed. The female subject, committed to her relationship with the man, exercises a passive form of power, and embodies the traditional female power of resignation. Here the subject position is the traditionally feminine and heterosexual.

A related poem inscribing power and its adverse effects is "Afterward," where the strong direct address comes from an inventive second-person perspective: the speaker sees "your" hopes are shamed, "you" are alone, defeated, and resigned (*CW* 43). Here "the finely poised paradoxes...note ruefully that a fond innocence must fall, as it will, to a recognition of limits" (*ARP* 284). Given the constrictions of the female sphere in the late 1940s and early 1950s, no wonder an exceptionally accomplished woman, knowing she is intelligent, would likely be shy and not suspect high professional achievement. Evocative of A. E. Housman, this poem communicates the sense of doom or fatalism understood by anyone who has competed for a high prize and lost; this experience often figured in the late nineteenth and early twentieth centuries in the epoch of the World Wars. And the situation of this poem is the exact opposite of that of the foregoing poem—there, the woman congratulates herself for not using all her power, and here the subject is chastened and disappointed because pride led him or her to think s/he could succeed at some task where failure ensued instead.

Ironically, although the poem "Afterward" was ostensibly first written to and about a man who has had to scale down his hopes and dreams, in the 1975 Norton Critical Edition *Adrienne Rich's Poetry,* Rich changes the pronoun in the last line of the poem "Afterward" from "his" to "her," adding the note saying she altered the pronoun since it altered for her "the dimensions of the poem" (*ARP* 4). From our critical perspective, this is of course a meaningful change: a formerly highly idealistic, traditional woman rises to meet her *doom:* when her efforts at winning fail, her perspective must be readjusted. In writing a poem like this, Rich reveals her mastery of taut Anglo-Saxon rhymed verse, making caustic points about woman's sphere by choosing strong masculine rhymes like *proud* and *crowd,* and *room* and *doom.*

The French feminist critic Luce Irigaray expresses women's striving unsuccessfully to conform in a male world:

> On the outside, you attempt to conform to an order which is alien to you. Exiled from yourself, you fuse with everything you encounter. You mine whatever comes near you. You become whatever you touch. In your hunger you find yourself, you move indefinitely far from yourself.... Assuming one model after another, one master after another, changing your face, form and language according to the power that dominates you.[25]

Similarly, the lyrical "I" of this poem faces his (her) doom with resignation and a sense of fatalism since a woman can expect nothing else in a man's world. Politically and culturally, her function is to accept shame and defeat nobly.

BEACON HILL, ALCHEMY, AND METAPHYSICS IN *A CHANGE OF WORLD*

One of the only poems in *A Change of World* clearly set in Boston in America is "Five O'Clock, Beacon Hill" (*CW* 47–48), a witty parody of Boston's intellectual poseurs. The speaker is the (probably female) "I" of the sherry-drinking couple enjoying the "green receptive twilight" amid vines on a quiet evening. The displacement of "receptive" from the speaker to the "twilight" is an example of pathetic fallacy. This lyric "I" is the observer who studies Curtis and his aristocratic, avant-garde anger at boring conventional people and their bourgeois ideas. Curtis diplomatically puts down "elder values" scornfully while the lyric "I" sits resignedly, patiently, quietly observing the twilight cast a greenish light over his face (*CW* 47).

The *abba* rhyme of these five stanzas, a rhyme scheme traditional in sonnets, subtly emphasizes Curtis's passivity and inconsequence in the larger schema, stressing as it does how neatly his rebellion fits into traditional structures. Although he purports to protest against the status quo, she doesn't: the lime green often associated with him here may be the color of cowardice, while in contrast the glowing auburn of her sherry expresses passion, security, and commitment, the warmth of a living tradition. Although the observant "I" never speaks to Curtis, she shrewdly notes that his Puritan nose is dignified, discreet, yet definitely an aristocratic nose, often seen in family portraits (*CW* 47). In other words, his classically Puritan features belie his hypocritical, feigned stance: his skin and the shadows of leaves falling on it show his true colors.

As before, when she is honing in on a telling philosophical summation, she asks herself probingly if a rebel heart beats beneath his "mask" and comments, "Avant-garde in tradition's lineaments!" Her ability to satirize Beacon Hill aristocracy of Boston evidently spoke of her sophistication and the fact that this was a member of the publishing elite speaking to other members of the elite.

While strength, dignity, and power are important themes, love is almost wholly absent as a theme in these poems. True, it figures in "At a Bach Concert" where they realize that life and art are opposites. Yet in hearing Bach's music, they become aware of a love with no roots in pity (*CW* 54). Love figures in this poem as an abstract quality residing in the music rather than as a presence in the sophisticated scene. Only in Bach's music does the speaker feel an aesthetic love and beauty, disciplined, and pure. In true formalist mode, form is conceived of here as love's highest offering. The poem's argument resolves itself in the final stanza by stating that art, in order to remain art, cannot be overly sensational or emotional (*CW* 54). Art must contain an element of hardness, purity, sternness because "proud restraining purity" alone of Bach's music can revive the sensitive heart (*CW* 54). Only the purest art uplifts the spirit and the heart and assuages the pain of the ordinary betrayals humans are subject to.

Earlier, the influential Modernist critic T. S. Eliot had defined poetry as an escape from personality and emotion in "Tradition and the Individual Talent," claiming that *"only those who have personality and emotions know what it means to want to escape from these things."*[26] Paradoxically, intensity of a poet's passions demands *form* since without form the emotion would overwhelm the creative process. The Neoclassical protectiveness and conservatism referred to above manifest themselves again here in this aesthetic credo: art must be pure, not too compassionate or full of pity, or else it cannot restore or revive the vulnerable heart. According to Rich, the source of this restraint is proud purity born of the poet's (or musician's) love of the craft, love for the discipline and its tradition. Within the strictures of form, love and the creative impulse feed each other directly to produce such chiseled poetry. Modernist and Neoclassical critical theory imbue this conception of an art that reflects ancient discipline, immaculately pure (*CW* 54).

The one poem in the book that may be said to be about relationships, the last one, "For the Conjunction of Two Planets" (*CW* 82–83), might be read as a heavily disguised augury for the conjunction of two lovers. Certainly it more closely resembles an elaborate Renaissance conceit than a modern poem. In most of the stanzas the lines are not end-stopped but break the bounds of the line. In this, one of the best poems in the book, Rich weighs the medieval man's belief in astrology against modern astronomy's mathematical approach to the stars with slide rule and a photographic plate (*CW* 82) rather than with the awe stars inspired in the ancients. Despite the allure of each way of viewing them, the poem explains, the stars each retain their essential mystery. At the end of the poem, reader and narrator alike remain unable to resolve the schism between astrology and astronomy, the dichotomy between science and wonder, so again the poet ends with a question in iambic tetrameter: can any light so proudly "thrust" signal something we can "trust?" Or is this merely a figment of the imagination that enables us to see the things we want to see in "fiery iconography?" (*CW* 82) Are the constellations in any sense truly bears, women, or scorpions, or is the drama of the stars pure wishful thinking?

The poem's skillful allusion to astronomy, a modern science, balances "unresolved dualities" (*ARP* 284) reminiscent of the Metaphysical poets' treatment of contemporary science in similar *ababcc* rhyme schemes, as John Donne does in "The Good-Morrow." But such craft and verbal dexterity can come to seem hollow when sustained for too long: Gelpi wonders whether or not this artifice, however "skillfully wrought," could serve as a partial evasion of the conflicts which are the subjects of the poem. He imagines that poems provide a perspective on "a changing world divided . . . against itself" (*ARP* 284).

Her stunning verbal style camouflages a refusal to do what "The Ultimate Act" urges—to commit an act "beneath a final sun." Limits which are hard to accept may become, in the end, too easy to accept. The precariousness of one's situation makes for the insistence on remaining remote and unharmed; hence the decorous reserve of the woman toward the man in "An Unsaid Word"; there's a cool geniality between the couple.

Yet Rich's desire to pose metaphysical questions, profound questions about the nature of our being in the world, while practicing this brinkmanship in metaphysical imagery, is a desire John Donne, the poet's poet, would have enjoyed. Like Metaphysical poets, Rich risks asking—though not resolving—challenging questions in response to contemporary events in America's changing cultural climate. She dares to see and learn from empirical reality. Though she will continue for almost another decade as a formalist, her poetry embodying what she later calls *silences,* the reader can observe her deliberate detachment, her conscious craft, and the hard-won, seemingly effortless skill of these early poems.

"AUNT JENNIFER'S TIGERS"

The popular favorite in *A Change of World* is "Aunt Jennifer's Tigers" (*CW* 19), a poem foreshadowing ideas about herself and women that is in general characteristic of her later feminist work. It is perhaps the most important, most frequently anthologized of all her early poems. Though it lacks the Neoclassical style or tone, it is replete with memorable imagery and a fluent rhythm that vividly conveys the dynamism of Aunt Jennifer's needlework tigers. The tigers' aesthetic energy, taking on a symbolic dimension and energy from William Blake's "Tyger," contrasts sharply with Aunt Jennifer's inner fears, her outer silence, and submissiveness. The point of the poem appears to be that while her actual life was "ringed with ordeals she was mastered by," her cherished embroidered tigers somehow escaped any such domination: the tigers in the panel she embroidered continue prancing and "unafraid" (*CW* 19)—unlike her, her female forebears, or successors. Adrienne Rich questions her female inheritance. Many critics argue along with Rich that strong respectable women, the "Aunt Jennifers," of former generations were frequently overpowered by ordeals imposed by fathers, husbands, sons, or male authorities in general, yet they have been able through their art—through quilting, knitting, gardening, or in this case needlework—to produce something beautiful and memorable, something eternally alive. "Aunt Jennifer's Tigers" is written in perfect quatrains in iambic pentameter: only three perfect stanzas, it is a jewel of completeness.

Of Aunt Jennifer, all we know is that her terrified hands were in life ringed by challenges (*CW* 19) that "mastered" her: the word *master* of course is significant in that it attributes to mastery or domination a male gender. In the last quatrain, we do not see her alive at all since she has been overcome and mastered by trials, symbolized by Uncle's very heavy wedding ring. One descriptor of Aunt Jennifer herself, when alive, is hands "fluttering," delicate as butterflies—qualities of the nervous Southern belle. Her hands seem too gentle and are eventually too weak to pull the ivory needle through her wool. If Alice Walker writes about the creative inspiration and encouragement her "foremothers" offered in "In Search of Our Mothers' Gardens," Rich portrays their silent suffering and targets their art as mute witness to the triumph of their spirits. In "When We Dead Awaken," she says of her origins as a poet and the genesis of this poem, that when she reviews these early poems, she is "startled" to discover in them the obvious split between "the girl who wrote poems, ...and the girl who was to define herself by her relationships with men" (*ARP* 171). This manifests itself clearly, for example, in "Aunt Jennifer's Tigers," whose heroine is "mastered by" and "ringed with ordeals" and obstacles to her being her authentic self, and corresponds with what she would later call her sense of being *split at the root.* This state of self-perceived duality between the poet's intrinsic selfhood and her external social selfhood, described in the passage above, is one that Borges explains in "Borges y Yo" ("Borges and I"). It is a condition of divided consciousness experienced by many writers of poetry and prose in the late twentieth and early twenty-first centuries.

Her poetic ability to look with deliberate detachment at this split reveals an unconscious proto-feminism in her craft in Aunt Jennifer's suffering from the "opposition of her imagination," embodied both in her embroidery and in her actual life (*ARP* 171). Aunt Jennifer is merely the shadow, a dream image, of the poet herself, an image or self she was as yet unconscious of. But Aunt Jennifer startled her creator 20 years later because she is far less distinct from the woman who created her than Rich at first thought. Would now Rich think that one of her ideal readers might be Aunt Jennifer? Possibly. In the next paragraph of her essay "When We Dead Awaken," she clarifies her attitude toward Aunt Jennifer: then formalism was "part of the strategy—like asbestos gloves, it allowed me to handle materials I couldn't pick up barehanded." She adds in a note that this strategy resembles another she adopts later using what she calls the *persona* of a man instead of a woman, as she does in "The Loser" (*ARP* 171).

The radioactive material originated in the shadow of the poet's psyche: the rejected, feared, and suppressed image of mastered, subjected, subverted womanhood, Aunt Jennifer, was anything but the strong competent professional woman Rich is. Her craftsmanship rivaled that of the great Modernist poets, her mentors and models. In *The Aesthetics of Power: The Poetry of Adrienne Rich,* Claire Keyes portrays Rich as imitating them in her early work:

> Within that imitation,... she devises 'a mode of assertion' undetected by Auden and, most likely, unconscious to herself. The subtlety of this assertion contributed to the ease with which Auden accepted her into the circle of men poets, without, it seems, too much attention to her being a woman.[27]

Rich's "mode of assertion" consisted in depicting ironically restrained, demure, intellectual women who had the good sense not to air their dissident views before men, especially before avant-garde connoisseurs like the Beacon Hill poseur treated above, the men who wielded real economic power. Her irony allows her to grasp political material with sternness and impersonality that does not give away the poet's own allegiances but merely points up incongruities, absences, fissures in the social structure.

A second, contrasting mode of assertion is the vertiginous, mad mode of the crazy woman who speaks in "Vertigo," the poem immediately following "Aunt Jennifer's Tigers" in the book. Reminiscent of W. B. Yeats's "Crazy Jane Talks to the Bishop" or T. S. Eliot's "A Game of Chess" from *The Waste Land,* "Vertigo" ends with uncharacteristic levity of a streetcar, not named Desire, but one that goes to Mars. The speaker then addresses a friend, explaining she will either meet you there, or at the "burning bush" in Harvard Square (*CW* 20). In conscious self-parody, the female subject of this poem evokes Yeats's Crazy Jane, standing, as it were, alongside Moses. The shock of this poem full of metaphysical imagery, set amidst others written by a cosmopolitan formalist, shows certain fissures in the image of traditional womanhood and obliquely asserts the secret subtext of formalist female selfhood, the madwoman whom the controlled poet can barely handle, even with asbestos gloves. Many confessional and post-confessional poets of the 1950s and 1960s—Robert Lowell, Sylvia Plath, and Anne Sexton, to name the most famous—also dramatically assumed this pose of madness, following Rich.

THE DIAMOND CUTTERS AND OTHER POEMS (1955)

The same formalist style persists in Rich's second volume, *The Diamond Cutters and Other Poems* (1955), where the air of modernity, the slightly more fragmented lines of some of the poems—in the famous "Living in Sin," for example—chronicle the winds of change. Still, generally speaking, the book is full of European travel poems she wrote while on a Guggenheim or "tourist-views" of Walden or the Charles River. What sets them apart, though, is "the developing metaphor" suggesting that "we are all aliens in a fallen world" (*ARP* 284).

Rich's poems still present the "neatly and modestly dressed" female subjects Auden welcomed into the company of the best poets in America in 1951 in his foreword to *A Change of World:* they "speak quietly but do not mumble, respect their elders, . . . are not cowed by them, and do not tell fibs" (*CW* 10). Still, Carmen Birkle has argued that Rich at this point was only *just* able to obey "these . . . rules of poetry and art and was therefore, praised by her male critics and her audience. The mere fact that she felt the urge to make aesthetic statements indicates that she did not feel quite at ease with them."[28] In 1993, in *What is Found There,* an illuminating collection of her critical writings, she declares that *The Diamond Cutters* was "a last-ditch effort to block, with assimilation and technique, the undervoice of my own poetry" (*WF* 233).

The Diamond Cutters and Other Poems closely resembles, with subtle variations in theme, style, and content, *A Change of World.* In *The Diamond Cutters,* some poems parody our famous forebears—literary and historical: "The Strayed Village" (*DI* 69–72), for instance, clearly plays on Matthew Arnold's "The Strayed Reveler," ironically imagining the possibility that a villager could return after a long voyage only to find his village gone. What is unique of course is that home, the village, is not there when the voyager returns. Is this an objective correlative of the many soldiers, prisoners, and family members who were lost during World War II? It can be seen as both a tribute to a literary forebear and a last gesture toward the exotic and aesthetic realm of the classical poetics, a realm she was about to leave forever.

The Diamond Cutters and Other Poems was conceived while Rich was studying, teaching, and writing abroad; thus, it is full of Europe—English country villages, Italian villas (cf. "Villa Adriana"—perhaps Adrienne's villa?), references to harpsichords and Purcell's masques. Written in traditional rhyme patterns and formal meters, the poems generally evoke high culture, as "For the Conjunction of Two Planets" (this poem may itself have inspired a poem by a similar name by W. S. Merwin, the 1952 winner of the Yale Younger Poets Award).

Significantly, the first poem in the collection, "The Roadway" (*DI* 15–16), dedicated to her husband, begins with a road washed away, suggesting that some of the traditional patterns—or poetic "roads"—she has followed may be discarded, if not in this volume then in the next. Concerns with erosion of established paths, disappointment, sites of aristocratic retreat, madness,[29] all seem to echo the voice and sensibility of Emily Dickinson, the woman poet whose life *was* language. These obsessions and poignant loss (cf. "Annotation for an Epitaph") are material themes in *The Diamond Cutters.* Here some of her dramatic monologues are reminiscent of those of Robert Frost (cf. Frost's "The Death of the Hired Man"), chief among them "Autumn Equinox" (*DI* 62–68) and "The Perennial Answer" (*DI* 73–81).

"Autumn Equinox" is notable for its dramatic realization of a repressed, mutely frustrated wife whose entire life has been invested in furthering her husband's academic career without, in the end, any discernible reward—not that she is asking for any. The wife in the poem cannot find the reasons for her dissatisfaction, but possibly it is the fact of her having felt prevented from pursuing her own talents, ambitions, and career.

The style of the dramatic monologue resonates with that of Frost's "The Hill Wife," also about female loneliness and isolation in rural communities and how they can drive one mad, and "The Death of the Hired Man," about the Yankee concept of the social responsibility of one human being to his friend and fellow worker or hired man. In trying out new forms like the dramatic monologue, Rich explores new realms of the psyche: we can see her maturing as a poet here, able to enter into and render the psychological experience of the lonely frustrated wife, though doing so with ironic detachment. Later she will treat such women even more sympathetically, portraying them as victims of a sociopolitical system that nullifies women's talents, careers, and aspirations; here she merely gives voice to an isolated woman's sense of dis-ease.

"LIVING IN SIN"

Only two poems from this book were chosen to be anthologized in her *Collected Early Poems*—"The Diamond Cutters" and "Living in Sin." The same vague sense of dis-ease of "The Hill Wife" permeates "Living in Sin" (*DI* 60–61), the best and most famous poem in this book. Rich captures here, with style and class, the sense of disillusionment women—and men?—may feel on "the morning after" when they realize they are "living in sin."

Of course, she is quietly mocking and hence distancing herself from the speaker by using pejorative Christian rhetoric like *living in sin* and *jeered at by demons.* These phrases bring to mind a Christian hell and eternal damnation for sexual sins. Just as Rich, like many other upper-middle-class women, had been raised to value her virginity and avoid sexual impurity, so here the language invokes the dominant culture's stigmas against sexual impurity and its connection with eternal damnation and possible death—either the soul's death in sin or real death in childbirth.

As a girl, she had been for several years an Episcopalian, but her parents had sent her to the church for upward mobility, not for spiritual reasons. She attended "...without belief. That religion seemed to have little to do with belief or commitment. It was liturgy that mattered, not spiritual passion" (*ARP* 227). So in "Living in Sin," a more worldly textual "I" takes on the questions of the hypocritical morality of the age, its public stress on sexual purity, and the contrast between private, possibly archaic, notions of romance and public transgressiveness. In retrospect, Rich might have suggested that the phrase "living in sin" had been created to control women's sexuality. Here, however, the protagonist speaks refreshingly of that uncomfortable experience, a subject so little commented upon publicly by women poets in the 1940s and 1950s.

Now, with the publication of Sylvia Plath's journals and letters, the young American woman's angst over the dual academic pressures to succeed and the sexual pressure to give in to men has become common knowledge; however, women experiencing it in the fifties and sixties nearly always suffered alone. This is another manifestation of women's sense of intrinsic aloneness, isolation, and what some have called their invisibility.[30] About this, Rich writes, at that time she needed to prove to herself and others that she could enjoy a "'full' woman's life," she "plunged" headlong into marriage and rapidly into child-bearing (*ARP* 173).

For her, a conflict emerges between her perfect public self and what was then called a full life, on the one hand, and her unique career as a woman poet; and this conflict dominated her personal life and public poetry. Decades later, in *The Way We Never Were* (1992) and *The Way We Really Are* (1998) Stephanie Coontz deconstructed the romanticized image of the *real* woman's life, revealing it to be more romantic ideal than reality. This is not to say that the urge to build the perfect family *and* a growing career was not in itself admirable; but for Rich personally the effort to do everything perfectly herself ended in her feeling that "I had either to consider myself a failed woman and a failed poet," or she had to "find some synthesis" or perspective to enable her to comprehend "what was happening to me" (*ARP* 173). Hence she crafted that synthesis in a new poetry of liberation and female consciousness.

Correspondingly, in "Living in Sin," the deep fissures in the romantic relationship the speaker has apparently expected to enjoy but did not are evident in the language, tone, and rhythm: the poem's opening line is a rough iambic pentameter: "She had thought the studio would keep itself" (*DI* 60–61). Using religious rhetoric again, the speaker labels her not wanting to keep house in the studio a heresy, and this sets the tone for a poem about the domestic stresses brought on by entering fully into a passionate relationship out of wedlock. In the first verse paragraph of this poem in free verse, the alliteration of plosive *p*'s emphasizes posh aristocratic luxury: "A plate of pears, a piano with a Persian shawl"; but when next a cat arrives chasing "picturesque amusing" vermin (*DI* 60), we sense more trouble in paradise. *Picturesque* and *amusing* might be descriptors from scenic eighteenth-century tableaux in poems set in exotic spas or at casinos where the glasses and laughter ring. Here those adjectives echo deliberately falsely, provoking her realization that these are not actually such amusing or picturesque sights—mice are vermin, potential carriers of death. Finding a mouse in a studio on the morning after affects her view of the lovemaking of the night before. It may be seen as illicit, possibly dangerous; like the mouse, it may connote disease. Given the poem's rhetorical mode and meanings, it connotes spiritual disease.

Next in the poem comes a series of concrete physical observations whose undertone of sordidness works against her cultural mandate to be in love. Although she had expected no housework in this lovers' hideaway, all the details she is obsessed with haunt and negate that expectation: real life and real dirt make her aware of real guilt—or that at the very least she is being observed by judgmental eyes. Before, she could not have known that looking back at her from a kitchen cabinet, she would find a pair of "beetle-eyes," those of an insect intruder (*DI* 60). It is also remarkable that here Rich finds for the first time a more informal voice and stops capitalizing each new line. Even as this poem is about breaking down of the conventions of lovemaking between single men and women, so too her poetry adopts the more unconventional form of radical or revolutionary poetics.

In the poem's conclusion, there is not so much a perception of a breach of faith as a sad, stark recognition that the traditional female roles still obtain, even here; it is a realization that the woman romanced as a lover the night before is still expected to do all the dusting and cleaning of the furniture of love. The subtext of the poem is antiromantic, deflationary, even anti-heterosexual; it effectively registers how a woman entering into living in sin can feel mocked by minor devils. For her, this romance has become a torturous lie and a sin.

Now, switching to observing the man, the speaker's romantic counterpart, in the verse paragraph after the one on the mouse and beetle, the poet moves to a truncated line where strong caesuras stress the discontinuity between male and female perceptions of this love nest: he yawns and plays notes upon the keyboard, but then pronounces it in need of tuning, shrugs at himself in the glass, and having rubbed at his beard unceremoniously, goes out for cigarettes; his actions are active, even egotistical and self-indulgent. But when she rips off the sheets and makes the bed, her work is not only necessitated by a sense of the woman's duty, it is also mindless, routine. While she is dusting the table with a towel, the coffee boils over (*DI* 61).

The succession of active verbs describing him indicates his edgy restlessness, followed by his escape, and her angry dynamism, powerlessness to keep him in; the speaker keeps house instead, pulling sheets, making the bed (not love), and finding not romantic passion but a towel. Consequently, in self-absorption, she allows the coffee-pot to boil over, wasting what she has provided. Perhaps her anger at having been left with all the cleaning up is displaced and rendered concrete in the image of the coffee-pot boiling over on the stove. Since she cannot boil over, she lets the coffee-pot do it for her. The mind-numbing repetition of boring household tasks is emphasized in the linking of her acts paratactically with *and*'s instead of listing them with commas in-between in a more plausible sequence.

In "When We Dead Awaken," Rich relates her own sense in young womanhood of "female fatigue of suppressed anger and loss of contact with my own being": the required constant attention to trivial tasks or duties that had to be done over and over since young children constantly undo what their mothers do (*ARP* 173). For Rich personally, the loss of contact with her own being—the loss of selfhood and a living connection with both the contemporary world and her own imaginative life—were sources of shock and pain. In the poem, each of the lovers performs a sequence of activities, but the man's are the more picturesque, dashing, and romantic, far freer and more active; hers are determined, generic, ordinary, servile even. And because he effectively abandons her, going out for cigarettes, she must go back to being merely an ordinary woman and a drudge while he can flit off, stylishly insouciant, typically not having to deal with the mess. Most telling is that final verse paragraph's facing up to the denial of her resentment: the speaker asserts that the romance was restored to their relationship later that night, that she was back in love again, but the perfect rhythm of the poem's last line is jarred by the swift addition, in imperfect rhythm, of "though not so wholly." Overnight instead of sleeping, this woman wakes up occasionally to feel the daylight coming in ironically upon the lovers like a "relentless milkman" stomping upstairs (*DI* 61). Denial, guilt, and desire play in this romantic interlude revealing the woman's lack of equality and freedom in the game of love and romance.

Some critics have offered ingenious interpretations of this final motet: "The coming of light is associated with a man. And it is perhaps significant that he is a milkman, suggesting obliquely that women have been alienated from their natural condition."[31] The coming may have sexual implications reflecting an alienation, but central to the resolution is the relentless arrival of milkman equated with daylight, the dawning moral consciousness that she is living in sin, and it does not give her the happiness she dreamed of. Noises in the taps and on the stairs disturb what should be ecstatic slumbers, and the pears are merely scraps in the morning. Heterosexual love, too, is reduced to scraps and messiness and a new awareness of dis-ease—in short, disillusionment, perhaps a guilt, that she could impart to no one without loss of face. She confides that American culture dictated that in the 1950s, life was "extremely private"; and women were isolated from one other by the "loyalties of marriage" and never spoke together "about their secret emptiness, their frustrations" (*ARP* 173). Women were reluctant to confide in one another, afraid to confess their inner discontent in a time when they were supposed to be living their lifelong dreams. It later became one of Adrienne Rich's purposes to break down women's isolation and lack of communication by the force of her poetry. She ventures to speak to the woman isolated at home and/or oppressed. In the end, the milkman, coming up the stairs, and the conquering chivalric lover's absence awaken her to a knowledge that the real world and man's dominance, sounder than any lover's illusion, will prevail, despite her fantasies.

Visiting the classic scenario of woman seduced and abandoned (without a hint of tawdry sentimental melodrama), this realistic, practical woman poet compares her perceptions with what Simone de Beauvoir and Gayatri Spivak call "the Other." Experiencing oneself not as the acting subject but as the passive—yet experiencing—object in male-female relationship, she gives voice for the first time, if mockingly, to a legitimate angst felt by many women. For the first time, here she writes personally of the universal female pain of disillusionment and unexpected loss, her sense of "secret emptiness" and frustration. Yet the wonder of the poem for the reader is a quality she has commented on in other women's poetry that "the source of the fascination and terror is, simply, Man's power—to dominate, tyrannize, choose, or reject the woman" (*ARP* 168). If the speaker of "Living in Sin" is not tyrannized over or rejected, she is dominated and, ironically, chosen. This is the situation, she suggests, of even the intellectual woman, desiring a freer life, one un-countenanced by culture and tradition.

Her poetic interest in the limits of language, in the tension between language's potential for containment and for liberation of meaning, is another abiding focus for Adrienne Rich. In an interview with David Montenegro, she says that "one of the underlying themes of my poetry is the tension between the possibilities in language for mere containment and the possibilities for expansion, for liberation" (*ARP* 258). The new dynamism of her poetry opposes women's traditional confinement to restrictive social and political spheres and seeks to face the difficult questions of women's authentic experience in liberating poetic language, rhythms, and forms.

For Adrienne Rich, this period, 1949–1955, was one of subtle, deep inner exploration of the tension between containment and liberation, purity and danger, social/sexual risk and its consequences. Her poetry had previously embodied containment: her former emphasis had been on saying what she could in the most elegant and succinct way. But here and there in the familiar poem "Living in Sin," the discordant, liberated note of her future voice, what she calls her undervoice, sounds.

"VILLA ADRIANA" AND WALLACE STEVENS

The last stanza of "Villa Adriana" displays an imagery of excavation and reconstruction, imagery that will become central to Rich's poetic poetry, from *Diving into the Wreck* through *Midnight Salvage:* the perspective is often that of dreamers searching for an answer, searchers who are "[p]assionately in need to reconstruct..." (*DI* 44). Cool and composed, the poem completes this image of archaeological and psychic reconstruction, all occurring in a dream state: some dreamers dig in dreams under the "high noon" of deepest sleep at the site of love but find their Hadrian has slipped away and vanished (*DI* 44). Here in a charming conceit, Rich neatly combines the tropes of passionate lover and spiritual seeker at the same time that she builds a sense of urgency. In this way, she subtly makes the ancient contemporary, balancing timely desires and current interests. In her mind's eye, Hadrian's villa is repopulated with his lovers and liaisons. Persons of high rank in higher intrigue, facing their own high noons, effect her realization and understanding in sleep's high noon of their thrilling lives. The work of excavation is another central theme in her poetry, one linked with her other work of exploring and later exposing the limits of language. Another poem in the book named "The Explorers," similar in style to "Villa Adriana" (tr. *Adrienne's Villa*), dwells on the exploration of the Mare Crisium on Mars. The focus on exploration and excavation culminates in *Diving into the Wreck* and in later books.

This sort of time travel or mixing of diverse spheres of reference also occurs in the work of Wallace Stevens, one of her mentors in this period. "Although," as Jaqueline Brogan reminds us, "Adrienne Rich certainly [in later years] indicts Wallace Stevens for his reductive uses of racial stereotypes and slurs; in her essay, 'Rotted Names'...she also suggests...that it is from Wallace Stevens that she first learned a 'radical or revolutionary poetics.'"[32] From Stevens, she learned to connect the reality of her female subjectivity with the local place or event and render this connection in contemporary poetry.

A poet of Auden and Eliot's generation, Wallace Stevens was the poet Rich chose as poetic mentor or muse, especially while writing *The Diamond Cutters and Other Poems.* Even though she rejects him later when committed to a poetry of witnessing for what she calls his "compulsive reiterations" of a racist word, still much in his language and in the scope and range of his poetry attracts the young poet. In his poetry Stevens discusses philosophical and aesthetic ideas in poems in free and blank verse, always employing a carefree, if formal, tone. The imagination itself is his central inspiration and subject. In "Not how to write but wherefore," an essay from *What is Found There,* Rich describes her beginnings as a poet: she was "well grounded in formal technique, and...loved the craft"—yet she was trying to find a sense of vocation, "what it means to live as a poet—not how to write poetry, but wherefore" (*WF* 195). So she took as her mentor Wallace Stevens, an insurance executive, "a poet of extreme division," who was an excellent choice, given the fact that she had to write herself out of her own divisions (*WF* 16).

Choosing as her mentor a poet obsessed with resolving his own internal divisions was actually intellectually stimulating for a poet riven with the internal divisions many women were secretly then experiencing. Acting as a seismic register for the tensions and pressures privately experienced by young married women wanting lives fuller than their mothers', yet seeing little possibility of achieving them, her poetry records the shifting subterranean plates of women's dawning consciousness of themselves sharing common goals and common pain, hence her need to write herself out of her divisions. Since the pressures on the poet and her poetry were intense, the poetry itself had to change, break into free verse and blank verse, experiment with different kinds of rhythms and rhymes, other modes of making music in order to record a shift in women's consciousness. Eventually Rich would create her own version of Charles Olson's projective verse; however, in *The Diamond Cutters,* her aesthetic credo is best articulated in the title poem.

RICH'S AESTHETIC CREDO IN "THE DIAMOND CUTTERS"

After the first book of poetry, *A Change of World,* and its successes, Rich continued to write assiduously; the impetus to find her voice and identity, to build a poetic selfhood, drove her to write and express her aesthetic credo. In "The Diamond Cutters" (*DI* 118–19), a poem whose title invites comparison with Robinson Jeffers's *The Stone Cutters* published 30 years earlier, she articulates her credo, a poetic testament of the sort Robinson Jeffers himself had created. This poem is about craft, likening the poet's art to the diamond cutter's.

The qualities of precision, intellect, and planning it takes to cut diamonds are delineated here. Combined, they produce a prescription for writing poems; it is fitting, though somewhat surprising, that the poem should be a series of direct commands, beginning with a stress on adopting a matter-of-fact tone and realistic attitude. Intelligence is personified and addressed here; like the diamond it is recently unearthed (*DI* 118). Here the intelligence is both the poet's and the stone's: a relationship of respect and love exists between the poet and her medium—words. A chain of commands ensues to be serious, and hardhearted—oddly personifying the stone, stating that the stone may become contemptuous if the poet's hands are overly familiar (*DI* 118–19) since only in keeping the proper aesthetic distance does the poet achieve a successful poem through crafting the perfect form. The craftsman/poet must remain tough (*DI* 119), since eventually the artisan must part with her creation: since the poem will go out into the world to be read by strangers, a writer must stay aloof from human pride or vanity. But women writers must be single-minded, loving only the craft and what they are now creating, not staying attached to what has already been created (*DI* 119). Let go of the past as now it is beyond change or redemption.

Discussing this poem in a later interview, Rich courageously acknowledges that at the time she wrote it, she had had no idea of the actual living conditions of those who worked the diamond mines in South Africa, or of the human rights issues she was failing to engage in this stoic, even *macho,* statement of the craftsman's creed. There is a strong division between master and material here. Again, the distinction between subject and object, craftsman/woman and words, actor and the acted-upon claims center stage while the individual speaker is neutral, cold, impersonal. If the artist's sole purpose is to shape the materials in the process of creation, here the oracle of critical theory, the shaper of the poem on how to write, explores the metaphor of poem-making as diamond cutting, since poems are as hard, brilliant, and as difficult to cut as diamonds. Through a creative detachment and formalist dissociation, the poet wields disparate materials into the perfectly formed, unified product, the verbal icon of the poem: use refined tools and claim a good price (*DI* 119), since refinement increases a poem's worth. Just as the diamond cutter liberates the best form for each unique stone, Rich's advice to the poet is to liberate her (the poem's) purity but still to remain impassive, detached (*DI* 119). Although Marilyn Monroe sang, "Diamonds are a girl's best friend," here Rich insists that the true poet must remain aloof from desire, in true Modernist fashion. Still, *The Diamond Cutters* is one book the mature Rich has said she might want to disown from time-to-time.

Speaking authoritatively to a new generation of poets as a now well-established poet, Rich exhorts her audience of would-be apprentices to "Be proud." In lines reminiscent of the late W. B. Yeats, she orders them to leave the work aside when finished and refrain from the craft, knowing another day will give them fresh inspiration and new works of art to create (*DI* 119). The poet explores the possibilities of language for containment rather than for expansion in lines glorifying the craft and the poet's adamant dedication to craftsmanship, for its own sake.

In a 1991 interview, David Montenegro asked her if she now felt she had taken responsibility for what some might now think was the socially and politically irresponsible emphasis on the *travail* of diamond miners and cutters, figments of her imagination. In a rather far-fetched image, embarrassingly she equated by her own admission "the travail of craft with a very different kind of labor—virtual enslavement, peonage" (*ARP* 259). Now, she wishes she had not.

Whether or not one deems it successful, what the poem attempts to convey is a sense of the travail and craft of writing poetry, that poetry-writing is hardly something to be taken lightly: it is a profession necessitating a vocation, even a high calling. Even though one may doubt the contemporary effectiveness or political correctness of the metaphor, one can respect the courage it must have taken to reprint the poem anyway in the second Norton Critical Edition *Adrienne Rich's Poetry and Prose* (1993), despite what may be some embarrassment about its callow association with the exploitation of Black South African miners.

Giving her own assessment of *The Diamond Cutters* in 1993, she writes,

> The one book from which I was tempted to delete poems is *The Diamond Cutters,* my second volume. It received much praise; but too many of the poems were, at best, facile and underground imitations of other poets—Elinor Wylie, Robert Frost, Elizabeth Bishop, Dylan Thomas, Wallace Stevens, Yeats, even English Gregorian poets—exercises in style.... Many of the poems in *The Diamond Cutters* seem to me now a last-ditch effort to block...the undervoice of my own poetry. With the poems in *Snapshots of a Daughter-in-Law* (1963), I began trying, to the best of my ability, to face the hard questions of poetry and experience. (*CEP* xix)

Having achieved a consummate mastery of rhyme and meter at the beginning, in later books Rich will experiment with open forms and free verse. She will gradually leave behind the former extreme poetic restraint for a more direct confrontation with the subjects of the poems and of woman's selfhood, facing with greater awareness the hard questions of poetry and experience (*CEP* xix).

Chapter 3

Eruptions of the Female Psyche

The publication of Rich's next book, *Snapshots of a Daughter-in-Law* (1963), marked an utter departure from anything she'd written before, a transformation in poetic sensibility and style. It demonstrated a marked evolution in her poetry and feminist consciousness.

Affirming that poetry can unite those "parts of us which exist in dread and those which have the surviving sense of a possible happiness, collectivity, community, a loss of isolation" (*ARP* 164), Adrienne Rich now addresses the dislocation of the world and of her own psyche; her new poetry explores the gap between what is public and what is private in contemporary America. She conceives of her poetic mission as an effort to bring women's secrets out into the light in the belief that women's secrets are not only the same, but that if they are painful they are wounds that can be healed once opened to air. When women stop hiding in fear and dread, keeping up appearances, Rich asserts, they can forge a "possible happiness, collectivity, community," and hence, end that particularly female isolation of the middle-class housewife (*ARP* 164).

Reading the new book makes Rich's first two books, *A Change of World* and *The Diamond Cutters and Other Poems,* seem somewhat inauthentic for the present time. In the books of poetry published in the 1960s, she writes as a more contemporary, if erudite poet, less concerned with the strict observance of rhyme and conventional classical subjects, less attracted to or imitative of her forebears. She is far more original and adventurous. Here Adrienne Rich is a woman giving birth to her own unique voice, what she calls the undervoice of her own poetry. She is emerging from female invisibility into self-exploration and self-definition of her identity.

In his book on the writer's vocation, *Life Work,* Donald Hall tells of their discussions of poetry writing during the period when Rich awaited one son's birth and he was caring for young children:

> Once a week, Adrienne Rich came to the apartment for a three-hour visit during baby-care. She was pregnant with her first child, and although we talked poetry most of the time, we did not talk only poetry. Like anyone awaiting her first child, Adrienne was nervous about the fragility of an infant, and about the nurturing tasks ahead of her. Twenty-five years later, when so much had happened in our lives, Adrienne and I talked about gender politics in the 1950s; I claimed I wasn't nearly so bad as I might have been. "Don," Adrienne reminded me, "you taught me how to bathe a baby."[1]

Does Donald Hall record this out of friendship, or to reveal his helpfulness to her or how he taught her, or to show how poets could stay in touch with their work even in the course of child raising? Probably he seeks to show her dedication to her vocation and efforts to continue writing poetry despite her personal circumstances. Whatever his reason, this rare glimpse into her life as pregnant wife reveals a professional poet regularly scheduling visits to a fellow poet and building discussions of poetry into her traditional married life and her perseverance in this in the face of imminent childbirth. That she kept on writing throughout the entire process of childbearing and raising her children is clear from her poems in *Snapshots;* the experience of motherhood tested the dedication of her professional commitment to the poet's vocation and ambition, and her vocation emerged as her proven life's commitment. Still, she has always objected to poets who place their loved ones in their poetry and make poetic capital from their domestic experiences, so there are few poems focusing their gaze solely on the domestic experience of being a wife and mother. Rich might consider this an exploitative invasion of their privacy.

That she may have endured the constant pressure of daily childcare as virtually sole caregiver to her three boys seems probable both from contemporary reports and because of the sex-role stereotyping normal in the 1950s. The experience certainly led to growth and fuller self-discovery, and from this new self-knowledge and consciousness of motherhood she crafted a new poetry in more open forms and fields, creating new female subjects to give symbolic embodiment to difficult personal conditions and the inner changes motherhood thrust upon her. The extreme psychological pressures of motherhood, especially strong when the children are spaced at two-year intervals, force the entire family to examine its priorities, and each parent to explore his or her limits of sanity.

Although she had deliberately chosen motherhood, at times caring for so many small children made it difficult—even impossible—for her to write because it greatly curtailed the time and effort she could put into writing. Of this period she wrote in 1971 that the poets' imagination must testify to the lives they are living: the imagination must be honest, imagine oppositions in dialogue with one another and alternatives. This does not mesh well with the day-to-day maternal care of youngsters (*ARP* 174).

Her poetry of this period reflects a woman's earnest desire to fulfill all the prerogatives of a "full" life, "the life available to most men, in which sexuality, work, and parenthood...coexist" (*ARP* 174). She sought to be the perfect traditional wife. In her poems the "human relationship is presented in geographical/spatial terms."[2] The woman's sphere is indoors, maintaining the home, caring for the sometimes-quarreling children; as in "Living in Sin" the man's sphere is outdoors, away from domestic responsibilities. Because she coped honestly and energetically with the challenges and frustrations faced by any mother with very young children and a vocation and because practically alone of her generation of women poets she survived this period of her life (while Sylvia Plath, Anne Sexton, and many other women poets foundered on the shoals of motherhood), her poetry of this era and its psychic transitions are important both intrinsically to Rich and extrinsically in bearing witness to the female undervoice of motherhood, previously so long suppressed.

Except for Edna St. Vincent Millay, H.D., Sarah Teasdale, Mina Loy, Marianne Moore, and Elizabeth Bishop, serious women poets did not dwell on their intimate psychic, spiritual, or psychological states in informal personal voice or create female characters who occasionally wondered if they were going mad until the generation of Adrienne Rich, Denise Levertov, Sylvia Plath, Robin Morgan, and Tillie Olsen gave younger poets (and a post–World War II audience) inspiration and impetus to write in this more daring vein. Because Rich charted her way poetically through the turbulent waters of this transitional time both in her own life and in women's lives in American history, *Snapshots of a Daughter-in-Law* represents a turning point in her poetic development and in American women's poetry; it contains the seeds of her later, more mature, poetry.

SNAPSHOTS OF A DAUGHTER-IN-LAW (1963)

If Rich could say of *The Diamond Cutters* that it was her "last-ditch effort to block...the undervoice of my own poetry" (*CEP* xix), in *Snapshots of a Daughter-in-Law* she removes all block to or mutings of the undervoice of her poetry. In her third book her real female voice speaks. The incipient radicalization of the traditional woman who will become the foremost American feminist poet and critic announces itself with the advent of this book.

One might say that at this point in her poetic life the education in what it is to be a woman supersedes the education in what it is to be a poet. Rich changes subject positions and enlarges her perspective on womanhood and its potential—personal and poetic. The fractured lines of the title poem and other major poems like "The Roofwalker" betray a new consciousness and momentum: her goal is "To give birth to—a recognizable, autonomous self, a creation in poetry and in life" (*OWB* 26–27). The poetry betrays a new urgency as well, and it is important to note that her next volume of poetry would be called simply *Necessities of Life,* emphasizing the need to be of use—for both poem and poet to be useful. In *Snapshots of a Daughter-in-Law,* the highly creative, original poems in free verse reflect a mind in the process of conscious evolution along with a consciousness in the process of that evolution; these are Rich's first feminist poems. As Betsy Erkkila explains, she was "unit[ing] the divided energies of body and mind, woman and poet, relation and creation in order." Moreover, "Rejecting her 1955 volume of poems *The Diamond Cutters* as 'mere exercises for poems I hadn't written,' in the late 1950s Rich was able, as she says, 'to write, for the first time, directly about experiencing myself as a woman' [*On Lies, Secrets and Silence,* 42, 44]."[3] Rich speaks from the duality of needing to find a mesh between woman and poet. She is a woman who as part of her "resistance" wants to clean up her act and become more aware of her behavior as it reveals her politics (*ARP* 239).

Her early poems had been rightly praised for their mature perspective on mutability and their cultivation of "'detachment from the self and its emotions,'" which was T. S. Eliot's definition of *craftsmanship.* But in *Snapshots,* her voice becomes at once more intimate and personal yet ironically more poignant in its expression of her consciousness of what it is to be a woman. Her undervoice is expressed for the first time, so the poems are more graphic and particular in their focus on telling detail. In this poetry, "body and mind, woman and poet, relation and creation" are united for the first time.

In tone and style, the new poetry is far freer. The poem here is not a means of containment of the idea and craft but a liberation of word, thought, and woman. It is as if the doors of the mind have been thrown open and the fresh air of viscerally experienced thought and emotion is blowing in; the former poetry had striven toward a universal consciousness and maintained what was essentially a neutral tone and voice. Conversely, here the lyric "I" may be either a man or a woman ("The Loser"), or a woman commenting sarcastically about the fate and limitations of women ("Snapshots of a Daughter-in-Law") or a woman reflecting on common humble household chores, ironically weeping while doing them ("Peeling Onions"). In "Peeling Onions," she mocks a housewife's plight in the first line: if only she had a grief that was equal to all this weeping (*S* 54). She mocks herself since, in reality, she isn't sad at all (*S* 54). In fact, she is tough as Peer Gynt, the stoic picaresque hero of the Norse epic. And at times in her life her extreme sensitivity made her so vulnerable that even the gaze of an animal burned into her consciousness (*S* 54). The speaker feels her eyes stinging in her head;

hence she imagines clerks would notice her (*S* 54). This image invokes another epic image, that of Oedipus: although before she had said to herself that she is not a hero, only an onion chopper. Blinded like Oedipus, she knows she is hardly in his league since she has been blinded by onions, not epic spears or a tragic destiny. Again, she mocks women's pretensions to epic heroism; yet ironically heroism takes up space in the poem and becomes its focus.

Here women's pretensions to male spheres and status are portrayed ironically, perhaps for the last time in her poetry. Still, despite the irony, she also speaks as a woman on behalf of all women in this book for the first time. She speaks of the situation of women frequently relegated to *peeling onions*, a common household chore. Such earthy humor has hardly figured in her poetry before, nor has self-mockery. Her moral sensitivity, with its attendant pain, lies stuffed in her lungs like smog (*S* 54). The textual "I" may have had no legitimate outlet for her psychological or physical pain, no break from her labor, or respite from drudgery in *Snapshots of a Daughter-in-Law* (1963).

In *Snapshots of a Daughter-in-Law,* her highly original poems in free verse reflect a mind in the process of conscious evolution along with a consciousness in the process of that evolution; these are Rich's first feminist poems. They reflect her dawning awareness as a poet that the acculturation of the traditional female denies women's creativity and originality: as she said later of this time, "But to be a female human being trying to fulfill traditional female functions in a traditional way is in direct conflict with the subversive function of the imagination" (*ARP* 174) which must have total freedom to work efficiently in a poet. Her early poems had been rightly praised for their sophisticated perspective on mutability, but as she was changing within so her style of poetry had to change.

Even the title of this book is far less abstract and allusive, more informal and intimate, than any previous Rich title. And the term *snapshots,* while it brings to mind risqué photos stuck in the cockpits of planes during World War II or photos on refrigerator doors, is an informal term that distances and objectifies the daughter-in-law. Not quite real, the daughter-in-law is merely the subject of the photograph: she is accorded her title only by marriage, not through any qualities she herself possesses. The casual word *snapshot* implies she may be unimportant; moreover, she is defined in terms of her legal relationship with her husband; she is not given a name or an identity. She is depersonalized, objectified, yet the very act of capturing her on film in a snapshot presents her as a potential lure to the gaze, even a sex object. Romance or sex, however, seems strangely lacking here in the title poem.

Having completed what may be called her poetic apprenticeship, Adrienne Rich is no longer writing in the Eliot-Tate-Auden formalist style, her style of the early- to mid-1950s. In "When We Dead Awaken," she describes the whirlwind changes in her life, first a Radcliffe undergraduate, then published her book of poems "by a fluke," and engaged in all the activities of a typical college graduate—breaking up with a love, starting a job, living alone, falling in love again, and energetic, even exhilarated, because everyone concurred she was a born poet (*ARP* 173). Her candor in the essay is both surprising and disarming since it indicates that before the world acknowledged that she was a poet, Rich herself may not have been quite sure.

In and after writing her second book she awakened to a truer sense of her mature poetic identity in poetry: but by the time it appeared, it seemed to her to be full of "mere exercises" for potential poems, and it grated that *The Diamond Cutters* was praised for its "gracefulness" (*ARP* 173). To make matters worse, Randall Jarrell, another important Modernist critic, had called her "sweet." Her wistful and frustrating sense of having been patronized is not lost on the modern reader, male or female.

Having fulfilled, like so many young girls of her time, the American Dream, she felt vaguely guilty to be bored occasionally or depressed with both a fine husband and son. When she had these bouts of depression, she felt it was a sign of ingratitude or insatiability: she feared she might be a "monster" (*ARP* 173). Not surprisingly, *Snapshots of a Daughter-in-Law* is written in this spirit of fear and doubt: it reflects the consciousness of a woman who "sleeps with a monster" or possibly the one who might think she is a monster. She had succeeded at all she'd aimed for and was supposedly living the American Dream of the perfect mother and housewife, the woman who has it all. Still, she was beset by self-recrimination and guilt. She likely blamed herself for her misery and could not yet see the larger reasons for this very natural state of mind. Postnatal depression was still unheard of.

Having three sons in six years, she suffered both the physical, mental, and psychological shock of many childbirths in a short time and the constant exhausting, seemingly futile work of nurturing small children. Possibly at some point every mother who has worked before giving birth may have fears that her brain may be moldering. Thoughts of Miss Havisham's madness might evoke in any young mother a panic that she too would go mad, plagued by her sense of loss and anger at a sense of lack of fulfillment and undiagnosed, possibly postpartum, depression. Now, society's awareness of women's psychology during and after childbirth may make it easier to cope with the dull depression, the frustration of maternal isolation, or feelings of displacement. These feelings are even greater challenges for the woman poet, however, since only the free life of the imagination can produce good poetry, and imagination may become, by her own account, inaccessible for periods of time during maternity. While husbands in this era could always leave the home either for recreation or work, a wife was solidly bound to the home and children and to domesticity.

Still, in the 1950s, political and religious leaders alike perceived and denounced women's rebellious feelings as running counter to social expectations. The very qualities in her work which W. H. Auden had praised and personified—conformity to tradition, self-restraint, modesty, and detachment—were not qualities that best equip one with what today are thought of as "survival skills" for motherhood. And in other marriages (not Rich's), a wife's talent—or lack of it—for leaving the "unsaid word" unspoken has led to many divorces. It is understandable that creative women possessing these and other poetic talents might find it hard simply to have babies and keep house while trying to find the time and mental space to write.

"THE ROOFWALKER"

"The Roofwalker" in *Snapshots of a Daughter-in-Law* is a fine, poignant poem about a daring person walking across a roof, a person whose situation parallels that of the feminist poet; its conclusion reads like the inner monologue of an artist unwillingly fallen into the wrong role or career in life. The ruminating speaker, an architect, wonders why he drew blueprints, those and calculations (*S* 63). Why such care and attention to builder's specifications and all details? Why did he do so much figuring—just to be so unhappy with the outcome? The poem continues, stating that what she found herself living was a life she had not anticipated or chosen (*S* 64). What's more, her tools are the wrong ones for this enterprise (*S* 64). Young women are trained to be beautiful, obedient, and quiet before marriage; but they are given education inappropriate to the new roles they will fulfill. Indeed, Rich's opening for part nine of "Snapshots of a Daughter-in-Law" is the statement of Samuel Johnson, who elsewhere equated the phenomenon of "*a woman preaching*" to that of "*a dog's walking on its hind legs*": "*Not that it is done well, but / that it is done at all*" is astonishing to the misogynist critic Dr. Johnson (*S* 24). To which the textual "I" replies sardonically that one should think of the odds against the weaker vessel's succeeding in the real world of the professions (*S* 24). Here she alludes to the traditional image of the woman poet as invalid inherited from nineteenth-century England, reminiscent of poets like Elizabeth Barrett Browning, an invalid, kept sequestered by her tyrannical father. Still, she was a brilliant poet, one who nearly became poet laureate of England.

In another part of the same poem, part four, Rich focuses on one of her own heroines of poetry, the reclusive Emily Dickinson, whose gifts for writing poetry are seen by Rich as not necessarily pure bliss, but a curse; and the gift makes her defensive and proud to the point of being sensitive to any hint of scorn (*S* 22). She envisions Emily Dickinson reading in the kitchen waiting for an iron to heat, then writing her line "*My Life had stood—a Loaded Gun—*." Rich makes a point of rhyming the strong Anglo-Saxon monosyllables "gun" and "scrum" when she speaks of Emily Dickinson as loaded gun in that Amherst pantry tending jellies that boil and "scum" (*S* 22), showing how Dickinson's own life may have been silently in turmoil, heated by suppressed indignation as she stirs and writes—about to explode?

Confined to domesticity—all cooking and cleaning—Emily Dickinson, whose line "*My Life had stood—a Loaded Gun—*" Rich incorporated into her poetry, is for Rich the classic original poet, "THE American poet" as she puts it, not an invalid but a genius. Still, she is a recluse, a woman in white seldom seen outdoors, never a bride, but definitely a cook, housekeeper, practical provider, and gardener for her family. It testifies to her thrift that many of her poems were written on torn envelopes or the backs of grocery lists or friends' letters.

Dickinson represents another traditional archetype of the woman poet—the eccentric solitary (possibly mad or cracked?, asked the gossips with their "Dimity Convictions"): Dickinson is a poet who in previous centuries might have been branded an outcast by an uncomprehending public or even burned as a heretic or witch. Rich imagines her imprisoned in her father's house, nursing a rage that may have boiled and scummed over, since she herself had suffered through a childhood with an overbearing father and even had been locked in a dark cupboard or closet when she was naughty, as Dickinson was. Both had been abused as girls—not physically, but mentally, spiritually, and psychologically.

On the contrary, my own reading of Emily Dickinson indicates that her isolation was pleasant freedom from the social duties of the Amherst middle-class lady; it was self-chosen and self-imposed. Certainly, though, like many other nineteenth-century women writers, Emily Dickinson had to fit her poetry writing in around daily household chores that took precedence over poetry in her family's—and even more important, her father's—eyes. As Paula Bennett, Betsy Erkkila, and others have indicated, Adrienne Rich may have been able to identify with what she saw as Dickinson's domestic repression.[4] Rich sees that Dickinson was determined to live her life on her own "premises," playing on the double meaning of premises; and this would likely have emboldened Rich to attempt what has never been attempted—to reinscribe the female subject in history and poetry.

In "The Roofwalker" (*S* 63), the title character embodies the revolutionary spirit of a person unafraid to leave the security of home and family, the psychic and spiritual ethos of a person bold enough to be a poet. This (male) roofwalker has escaped middle-class complacency, domesticity, potential mediocrity, and the traditional, culturally prescribed roles, in that the speaker is naked, ignorant, and fleeing at night over roofs, but this is a person who might *just* as well be sitting in a comfortable chair in the lamplight reading—with great interest—about a naked man running across roofs (*S* 63).

The lyric "I" stresses the ironic Escher-like reversibility of speaker/writer and reader, since the poet is a radically changed woman and hence her readership is new now.

Although the roofwalker is male, the speaker anticipates the androgynous "I am she: I am he" speaker of "Diving into the Wreck" (*DW* 24). Rich may suggest that although the traditional position of women might have resembled that of the person relaxing under a lamp, reading, ironically eagerly, about the daring original feat of creation the roofwalker now achieves, the fact that a woman poet may just as well have created a physically active naked female subject signifies Rich's realization through poetry that woman is capable of emancipation from domesticity or confinement or imprisonment—of the imagination.

Just as the author here is female, so here the roofwalker, the original one who takes risks, is probably female for the first time as well. In the past, the women in Rich's poems were passive and resigned: they read, praised, and reacted to men's creative efforts while men had adventures. Women's chief value inhered in their docility, passivity, and their sensitivity to men's needs, even in their ability to do the household chores men never thought to do, as in "Living in Sin." With the change in the air brought about by the passage of the Civil Rights Act of 1964, the Black Civil Rights struggle, and women's liberation, minorities and women began challenging formerly all-male bastions in the sciences, arts, all professions, and in every walk of life. But since each resisting woman tended to see herself as unique, a pioneer, it could seem lonely and dangerous out there.

The alienation from society and isolation symbolized by walking naked and alone on rooftops might be terrifying—or exhilarating—depending on one's perspective. Having rendered in "The Loser" the stresses of the claustrophobic existence of the isolated suburban wife, Rich now imaginatively experiences the distinct thrill of being an outsider. Displaced and voyaging alone in the spheres of the imagination, through the medium of the poet's transcendent perspective, she can almost look down into her own living room and see herself.

WHO IS "THE LOSER"?

Paradoxically, up to this point, Adrienne Rich's poems had depicted *men* reading, thinking, studying; these are the natural, expected activities men engaged in while women did the housework. "Ghost of a Chance" opens by focusing on a man attempting to "think." At such moments, one wants to tell the world to stay away from him, to allow him space (*S* 55). But she believes in every person's right—the universal right—to study, read, and *enjoy* learning and thinking, not only men's right to those intellectual pleasures and pursuits, but everyone's. This is another poem where "he" could have been be substituted for "she." So, significantly, his attempts at thought (like Claudio's attempts at prayer in *Hamlet*) end in devastation as if the speaker had to punish herself for the transgressive act of stealing the language, stealing thought itself, and creating a good poem. In addition, the poem registers the wave of angst some women feel at times upon realizing they are more intelligent or talented than some men are.

In 1962, "he," not "she," was the generic pronoun. Later Rich wrote of this time, "I hadn't found the courage yet to do without authorities," or even to use the pronoun "I" (*ARP* 175). In "Diving into the Wreck" Adrienne Rich will write sardonically that the very act of poetry writing may be seen as an unnatural act (*DW* 31)—for a mother, for instance, who has other claims on her attention; yet it is not unnatural to a woman whose vocation is poetry. Yet to a woman whose vocation is poetry to forfeit poetry writing altogether as culture and society seem to necessitate is to become unnatural—a loser.

In the late 1950s, the time when Adrienne Rich was writing *Snapshots,* women were seen primarily in their sex and social roles, and unlike her male counterparts, every little girl was not raised to believe she could achieve success in a profession or be president. Women were assured of being the world's future housekeepers or its mothers, sisters, but not necessarily its poets or leaders; thus, it is not surprising that Rich might feel some concern about her future in poetry. She may even have feared losing her ability to write through the loss of her craft: terrified by the "sense of drift" she experienced, pulled along by life to invest all her time in the children, she felt she was losing touch with her own being (*ARP* 173).

The horror of becoming isolated, of losing touch with one's own inner life, the life of the imagination, is frightening. That her real life was filled up with what may have felt at times like futile domesticity and drift could itself be a motivation to write, in another poet. Finding a way to deal with all these complex issues, Rich writes in the third person perspective of a former lover or friend of a young housewife, and later she inserts the poem "The Loser" whole into the essay "When We Dead Awaken" to indicate how she was wrestling with the gains and losses of marriage and motherhood just before the birth of her youngest son, Jacob Conrad, in 1959. The poem assumes the classic stance of the rejected lover longing for a lost love, seeing the young woman, the poem's subject, as a bride and, now again, nearly nine years later. He still sees her beauty and strength, admiring them.

Cut off from her father, for whom she had written poems for the first 21 years, and cut off temporarily from her studies and career as a poet, Rich is now forced to fall back on her own inner resources, to change her approach to poetry, and consequently her poetic style because *she* and her audience have changed, and she needed to write herself out of her divisions. All the while she ironically resented her seemingly self-imposed dilemma and felt a mixture of self-loathing, guilt, and anger at herself and others, experiencing an abiding exhaustion of "suppressed anger" (*ARP* 173).

In 1959, when her third son was born, she felt impelled to take strong measures to recover her selfhood and the poet inside, who was drowning; hence she transformed the raw materials of these profound conflicts and questions into a new more fissured poetry reflective of her less-assured or poised life. In "The Loser," Rich envisions a young wife being watched by a man who has once loved her and lost her. The woman is strong, capable, hanging washing on the line on a cold morning and leaning into the wind, putting all her intelligence into that act. I see the poem as wry cultural commentary on romance, courtship, marriage, and its aftermath.

A note of bittersweet regret pervades the poem, which might be read as a loosely drawn sketch of her life as it was at the moment of composition or might be an exercise in the new ideology of the dawning feminist movement. The first lines are reminiscent of A. E. Housman and his concern with death, loss, and mortality; the noun in direct address is oddly linked with its modifying "lost" by an "and": it begins lyrically, rhythmically, yet oddly ungrammatically: "I kissed you, bride and lost" (*S* 15). He returned from the wedding with the cool taste of her cheek on his lips (*S* 15), expressing his sense of loss in an ironic barb, playing on the double meanings of "cool," "cheek," and "lips."

The lack of end-stops and the passion in the lines countervails the classical rhyming couplets and cavalier tone of this poignant stanza, whose culmination comes in the second stanza, where the speaker symbolizes her loss to him as one more golden apple has fallen (alluding to the judgment of Paris): he envisions the apple falling silently and uncomplainingly, then she would lie windfall, a beauty wasted—and soon forgotten (*S* 15). Lost to a certain world when she married, her loss as a windfall, but how could golden apples be windfall? She is the fallen, wasted, golden apple since she, the one who shone for him, is now reduced to purely menial tasks, unaware of her seemingly eternally divine potential or her intelligence.

In the third stanza, the speaker continues cynically, observing that all beauty is given away profligately, indiscriminately (*S* 15). The sadness of a brokenhearted suitor who may have lost a true love emanates from these lines, yet in the final three are references to Helen of Troy and her face that launched a thousand ships: here he comments that the wife's face could never be loved seriously enough (*S* 15). This romantic line acts as a kind of consolation for the harsh winds and hard domestic work the former bride now has to perform. Clearly the subtext is that she has thrown herself away on the man she did marry, as this marriage has apparently not been successful. Why is one so beautiful forced to do so much hard physical labor?

In the second section of the poem, in a clever gambit, the young wife strikes admiration in the lover/speaker, anticipating a proto-feminist perspective: he sees that she is tougher than he imagined (*S* 16). But on this icy Valentine's Day morning, her mind is not on romance but laundry: this fact is stressed by the ironic rhyming of "Valentine" and clothes-"line." Apparently an unobserved observer, he sees all her strength is thrust into this energetic stance (*S* 16).

Even though the line might be a tacit complaint that all her intelligence goes into doing menial work; and he admires her strength and tenacity in elegant, formal lines that belie the occasion described, affirming her beauty even now, although the nine years have made her more solid (*S* 16). Her body reveals her history of childbirth—she has borne three daughters but miscarried a son (*S* 16). The years have tested the mettle of this female subject, but they have not conquered her. Childbearing has merely matured her and made her stronger, more confident, but the pull of the intervening years and motherhood have thickened both her body and her approach to life.

Undaunted by harsh weather, engaged, and apparently unnoticed by anyone else, in an unromantic occupation on the morning of St. Valentine's, the young woman seems proud to be fulfilling her work as a wife and mother. She puts all her mind, energy, and will into performing the tasks expected of a good traditional wife and mother, the poem ironically emphasizing that it is not intelligence at all but physical strength woman needs to keep house and bear children. But perhaps this effort has taken its personal toll; at the end, the speaker quietly sees her stumble homeward, bending into the wind. Although she is as yet "unwearied" since she is only 30, her pose is still a stance, not real. Like the stance itself, her role here is a performance, a successful poetic performance and a strong performance by the female subject, ably filling her traditional role, against the harsh February winds, which like life and childbirth itself, have worn away at her natural beauty.

MOVING INTO A NEW POETRY

During the time when *Snapshots of a Daughter-in-Law* was being written, in an act many have remarked was political and personal, Adrienne Rich began giving her poems dates, so as to ground them more firmly in history: she wanted her poetry to partake of what is called reality, with events in history. Aesthetically, she opposed the Modernist notion that poetry was separate from life. She saw it as part of a "historical continuity" not transcendent, superior, nor inferior, just that texts are part of the world, too. Later she comes to believe that poetic texts are not even necessarily better or worse than other texts, just that all are rooted in history and have a responsibility to show where the hands of the clock stood in the republic, each year and each milestone of history (*ARP* 174). Although Rich is an unlikely prophet, she has remained one since *Snapshots.*

Poems, then, arise naturally, imaginatively from their grounding in history; they form part of it, she believed along with Wordsworth. In the next book, *Necessities of Life,* there will be more about poetic grounding and rooting, but from *Snapshots* on, each poem is an act of self-discovery although the self discovered may be—and often is—an imaginary one, a mask covering the true face of the searching poet.

Analyzing her statement that poems needed to be dated and grounded in historical continuity, Craig Werner writes:

> When Rich introduced her *Poems: Selected and New* (1974) 'not as a summing-up or even a retrospective, but as a graph of a process still going on'..., she sounded a note which echoes down through 'Contradictions: Tracking Poems,' the final section of *Your Native Land, Your Life.*[5]

Over her poetic career, Rich's constant effort is to chart the graph of this thought/fear process and share her emotions and ideas about inner change with a sensitive, intelligent reader, who may have been experiencing the same anger she has at the subjugation of women throughout the world. Indeed, her own poetic and imaginative progress through all the roles a traditional woman fills has likely been a vivid source of inspiration and knowledge to her, as well as a source of strength and conviction. In recent years, no woman poet who lived single and childless has commanded so strong a base of power and respect as have the poets like Adrienne Rich, Maya Angelou, Sylvia Plath, Anne Sexton, Maxine Kumin, and Rita Dove—all poets who have given birth to children and experienced the sexual politics of male-female relations. Having first been a heterosexual woman and then a lesbian advocate for women's rights, convinced of the need for women to affirm one another, Rich has run the gamut of subjectivities possible for contemporary women in America. At different times her poems appear to speak from the perspective of each and every female role—daughter, wife, lover, mother, revolutionary leader, professional woman—that a contemporary woman might fulfill.

This is the case with "Snapshots of a Daughter-in-Law," where the speaker is different in each of the poem's 10 sections. In response to a sense of loss, a disillusionment borne of isolation, overwork, and a corresponding sense of futility, Rich writes the poem "Snapshots of a Daughter-in-Law," written in 10 parts over two years, and experiences "extraordinary relief": her sense of unique selfhood and identity returns. By her own admission, she was still stealing from her masters, or poetic mentors, and could not yet forfeit her authorities—the work is replete with quotes from everyone from Campion to Dr. Johnson. Like many graduate students, she could not yet use "the pronoun 'I'," but still she writes herself into the poem as a woman who believes she may be going mad, a daughter-in-law, and another female subject who hears voices prompting her to "resist and rebel" (*ARP* 175).

"SNAPSHOTS OF A DAUGHTER-IN-LAW"

In Part One, the first woman introduced may be an image or imaginary alternate of Rich's own mother. Establishing the speaker's identity from the start, the poet opens the poem in second person in direct address to "You," who was a debutante and Southern belle, with dyed hair and soft skin. The "belle" still makes sure her dresses are copied from the fashions of those days (*S* 21); sadly this belle is an anachronism, with a brain rotting like an old wedding cake now, and the world she inhabits is faintly reminiscent of the salons evoked in *A Change of World*. Her mood is expressed oversentimentally in a line from Cortot: "*Delicious recollections/float like perfume through the memory*" (*S* 21). This is the stuff of romantic illusions, the world of fantasy that reality destroys—like Miss Havisham's hopes for marriage, her fantasies of a romantic future may have moldered like her wedding cake in *Great Expectations*, where the old lady symbolizes patriarchy's buried woman, the woman frustrated in and negated by her own (great) unrealized expectations. Rich keeps an ironic distance from this somewhat grotesque caricature of a belle.

Here the debutante's mind, with its training for the role of Southern belle, is now full of useless experience and knowledge, full of illusions that fragment under the knife blade of reality (*S* 21). The fact that her mind is rotten is due to the belle's inappropriate education (*S* 21). Romantic hopes with no basis in reality, hopes that have foundered and confused her mastery of facts—indeed the cognitive dissonance generated by a woman's training to be a belle—have left her with a mind incapable of dealing with reality. That she has served merely as a negative example to her daughter becomes apparent in the last part of this section, where the daughter is depicted as edgy, sulking, dutiful, but rebelling inwardly (*S* 21). There will be no more Southern belles in this family!

In fact, the subject of the second section is the daughter, now a daughter-in-law several years later. This is the woman on the edge of a nervous breakdown, the young mother who is not crazy but who senses she may be losing her sense of selfhood and perspective. The early 1960s were the years when suicide was on the rise for female celebrities and poets—anticipating Marilyn Monroe's and Sylvia Plath's in 1963. The heady joy of life in America the late 1940s, with "heroes" returning victorious from the War, the exhilaration of the generation that had "won" World War II: this had a role in creating economic boom in the early 1950s. Ultimately, the boom precipitated women's recognition that they were truly no better off now than they had been before World War II, but they had lost their idealism and their hope that their lives might fulfill their professional as well as their maternal potential.

Arthur Miller's *Death of a Salesman* had suggested that the American Dream had lost its innocence and its credibility. Some of those who had enjoyed the post-war boom and the excitement of starting a new life in the 1950s were now rather jaded: men were enjoying business success and its perks, but women were still facing the lack of professional choices and, in some cases, the monotonous day-in-day-out of cleaning and caring for youngsters. Few new careers were opening up to women, and some intelligent women at home with children all day may have felt they were slowly going mad or losing contact with their own being, lacking the escape valve of adult connection with the world. Rich writes in *Snapshots* that like a cat, Emptiness sidles around the door seeking to enter the middle-class housewife's home (*S* 26). Another poem, "Always the Same," speaks of women becoming hysterical in the later years of a marriage while consequently their husbands become silently alarmed (*S* 61), not understanding why their wives are hysterical. For a decent woman to need to discuss personal matters with a psychiatrist was thought by some to be scandalous in polite society: the pillars of society deemed it a sure indication that one was "crazy" in the 1950s and 1960s—and this remained true through the next decades as well. While some female poets like Anne Sexton were clearly not put off by the stigma, Adrienne Rich, who came from a different social class, ethnic background, and moved in higher academic circles, may well have been.

Dominant in the male Modernist tradition was the disjointed epic poem expressing fragmented states of consciousness; T. S. Eliot's "The Waste Land" and "The Hollow Men" were excellent examples:

> We are the hollow men
> We are the stuffed men
> Leaning together
> Headpiece filled with straw. Alas![6]

During the period of "Snapshots," however, poetry was still a male-identified profession and vocation. As male poets like Stevens had been Rich's early poetic mentors and those she wrote for, likewise she consorted with other poets who, like Donald Hall, were male. But Rich was also reading and discovering Muriel Rukeyser and Denise Levertov, beginning to dedicate poems to them and other women poets she admired.

In the poetry of such forerunners as T. S. Eliot, W. H. Auden, Robert Lowell, and Anne Sexton, along with Sylvia Plath, an occasional sortie into madness freed the poetry to express new freer barbarous states of consciousness inexpressible before the publication of "The Waste Land" in 1922. Having read the madsongs, the account of the vulgar typist, and the fortuneteller's monologue in "The Waste Land," Rich writes in the fractured "Snapshots of a Daughter-in-Law" what is effectively her "Waste Land" in this poem which chronicles the demise of the old-fashioned women's happiness in romance and marriage. The subversive subtext of this poetry is that "the American Dream" could drive the middle-class women who subscribed to it mad and occasionally render them incapable of positive action or it might make them turn their energy in on themselves in negative ways.

The second section of "Snapshots of a Daughter-in-Law" opens with a most un-belle-like gesture: crashing the pots and pans while washing them, she believes she may hear the "angels chiding" (*S* 21), and she "looks out" into the tidy garden and up into a "sloppy" sky. The pathetic fallacy (how can a sky be "sloppy?") projects the sloppiness of the narrator's house onto the sky following her hearing voices understood to be angels' voices giving her commands. Are these the voices of madness heard by an exhausted daughter-in-law clinging to sanity, overburdened with housekeeping tasks? Oddly, these commands echo semantically the orders given in Rich's aesthetic credo "The Diamond Cutters." While before the artistic orders had been to be proud, serious, and hardhearted, now, in parody, the angels command her to be impatient, insatiable, and to rescue herself alone. The parodic placement of these sparse, staccato orders calls into question the sanity of her earlier barrage of orders as they reflect a harsh aesthetic position or critical stance that she can no longer maintain.

If in "The Loser" several long years have passed, the equivalent in psychological duress has transpired for the daughter-in-law, whose experiments with self-torture in the steam of a kettle or with matches burning into her thumbnail reveal a sinister, sadomasochistic side. This daughter-in-law housewife is half-mad and ignores the chidings of her angels since to obey them would be to violate all she has stood for as a wife and mother, and to lose all she has worked for since the days of courtship: in desperation she now burns herself deliberately in a stream of water or burns matches down to her thumbnail (*S* 21). This self-torture signals that she is denying her unhappiness and indulging in self-abuse as a means of exorcising her demons.

Hence the next lines seem incongruous, consciously evoking madness: she assumes they must be angelic voices she hears since now she is numb to all pain or emotion (*S* 21). Does this indicate a change in consciousness—a change of world? The textual "I"'s perspective combines self-loathing with a depressive's meticulous, unenlightening self-absorption. Thus, the poet forces the reader, as yet too afraid to own this madness or this daughter-in-law as a part of herself, to leave her demented in exhausted isolation, and see her as a victim of the solitary confinement of the intellectual suburban wife who ironically has fulfilled society's dream for her: she has won her man, had the children she desired, yet is at moments now supremely miserable. She is a woman Rich or anyone could sympathize with. Here the subject position of independent woman and wife is beginning to emerge from the traditional role, challenging it and sex role stereotyping generally. Her consciousness of her own emerging identity and of sexual politics is growing along with a self-involved self-awareness.

Before they were married Rich's husband had spoken excitedly about the children they'd have, and there was unconscious pressure all around for her to become pregnant immediately—she did—but she had no idea what her rights and choices were in this situation. The Jewish culture was just as heavily patriarchal as her "Christian" upbringing had been, and no one had prepared her to be out on her own, the roofwalker of Cambridge, Massachusetts. Hence, though privately unsure, she flung herself into full womanhood and all it entailed expecting all would be as successful as her writing career and academic life had been up until then, only to find child raising much harder than she anticipated. Later, Rich writes, "My politics is in my body," in part at least referring to women's traditional lack of choice about their own bodies paralleling their lack of control over their bodies.

The harsh order *"Be hard of heart"* closely resembles the other voices Rich hears—possibly that of postpartum depression—in her head. Of these commands, Judith McDaniel writes, "These are not the voices of angels, but of monsters, the inevitable accompaniment of growing self-awareness and self-involvement for women. And these monsters do not come from another sphere; they are from within" (*ARP* 319). They are the voices of the suppressed Furies, or the unconscious drive to selfhood desiring creative expression, what Rich calls in later poems "the Erinyes," the anti-patriarchal voices of female rebellion of the Greek playwright Aeschylus.

Rich wrote later of how one section was devoted to the madwoman and another to one haunted, not quite guided by voices (*ARP* 175); the lines express or vent what she calls her "undervoices." None of the compulsive orders to be harsh, to *"save yourself,"* are consciously understood by the lyric "I"; none is imbued with anything prophetic or any openness to divine revelation, but the voices seek to control her. The female subject inertly attends to them because they might ultimately lead her out of her current hopelessness and self-alienation. Perhaps these are not angelic voices, as she says, but rebellious demonic voices. The only sign that the speaker is in fact still alive is that she still feels pain every morning as the grit in the wind blinds her, a concrete symbol of the obstructions she faces. Life itself appears to be blowing symbolic grit into her eyes in the form of all the work, painful experiences, and inexplicable, yet imperative, voices assaulting her. This is one of the first articulations of the ordinary housewife's madness, the malaise of the 1960s middle-class housewife, bored and stifled by domestic tranquility and overwhelmed with the many small tasks caring for three small children requires.

At that time, it was dangerous for a woman (or anyone) to be or seem discontent, so this poem's rebellious outcry amid her fate in domesticity must be cloaked in the guise of madness; at the same time, Rich is expressing the feelings of many housewives in this era, and Anne Sexton and Sylvia Plath, both suicides, expressed similar existential anguish in their poetry.

In Section 3 of "Snapshots," Rich exposes other chimeras, false idols, and transgressive, if not supernatural, messages. Appropriately, the segment begins dramatically with a kind of explanation of the fractured consciousness of the prior part, announcing that a thinking woman lies with demons. Her body becomes a beak that seizes and holds her (*S* 22): it becomes a source of pain and out-of-control change. On one level, this can be read as a reference to Leda and the swan in classical mythology, except here the beak is a part of herself, her own thought process interacting with her objectified body, and the image refers to the punishment of Prometheus. Could the lines suggest that thought or creativity itself is detrimental to women? Is she being punished like Prometheus because she seized the flame? Rachel Blau DuPlessis sees the line about monsters and beaks as an answer to W. B. Yeats' famous question in "Leda and the Swan":

> When Yeats asks, "Did she put on his knowledge with his power/ before the indifferent beak could let her drop?" Rich responds, "A thinking woman sleeps with monsters. / The beak that grips her, she becomes," turning the question back, and showing an ambivalent judgment about the possession of phallic power and knowledge. Anger, rupture and a wounding self- initiation define this text.[7]

Rich assumes the rebellious subject position of the consciously female poet for the first time here and gives voice to the creative or demonic voices urging her to rebel.

In the heyday of the Kennedy presidency, when this book was published, the expectations of American women were gradually changing: there was more hope for the smothered housewife because women were beginning to move into a variety of new careers, and women's achievements were more valued in the marketplace. The entirety of "Snapshots" registers this historical shift in women's consciousness, a change that was later articulated in books by Betty Friedan and her successors—Gloria Steinem, Robin Morgan, and Starhawk. But Adrienne Rich is among the first of the women poets to detect and speak of it in her poetry.

The third and fourth sections of the poem explore that shock of recognition that change is afoot, that thinking women may now find a means of varying the traditional woman's role. The intelligent woman lies with demons—and the line has the many levels of meaning, playing on the lovers a woman may sleep with and the horrifying, unladylike thoughts that give her nightmares because she is haunted by her unfulfilled dreams.

Nature has added to her dilemma by making her a creature that her culture assumes must be constantly improved on: nature, the enormous repository of custom and conformity (*S* 22), bears the load of traditions that determine the ways women see themselves and behave growing up. Women apply and ingest such a lot of adulterations of nature: they take the traditional debris and take pills (*S* 22)—are these diet pills or pills for female ailments? This is too early for birth control pills, but they may be diet pills, Valium, or tranquilizers. The lines signal the fact that women inflict upon themselves a variety of pills and remedies. The lyric "I" declares menacingly, they have breasts of Boadicea, the avenging British queen, under the fox stoles and flowers they wear on their queenly occasions (*S* 22). Boadicea, the feared Saxon warrior who defeated her tribal enemies, may have cut off one of her breasts like the Amazons, the better to shoot her arrows. Her statue standing at the entrance to Buckingham Palace, home of the queens and kings of England, is a daily reminder to each successive English subject of the bravery inherent in women and especially royal women. Is she the daughter-in-law's inspiration?

Other monsters the thinking woman sleeps with are the monsters of guilt and angst since no matter what she does or how hard she works, she feels guilty that she ought to be doing something more; and a thinking woman is acutely aware that she may be expected to do most of the domestic work socially ascribed to women instead of doing the work her mind or imagination envisages.

Hence, since the daughter-in-law prefers the life of the mind, she may feel anguish and guilt whenever she *thinks* or *writes* instead of doing something useful, doing manual work because she is conscious of neglecting some womanly duty or occupation. She writes that at 29, she felt guilt both toward her next of kin and toward herself (*ARP* 175). I would submit that this is significant not just because it reflects Rich's own frustrations in life, but chiefly because she records so aptly the frustration of a good number of American housewives in this era. Enjoying the life of the mind only intensifies their anguish or despair that life would seldom offer more to a woman than pain, childbearing, and hard, repetitive, unrewarding domestic work.

In contrast to the way physical limitations team up to conquer the woman in "Snapshots of a Daughter-in-Law," the second stanza of "Snapshots" focuses only on what might be considered women's mental and spiritual limitations or ills, their ability to fight with other women, what Rich humorously calls the argument *ad feminam*, women picking on other women in a none-too-noble fashion (*S* 22).

The pre-feminist speaker does not seek to remove the knives in her back or forgive the attacks but instead seeks revenge—to stick the knife into another woman's back, addressing her as her hypocritical sister (*S* 22). That subject position and women's cultural objectification necessitate that women be pitted against one another in competition for men; hence they drive knives in one another's backs, where they rust. Rephrasing Baudelaire's address to his bourgeois reader, "*hypocrite lecteur*," who is identical to himself in secret sinful self-indulgences, his brother in sin, the poet ironically inverts the Prometheus story and implies that all warring women, especially all who fight one another and drive knives into one another's backs, are equally hypocritical and evil. But the loss of innocence coupled with dissent does not induce any convivial sense of community in a pair of women gripped in heated discussion (*S* 22), as Prometheus's beak grips and devours the liver and substance of the thinking woman here. Instead of being self-conscious or witty enough to perceive how ridiculous this specter of women fighting is, they scream, their shrillness tearing across the middle-class Victorian cut glass, acting like Furies (*S* 22).

The evocation of Greek tragedy again ironically reinforces and emphasizes the unheroic nature of women, since in Greek tragedies the Furies are unconscious embodiments or spirits of female revenge. Clearly these are true pre-feminist sentiments of the 1950s and early 1960s, the decade before the birth of the women's liberation movement. "Snapshots" attempts to render womanhood's shadow side, not simply her shining public image, but the shadow side, as if Rich wished to bring to light and purge these negative aspects of the female psyche, as though she wished to evoke and then banish them through the vehicle of this dark poem.

These negative mythic images of women exorcised, Rich introduces the first potentially positive image, that of the spinster poet Emily Dickinson; in the fourth section the lyric "I" speaks more intimately of a person reading and writing in her kitchen as the jellies boil and "scum" (*S* 22). The half-rhyme and assonance here, rhyming "Gun" and "scum," uniting the weapon with the housewife's oppression; the boiling and "scumming" betray activities of the newly fermenting, changing female psyche. The image symbolizes danger: all the creativity mandatory domestic chores have repressed is now set to begin to boil over, exploding in a rage of poetry.

In conclusion, "Snapshots of a Daughter-in-Law" is a series of poetic sketches embodying mythic, historical, or literary women, only some of whom are daughters-in-law. Most important, these are for the most part women who have defined themselves in and through their relationships with men. The outcome of this self-definition has been inauthentic, repressed, or self-abusive identity, the identity of the contemporary American woman who has lost her selfhood amid the work of childbearing and child raising; the poem exorcises all negative images of the feminine embedded in Western culture, myth, and tradition. Some quasi-mythic characters, like Emily Dickinson, are merely alluded to, hardly identified, only seen from a distance, or snapped as daughters, never even technically daughters-in-law. A feminist reading of this poem might assert that marriage is a purely economic arrangement for appropriating women's wombs and labor and for the production of children. The title lends a false or ironic semblance of objectivity to a truly revolutionary poem.

In dramatic contrast to Emily Dickinson, the shy daughter apparently driven into spinsterhood, are the nubile young girls of Latin lyric poetry, the Corinnas who sing and play the lute. Section five of the poem begins with a frequently quoted line from the great pastoral poet Horace's Latin, which translates "*sweetly laughing, sweetly speaking*" (*S* 22). Here the daughter-in-law or marriageable girl is conscious that she must be beautiful to attract a mate. To that end, her shaved legs gleam enticingly, as brightly and unnaturally as petrified mammoth-tusks (*S* 22). In this short stanza, Rich mocks the unnatural lengths women go to to make themselves look beautiful and the gleam of legs polished to perfection. Indeed, she poses the question: Which is worse—to grow old and wear out in service like Emily Dickinson (possibly retaining a certain personal independence, autonomy, and inner freedom) or to adorn oneself for men, catch a man, become a daughter-in-law with a rotting mind and risk going insane like the speaker, hearing voices that urge one to defy the social order and break free of domesticity? Rich seems to side with those who choose domesticity and the single life along with covert poetry writing.

Still, in section six, she gives new life and form to the flirtatious Renaissance maiden Corinna playing her lute. In Western literature Corinna was first seen as the lovely nymph in Ovid; later, she was the subject of many Renaissance poems, art, and music. In the first line, Rich quotes from the first line of the famous poem "When to her Lute Corinna Sings" by Thomas Campion, as master lyricist and lutanist, yet the irony hits hard in the second, where Rich assures the possibly resisting reader that when her Corinna sings, the song is hardly original. Corinna could not *be* original or spontaneous. She is merely living out society's expectations of the nubile girl, fulfilling her destiny within the parameters of the possible, without creativity.

The next lines in this sequence echo in chilling fashion the seduction or rape scenes in T. S. Eliot's *The Waste Land* in their lust and sensuality. The poem implies that nothing about Corinna is her own, except her sensory experiences of hair touching cheek, silk touching her knees. The ultimate affront, however, is that even her body and its movement are judged in the reflections of others' eyes: others determine her accomplishments, graces, and position in society. Her very selfhood and being are objectified and judged by the reflecting eyes of men and other women; in that judgment, not in her self-judgment, inheres the value of her existence. In the end,

Corinna is purely an artificial literary construct: readers, like her observers, create her meaning and significance in the act of reading.

In the following stanza a sensual drama ensues, but it is not fully traced for the reader. We view her hesitating and unfulfilled in front of an unlocked door she seems just about to open. The openable door is in fact a strong cage, since presumably she is here voluntarily; even though she is unsatisfied, where might she go? She has been raised to this. The narrator asks her archly to reveal to us if this is fruitful, creative pain she is experiencing (*S* 23). The question is, *Is your sorrow productive? Or life-giving*?, as the notes to the Norton Critical Edition *Adrienne Rich's Poetry and Prose* define it (*ARP* 11). Is this fertilizing pain or sorrow, not intellectual or spiritual? The act of love fixes and arrests her here (*S* 23), and this act is the only natural act for her.

Then the objective narrator inquires if woman is naturally more sensitive, intuitive, or perceptive than man? Or if Nature has revealed her secrets to woman alone (*S* 23)? This is a common assumption of patriarchal institutions, Rich declares in "The Anti-Feminist Woman," an essay published a decade after *Snapshots of a Daughter-in-Law* in the 1975 Norton Critical Edition *Adrienne Rich's Poetry* but deleted from the 1992 edition. Patriarchy asserts that women are somehow "special" and more in tune with nature; therefore, it was thought they were ill suited to lives in business or the professions.

Earlier in the essay Rich had defined "patriarchy" thus:

> I mean to imply not simply the tracing of descent through the father,...but any kind of group organization in which males hold dominant power and determine what part females shall and shall not play, and in which capabilities assigned to women are relegated generally to the mystical and aesthetic and excluded from the practical and political realms. (It is characteristic of patriarchal thinking that these realms are regarded as separate and mutually exclusive.) (*ARP1* 101)

Hence, some Muslims' insistence on women's keeping covered from head to toe and the common prohibition on women's baring their breasts. Rich might agree that women's enslavement and physical isolation under patriarchy in countries like Afghanistan may stem, in part at least, from men's need to preserve them for themselves and safeguard their homes and families.

Next Rich clarifies patriarchy's position on women in the West:

> The patriarchy looks to its women to embody and impersonate the qualities lacking in its institutions—concern for the quality of life, for means rather than for pure goal, a connection with the natural and extrasensory order. These attributes have been classified as "female" in part because the patriarchy relegates them to women and tends to deny them—with a certain fatalism—to men. (*ARP* 102)

It is significant that the great Greek prophetess Cassandra, the woman who predicted the Trojan War but was not believed, and many of those with psychic gifts in ancient times were female.

Critic Helen Vendler is aware of the influence of patriarchal views in "Snapshots of a Daughter-in-Law," and she assesses the marriage envisioned in "Snapshots" as "more bitter—a separation under the same roof, a sense of separate-and-not-equal lives bequeathed to men and women, with women's only claim that of a more arcane insight into Nature" (*ARP* 304). But the poem does not even necessarily affirm that nature has revealed her innermost secrets (*S* 23) to women—in other words, that women are more natural than men– it only asks if she has. The answer rests in silence, though certainly the later Rich would probably affirm that women are definitely more intuitive, sensitive, and natural (*S* 23). Vendler comments on the fate of the daughter-in-law in marriage, noting that here the silent mental isolation brought on by marriage yields to only "a choking, deprived speech" (*ARP* 304). Once married, Corinna is silent: the rest of what a patriarchal woman might say publicly about sexuality and their artistic originality is silenced or ignored.

Mary Wollstonecraft's lines about the need of a woman for a *"stay,"* (like Eliot's *"momentary stay against confusion"*), for something of her own, begin the seventh section of the poem. This is Mary Wollstonecraft's answer to Virginia Woolf's requirement that a woman who wants to write must have a room of her own. In the poem, Wollstonecraft is styled engagingly as a woman who was not perfect, who fought for what she imperfectly understood (*S* 23). The rhythm of the ditty or hymn throughout the whole stanza underscores the nursery rhyme quality of distancing Rich creates here and subtly echoes the hymn-like rhythms of some of Emily Dickinson's poems. The poem defends the liberated Mary Wollstonecraft, the mother of Mary Shelley, she claiming that she was a victim of male rage, categorized as an immoral outcast (*S* 23). Here the stock misogynist labels are hurled at her; and the ironic rhyming of *more* with *whore* defines the way women who do listen to their rebellious or angelic voices are typecast and ostracized. A Neoclassical couplet neatly sums it up. The daughter-in-law seems to perceive the problem, now yet remains silent.

In early English and American literature, the stigma against women's publication made it almost indecent for a lady to publish and difficult for women to express dissent or advance original thoughts. Rich may think that Mary Wollstonecraft realized only a small part of her potential, since she died early, bringing the baby Mary—later Mary Shelley—into the world. Section seven of "Snapshots" records a telling line from Mary Wollstonecraft: *"To have in this world some stay which cannot be undermined, is / of the utmost consequence"* (*S* 23). Ironically, the passage evokes a recollection that this eighteenth-century writer of genius never had any real "stay" or security of this sort except in her writing, and her fierce independence may have contributed indirectly to her early death.

In the next section the misogynist French philosopher Denis Diderot enters to accuse women once again, saying, "You all die at fifteen" when they lose their virginity (*S* 23). Still imprisoned in her steamy suburban kitchen, the lonely daughter-in-law attempts to look out on freedom through foggy windows. A keen guilt or angst at the thought that her life is probably now over, a regret in thinking of her wasted potential disturbs her like thinking of adultery refused or other chances missed (*S* 23). Dutifully confined inwardly, she may regret the choices she has made that led to her imprisonment in this steamy, impenetrable prison. Or has she been involved in a "flight from connection," as Craig Werner indicates?[8] Does the memory of unconsummated adultery represent a true intimacy refused? Because Rich conceals essential aspects of the scope of the domestic or romantic drama, we cannot say for sure. But the poem's passion awakens keen interest and evokes the feelings many in unequal marriage have felt down the centuries.

The litany of slights against women accumulated from the writings of European scholars persists in the ninth section, where Dr. Johnson's words liken a dog's walking on its hind legs to a woman preaching: one is surprised, Dr. Johnson wrote, that a woman even makes that effort or amazed "*Not that it is done well, but that / it is done at all?*" (*S* 24). Johnson's are fighting words, designed to enrage the reader, so at last the speaker openly expresses her indignation at his arrogant dismissal of women's claims on an intellectual or creative life like men's (*S* 24). She retorts in internal monologue. In her way of letting ideas flow and free-associate, Rich sums up the woman writer's (her own?) talents, trivializing them as though reporting them from the male perspective, asking if "we" would give up our token status: the "we" here are women admitted through privilege or birth into a man's world. The products of our talents lie about us in drafts and ruins (*S* 24). Here she mocks the conforming traditional woman for her lack of ambition, asking who of her sex has produced a masterpiece. We recall that at the time this poem was being written Judy Chicago had yet to produce her artistic masterpiece *The Dinner Party,* and the field of women's studies had not yet come into being. In a marked change in tone from the former stanzas, here the speaker appears to be a privileged woman addressing other privileged women who have been educated and given a sinecure, a secure place in the professions. She assumes the subject position of the token woman professional, asserting that the dominant culture consigned women's writing to the status of rough drafts and scattered pieces, dismissing it as dazzling yet incoherent; still, the subject ingratiates herself with Diderot, Johnson, and other early philosophers and critics whose *machismo* and male arrogance seem to have necessitated the subjugation of women. Rich was familiar with patriarchal arrogance, after all, since initially she wrote poetry for her father. In another poem in this volume, "Juvenilia," she speaks humbly and self-critically of reproducing her dutiful verses (*S* 32) and of being allowed as a child to read and write in her father's study among his gold-embossed leather Ibsen collection (*S* 32). Men's books flake in gold bindings, but women's writing shines and glitters, despite its fragments. The lyric "I" may assume the reader understands the humor in the fact that Ibsen, author of *The Doll's House,* was the first major playwright of women's liberation in pre–World War I Europe.

The poem then shifts into a Renaissance mode at the start of the next stanza, with a reference to the song "Sigh no more, Ladies," the first line of a Shakespearean song from *Much Ado about Nothing:* the song is sung when the star-crossed lovers appear not to have any hope of uniting. After "Sigh no more," the significant next line affirms

> Men were deceivers ever, . . .
> To one thing constant never.
> Then sigh not so, but let them go,
> And be you blithe and bonny,
> Converting all your sounds of woe
> Into 'Hey nonny, nonny!' (*Much Ado about Nothing* II, iii, 64 ff.)

Apparently the daughter-in-law does let them go, but in an objective voice speaks in the ensuing lines in Augustan periods and rhythms (*S* 24). Speaking to all women in power, the lyric "I" says elegantly and self-deprecatingly in these lines that men praise women for all the wrong reasons, celebrating them chiefly for passivity or indolence rather than for any positive accomplishments (*S* 24). Men in power value only weak or malleable women and praise them for remaining docile. Later the poet spoke of how she herself disliked the way she had been forced as a child to write and *learn* sedulously.

Since she had the pluck, intelligence, and extraordinary talent—in short, because she was already considered one of the best female poets writing in America (as Plath said in her diaries)—she had been lucky enough to be chosen as a token woman, to be lionized as an exceptional poet by the Auden-Eliot generation. Having earned a strong reputation in the world of letters, she now speaks out against that world, hence this poem—and the entire book of poetry—were called bitter and strident at the time by some critics who formerly praised her.[9]

Women, as she says in the last lines of this sequence, can sin by adopting a superiority complex or by being rebellious or too large (*S* 24), speaking stridently against convention. The penalties for violating the patriarchal establishment's rules are dire: women are ostracized, expelled, even tortured and shot at; hence, few choose this (*S* 24).

The sardonic last lines complete her appraisal of how intellectual women—philosophers, protesters, and poets—have been castigated down through the centuries since Roman times. The lines have shown how hard it has been to survive mentally and creatively for all women but a few.

Turning its gaze toward the future, the rest of the poem projects a more positive image in lines translated from Simone de Beauvoir's *The Second*

Sex, heralding the mythic arrival of the New Woman, the woman free from exploitation or domestic slavery. Significantly, she is described as being equal to a boy in beauty with a keen mind open to the future. She lands like a helicopter, self-assured, still full of potential. In a change of tone, she is now no longer the daughter-in-law, but the free New Woman, as she describes this new womanhood as *delivered* and *palpable* yet *ours* (*S* 25). Exactly whose? She belongs, the lines imply, to women, but why? She embodies the New Woman, woman's exotic intellectual, professional, and even erotic or visionary desires and potential. She can employ ambitions, strategies, and all the liberated female subjects to come.

Like *The Waste Land,* which it resembles, this long poem ends with an apotheosis, the appearance of a female god, the New Woman who will save women. In this case a real dea ex machina arrives in a helicopter! But having navigated the sterile streets of the ordinary woman's difficult life up until this point, has the poem earned the right to open out into this view of god—or goddess? Surely the shift in tone comes as a shock, a shock too abrupt for some contemporary reviewers. Those unprepared for this changed Rich found the climactic section too abrupt a turnabout and the entire book too bitter and too personal.

Although "Snapshots" was a personal liberation for Rich to write, it was passed over by the critics, considered too personal, bitter, and fragmented, too dramatic a departure from her former style to be praised. Expressing a rebellious selfhood, yet not venturing into the territory Muriel Rukeyser was exploring already, in this volume Rich has at least begun to speak out and to explore the reality of woman's alienation without actually abandoning the safety of conventions—literary or social. In *Writing Beyond the Ending,* Rachel Blau DuPlessis reminds the reader that Virginia Woolf summoned women writers to

> aggressive truth-telling from female experiences,... The expression of woman's feelings can be achieved only by delegitimating [*sic*] narrative patterns embodying the social practices and mental structure that repress women.[10]

Certainly this describes Rich's effort here—to craft a new structure for the first revolutionary American epic poems of the women's movement of the late twentieth century.

"Snapshots" accomplishes this "delegitimation of narrative patterns"; thus, DuPlessis calls the poem "an outstanding example of this critique of consciousness."[11] DuPlessis adds, "As Rukeyser and Levertov confront canons of respectable language, so Rich pits herself against acceptable notions of the subject and of womanhood." DuPlessis recounts her words: "'I had been taught that poetry should be "universal," which meant, *of course,* non-female'" [*emphasis added*].[12] Critics like Craig Werner, Alicia Ostriker, and Deborah Pope greeted "Snapshots" as Rich's "transitional" or breakthough poem, the poem that forms a bridge to her later work where she treats far more unconventional subjects and adopts more threatening selves, using the new more direct style.

Certainly the poem does announce the new direction her work will take in later books and presents the reader with a new subject positioning, that of the dissident daughter-in-law, the female subject daring to question and criticize and bring portions of satiric writings against women into the poem, thereby announcing that the work is political. "Snapshots of a Daughter-in-Law" is a collage of literary portraits of women, who, as Rich wrote of Emily Dickinson in her essay on her "Vesuvius at Home," are exploring what one critic called "states of psychic extremity" (*ARP* 192), risking venturing into the dangerous areas of the psyche. These more personal poems are daring and modern in their tracking the dawning consciousness of the identities of the poet's multiple voices and selves.

"ANTINOUS: THE DIARIES" AND "A MARRIAGE IN THE SIXTIES"

Also important among the final poems in this collection *Snapshots* is "Antinous: The Diaries," evoking T.S. Eliot and perhaps imagined as a poem scrawled by the indulged favorite of the Emperor Hadrian, Antinous, a beautiful boy who was later found dead, assumed to be a suicide. Coming four poems after "Snapshots of a Daughter-in-Law" in the book by that name, it too speaks of the end of an era, the receding tide of a love or a marriage.

Linking the season of autumn and decadent sexuality, starting on a jaded note—it depicts the time of the year's death, the fallen leaves, the waste they strew on the pavement at the same time they strew him with flesh-colored flowers (*S* 30). This is a poem about being made sick by what one has repressed: yet the speaker is nauseous and exhausted (*S* 30). But this is not surprising since the subject—Antinous—has brought it on himself by what he has allowed others to do to him, the court has objectified its darling, and this special status as the Emperor's favorite ultimately causes his sickness unto death.

Asking, tellingly, why I "*miscarry?*" and thus invoking the language of childbirth and its failure, the subject replies that it is what the speaker has undergone in order to conform, to remain part of this sophisticated imperial city that is now sickening him (or her) to the point that he or she is left stranded, ill, and abandoned like stillborn babies (*S* 31). Again, parts of the self that will never be realized now are spewed forth, spit-out fragments. Written in 1959, "Antinous" is about the same favorite to the Emperor, another testament to despair. The boy speaker cannot envision any means by which he might escape the prison of this gilded net of privilege that forces him to swallow the unmentionable, forfeiting his own selfhood.

This secluded, debauched life leaves him miscarrying and vomiting, feeling ill. He dies solitary and neglected (*S* 30), as the daughter-in-law feared she would die, never having realized her full potential or having truly lived. Both the emperor's favorite—and perhaps the daughter-in-law—have much unrealized potential.

According to Albert Gelpi, "Antinous" presents a logical progression and evolution in Rich's subject position, from beleaguered female to beleaguered "favorite... the object of male lust... [in] a decadent society" (*ARP* 288). Gelpi clarifies the resolution Rich has found in this poem:

> In reaction against the definitions of "woman" allowed by the rules of the game Rich at first identifies the new possibilities of self-realization with "masculine" qualities within herself and so with images of men.[13]

Around this time the Jungian concept of the animus, the male aspect within the female psyche, entered her poetry and became a constant presence in later poems like "Orion." She experiments with the male subject position in more personal, intimate narrative poems. This is the progression from the apotheosis, ablaze with de Beauvoir's own language and imagery, at the end of "Snapshots," the image of the female helicopter, her mind open to the wind and new ventures, she is beautiful as any classic youth (*S* 24). Here in comparing woman with boy, Rich was moving toward androgyny as a way of experiencing the masculine dimension of the female self.

In a striking, already discussed poem in this book, "Peeling Onions," (*S* 54) Rich treats pain—or crying—comically. When one is peeling onions, the tears are purely physiological, due to peeling onions, not to pain; inside she is as unemotional as Peer Gynt, who first likened each stage of life to the peel of an onion: in being peeled away, the onion merely leaves a person with the next layer to live through and remove. This is yet another conception of selfhood—self is a series of removable layers. This sardonic parody of other subject positionings in the book calls the reader to question, *Which is real?*

In "A Marriage in the Sixties" (*S* 45–46), Rich describes the husband in the poem as half Roman emperor, deftly linking him to Hadrian (who may have driven his favorite to suicide) within the compass of this collection of poems, *Snapshots of a Daughter-in-Law.* As in the poem by that name, the personification of "Time" once again assumes a subject position and voice; now it treats him well. He is aging gracefully, with his memorable noble face (*S* 45). Clearly now, romantic passion is gone, but his first love letters thrilled her on Magdalen Street (*S* 45) (note the interjection of the name of one of Jesus's only possible female disciples). Not so today: the couple stalks through the house, each feeling alone, angry, competitive, self-absorbed, lost in the outer echelons of thought. Playing on Shakespeare's line from *The Merchant of Venice, "The quality of mercy is not strained, but passeth as the gentle dews from heaven,"* the speaker here states that their one drop of mercy is that they know of each other's presence, and that in itself is comforting (*S* 45–46). But apparently that drop does not produce enough mercy to afford them any release from this torment.

One image for a marriage here is that of two fellow creatures profoundly divided from one another, yet stranded together eternally (*S* 46), yet the lyrical "I" conjectures that their marriage still may have a future: they still have excellent discussions of ideas or clashes of wits that language aches for, but their alienation seems to preclude that (*S* 46). If the couple in the poem cannot now remember why they married, still they can enjoy the friction of minds in rousing talk. In the last stanza, the narrator addresses the husband coyly, if anti-romantically, as loved "fellow-particle" (*S* 46). Hanging in space, revolving like electric atomic particles blown together, their asexual intellectual union occasionally scintillates with perfect talk. The poem envisions modern marriage, a suspension in time and space as fellow-particles suspended together in space forever, a parody of a constellation. This portrait of a marriage affords a view of friction and solitary angst, but from time to time the "furious" domestic resentments, occasionally felt in marriage, suspend their dance. Each partner is suspended beside the other, twinlike, so they have the solace of each other's presence. In itself, that constitutes an idea of order that Stevens himself would have acknowledged as valid, yet while at first his hot words melted the narrator, here each, while acknowledging each other's presence, each stalks his or her own passionate thoughts (*S* 46).

In a 1972 poem, ironically titled "For a Survivor" and addressed to her now-dead husband, she describes the leap she has made into her new womanhood, her new life, conceived of as the leap that they spoke of attempting, a sequence of wondrous acts and ventures, each step enabling the next (*DW* 50). These lines in fact reflect the actual structure of "Snapshots of a Daughter-in-Law," which is a tour de force, a chain of successful daring steps toward the unknown. At the same time, the poem's ending presages the leap into the future she could make, so courage and change would become necessities of life.

Toward the end of the book comes the symbolic "Prospective Immigrants Please Note" (*S* 59), a consideration of the door through which prospective immigrants must pass to enter their new chosen countries, a portal through which Rich has not yet passed, but is about to. The symbol of the portal reverberates and recurs throughout her later poetry: it returns in "The Fact of a Doorframe" and many other poems. Its relevance stems from the fact that Rich, continually transforming herself, shedding the skins of old lives and becoming new, must open and pass through many doors in her successive transformations, some of which open only one way. Conceived symbolically, this gate is a point of no return.

Whether or not to go through is a genuine choice the reader or poet will have to face. To go through is in some way to be obliged to remember or forget one's name. Still, if one passes through, one might, ironically, actually remember one's own name and former selfhood afterward (*S* 59). Here she may be alluding to those who have emigrated to forget or leave behind their past lives and selves or to the many immigrants or divorcees or brides who have had to change their names in the process of going through the gate into the new country and identity. Many immigrants had their names butchered by immigration authorities. The poem may suggest that it would be painful to lose such a vital part of oneself as one's own name, an intrinsic part of one's identity, and then still remember yet be denied it in the new country. The immigrant's musings are deliberately ambiguous, multidimensional in meaning. Similarly, were Rich to leave her secure "homeland" or native land of marriage and identity as a married woman, she would be passing through a gate into an unknown, frightening territory, crossing into an alien land from which there is no return. There, reality does a double take, and the immigrant has to let it (*S* 59). "You" must interact with reality and experience events that will change you.

If the first three, three-line stanzas here deal with the consequences of going through the gate, the second three stanzas deal with assurances of the possibilities for a life that refuses the passage through the gate. More and more, the gate appears to be connected with the immigrant's (or self's) assimilation into a new culture on one level and a refusal to change or assimilate on the other. The advantage of remaining a traditional Jewish wife has its attractions—the respectability, dignity, and honor of an acknowledged role. The lyric "I" may be contemplating entering the unknown country Sandra Gilbert and Susan Gubar have called "No Man's Land," where she does not (yet) speak the language. It is a venture into a land of no return, a place one may live to regret venturing into (*S* 59). So to enter through this door is to open oneself to danger, to open up the possibility that one might or might not remember one's own name, that one's identity, hence one's life, may change.

Elsewhere Rich described powerful poetic writing thus: it is "as if forces we can lay claim to in no other way become present to us in sensuous form."[14] The poet accomplishes this task and communicates with these forces in *Snapshots of a Daughter-in-Law,* whose fractured lines reveal an emerging feminist consciousness and new urgency.

If W. H. Auden patronizingly extolled Rich's first book for being "neatly dressed," and speaking low and respectfully (*CW* 11), the poetry of her third book is anything but quiet or neatly dressed. The younger Rich was evidently dissimulating before, in effect lying to herself, forcing herself into a pose of obedience unnatural to her. Now she gives voice to her feelings, is not silenced by anyone. It is important to note that her next volume of poetry is called simply *Necessities of Life*; here the transformed, revisionist self crafts a new more practical and useful identity. The lyric "I" experiences a hesitancy about entering this frightening new country and crossing some sort of border or point of no return—this new realm is the open territory of women's liberation and equality in America. In *Necessities of Life* she reduces her subjects to their most basic elements and reduces the poetic forms.

Rich now turns from a focus on marriage to a focus on death. Gone is her former "detachment from the self and its emotions." Gone is the self-alienating mask her first books of poetry wore. Her poetic subjects now wear more human faces and occupy more real and convincing contemporary subject positions. Most speak in clearer female voices, and they can now make the leap of faith into an unknown zone. The future of American women's poetry lies in the balance.

Chapter 4

New Poetry Enters the World

A raw sense of beginning anew in a wholly different direction communicates itself in the opening lines of the title poem in *Necessities of Life* (1966): the "I" returns to the world, as one waking from sleep gradually, only little by little (*N* 9). First, the speaker in the poem conceives of the self as "a small, fixed dot" (*N* 9). The old self is perceived as a dark-blue thumbtack smashed into this scene but not authentically part of it (*N* 9). The speaker, monadic, solitary, and fiercely independent, assumes the work of creating an authentic self in this poetry. Vibrant colors become more important to the poems here as the speaker sees the physical world directly, as if for the first time.

The former self is viewed as hard and definite: its jaunty top sticking sportingly out of a pointillist's frenzy of points and dots. Yet that self could not remain static. Try as it might, this self could *not* stay fixed forever in life like a dot in a Seurat painting in pointillist style. Lives full of passion and intellectual activity forbid some selves from continuing to play a static role. Similar to the way she had engaged in *Snapshots* in a debate over whether to observe change passively or to engage in change actively, here she envisions a textual "I," a solitary monadic selfhood, first as a dot; and then as the dot starts to melt, it is a dot oozing and sprawling (*N* 9).

Psychic heats of the sort generated by a complete transformation of the self cause this formerly hard little dot to blur into ranges of abstract form, as in abstract art, arrays of red, vibrant green (*N* 9)—burning colors the poet had formerly been too restrained to use. But as this poem, significantly first entitled "Thirty-Three," indicates, a woman of 33 may no longer feel like a yielding young daughter-in-law or like the graceful

Corinna, nor can this lyric "I" remain a docile wife. The self now has to begin again, as the world begins anew in Genesis, with the blurring indicating her questioning of her sense of the role she must fulfill in life, bringing her new selfhood into focus. With this comes a new access to imagination in this poem, appropriately named "The Necessities of Life," since here the self is debating what is absolutely necessary to its own renewed life. Stirred, even stunned, by many internal changes, Rich writes a very different sort of poetry now. Of this process of reintegration of the self and communication of a new vision, she explains, "something in me was saying, 'If my material, my subject matter as a woman is going to be denied me, then there is only one other subject for me and that is death.' " Hence the stated topic—just one topic—of *Necessities of Life* is death, the death of love or illusion, and the death of the old self or selves: I interpret this as death as it is commonly understood, death to conformity in life or in poetry, and death to former poetic selfhoods.

W. B. Yeats said that *"out of the quarrel with others we make rhetoric and out of the quarrel with ourselves we make poetry."*[1] Alicia Ostriker, in *Stealing the Language: The Emergence of Women's Poetry in America,* an account of the progression of American culture's perception of women's poetry and how it "stole the language" in Promethean fashion, says that

> Within the symposium of the self, woman poets evidently wish to reverse Yeats' dictum that from the quarrel with ourselves we make poetry. Instead they struggle to make poetry about healing the self through reconciling spiritual antinomies.[2]

While maturing as a poet, Rich did have to reconcile spiritual, sexual, psychological, class, and racial antinomies and fissures within the self. To survive, she had to put together, like Psyche in the myth of Eros and Psyche, the scattered pieces of her identities, selves, and voices. Even though her beloved father was raised as a Jew, she came to resent the fact that she had been denied the choice to become a Jew, too (*ARP* 227). Her mother told her to write "Episcopalian" since not to list any religion was "dangerous."

Her parents raised her as an Episcopalian "without belief"—an Episcopalian for social purposes, with a strong faith in education, rather than in religion. As a young women, she experienced a new urge for a strong faith and a sense of heritage along with "belated rage that…[she] had never been taught about resistance, only about passing," and in the words of Sylvia Henneberg, "that rage is as much directed against her mother as her father."[3] Perhaps even more so. Her father was arbitrary by nature, but her Christian mother could have been more open with her about the decisions they had made on their children's behalf, possibly before they were born.

Though it was socially unacceptable in the 1940s and 1950s, in fact many formerly Christian families were becoming quietly agnostic, stopping attending church; the younger generation's horrific experience in

World War II had deeply estranged some veterans from organized religion. Changing social conditions and lifestyles affected others. Indeed, in the 1960s, religious observance quietly became increasingly unfashionable in America, intellectual circles, except in T. S. Eliot's set and High Anglican circles in England.

At university, independent of parental control, Rich saw that Judaism and "roots" were more than words (nonexistent) on a form and that an entire life must be grounded on a bedrock of values. The pressure to discover her true individuality, multiple voices, and identities and society's "compulsory heterosexuality" coalesced in her becoming a traditional Jewish wife, gratifying her need for identification with and belonging to a larger community and an ancient religious tradition, and her desire for fulfillment in the socially endorsed goal of marriage to a successful young Harvard economics professor.

It is significant that she says in an essay both her gentile mother and her mother's mother were "frustrated artists and intellectuals"; her grandmother was a lost writer, while her mother was a lost composer (*ARP* 225). At this point in her feminist awakening, she realizes she is following in the footsteps of her maternal and paternal grandmothers and mother and fulfilling their unmet goals, while moving away from the tradition of her Jewish mother-in-law and husband, intellectually, professionally, and aesthetically. Around this time of transformation, Rich becomes more conscious of the cultural and ethnic split, aware that she senses she is more radically self-divided than she had previously understood she was in her early conventional roles as daughter, student, wife, mother, and daughter-in-law. She sums up her split thus in 1982:

> Sometimes I feel I have seen too long from too many disconnected angles: Jewish, anti-Semite, racist, anti-racist, once-married, lesbian, middle-class, feminist, exmatriate southerner, split at the root—that I will never bring them whole. (*ARP* 238)

I can sympathize with her feeling of being split and out of touch with her own being—after all, what is integrity and wholeness, belonging, identity, or selfhood for one from such a diverse, multicultural, polysemic background? Still, to be an authentic person, she must "bring them whole." Throughout her life she has asked, to cite the Duchess of Malfi she played in a school play, "*Who am I?*" (Surely, too, her sense of being "other," different, self-divided, and split was compounded by a private recognition around this time that she was a lesbian.) Even if she had not yet "come out," internally the realization may have dawned, and the anxiety implicit in this and the previous book reflects the anxiety of confronting disparate internal differences. Of course, feeling split is not something unique to women writers: in 1976, in "Moving Around," the poet William Matthews discussed a similar sense of being separate that dominated his dreams. He understood that a recurrent dream he was having was as much "about my urge to be separate as it was about my fear of separation," and it is this territory Rich inhabits in *Necessities of Life* and *Leaflets* (1969). But, as Alicia Ostriker points out, healing this split must involve the woman poet—in this instance Rich—in a spiritual, psychological, and political quest:

> For many women writers, the quest to re-integrate a split self is simultaneously a drive to topple the hierarchy of the sacred and the profane, redeeming and including what the culture has exiled and excluded.[4]

This rebellion contains an aspect of adolescent rebellion, too: having never been free to do as she pleased in her entire life, now she begins to realize that she might have some say in the direction of her life. For Rich at this time, the process might have seemed just as Promethean or violent as Ostriker's claim implies; it meant opposing hierarchies constructively and reexamining the subjects and female/feminist subject positioning in her poetry, discovering the new identity or identities of the authentic speaking selves there. For writing is re-creating, recreating the world, she declared, as Whitman and Emerson had said a century before: to express one's authentic, original selfhood in poetry is to create the world anew.

As signaled in the previous chapter with *Snapshots,* around this time Rich began dating each poem as if to root it individually in the soil of history because Rich herself until then or at that time may have truly felt rootless or in such a restless time needed to feel more rooted. A president had been assassinated in 1963, others were being assassinated as she wrote, absolute change and possibly revolution were in the air. In *Necessities of Life* Rich goes beyond self-reinvention and grounding in history, writing consciously anti-literary poetry, at first privileging her own private history over recorded public history or literary history, then moving at the end of the decade into a dialogue between herself on the one hand and American history and culture in the throes of the Vietnam War on the other. Kevin Stein has commented of her poetry of the mid- to late-1960s onward:

> Through the work of Lowell and Rich, readers of American poetry gain a singular notion of the way poets may effectively hold dialogue with culture and history. Their poetry stands as an antidote to the enticing insularity of the "hermetic" mode by which poets hope to abandon their communal function in favor of the pristine woodlands of "pure" art.... For Rich, however, living "with what was here" means precisely to change the present, to alter and remake its conventions for our future's sake—essentially, choosing not to live passively with history's inheritance.[5]

Indeed, this is the central fact for Rich in the 1960s: she seeks to embody and even influence contemporary history, reflections on death, and all the contemporary cultural and social issues impacting women, to launch challenges to the patriarchy and provide a kind of seismic or literary record of the reintegration of a female psyche in transition toward a more adventurous, freer life at this time of feminist revolution. If at the end of "Snapshots," the new woman of the future is said to be taking her time coming since she is more merciless and exacting to herself than history will be (*S* 25), *Necessities of Life* and *Leaflets* record journalistically spare expectations and harsh labor pains of this cataclysm of rebirth. But if Rich had faith in nothing else, she may be said to have faith that the newly empowered American woman will have been well worth waiting for since she would possess a more creative, integrated, adventurous, fully alive self and soul. Hers would be a generation of women: she would advance boldly into the professions. The end of "Snapshots" anticipates female astronauts and even heralds female heads of state. In fact, seeing it now over 40 years later, we find her faith in women's greater potential has been vindicated.

Necessities of Life embodies poetry "[n]ewly freed from the metrical conventions of her earlier books."[6] Helen Vendler comments that this book encompasses all her prior "phases" or styles of poetry, "If, as Rich's early pattern suggests, blunter poems are followed by subtler ones, *Necessities of Life* derives its power from its absorption of all past phases into its present one" (*ARP1* 166). This volume skillfully subsumes what is most powerful and characteristic in early phases of her poetry; moreover, there's a refined focus on nature, on colors, and explorations of selfhood here and a stronger sense of place. In this book it is as if she is seeing the world for the first time, and this sense of wonder invites a contemplation of both the world's beauty and, more arrestingly, its ugliness. These poems seem to physically assault received American notions of traditional womanhood and proclaim that she refuses to write like a proper lady ever again.

One can watch a multivalent emancipation in the short, urgent, almost breathless lines of "Necessities of Life," where the lyric "I" renounces "'*Difficult ordinary happiness*'" (*N* 11). In lines reminiscent of Theodore Roethke's "Root Cellar," she describes her self as peeling, "scaly" as an old bulb tossed in a "root cellar" (*N* 9). She assumes the subject positions of a discard, and a person with as many layers to peel off as a bulb, along with one who henceforth will never be used by anyone or anything: in a partial divorce from domesticity the bulbous "I" uses herself since she was her own possession (*N* 11). Obviously weary of being used by others in her roles as mother, wife, obedient daughter, the speaker rejects the traditional womanly role of self-sacrificing nurturer, rescuer, and helper. Instead she hovers poetically from time to time, brooding over life's bare necessities, the little one needs to live (*N* 10), evoking Genesis, chapter 1, where God hovers over the universe while creating it.

As if starting from Roethke's "Root Cellar" or Yeats's place where poems start, the "*foul rag-and-bone shop of the heart,*"[7] she returns to basics here to risk dwelling in her new world (*N* 10), even as she stays trenchant, motionless (*N* 10). The speaker is an ungendered or androgynous self, opaque, stubborn, and hard as a cabbage or rutabaga (*N* 10). Still, the textual "I" has opportunities from nature: watching a field, she sees mist steaming toward the sky (*N* 10) reminiscent of the mist or steam that burned the daughter-in-law's hand in "Snapshots." It appears that on the road, homes wait "breathless" with the desire to tell their stories (*N* 10). No, the textual "I" will not accept all these invitations but, through the exercise of her perceptions, fends off self-pity, desire for revenge, or loneliness, even adding some humor to the assertion of selfhood.

Everything else in this book, though, has an eerie quality that John Ashbery calls "metaphysical" with a positive spin. Ashbery also identifies Rich with the tradition of T. S. Eliot's *The Waste Land* and says she is "a kind of Emily Dickinson of the suburbs," who is "bleakly eyeing the... pollution around her." Ashbery mocks her not so subtly in this review, probably not fully understanding the revolutionary dimension of her book: "Sometimes" she is "shocked into passionate speech."[8]

After all, Ashbery's incomprehension is not surprising: what is more serious, more thought provoking, yet more inappropriate to speak of socially than death? He was a male of the New York Establishment; she was a New Woman whose new writing for the most part her former colleagues *could not understand.*

Fortunately John Ashbery also comments on the way her "hard and sinewy new poetry...tack[s] between alternative resolutions of the poem's tension and of leaving the reader at the right moment, just as meaning is dawning."[9] He notes how this moment of epiphany is skillfully accomplished in "Mourning Picture," a meditation on death and the spirit, written on two parents who watch their drowned child's spirit. The dead child, Effie, is the omniscient witness, the selfhood of the poem.

What is profoundly original here is that the poem is narrated from the dead child's perspective; in fact, Effie is the creator of the vision: the poem is told from her vantage point as she wonders whether or not to remake her parents' world: Effie was the creator of their world, and they were *her* dream (*N* 32). In a surprising reversal of the typical parental idea that the child is purely their creation, little Effie, the speaker in the poem, insists that they were *her* creation, *her* dream, utterly reversing our set ways of thinking of the parent/child relationship. This is a perspective so ingenious that one wonders at its originality as well as at Rich's sympathy with parents who have lost a child.

Thinking horizontally, too, one might liken this nostalgic perspective to that of a lesbian who sees she must renounce traditional marriage: the subject's poignant look back at her parents before she walks out into the realm of death resembles the last look a traditional wife might give her marriage before stepping away forever.

Equally poignant is "Like This Together" (*N* 16–17), a 1963 poem for her husband, chronicling the benefits and estrangements of a marriage. It celebrates the unusual modus vivendi the couple has established. She comments archly that they have some tastes and predilections in common. But they seem to hold no qualities or ideals in common. The poetic gaze encompasses only the children they share and their slate rooftop where frozen pigeons stand grouped together for warmth. Along with being antiliterary, this image is also antiromantic, self-parodying: ironically, the married couple is likened to huddling pigeons.

Once in a while in dreams the husband seems to become her mother and disturbs her reveries (*N* 17), says the subject to her husband. This candid speaker ridicules the strangeness of marriage's bedfellows: "Miscarried" information—misunderstandings and suspicions—disturb and "twist" them "like hot sheets thrown askew" (*N* 17). Is it *miscarried* knowledge that now keeps them together rather than sensuality, love, or passion? Does only talk sustain the marriage, as they huddle together like cold pigeons on a roof, as safe and accustomed to routine as the person reading in the lamplight in "The Roofwalker"? Not doers or actors, they are just passive observers of real life. Waiting, they hope for an hour of perfect conversation. The couple's shared tasks of fostering their sons' growth and gardening, a mutuality of watching and observations, are balanced against their misunderstood—or misunderstanding—words.

The former sensual and sexual consolations of marriage no longer obtain; what was natural before is now forced into being by attention to it (*N* 17): as if only the couple's careful tending and attention can "grow" the marriage out of the lumps of earth or deadlock it has fallen into. Total attention alone now swells the wet buds along a stem's entire surface (*N* 17). Helen Vendler comments that this ending itself seems forced and unnatural since here "Rich declares that love can be kept alive by our working at it, that the dry scaly bulb can be pried into life" (*ARP1* 168). If love can only be kept alive by "our" working hard at it, how is marriage viewed here? Is Rich merely paying lip service to or mocking the convention of marriage, or is this an attempt to salvage the marriage, metaphorically speaking at midnight when its time is just about over? The poem seems to ask, is fear of the unknown all that holds the marriage together? Later, in *Of Woman Born* Rich questions marriage, seeing problems with that institution, its problems caused by Western culture.

Omitted from the poem when it was published in *Necessities of Life* in 1966 was a last stanza that appeared when it was published in *Poetry* in April–May, 1965 (*ARP* 24). Rich may have left out the last stanza because it states a severed limb retains sensation, keeps on suffering "in the ghost limb beyond." It ends by asking poignantly how "we" can stand the bursting forth of new life in spring, recalling Eliot's *The Waste Land* in its opening, "*April is the cruelest month.*" But this ending may speak to a reenergized marriage, likening it to a tree's stump that is putting forth new shoots and sucking power from our roots; thus, all we have to do is cling to what we know for sure. That means, "we" must hold on (*ARP* 24).

Helen Vendler, who commanded considerable respect in academic circles and later was appointed to the English faculty at Harvard University, believed that "Like This Together" and "After Dark" fall into "increasingly expedient 'literariness' " (*ARP1* 168), Rich's old means of escape from the personal. No doubt Vendler detected the hints of Eliot and other former mentors Rich was in the process of jettisoning here, too. Vendler's essay, "Ghostlier Demarcations, Keener Sounds," also omitted from the second Norton Critical Edition, *Adrienne Rich's Poetry and Prose,* argues, "Better a change than the falsely 'mature' acceptance of the unacceptable, a stance that Rich falls into off and on in *Necessities of Life*" (*ARP1* 168). The falsely mature mask is fragmenting, and at last her true poetic undervoice can be heard. A new self is revealed, the self aware of death and what it means to be a woman, the selfhood that will play a larger part in her poetry as it progresses. Rich no longer evades expression of her own real feelings in the poetry but writes a revolutionary poetry of what could be. Around this time, she leaves Boston, where she has been educated, has taught and written, and had her children, and moves with her family to New York, at that time the hub of intellectual life in America.

FAREWELL TO FATHER

"After Dark," a poignant poem addressed to her dying father ("You," Dr. Arnold Rich), is one of the better known and most successful of her poems in this book about death. Significantly, for her the experience of watching him die is naturally heartbreaking, even gut wrenching: she is uprooted (*N* 29). His former droning, broken-record-like repetition that he knows her better than she knows herself (*N* 29), once hated by the girl growing up, now become what she dearly wishes he could say as he lies dying. This recollection pulverizes her heart (*N* 29).

After college, she had "limped off, torn at the roots," in an effort to separate herself from him; she even gave up singing a whole year, even acquired a new body and new breath (had a baby) and "croaked" for words (*N* 29). This modest self-disparagement masks the speaker's gnawing pain. Now at last she has won a Pyrrhic victory in this feud with her father, yet now you surrender of your own accord. While he is losing his life, the speaker is keenly aware that he gave her life and that she would willingly give it back to him. At least, she would sacrifice "something" just to prevent the end of their quarrels (*N* 29–30). The death of her father constitutes for Rich a generational rite of passage. Later in prose passage in *Sources,* she described their relationship thus: "*He and I always had a kind of rhetoric going with each other, a battle between us, it didn't matter if one of us was alive or dead*" (*S* 32). The battle with her father that had defined the first half of her life is over, and she must now define a new field for struggle. What better challenge than the cause of women's liberation?

Her mother's death is captured in "A Woman Mourned by Daughters" (1960) in *Snapshots of a Daughter-in-Law*: she recollects fondly more than once in the poetry how they successfully, gleefully ignored their mother (*S* 35). In another poem her mother is said to be "crisp" as a dead bug. Elsewhere she addresses her equally dismissively (*N* 20). She could more easily accept her mother's death because she'd resented her, if anything, more than her father. Rich wrote, "For years, I felt my mother had chosen my father over me, had sacrificed me to his needs and theories" (*LS* 222). Hence she deplored her mother's seemingly mute, mindless submission to her father, knowing that she had been "mothered by a strong, frustrated woman" (*OWB* 221), whom she never got to know or understand fully since her mother had renounced her own selfhood in order to be the perfect wife.

How does the independent prodigal daughter survive the loss of the one against whom she has rebelled (or wanted to rebel) all her life? Their relationship is transformed from an interplay of love and strife into one of pure love by her desire to preserve the life of her departing father, a man whose character she can respect even if she cannot accept his values: her poem "After Dark" is a way of celebrating his strength, his life itself, and giving him a measure of immortality beyond the boundaries of his professional life in medicine. It also declares the purity of her love for him and gratitude to him: he had been the first to detect her talent and force her to cultivate it. He had been the one who first insisted that she learn the craft of poetry, master rhyme and metrics, become the skilled poet and woman of letters she is.

ECHOES OF SYLVIA PLATH AND EMILY DICKINSON

In a review in the *Washington Post* in 1972, in which Rich wrote on women poets and what I have called the female tradition in Anglo-American women's literature, Rich assesses the history of women poets over the last century, running from Christina Rossetti through Emily Dickinson, past Sara Teasdale, Elinor Wylie, Marianne Moore, and H.D., to contemporary poets like Carolyn Kizer and Denise Levertov. Most notably she comments on the fact that "[p]sychoanalysis, increased verbal and sexual freedom, a more organic and open poetic mode" like Kizer's and Levertov's now "release women's poetry from the discreet, the melancholy, the sentimental, the merely ethereal." The new forms liberate women's poetry even as women themselves are quietly in the process of being liberated. Concurrently "Anne Sexton and Sylvia Plath...began to speak of the quarrel with themselves—which was found to be also the quarrel with others."[10] That anger and rage now streaming out of contemporary women's poetry takes two forms, however: there is the purely subjective rage verging on madness of Sexton and Plath and Diane Wakoski, and the rage in feminist poetry, which is curative, restorative, cleansing, and ultimately salvific. Barbara and Alfred Gelpi determine that because their rage is not purely personal but is also political, Adrienne Rich and "[Robin] Morgan are feminist poets, and Plath and Wakoski are not" (*ARP1* xii). As Rich expresses it, "in Plath and Wakoski a subjective, personal rage blazes forth, never before seen in women's poetry. If it is unnerving, it is also cathartic, the blowtorch of language cleansing the rust and ticky-tacky and veneer from an entire consciousness."[11] And not surprisingly, rage is at the core of Rich's interpretation of Dickinson's poetry, too. Rich identifies with the earlier poet, whose options were so much more limited than her own have been, and sympathizes with Dickinson's desire for an aesthetic and literary seclusion, wishing not to be part of the coercions of society as it was understood in the nineteenth century by those with "Dimity convictions," the fashionable ladies of Amherst. In Dickinson, Rich may have consciously or subconsciously seen another rebel, but a quieter one than she herself had been. If Dickinson did not shout and quarrel with her domineering father, still she wrote subversively, criticizing and questioning the mores and very cultural and spiritual foundations of the world into which she was born. From her the young Adrienne Rich seems to have received courage and inspiration: if Dickinson could become America's greatest poet although cut off from academia and from the society of the great men and thinkers of the day, certainly a woman with Rich's privileges and superior education could excel as a poet in the twentieth and twenty-first centuries, especially now that there was no one to stop her, neither father nor husband, neither lack of money or a place to write—woman's typical quandary and the one Virginia Woolf signaled.

From Dickinson Rich draws intoxicating inspiration, since Dickinson's work in the female tradition prevailed over all the poetry of men writing in her day, with the exception of that of the free spirit Walt Whitman. Genius that she is, Dickinson cultivated her poetry exclusively and in isolation, unhampered by children or a husband or onerous domestic duties. Rich may have realized that if Dickinson could be a superior poet in her hermit-like existence, so, too, could she herself, since she had unprecedented freedom now, a strong will to change not just herself but the lot of all women. As a feminist with these abilities, then, she knew she had the responsibility to make sure her voice continued to be heard for as long as she could speak out.

In the review, Rich states, "In Robin Morgan's *Monster* this same force is politicized, shared with other women, offered to them as a sounding board, a voice at the end of some hotline. Morgan writes not simply out of her personal intention to survive but out of a vision of the survival and transformation of all women."[12] Commenting on this, the Gelpis state that the crucial distinction Rich makes between feminist rage and pure woman's rage is that the feminists make their insights, growth, and personal experiences and feelings available to other women, not just in the hope of helping others survive, flourish, and understand their lives better but also in order to bring about the "'transformation of all women'" (*ARP1* xii).

The Gelpis continue, "In Rich's development the private poet becomes a public poet without sacrificing the complexity of subjective experience or the intensity of personal emotion" (*ARP1* xii–xiii). Rich's poetry explodes from the same depth of repressed emotion and irony as Dickinson's does; both reflect on woman's estate and wonder why woman must be the subordinate sex. In Rich's poetry, the Gelpis note, "We can hear Dickinson's quandary breaking out, reaching into rhythms which reclaim, on women's terms, Whitman's prophetic call to a society of individuals" (*ARP1* xiii) to be free and independent co-creators of the American nation, working to form the feminist nation, and the lesbian/feminist nation in the fullness of time. If woman were effectively excluded from the Declaration of Independence and the Constitution, today women are free to build any number of new nationhoods, with and without men. And they can re-envision American poetry, creating visions more heartening to and inclusive of women. Rich is an example of a person situated at precisely the right historical moment to make sweeping changes in the way America and the rest of the world think about women. She saw that and grasped her opportunity to speak for all women in *Necessities of Life* and the next books, and in so doing, she produced some of the best poetry written in the twentieth century.

Having earlier followed the tradition of Emerson and Whitman, Rich is now free to cultivate her poetry in the female tradition more fully and creatively: before, during, and directly after the death of her father she begins to hear her developing poetic undervoice, her feminist consciousness. This she first experiments with in "Snapshots" and there assumes a variety of new female subject positions, exploring every possible traditional female role, perhaps in an effort to find her newly transfigured self. Looking around at the work of her peers and female contemporaries, she gains inspiration for new poetic modes and forms, even as she deals with her father's death in a poetry reflecting her sense of loss, fragmentation, and dislocation. At 35, she mourns the death of her youth, too, along with the death of her marriage and the nuclear family she had worked so hard to build and nurture earlier in life. The violence of Alfred Conrad's suicide jarred her to her very foundations; yet for once in her life, too, she is at last free to determine her future entirely independent of marital, religious, and patriarchal ties or bonds.

Many poems in *Necessities of Life* reveal another side of the preoccupation with death, and some, like "Breakfast in a Bowling Alley" (*N* 18–19) and "The Corpse-Plant" (*N* 11–12), resonate with the tone and vocabulary of some of Sylvia Plath's poems and echo Plath's direct addresses on, from, and to the body ("Smudged eyeballs" could be one of Plath's phrases), along with her preoccupation with morbidity—she states she's a corpse (*N* 18). And in "The Corpse-Plant" where the terror is abated (*N* 14), she likens death to an "intolerable" photographic negative (*N* 14), life's grim opposite—or is it a metaphor for the spiritual life?

The fascination with what is difficult, dead, grotesque, spiritual, or hard to name makes these poems seem haunted, full of negation or chilling imagery—death has an insectlike lack of color or blanched quality (*N* 14). Here, Rich arrives at a sense of *huis clos,* no exit. There seems no way out of this impasse or dead end, this hell, yet she must stay faithful to the necessity of expressing oneself truthfully and render into poetry the reality of her frustration at her limitations and her pain.

Like Emily Dickinson, of whom she writes in "I Am in Danger—Sir" (1964), Rich chooses "to have it out at last" on her own conditions, living according to her own assumptions, her own ideals, self-concept, and initiative, on her own "premises" (*N* 33), embodying Dickinson's daring decision to create and write her truth, no matter what. Emily Dickinson separates herself from the world around her; even though her poetry did not meet with national acceptance and fame, and even though "Higginson complained that her meters were too 'spasmodic,' that her poetic rhythms were rough and untutored" still she persisted in "lonesome glee." Wendy Martin points out that it is "this highly individual verbal timing that makes Dickinson's poems so vivid and charged."[13] They make her work daring and original. Working virtually alone, Dickinson enjoys her home as a private paradise which affords her the privacy to develop her craft.

Rich, on the other hand, savors the sustenance of a poetic dialogue with her peers and public in thriving as a poet, the evolution of her poetry draws her further and further away from the docile Victorian Lady or "Angel in the House"[14] or Southern gentlewoman she had been raised to become, and she remakes herself into a politically engaged woman poet, accountable only to her country, immediate family, and other women. Having encountered Dickinson's poetic mastery, her gnomic yet still queenly style, and driving, zigzagging rhythms,[15] Rich now writes more openly of female selfhood against the backdrop of American history—current and past. Upon discovering Dickinson in the raw, as it were, Rich breaks "the bonds of traditional versification"—and traditional womanhood—as she "begins to probe her experiences more deeply to discover the sources of her conflict as a woman writer who is also mother and wife."[16] In *Snapshots*—and, I would submit, *Necessities* and *The Will to Change*—she declares "her intention to move away from social forms in which she feels the lives and energy of women and men are essentially controlled by a masculine ethos."[17] This movement beyond conventional society is mobilization of her dating inner roofwalker bursting out into the fresh air of an authentic reality, where "the moment of change is the only poem" (WC 49). This is how Rich "has it out on her own premises" (N 33). In this act her poetry shares Dickinson's daring, originality, and determination to survive as an independent, creative spirit. Dickinson's poetry and life assure her that survival is not only possible but admirable and inevitable. With the focus on the future alone, her poetry of this time can appear to imply that all women ought to take the initiative and have the integrity to be survivors—and roofwalkers themselves.[18] The poetry now centers on the process of discernment of her newly emerging feminist selfhood at the same time that she reads the unbowdlerized Dickinson and is impressed by "*the unquestionable power and importance of the mind revealed there*" (*LS* 168). She also finds in Dickinson's verse a way to link her personal experience as a woman with the more public sphere of life lived by mature late-twentieth-century women. "More than any other poet," writes Rich, "Emily Dickinson seemed to tell me that the intense inner event, the personal and psychological, was inseparable from the universal; that there was a range for psychological poetry beyond mere self-expression" (*LS* 168). This was a turning point in the development of a new consciousness and of a new poetics more true to her private and public female selves.

Rich does not read Dickinson's poems as the seismic record of a specifically female psychology or sensibility: in fact, she appears to look at such readings as part of the problem rather than as the solution to understanding female poetic expression. It is because Dickinson appears to redeem and validate women's psychic and psychological experience for universal purposes that Rich is drawn to and enabled by her work at this point in her poetic career. For if the intense inner female event is not part of a separate sphere but part of a universal sphere, then the woman poet can command a "range beyond mere self-expression." This is not to say that Rich was deaf to cultural difference, but that her poetry of this period aspires to communicate with and speak *primarily* for women. Later she addresses all readers.

In *On Lies, Secrets and Silence,* Rich praises Dickinson for appropriating and employing this range of experience, ideas, and feelings, declaring: "she was determined to survive, to use her powers, to practice the necessary economies" (*LS* 160). For her, Dickinson is not only a model of female survival in patriarchal culture or "phallogocentric tradition,"[19] as Betsy Erkkila calls it, but also a figure of female poetic power, creating herself and recreating the world through the power of language. As a woman poet who was herself struggling to challenge and dislodge the "phallogocentric" and sexist assumptions embedded in language and culture, Rich found in the boldness, the slant rhymes, paradoxical cosmic vision, and fractured rhythms of Dickinson's poetry a clue to the ways patriarchal language might be used as a vehicle to express female creation and transformation. Rich's rediscovery of Dickinson as a source of linguistic renewal corresponds with a transformation in her poetics.[20] Along with her embrace of a new "personal lifestyle, poetic strategy and political vision [comes] her effort to reclaim Dickinson as a poetic mother."[21] Strange as it is to think of Dickinson as anyone's mother, possibly this is her function for Rich, who in the 1960s was immensely influenced by Dickinson's poetry and sought to probe the extreme reaches of consciousness and truth just as Dickinson had.

Despite the fact that Rich has often made her living by teaching and has been at times a radical activist, basically she derives her personal identity from her vocation as a poet, though she is also famous as a founder of women's studies, a feminist theorist, and "a figure of female poetic power."[22] sing language as a vehicle of creation and transformation. In this she is definitely a successor of Emily Dickinson, true to her own real voice and vision:

> In 1965 Rich wrote "I Am in Danger—Sir—," in which she celebrates Dickinson's creative potency; in the same year, in "Poetry and Experience," she declared her break with her earlier concept of poetry as a predetermined arrangement of ideas and feelings and her move toward a new concept of poetry as a means of renaming, reknowing, and reconstituting the world[.][23]

That essay explains, "In my earlier poems, I told you as precisely and eloquently as I knew how, about something; in the more recent poems something is happening, something has happened to me, and...something will happen to you who read it" (*ARP1* 89). Her new poetry records the actual experience that has shaped her consciousness and each poem ends at the precise moment of realization of a new truth. This poetry is designed to have—and often has—a transformative effect on both writer and reader. Using poetry to challenge the forces that would subvert or dominate her, the speakers experience visceral challenges and triumph, to be born into a new consciousness or a way of seeing women's place and selfhood in the world.

As tribute to Dickinson, her first female mentor, Rich writes "I Am in Danger—Sir" (*N* 33), which title quotes Dickinson's words to Thomas Higginson, her "*Preceptor,*" upon hearing from him that he found her verses eccentric and her "*gait spasmodic.*"[24]

It is true, too, that to his friends he spoke of Emily Dickinson as "*Half-cracked,*" but even today we do not completely understand her life or poetry. As Rich expressed it some years ago, it is surprising "how narrowly her work, still, is known by women...writing poetry, how much her legend has gotten in the way of her being repossessed, as a source and a foremother" (*LS* 167). Her fame and charisma may block many readers from getting beyond the myth of Emily Dickinson's mysterious solitary life to the tougher negotiation with her poetry.

One of Rich's purposes in "I Am in Danger—Sir" is to reveal that all who disparaged Emily Dickinson, called her eccentric or odd or *"half-cracked,"* are now suspect themselves since they misjudged her worth as a poet—or a Poet, as Emerson defines him or her. For her the *"word was more than a symptom—"*: the word was *"a condition of being"* (*N* 33), as it is for Rich herself. Her home was not chosen as a refuge out of fear: in fact, in deciding to limit herself to its sphere, she displayed the ultimate sanity in choosing to live an independent life, and writing poetry for a intimate few, to live with integrity on your own "premises" (*N* 33). Earlier in the poem, Rich wrote metaphorically of "the air [around Dickinson] buzzing with spoiled language." To Dickinson, it rings of "[p]erjury" (*N* 33). Erkkila comments on these lines:

The perjury that sang in Dickinson's ears is the false witness of female lives embedded in patriarchal language and culture. Rather than perjure herself, Rich suggests, Dickinson chose withdrawal and silence as a means of surviving as a woman poet in nineteenth-century America. The repetition of "half-cracked" at the end of the poem stresses the disjunction between the "cracked" image of Dickinson and the absolute sanity of her choice: her life and her poems only appear "cracked" in the spoiled and perjured context of the phallologocentric tradition. The repetition of "chose" at the end of one line and at the beginning of another further underscores Dickinson's powerful will to survive. No longer dwelling on the image of Dickinson pinned between the boil and scum of jellies in her Amherst pantry, Rich underlines the connection between her decision to stay at home, her determination to have her own will, and her power to create herself and recreate the world, by yoking the three ideas in the final image of the poem: "on your own premises." Unlike the house of "Snapshots of a Daughter-in-Law," here the house has become the site not of destructive female energies, but of potency and necessary economies.[25]

But society cannot be expected to understand her "potency" at once. This poem and others in the book contains an image of women browbeaten: in "I Am in Danger—Sir," Dickinson's forehead is described as being beaten "paper-thin" by her culture, "you, woman, masculine" with regard to her single-mindedness (*N* 33); the juxtaposition reveals Rich's valuing of single-mindedness and its importance to women poets. It is significant, too, that she yokes "woman, masculine" directly together, reasoning or "figur[ing] Dickinson's powerful will as male."[26] Her style reflects these changes in gender consciousness in that it is more fissured, disjointed, mirroring political and aesthetic breakups, new wave cinema, and Olson's projective verse:

As in Dickinson's poems the drama of Rich's new poems is created not by logical development or narrative line, but by verbal compression and the dynamic tension generated by the splitting of syntax, image, line and unit. Thus, Dickinson was an early model for the poetics of process that Rich pursued in *Leaflets* (1969) and *The Will to Change* (1971) in which, through the ghazal couplets of Mirza Ghalib, the projective verse of Charles Olson, and the new wave cinema of Jean-Luc Godard, Rich sought a form commensurate with an age of cultural and political breakup and collapse.[27]

Returning to the image of browbeating, the last poem in *Necessities of Life* is the 1965 "Face to Face" (*N* 49), a poem David Kalstone describes as "breathless with tension and with the envy felt by the modern speaker for the frontier's stern isolated life" (*N* 138); it ends with an explosive image linking the repression of nineteenth-century heroes and heroines like Emily Dickinson with the image of browbeatenness—the brow beaten thin. The lines imagine how jubilantly people used to encounter one another when they were hungry for stimulating talk and the company of their peers (*N* 49), so eager for fellowship and good conversation after a winter of being snowbound, each with a God-given secret truth burning in the scalp (*N* 49). If scalps are bleached from the wear and tear of physical or psychic weather, are they more damaged by what their culture does not permit them to express than they are by the constraints of their milieus? Whenever they meet, their truth, their speech resembles *"a loaded gun"* (*N* 33). Human language can be as explosive and have as strong an impact as the report of a gun, and Dickinson's (and Rich's) poems frequently have the explosive power of a gun report: Rich likens this power to that of Vesuvius's eruptions in poetic power and magnitude. Kalstone is exuberant about this poem's dynamic movement: "Rich has provided a syntax of infinitives and exclamations, of elided main verbs, for these scenes of stress and expectation, of a loneliness which sharpens the senses."[28]

Understanding it somewhat differently, Albert Gelpi, writing about her work, has commented that Rich writes "a poetry of dialogue and the furious effort to break through to dialogue" (*ARP1* 145). Her poem "Face to Face" displays the sort of "furious effort" he is alluding to while at the same time it confronts issues of loneliness and exploding repression or imploding creativity.

This phrase *"a loaded gun"* is, of course, as noted above, taken from Dickinson's poem *"My Life had stood—a Loaded Gun—."* The exploding gun is the perfect image for the way a creative woman might feel at this turning point in women's history, this time of liberation—full of meaning and ideas and ready to fire. "Face to Face" conceives of early Americans' lives as so full of expressive potency and intensity that they seemed ready after a long, lonely winter to explode like loaded guns, ready to "fire" their pent-up thoughts, love, emotions, and desires for a new place for women in American society. Likewise Rich herself may have felt her life "exploding" in new intellectual, political, cultural directions, moving adventurously into new territories. Certainly many American women—especially the young—felt this change in the air and were stirred by a sense of new possibilities in store for them.

Later, in *Leaflets,* the forehead image returns, but now the forehead is not just beaten but also physically invaded: someone tries to go past her eyes into her head in "Orion" (*L* 11). Even if Rich has nothing left to offer in a dialogue with a man who overreaches her boundaries, invades her privacy, she still has not lost all faith in communication because she persists in writing and publishing poetry: she is now more prolific than ever, as if making up for lost time, giving a voice to dreams and women's unspoken truths.

This poetry envisions a utopia where all women can be free and equal: in "Autumn Sequence" in *Necessities of Life,* she predicts that this time and place "where so many nerves are fusing" (*N* 35) must exist or must come to exist—a place and time for a "purely moral loneliness" (*N* 35). Deconstructing "moral loneliness" recalls Greta Garbo, perhaps the first feminist film star, who said, *"I want to be alone,"* asserting her right to a female selfhood equal to and valuable as men's; this is what Rich claims aesthetically and poetically. Her poem seems to predict that one day the time and place will come when true equality between the sexes will be achieved, and everyone who wishes to can enjoy moral loneliness unmolested since this is a prerequisite for poetic creation.

COULD *SHE* BE A GENERIC PRONOUN?

Rich now crafts what she had predicted would be "a whole new poetry beginning here," using her two-space line (see "Nightbreak," *L* 49), more irregular stresses, a more elemental vocabulary, and more colorful imagery. In *Leaflets,* feminist and lesbian self-expression in poetry are deemed standard. Since, as the Chinese proverb goes, *"Women hold up half the sky,"* logically the pronoun representing humankind could be "she" just as well as "he." True to this advance in her feminist consciousness, Rich later changed the pronoun in "5:30 A.M." (1967) from "he" to "she," making the line exclaim on their beauty, fox and poet with their auburn pelts and, ever one for the shocking detail, bloody tracks (*L* 31). The poet gives this note of explanation when the poem is republished in 1975: "Very rarely, I've altered a verb or a pronoun because I felt it had served as an evasion in the original version" (*ARP* 33). Now she must come out as a lesbian as well as a feminist. Hence her celebration of shared femininity with the bleeding vixen: she and the fox, both refugees from the strategies of civilization, flee the expressionless murderer (*L* 31) who, paradoxically mindlessly "singleminded," wants to pursue and murder them (*L* 31). Each must escape the killer who would skin them, as patriarchal culture has been known to devour females. Later she will write,

I am a feminist because I feel endangered, psychically and physically, by this society and because I believe that the women's movement is saying that we have come to an edge of history when men—insofar as they are embodiments of the patriarchal idea—have become dangerous to children and other living things, themselves included. (*WF* 218)

Can they survive? Will they survive? Rich implies that women must free themselves, even if they only get away with their own skins. The vixen's orders sounds like the angels: "*Save yourself if you can.*" The urgency of desperation breathes through every syllable. It is the nightmare desperation of "5:30 A.M." As she had said in "In the Evening" in 1966, "The old masters," the dignitaries, and status quo are mystified by women's behavior at this time of quiet transformation, and cannot understand what we're doing (*L* 15). As Judith McDaniel calls it, "reconstituting the world" becomes the purpose of her poetry. In "Implosions" (*L* 42) the lyric "I" says she wants to find words that even "you" might be moved and changed by.

LEAFLETS AND "ORION"

In *Leaflets*, a book that reflects the social unrest of the anti–Vietnam War movement and the birth of the Women's Liberation Movement as a renewed political and social force, Rich's lyric "I" evolves into that of the revolutionary issuing leaflets from the front. Sending documentation of the struggle to free all women, she writes in rawer, more fragmentary two-space lines on topics of more immediate political consequence. And she employs Dickinson's psychological compression, her verbal dynamism, and common use of abstractions in unexpected contexts, and "[i]n fact, Rich's two-space 'zig-zagging' rhythm, which she employed for the first time in *Leaflets* to achieve fracture, pause, and emphasis, was probably a descendant of Dickinson's dash."[29] The brash spirit of these poems echoes Dickinson's "*lonesome glee.*"

Reading Rich's poetry of this era, one empathizes with her experience of living through momentous events and enduring the real dangers of political activism in the late 1960s: she is both rendering them in a precise poetic language and experimenting with new political subject positions. In the middle of "On Edges" (*L* 45), she writes of history as it is perceived in the making, history on the edge: holding a ripped-up letter and kneeling, she tries to piece together the fragments into a comprehensive whole; the speaker translates what bits she can, her brain working at top speed on a machine that translates "'*useless*'" as "'*monster*'" and "'*history*'" as"'*lampshade*'" (*L* 45). Of course, these last lines allude to the making of the annihilated Jews' skins into lampshades in the Nazi concentration camps even as the poem protests the ostracizing of the Jews during World War II. Relating various epochs of history to this one, her mind whirs like a thinking machine, only connecting, as Ezra Pound, the Modernist poet, had enjoined everyone to do, *history* with *lampshade*, and *useless* with *monsters*. This is the political reductionism of the oppressors: if Jews could be castigated as monsters, or useless parasites of the state, they could be reduced to lampshades by the Nazis. Her current task is to reverse the draconian logic of history.

"Orion," the first poem in *Leaflets,* dedicated to her "projected" imaginary half-brother who is the constellation Orion, sets the tone for the book. She speaks of it in her alarmingly titled essay "When We Dead Awaken," saying that the writing of that poem reconnected her with a male part of herself she felt she was losing: having seen women as largely passive and proper persons, 1930s style, up to this point, she now identifies or projects Orion as her "half-brother," "the active principle" (*ARP* 175) or part of her selfhood, her energetic imagination, the part of her that could rescue her as the knight in shining armor rescues the lost maiden.

In fact, "Orion" chronicles Adrienne Rich's own awakening from the dead, her awakening after what may have seemed for her were years of the mental lull of child raising; of course, she consciously takes the title from the Ibsen play by the same name, implying that the dead are now awakening and resurrected. In the poem "Orion" (*L* 11), the ungendered lyric "I" regains contact with the psyche's inner male, "my fierce half-brother," and reconnects with inner poise and confidence, along with driving ambition and a sense of purpose.

Raised in traditional Baltimore, Maryland, in a conservative, upper-class family, Rich experienced extreme sex role conditioning from her youth—hence the browbeating imagery of *Necessities of Life.* Her parents and relatives had taught her that women must be submissive and "womanly," giving "maternal love, altruistic love—a love defined by the weight of an entire culture" (*ARP* 175), the Judeo-Christian culture. If woman's province is love, then men's may be "egotism... achievement, ambition, often at the expense of others" (*ARP* 175), and justifiably so, she thought uncritically, when she was a traditional Jewish wife: "For weren't they men, and wasn't that their destiny [just] as womanly, selfless love was ours? We know now that the alternatives are false ones—that the word 'love' is itself in need of re-vision."

Indeed, just as it was necessary to rethink her concepts of masculinity and femininity, it has been one of Rich's tasks in poetry and life to reenvision love, sex roles, and sexuality, to claim for herself, as in "Orion," the qualities of her half-brother, Orion, the intrepid hunter, the fearless warrior. The poem's speaker exclaims: "No hurt, no pardon," as if hurt were inevitable. The locus of the poem is outside in the cold with you who have your back to the wall (*L* 11). To assume an enduring bravery, as the lyric "I" does in the course of the poem, is a conscious act of feminist liberation, a freeing of the active male principle in herself. She has signaled the poem as marking a turning point in her writing in "When We Dead Awaken," her tracing of the process of her evolution as an awakening feminist poet.

At the poem's opening, the speaker remembers herself as a small girl zigzagging in tamarack groves when Orion was her genius. He symbolizes pure strength and courage along with goodness and kindness. She calls him her strong Viking, her brother-rescuer, the "lion-heart king in prison" (*L* 11). Hence, she compares him with King Richard the Lion-Hearted, the popular Crusader King of England, who was captured by King Leopold of Austria and imprisoned but discovered by the faithful troubadour Blondel, who searched Europe for him until he found the dungeon where he was incarcerated. Here is the hero Rich might have sought in *Snapshots of a Daughter-in-Law,* the book of hidden female angst: King Richard the Lion-Hearted is another manifestation of the Orion/savior archetype, and a Viking known for his kindness, a good, courageous, generous man, worthy to be a strong woman's brother (*L* 11). Here the textual "I" is in the position of those anticipating liberation and his return from exile, yet she can still look up at his constellation in the night sky and find strength and bravery, despite his absence from their occupied kingdom.

The imagery of death and a negation of nourishment are conflated here in a dislocated poetry reflecting the cultural and political fracturing occurring around her in the late 1960s and a consequent sense of internal fragmentation. Are the children eating the crumbs under the table of the textual "I"'s life neglected or begging children? Or are they taking away parts of the poet's life? The tone makes it hard to say. This poem in regular six-line stanzas in tetrameter delivers a correspondingly powerful impact. Tight and lean, it progresses from focus on the speaker, a half-sister on the ground gazing up at Orion, to communication between the two, to her own ultimate transformation into a woman warrior outside, able to stand with her back to the wall.

Indoors the sisterly "I" is awkward (*L* 11), not leaving well enough alone; she betrays herself and others (*L* 11). But Orion throws down geodes, down the chimney into the grate, and the textual "I" is regenerated by Orion's rain of geodes.

The surreal image of seeing a female head resisting her gaze in the mirror (*L* 11) recalls a macabre scene from the contemporary film "The Exterminating Angel" by Bunuel, where a reflection ceases purely to reflect but takes on a life of its own. Similarly, the lyric "I" can no longer simply live unquestioningly according to traditional values, or assume the traditional roles of the good wife and nurturing mother to her children: she has gone outside—to the other side of the mirror (or role) as Mary Elizabeth Coleridge would have expressed it—and now communes with her half-brother Orion, appropriating some of his masculine qualities. She addresses him in the next stanza as he hangs "pinned," almost like a crucified figure in his crow's nest. The image incorporates an allusion to the cruciform shape of Orion, reminiscent of a ship's mast. He is accused of complacency, and in transference, she looks back at him "with a starlike eye shooting its cold and egotistical stare" out in space (*L* 12), but her gaze is directed for sight, not to wound him. She merely wants to be in visual contact, but now she also encourages and revitalizes him. Her piercing eye is now *starlike,* thanks to his divine influence, and it "shoots" its aesthetic stare spearlike at him and at her poetry. Here, she "projects her imaginative power as a masculine figure," Orion.[30] Her masculine side or animus is still displaced, distanced from her selfhood as a woman, since in Rich's mind a dichotomy exists between "womanly, maternal, altruistic love—a love defined and ruled by the weight of an entire culture; and egotism—a force directed by men into creation, achievement, ambition, often at the expense of others" (*ARP1* 175). In sum, men create, achieve, aspire, so they are the rightful possessors of egotism and altruistic love while traditional women usually love hearth and home—what's local—selflessly. The professions were thought to be men's domain and "destiny," while "womanly selfless love" was women's destiny. "We know now that the alternatives are false ones—that the word 'love' is itself in need of re-vision" (*ARP1* 175).

In the last lines, the speaker exhorts Orion to: "Breathe deep!" because there is neither harm nor forgiveness out in the night and cold with Orion, with his "back to the wall" (*L* 12). These lines echo phrases quoted in the Norton Critical Edition and originally found in Gottfried Benn's "Artists and Old Age" in which old artists are encouraged not to quit but to keep working boldly: "*Don't lose sight of the cold and egotistical element in your mission... With your back to the wall*" (*ARP* 30). Here the poet considers the condition of the poet in the modern world as one with "back to the wall," as Gottfried Benn describes it, and as "cold and egotistical." She speaks to all those poets and writers who are "*writing against the current*," as Virginia Woolf put it in *Moments of Being*. For Rich, this defensive stance is a necessary condition of being a feminist poet.

Alicia Ostriker and others see "Orion" as a poem of "self-integration through visionary integration with... [her] half-brother Orion"; it is a "healing the self through reconciling spiritual antinomies."[31] A healing and strengthening of the sisterly "I" are accomplished through the poem. And this image of the unified self builds on that of the strong-willed monadic "I," solid or stubborn as a cabbage in "Necessities of Life" (*N* 9), as well as on the metaphor for new womanhood descending from the sky at the end of "Snapshots of a Daughter-in-Law," as beautiful as any classic youth, adding strangely or "helicopter" (*S* 24). In this last image inspired by Simone de Beauvoir, she replaces the classical ideal of the naked youth (David, for instance) with the image of a beautiful, airborne woman who announces an age of women's liberation.

In the poetry of *Leaflets* there are frequent references to the tempestuous cultural and social changes taking place in late 1960s. In "In the Evening," a poem included in the 1975 Norton Critical Edition of her poetry but not in the second edition, published in 1993, Rich records the sense of enduring a transition from one era to the next that those who experienced the 1960s felt after 1966. There is a sense of the old order passing away and an apprehension about what will constitute the new order: huddling together in the twilight dimness of the 1960s, they exalt in how puzzled the powers-that-be are with their behavior (*L* 15). Hence the ominous tone and cryptic meanings of some *Leaflets* poems and the sense of foreboding that seemed to haunt the decade after the Kennedy assassination; the poems chronicle the end of a patriarchal era dominated by "the old masters" and outworn theories of women's physical, spiritual, and intellectual inferiority.

"THE DEMON LOVER," "IMPLOSIONS," AND OTHER POEMS

Leaflets registers this sense of change, loss, and foreboding experienced by many in 1966, along with a dread of political chaos many sensed just before the Watts riots, the 1968 Revolution in Paris, and the closing of many universities that spring in protest against the escalating Vietnam War. Predictably, in "The Demon Lover," whose title also echoes Coleridge's "Kublai Khan," the lyric "I" recalls: in a dream about the war, she and fellow collaborators sat in a kitchen in Chicago (*L* 20). At this moment, they hear over the radio that their state is the target (*L* 20). Next, the poem becomes a long conversation between friends engaged in the all-consuming incessant political debate that dominated the late 1960s. The sense of living through a momentous watershed in history resonates through the poem: ordinary women and men go along with their lives complacently while "Posterity" shivers and quakes (*L* 21). Then, emphasizing the point, she continues, insisting that they have to make the world according to "my coexistent friend," reclining in jail (*L* 21). The reader savors the delicious irony of the coexistent friend's saying that "we" must remake the world even though "we" are confined to jail. Poetic music, even the poem's message and humor, can be overlooked in the urgency of this mission. The sense of speaking underground, from a prison cell, our sense as readers of overhearing a conversation being recorded by secret police or possibly the FBI intensify the excitement of these lines.

The demon lover in the poem by that name connotes both a possible illicit underground lover and the "fatal attraction" of these political activities and resistance to the war themselves, all contraband, illegal, but necessitated by strong convictions and the moral loneliness integrity demands, described in "Autumn Sequence" and elsewhere in *Necessities.* If she found no connection with life in the old sources of comfort or in the traditional roles, she could still find communion with others in the dominant sadness of this time of anguish, of revolt, demonstrations, imprisonments, needless pain, and necessary protest: *"In triste veritas?"* she inquires [*Is there truth in sadness?*]. The poem ends in a faltering act of love and union, and like a drop she merges into oneness with the lover paradoxically, nauseated, seasick, falling into the depths of the sea (*L* 22). Dramatic effects, strident talk dominate this poetry of bold defiance to established order, of a changing of the guard, and Rich's poetry reflects the vibrant colors, emotions, and events that most adults and teenagers witnessed in the late 1960s.

The poems written in 1968 seem to dart off the page and grab the reader by the lapels: she wants to pick words that even you, the neutral or uncommitted reader, would be transformed by, the lyric "I" states in the radical poem "Implosions," which begins with lines from her student's poem (*L* 42). This is the first instance of her quoting from a poem by one of her students at the City College of New York, yet this strategy achieves powerful effects: the decade's headlong rush through frightening events began with the assassination of President Kennedy and, in 1968, that of his brother Robert Kennedy, the assassination of Martin Luther King, the deaths from drug overdose of Jimi Hendrix, Janis Joplin, Jim Morrison, and other rock singers, finally culminating in the Charles Manson murders in 1970, which brought to an end the Summer of Love in Haight/Ashbury in San Francisco and ended the Hippie Dream of a New Age of Aquarius. A decade beginning in much hope has culminated in mid–Vietnam War despair about the future. For Rich the sense of loss grows into a larger despair and rage at the loss of hope, of national ideals, and a communal sense of national honor.

She moves between fear and anger at the end of *Leaflets,* her first ostensibly political book; it ends with "Nightbreak," which opens with the poignant lines: "Something broken" that she has to have, broken by a loved one (*L* 48). The situation evokes what may be a frequent experience for a mother of three sons. The two-space rhythmic break takes the place of the dash; the form is what Olson and others called an "open field," Rich's own projective verse. The lines of "Nightbreak" have the strongest medial caesura she has used to date; the poem conveys a tone of division, irreversible loss, and brokenness: night breaks quixotically, not day (*L* 49). Dawn is not an illumination but a further darkening of the light; the depth of these, this loss and brokenness, may only be felt, not fully expressed in words.

Passing through this extremely difficult time is like walking on the edge of an abyss: as the ice shakes and cracks, *drowning* seeps into her (*L* 45); she cries in "On Edges," one of the best poems in this seismic book. Could there be a revolution or an overthrow of the government? Significantly, the image of new womanhood, the helicopter's turning blades return dangerously in this poem by way of warning: the "machine"'s blades could shred you, yet provocatively its function is humane (*L* 45) since its purpose is women's liberation. Siding with the revolutionaries, she states she prefers to draw and taste blood from a sharp cut rather than use blunt scissors on dotted lines (*L* 45), working obediently, as her teacher commanded (*L* 45). Quick, violent revolution, she says, is better than a blunt hacking away at established order. She wants to cut daringly and dramatically: verbal and perhaps physical violence are claimed as necessities of life along with the moral courage formerly denied her sex. She may have found a way for women to be legitimate warriors in this battle of the sexes being waged against the backdrop of the Vietnam War, but later poems explore how women warriors tend to be tortured and murdered.

Helen Vendler is not amused by Rich's writing about "ethical issues in the 'real world,' and ... tak[ing] a polemical or sorrowing position with respect to them. The chief imaginative act in Rich's work would appear to be the choice, from all the difficulties of this difficult world, of a set of difficulties to map."[32] Vendler criticizes Rich for choosing sexual politics along with ethical and class issues as her chief subjects, calling this poetry tendentious, monotonous, and boring, betraying self-pity or paranoia rather than anything constructive or, more important to her, beautifully literary:

> Rich is inclined to represent certain distinct kinds of social evil.... Such things as slavery, marital brutality, racist persecution, social discrimination, industrial crimes against health, and the conditions of imprisonment are her natural territory (rather than, for instance, the kinds of sophisticated moral evil that interested Henry James and Proust).[33]

Still, Rich might counter, How much interest did Henry James, Marcel Proust, or any other Modernists have in helping women to realize all their potential? Not much. Like many women of her generation, Rich might have waited quietly all her life for the time to improve women's global standing, or she could have become numb to the possibility of realizing the dream of improving women's status and condition worldwide. Instead, in her poetry, she speaks out boldly against all injustice to any marginalized groups. Conservative critics do not understand her extremism and deplore it. Many who formerly approved of her work snub her; some critics even satirize her,[34] or give her unfavorable reviews or none at all. In *Reviewing the Reviews,* Margaret Cooter gives this account of an experiment conducted around this time by the Writers Guild:

> At a meeting of the Writers' Guild, [Andrea] Dworkin and colleagues selected 'extraordinarily insulting' reviews of the works of [other] eminent feminist writers, such as Kate Millett and Adrienne Rich. But, when reading these aloud to the audience, they replaced the names of the women with the names of eminent male writers. The audience was stunned by the derogatory tone of the reviews and refused to believe they had actually been written—until it was proved otherwise.[35]

At this time, Rich may have become accustomed to—and possibly even somewhat hardened to—unfavorable reviews in the decades when eminent conservative critics called her too outspoken, shrill, hysterical, and of course unfeminine. Harold Bloom formed the opinion that she was one of the "hairy barbarians" at the gate of the Western canon and should be ousted from her former place in literary and academic circles.[36] Helen Vendler's snide words are representative of those of many conservative critics:

> [Rich] thinks it is the duty of the poet to bear witness to, and protest against, these social evils. She appears to manifest the reformer's faith that there is something that can be done against evil, and her poems invoke heroes and heroines ... who fought for social welfare.[37]

Though biased and disenchanted, this judgment does have a seed of validity: Rich does manifest "the reformer's faith" we shall see grow in future volumes of poetry. With a reformer's faith, in "Nightbreak" and other late poems in *Leaflets,* "Rich is breaking down language itself in order to... recompose it."[38] As a revolutionary who has finally found the true undervoice of her poetry, she is transforming and renaming the world in order to recompose and reunite it and the sexes. Later counterbalancing her criticism of Rich, Vendler affirms that

> The positive values Rich has embraced thematically in her books include female friendship and love, outspokenness, working for reform, truth telling, sympathy, conversation, moral outrage, persistence in work, introspection, and memory.[39]

Certainly these values and virtues emanate from this poetry. But, Vendler complains, "These [values] have as their aesthetic counterparts a devotion to plainness of style and to unremitting earnestness of tone."[40] When Helen Vendler joined the camp of those opposing Rich's work, mocking her feminist fervor, it may have seemed as though the establishment she had so cultivated early on had turned on her. But undeterred, Rich continues mining her own vein in the female tradition. Now any orderly "logical" sequence or succession of ideas is set aside, as is the basic syntax of the sentence. In 1965, she pens these prose jottings, directives to herself, in a notebook: "*Necessity for a more unyielding discipline in my life,*" to "*Recognize the uselessness of blind anger.*" She also resolved to "*[l]imit society*" and use the "*children's school hours better, for work & solitude*" (*OWB* 31). Finally, she vowed to "*Be harder & harder on [my own] poems*" (*OWB* 31).

Of her next two books, Suzanne Juhasz wrote, "a new quality of language irradiates Rich's poetry"[41] since at last she is free to "explore the sources of female power."[42] The hopes Virginia Woolf had for the writing women of the future would fulfill themselves over the next four years of Adrienne Rich's career and in the careers of many women who begin writing, inspired by her poetry.

Chapter 5

Seeing Is Changing, Writing Is Renaming

> In order to live a fully human life we require not only control of our bodies (though control is a prerequisite); we must touch the unity and resonance of our physicality, our bond with the natural order, the corporeal grounds of our intelligence.
>
> —Adrienne Rich

If *Leaflets* is not the pinnacle of Adrienne Rich's achievement as a poet, arguably *Diving into the Wreck,* winner of the National Book Award in 1974, is. The poem entitled "Diving into the Wreck" is considered by many to be the most important feminist poem of the twentieth century; it may be one of the most important and influential twentieth-century poems written by an American poet. It confirmed Rich's place as a founder of women's studies and feminist theory, and it helped release a tide of feminist poetry across the world, as others, hearing her voice, were inspired to break their silence.

But *The Will to Change* preceded her *Diving into the Wreck. The Will to Change* vents anger at cultures that subordinated talented women with the potential for professional accomplishment, simply because of gender. A centerpiece of *The Will to Change,* a book dedicated to her sons, is the poem "Planetarium," which opens onto an image of a monster/woman (*WC* 13). The subject is Caroline Herschel, the sister of the noted astronomer William Herschel. Helping her brother, who discovered Uranus, she was a brilliant astronomer in her own right, discovering "8 comets" and making many more astronomical discoveries; but while William became famous, few knew of Caroline's lifetime of outstanding work. The subject articulates both their existences: Herschel sees herself as a woman-shaped instrument, a person trying to translate "pulsations"—from the psyche, or stars?—into images for the body's sensual release—in the wholeness of a perfect image?—and "the reconstruction of the soul" (*WC* 13). This is the work of the feminist poet. Rich says of the composition of "Planetarium," "at last the woman in the poem and the woman writing the poem become the same person" (*ARP1* 264). The poet and poem are now integrated and integral.

This book, *The Will to Change,* is comprised of dreams and images of life, memories of dead loved ones and visions of dying institutions and people; it was written over the years of her husband's suicide; she presents the reader with vivid glimpses into her urban existence as alienated wife and loving mother, passionate friend, lesbian lover, and most important, intellectual champion of women's issues globally, a writer of women's manifestoes and foremother of women's studies. She is a writer achieving wholeness as both a woman and a writer. In these "experimental politically engaged poems Rich would begin to locate the sources of her creative power within herself and other women."[1] While she still spoke of women's experience in the third person in "Snapshots," in "Planetarium" she "speaks for the first time as a woman poet and an 'I' who identifies with the historical power and experience of other women."[2] To show how she arrives at this moment of commitment, how she unites the woman in the poem or lyric "I" with the woman writing the poem will be the purpose of this chapter.

Having been caught up in the political turmoil of the late 1960s, she emerges from this decade a changed, more radical woman; and of necessity, her poetry is a changed, more radical poetry. Albert Gelpi comments that the next three books are better than the second; "they move steadily and with growing success toward making a poetry which is not just an activity consonant with life but an act essential to it" (*ARP1* 291). Poetry's focus is now not the truth and purity of art, but the necessity of the interpenetration of poetry, history, and experience. A series of elemental transformations, akin to those of a butterfly emerging from a chrysalis, continues in *The Will to Change* (1971) (whose title is taken from Charles Olson's "The Kingfishers"—"*What does not change / is the will to change*") and *Diving into the Wreck* (1973), a book thought by many to be her best.

For *Diving into the Wreck,* Rich won but personally rejected the National Book Award: she rejected the award for *herself alone* but accepted it collectively in the name of all women, along with Audre Lorde and Alice Walker, the other two nominees, saying, "We together accept this award in the name of all the women whose voices have gone and still go unheard in a patriarchal world, and in the name of those who, like us, have been tolerated as token women" (*ARP1* 204). At last in 1974, she expresses her rebellion publicly, crystallizing the cultural role of the feminist poet as rebel. In this chapter we shall see how her desire to break the old poetic modes led her to experiment in open forms in part inspired by the projective verse of Charles Olson and by Emily Dickinson's poetics of fracture, pause, and emphasis, and how her revolutionary politics, Godard's New Wave cinema, and other sociocultural movements influenced her poetry. In this new evolution in her poetry, she joins the transcendentalist tradition of Walt Whitman, and the female tradition of Emily Dickinson, as well.

"PLANETARIUM" AND THE CULTURAL ROLE OF THE FEMINIST POET

The Will to Change was partially written during the time of separation from her husband (1969–70) before his suicide in 1970. It is a paradoxical blend of fear of and desire for liberation. Significantly, the first lines of *The Will to Change* begin in direct address to an unknown "you," stripped and starting float-free like a freed slave or wisp of smoke (*WC* 11). The identity of "you" is a mystery that must be solved in the process of reading: at first it is something like a spirit that could drift free over local fires, something that is part of the autumn burning away of all that is dead. "You" may be the part of the poet that is liberated, free. This is what is expected, what fall expected when all the cardinal fall colors are gone (*WC* 11). Employing the word "collapse" at the end of the eighth line and dating the poem 1968, Rich invokes the collapse of governments, buildings, and institutions. Yet what is coming into being here is something as elusive and important as a revolution in consciousness and perspective, in the way society sees half its population. To signal this, the poem engages the dimension of incipiency, the opening of the new age, more fully in the final stanza where she relates her own puzzlement at "your" origin in very short lines: about how "you" burst open; the lyric "I" is ignorant. Spirit bloweth where it listeth, and comes and goes mysteriously (*WC* 11). The subject only knows that nothing material will hold "you" and that only when all the old order's pillars of reason and standards have been torn down could "you" begin to rebuild from the foundation up (*WC* 11). The poem ends in awe, the "I" in awe of her ignorance as she sees "you" starting to give yourself away and merge with the wind (*WC* 11). Like pure spirit itself or like wind, the tracking of a change in consciousness in this book is subtle, powerful, hard to see happening. In blunter, clipped lines, she records her wonder at its movement, a movement nothing can arrest.

Rich shows that the poem "Planetarium" was important to her process of self-unification and her development as a womanist/feminist poet: written three years later, Orion's companion poem is "Planetarium," composed after a visit to a real planetarium, where she read an account of the work of Caroline Herschel, who helped famous brother William nightly with his measurements of the stars and astronomical calculations (*ARP* 264).

The effort here is to bring to the reader's attention both the merit and the contribution of this intelligent, productive, yet almost unknown woman astronomer, in the same way that simultaneously Judy Chicago was creating *The Dinner Party* to draw the public's attention to all the women artists, scientists, writers, painters, and others whose contributions had shaped human history but who, like Emily Dickinson, for example, may not have been invited to any dinner celebrating their contributions and whose works were at the time considered outside the canon. This poem parallels Judy Chicago's work of reconstructing our sense of women's history by creating *The Dinner Party* for all the mythic and real female creators of work of artistic or scientific merit in that "Planetarium" celebrates the accomplishments of Caroline Herschel, the sister of William, who lived to the age of 98, discovered eight comets, yet never in her own lifetime received recognition—or even acknowledgement or honorable mention. She was herself an excellent astronomer, yet history buried her, crediting her brother with all her work and discoveries. Furious at the way history overlooks great original women thinkers, Rich rescues Herschel's reputation in "Planetarium."

The vivid opening lines of this poem of resurrection are arresting in their monster/woman imagery and stark declarative style, replete with these women/monsters in the form of constellations (*WC* 13). In the earlier centuries in the South, decent, well-bred upper-middle-class women were not encouraged to have careers—indeed, a woman who tried to work was often deemed *monster*—an unfeminine harpy. Caroline Herschel had bowed to convention and relegated herself to helping her brother throughout his career. Read in another way, however, the line "woman in the shape of a monster" could also refer to constellations like Cassiopeia, Virgo, or constellations evoking the mythic monsters Scylla or Medusa, whose look turned men to stone. A fascination of these zodiacal women/monsters must have spurred the research of many astronomers down through the ages, but this is possibly one of the last times Rich will use classical references in a poem.

Having opened with shocking imagery of woman as monster in the first stanza, Rich next deflates the old mythology and astrology when she adds the real words of Caroline Herschel standing "*'in the snow / among Clocks and instruments / or measuring the ground with poles'*" (*WC* 13). This is Caroline Herschel's own description of her (hard) work of mathematical and scientific measurement—and silent suffering. The next quoted passage, however, is from Tycho Brahe (1546–1601), the Danish astronomer who might be construed as one of her international precursors: he describes his own eyes as "*'virile, precise, and absolutely certain,'*" yet if his eye could be described as "virile," so could Caroline Herschel's, Rich suggests. If Orion formerly constituted Rich's animus, the awakened creative principle newly invigorating her writing in *Leaflets*, now she deliberately resexes her animus, declaring it to be a virile female rather than an anima.

Even though Herschel's reputation had been eclipsed by her brother's, she had lived a life on the keen edge of scientific discovery, a long creative life devoted to finding the truth about the solar system. Her life was about seeing: and seeing is changing (*WC* 14). Playing on the two meanings of the last assertion, Rich asks, How is what we see changed by the act of seeing? This question is still vigorously debated by contemporary physicists, astronomers, philosophers—and poets. She has been standing all her life, confronting celestial flashbulbs, planets, and stars (*WC* 14), signals written in the most accurately transmitted and indecipherable "language in the universe" (*WC* 14).

Speaking in the voice of Caroline Herschel in the last stanza, she renders the astronomer's search in language that reveals her professional position—direct path—writing her poetry. The radio signals and light waves Herschel sought to translate were the hardest to translate in the universe; poetry, too, first emerges in indecipherable language of light waves, language only a creative or poetic intellect can translate. And here the poet is metaphorically linked with "a galactic cloud so deep" and dense that it could take almost a score of years for a light wave to travel through her. The notion of woman as object is standard in the Western literary tradition, but woman as instrument is a more original image: it combines a dual or triple symbolic meaning here. On one level, woman as astronomer is woman as channel for the radio impulses, signals, impulses of light exploding now from the core of stars and planets, "pulsations," all of which she receives, endures. Yet as a poet, she is an instrument shaped like a woman, one who creates images out of a star's or planet's pulsations (*WC* 14); thus, she is a faithful translator of pulsations of thought, emotion, and sense impressions into poetry.

These dramatic lines culminate in the most significant part, its definition of the purpose, "the relief of the body and the reconstruction of the mind" (*WC* 14). Whose body? Whose mind? Actually, the poet's, but potentially also of the readers—and hearers—of poetry, too.

Poetry heals, reconstructs, and integrates human minds and bodies. It reconstructs the mind so that it thinks more creatively and imaginatively. The poet, like an astronomer, receives the pulsations of knowledge or information from a higher source or spirit, "[t]he rhythms of this inner focusing are steadier, longer; pauses occur as breaths within the line as well as after it; statement is permissible—any language form that will translate 'pulsations into images,' as she [has] now identified the work that must be done."[3] The new forms will be anticlassical, fractured in that they represent a reality that is in the process of unfolding amid tumultuous change and growth.

In this book Adrienne Rich is committed to immersing herself wholeheartedly in change, in the dynamic evolution of women's growing consciousness of their own identity: this poem is an intimate, yet radical declaration of independence, documenting her own innerscape of the feminist revolution. She will record it, she asserts here, and she will herald the change in consciousness underway for all thinking persons experiencing the radical shifts in ideology of the late 1960s and 1970s; to Rich this is a revolution in consciousness just as important as the first American Revolution. While earlier, in "Abnegation" (*L* 38), the lyric "I," according to Vendler, "jettisons every past except the residual animal instinct of self-preservation, and every future except death" (*ARP1* 169), here she opens herself up to a bolder, more generous role and more fully realized subject position, that of woman poet with the will to change.

"FROM THE PRISON HOUSE," ANOTHER MANIFESTO, AND "THE BURNING OF PAPER INSTEAD OF CHILDREN"

Suzanne Juhasz calls the ominously titled "From the Prison House" (*DW* 17–18), a 1971 poem published in *Diving into the Wreck,* "another manifesto" in the same vein, "describing 'another eye' that has opened underneath her lids," a third eye or spiritual "eye that 'looks nakedly'" out on reality "at the light," receiving wisdom from a divine source; in critic Suzanne Juhasz's words, the "I"/eye

> observes the external world and sees "details not seen on TV," such as "the fingers of the policewoman searching...the young prostitute".... This eye looks out, not in, so that the two poems taken together are mirror images of the same process.[4]

"Planetarium" describes the view from and into space, while "From the Prison House" focuses more on the eye as agent of transforming sight: it is not for weeping, only for seeing what wasn't seen before, and is "unblurred" even though the lyric "I" has tears on her cheeks (*DW* 17–18). Still, its intent is clarity, like the intent of the poet's "I"/eye (*DW* 17–18). The poet's lyrical "I" desires to write and communicate with unblinking honesty of vision, with the lucidity of an uncut documentary film. Like a film or television camera recording everything not yet seen on television, this clear third eye must watch for transformation in the world in order to communicate those transformations into vital poetry. The staccato lines respond with urgency to the need for a strong recording "I"/eye to register the acts of mind and body in a desperate, changing world. It goes without saying that she protests the violation of the prostitute's body and the abuse of prisoners generally, the social injustice, and abuse of basic human rights she witnesses in prisons: the poem is her act of political protest. As "The

Blue Ghazals" explains: "seeing is changing" (*WC* 20–24). Seeing is changing both for the seer and the seen, the observer and the hearer of what is seen. Juhasz explains, "In order to succeed the sight must be unblurred, excruciatingly clear. One way to translate seen images into words is to pare language, likewise, to its essence, to reduce words to clear unshadowed counter, bone black on the white page."[5] This is exactly what we see in the naked poetry in this volume. Honesty is now her first priority.

More mainstream and more widely anthologized is her poem "The Burning of Paper instead of Children" (*WC* 15–18), closely following "Planetarium" in *The Will to Change.* Written at the time of the Vietnam War, this poem engages the topic of that war; its epigraph records both Daniel Berrigan's and her own sense of frustrating foreboding: *"I was in danger of verbalizing my moral impulses out of existence,"* said Daniel Berrigan, a fellow revolutionary, on trial in Baltimore as one of the Catonsville Nine, nine draft-record burners on trial for their acts of anti-war protest. Here Rich shows support for those who sought to help others avoid having to fight what she, Berrigan, and other protesters saw as an unjust, unnecessary war. A long poem sequence in five sections, "The Burning of Paper instead of Children" voices a sense of neighborly purpose mingled with exasperation at having to use the oppressor's language, a language she still needs to use to talk to "you" (*WC* 16). Here she opens what will be a continuing problem in linguistics and language: How does one subjected to oppression protest in the language of the oppressor? And why? These are questions many theorists including Rich will tackle over the years. Ironically one can protest, she determines, only by using the language of the oppressor.

The first dramatic sequence in "Burning of Paper" recounts an incident in which an angry fellow parent called to express his rage that his son and hers had burned a mathematics textbook on the last day of school. This act of simple defiance, possibly purely an expression of their distaste for school and mathematics, has led the father to ground his son for a week and forbid him from seeing her son because of the horror the act of burning a book arouses in him. In him it evokes recollections of Hitler's book burnings, the father says; to him, burning a book is the most disturbing act imaginable (*WC* 15). The reader quickly sees that the epigraph has a further ironic dimension since it derives from a trial of a man who has effectively burned a number of books, draft records, a trial in her hometown of Baltimore, a city known for its traditions of religious freedom and tolerance. The poem, then, is a subtly sardonic *replique* to the father who has no understanding of the sons' potential acts of protest and apparently does not discriminate between books. Rich's poem discreetly asks, Do any books deserve burning? The draft records for unjust wars might be good fuel for burning, as these papers contain the oppressor's information (*WC* 16).

Now, however, because her father had been her first oppressor, the poem revisits her father's library, a quiet, paneled study in that Baltimore family home, the study where she alone was permitted to work in her father's stately elegant library lined with "green Britannicas" (*WC* 15). But this is not just a sentimental journey into a past where reading was her life. She recalls some absurdities advanced by the writers of those books: "the crocodiles in Herodotus" (*WC* 15), said to populate unknown oceans, and the assignment of female sex to the quality of "MELANCHOLIA," a baffled miserable-looking woman (*WC* 15) by Albrecht Durer, the preeminent Renaissance engraver. Next, she sees the "*Trial of Jeanne d'Arc*," a poignant testimony to humankind's inhumanity to the brave woman warrior who was burned as a witch after leading France to military victory. But that book was taken away since she dreams of her too often (*WC* 15).

The gaze here is on her entire experience with books as a child, summing up the pure nonsense, misinformation one absorbs as a child, and the atrocities that excite one. Nonsense and atrocities may coexist between the elegantly gold-tooled covers of expensive leather volumes. The poem concludes by stating ironically that she is aware how much it hurts to burn (*WC* 16), a line that recalls both Joan and the half-mad daughter-in-law's burning her hand in the steam of a tea kettle in "Snapshots of a Daughter-in-Law," just in order to pierce through the "female fatigue" she feels or to prove to herself that she is alive.

Rich the poet, the now 44-year-old mother of adolescent boys who protest in their own right, reflects on "love and fear in a house" where there is "knowledge of the oppressor" (*WC* 16). Politically the lines may or may not suggest that at some point she herself has experienced womanhood as melancholia, as burning for one's imagined crimes or persecution.

In the second sequence comes a natural countermovement toward silence, as reading leads to philosophical reflection, pondering the depths of the implications of "coming out" in favor of burning books. The lyrical "I" revisits a sensual scene, imagining a time of silence and music. (*WC* 16). In times when sensuality prevails, words cease: we experience silence, yet next comes sure relief. The tongue changes into a speechless block of limestone, but what fanatics and traders—the first European Americans—dealt in was words. The green of the "Britannicas" of the first sequence links with the settlers and explorers stranded here on the green and red shore. Ours was a coast that first belonged to Native Americans, a coast where smoke signals blew in the wind (*WC* 16). At that time in early America, communication among some native tribes consisted of smoke signals borne by the wind; hence the reference in the last lines to the destructive force of the oppressor's knowledge and language (*WC* 16). These lines compound the ironies since the speaker cannot speak the Native American language, only the oppressor's—English. That language the speaker must appropriate to criticize the oppressor in, too, hence a sense of futility and rage reinforce the criticism of patriarchal language and knowledge (*WC* 16). From these lines onward, the poem becomes increasingly critical of political injustice since her poetry now occupies the domain of social protest.

The third section broadens the scope of the poem to embrace other oppressed minorities who must also use the oppressors' language. It begins with a prose passage, fugitive lines written out of desperation to explain the anguish and suffering of poverty and the toll they take. These lines are the more effective because they are written in the student's Black English: *"to hear a mother say she do not have money to buy food for her children and to see a child without cloth it will make tears in your eyes"* (*WC* 16). By incorporating the student's words into her poem, Rich demonstrates a sense of solidarity with the suffering of all families enduring poverty, as if to tell her son's friend's father that there are worse things than the burning of books, and that it is better to burn books than children. She comments in parentheses that here in the anguished outcry of the poor the sensitive reader sees that fracturing order and repairing speech in order to assuage and alleviate this suffering is the current poetic mission.

Just as the poem's second part retreated into the silence of sensuality, the fourth engages the quiet moment after lovemaking in which the lovers speak now of loneliness that is "relieved" and "relived" in a book (*WC* 17). Here the rhyming, near-rhyming, parallel structure and consonance echo the varied purposes of reading: we read both to escape from loneliness and occasionally to experience solitude and to learn from it. Hence, loneliness can be both "relieved" and "relived" in a book.

Over the centuries, she insists, books have described acts of lovemaking in the language of a male in pain (*WC* 17). His is the naked word, like a hand reaching from behind bars that brings deliverance, but for whom?

She continues with the argument: the existing books that tell about all this are useless (*WC* 17), since at that time they were nearly all written by men, for men, and do not express the feminine side of experience or history. In "Study of History," the poem before "Planetarium," for instance, the poet ruminates on all that has not been written, all that is yet to be written: but realize that all we know absolutely is that we shall "never entirely" understand or know what happened upstream in prior millennia (*WC* 12). In other words, the historical truth of what was done to women—and people of color, and others, too—is largely silence. If as "Study of History" says, "we" are at the beginning now, we are coming into a time of fuller awareness of what before was silenced, forgotten, what was done to them "upstream" (*WC* 12). She wonders which of your powers were ensnared, which channels, talents, or powers diverted (*WC* 12) and what "rockface" leaned over, staring into the victim's defenseless face (*WC* 12). This image of the dead female face staring upward will return in "Diving into the Wreck."

The image of a "rockface" suggests an adamant, but not necessarily male, face staring into the defenseless face of the oppressed, which need not here be only female; it is the face of anyone oppressed or trapped, suppressed, violated, subjected to cultural eradication, as the Native Americans were.

At the end of "The Burning of Paper instead of Children," she maintains the same line of ironic inquiry, adding sarcastically that no one knows what may happen (*WC* 18). So "*burn the* texts," commanded the surrealist artist, Antonin "Artaud" (*WC* 18).[6] The conclusion supports her son's action: she must endorse the burning of paper instead of children in a time when children are burning instead of paper in the Vietnam War, when Buddhist monks and protesters are setting themselves on fire, and when, as she says in the furiously uttered prose sequence ending the poem, our language can only record what we have lost (*WC* 18).

Isn't it better to burn paper instead of children and affirm peace instead of war? Even though the saint and national leader Jeanne d'Arc could not read, she was burned at the stake, an innocent female victim symbolizing the millions of women burned in Europe and America from the fourteenth through the seventeenth centuries. She repeats in the prose paragraph ending the poem that she knows it hurts to burn. Still, the lyric "I" reasons, why shouldn't files and records burn to make way for the possibilities of a world without oppression, hunger, or poverty? Although it is morally questionable, in the midst of what she sees as an unjust war, the choice is an easy one to make.

Furiously typing, the mother/speaker is poignantly aware also that African Americans have had to fight for even the simplest right (*WC* 18), the right to read and write (for example, even though Frederick Douglass wrote an English "purer than Milton's," he was forced to remain a slave for much of his life and only taught himself to read and write in secret) and that perhaps the greatest suffering is that of watching a child starve (*WC* 16). Quoting from an African American student's paper, Rich records his poignant truths, expressed in Black English: "*People suffer highly in poverty. There are methods but we do not use them*" (*WC* 18). Presumably here the student is referring to methods of eliminating poverty, hunger, racism, and starvation; this knowledge is excruciating to Rich because she is a mother, a poet, and a writer whose moral purpose is to say that suffering still exists and here in America we observe only the present tense (*WC* 18). Unfortunately, this is just as true of our country in the twenty-first century.

"I AM IN DANGER."

Since Adrienne Rich saw America as being in great danger during the Vietnam War, the burning of one book could not move her as much as the suffering of the poor and of starving children in the United States. To stress the ironic, "the oppressor's language" is now her only means of touching "you," the readers and citizens, perhaps likeminded people. In prose she writes, "The typewriter is overheated, my mouth is burning, I cannot touch you and this is the oppressor's language" (*WC* 18). Borrowing Dickinson's line, she announces, *"I am in danger. You are in danger."* Because of the larger social and economic problems America was engulfed in, a book's burning leaves the speaker numb (*N* 33). The words flow from the poem cryptically here like telegraphic messages in Morse code in an emergency rather than logically related thoughts, yet their overarching logical relationship is most apparent in this, one of the most important poems in the book. Finding a common cause with her son is just one of the links she is forging with others whom she might formerly have overlooked: it is the beginning of the bridges she will build throughout this and the next books to other women, children, all races—all oppressed or marginalized people.

Also written in the spirit of the revolutions of 1968 is "I Dream I'm the Death of Orpheus," another personal declaration of independence and political intent. "I Dream I'm the Death of Orpheus" is what Alice Walker would call a "womanist poem," centering on the female subject's self-definitions of womanhood: the speaker sees herself as in the prime of life, with certain powers, yet she is disempowered, "severely limited" now by authorities she almost never sees (*WC* 19). Here she returns to the focus on ominousness and honesty of prior poems since without self-knowledge and truth, nothing can be built up in the new civic order: Rich is a woman with a certain mission; she must follow explicit orders, orders that ensure her survival if obeyed meticulously (*WC* 19). But she herself may also be dangerous as a panther; she possesses the reactions and impulses of a panther, yet she also has contacts among Hell's Angels (*WC* 19), she says, as if to shock and shake off the genteel readers or any Aunt Jennifers around, still reading.

The textual "I" next envisions herself as the woman in the slow-moving hearse, a black Rolls-Royce, steadily, implacably driving Orpheus toward death in Cocteau's film *The Death of Orpheus* (1950), a film that had a profound impact on the avant-garde of the 1950s. The terror Death's entourage inspires can be likened to the terror felt in Western Europe a decade earlier when the combatants in World War II thought they were witnessing the death of all civilization. The same menace stalks in this poem, replete with self-definitions, most of them reminiscent of Allen Ginsberg's *Howl*, a cry of pain and outrage at the failings of American civilization.

In part, Rich writes for the political purpose of gaining support for resistance to the Vietnam War and to advance the women's liberation movement and in part she writes to save her own soul; but she fears her powers are greatly restricted although she is at the peak of her strength, ironically right at this time she cannot use them (*WC* 19). Frustration and honesty are her motivating principles because she defines herself as a woman sworn to lucidity, one who penetrates the chaos of the underground, the revolution in the streets (*WC* 19).

Even though she senses she is a poet with her back to the wall, she knows that her lover, her dead poet, Orpheus, is learning to walk backward against the wind, moving backward, against the current or the political status quo, on the wrong side of the mirror. She must move against the wind through her poetry and must learn to walk to the other side of America's mirror.

In Greek mythology Orpheus attempts to reclaim his lost love, Eurydice, from the kingdom of Hades, but he turns around to make sure she is following him, disobeying the gods' orders, hence he loses her again to death. Like Orpheus, the feminist poet must return to the land of the lost past to reclaim the lost female language and myths, lost customs and culture, women's lost history and traditions. But Rich may hope that this time, unlike Orpheus, she will be successful. In *Diving into the Wreck,* she is clearly successful in her descent into the underworld.

GODARD'S AND OTHER CONTEMPORARY FILMMAKERS' IMPACT ON RICH'S POETICS

Also noteworthy as experiments in the new open forms are her two other long meditative poem sequences, cinematic in style and focus, "Images for Godard" (*WC* 47–49) and "Shooting Script (11/69–7/70)" (*WC* 51–67), quite successful poems. Still, the latter does provoke one critic: Helen Vendler argues that "Shooting Script" may not be just "one poem" but several since it lacks formal coherence or any (to her) discernible structure. She argues:

> beginning as it does with fragmented single images, continuing with a translation of the Persian poet Ghalib, and going on to entire poems recognizably Rich-like... for all its awkwardness, [it] still seems to mark a conclusive new beginning, as the poem in which Rich is willing—in fact is compelled as by a vow—to let her descriptions float entirely free, uncoerced by any will to make things neat and orderly, whether for herself or for her readers.[7]

Vendler then concludes snidely: "It is ironic that a volume labeled *The Will to Change* should abandon the will to shape."[8] Certainly the lines are more broken and desperate in tone here since her own identity as a woman is breaking through. The entire book has almost no punctuation—only periods, which do not necessarily come at poems' endings. This is the influence of Godard's jump cut on her more open form. Since everyone's personal reality is now changing too rapidly and dramatically to be captured in any but filmic form, so she adapts her poetic form to the form of Godard's futuristic films, venturing into a territory not yet fully explored in her poetry, the erotic: loving is experienced as the body changes and moves, and to render love, like the New Wave films she loves and the films of Bunuel, the poem itself must move ceaselessly as it changes shape and consciousness.

The opening line of "Images for Godard" establishes that following Wittgenstein's literary theory, the textual "I" sees "language" as a "city" made of words. Since in the theatre those words exist mainly in the poet's mind, the poem asserts that the poem chiefly exists in the poet's consciousness (*WC* 49). Rich interjects a quotation into a filmic moment of erotic communion or merging: she sensed that for that moment she became him (*WC* 48). Film and poetry allow the reader and writer/director to unite momentarily in the same experience of ecstasy, and this poem evinces an eroticism Rich has yet to encompass in her poetry. Creativity and poetry are finely intermeshed through imagery for Rich; hence, the poem is a succession of discreet sense impressions and images, all of which join in the Godard-inspired poem, her mind.

Much of this book is about finding the similarities and differences between poetry and photography, poetry and film. In "Photograph of an Unmade Bed," for instance, Rich suddenly sees the difference between photography and poetry: while photography depicts what existed, poetry depicts a possible future (*WC* 45). Poetry proclaims what might be in the future if we use our imaginations and intelligence, while photography, at least in 1969, mainly bore witness to what the camera has seen, what was real.

Witnessing an interview Godard gave about his film *Alphaville,* he is discussing how the female character says, "*I love you*" at the end, yet there, according to the speaker, is exactly where the film begins. It is the one he vowed never to make because no one could since it was a film that embraces real life and emotions (*WC* 48). The film must henceforth be experienced inwardly by each newly convicted revolutionary leaving the theatre and taking the moment of realization into the world. Poetry, Rich attests, must now resemble film making in that it must reveal social, erotic, and political truth, political inspiration, or prophecy: this is the actual start of the film—at the point where his film ends, but Godard has not revealed that, so in pain they must depart (*WC* 49) because they are now forced to live out the film in reality as it projects each of their lives in the future. They are committed through the simple act of having seen it and understood its implications. Evoking the poetic monologues of Wallace Stevens at the end of "Images for Godard," Rich comments aesthetically, theoretically: the poem is the poet's interior monologue; hence, the notes for the poem are the poem itself (*WC* 49). Here the poetic form takes on the jerkiness of Godard's innovative handheld camera and jump cuts, hence the fragmentary nature of this collage of images melting and flowing into one another, progressing in freedom, the way the poet's mind moves freely in the dark, imagining Godard's dream, but differently (*WC* 49).

Adrienne Rich, who had addressed her husband lightly in an early book as "Fellow particle," now floats freely mentally in the theater imagining erotic love, woman's experience of sex with a man (*WC* 49), both in the Godard film and in life. In this evocation of the erotic fulfillment of heterosexual love, the speaker may be inwardly experiencing the joy of sexuality in marriage or merely experiencing a scene of the film. In the dark theater, images and words and scenes—what runs through the poet's mind—comprise the poem (*WC* 49), and the lyric "I" dreams Godard's dream along with him, at the same time revising it according to her own ideas, associations, dreams, and experience; while floating dreamlike, the speaker is aesthetically, mentally, and erotically in the dark, dreaming (*WC* 49). Dancing free in the projector's particle-speckled beam, the poet's mind changes while floating, realizing that the "moment of change" constitutes the poem itself (*WC* 49). Chronicling that moment of change in poetry is the only poem. Rich has thus come full circle from "The Burning of Paper instead of Children" to affirm the necessity of the poetic craft as a co-creator of the new reality of American women's lives and as reconstituting the world, the subject positions and selfhood of American women now.

In "A Valediction Forbidding Mourning" (*WC* 50), which title is borrowed from a poem by John Donne, the British Metaphysical poet, the lover/lyric "I" speaks as one bidding good-bye to a lover, perhaps her husband, for the last time, opening with an excellent image of the pain of parting: in parting the speaker feels her rushing desires but contacts only frozen lips (*WC* 50).

Still, as if that weren't enough, all the little things writers take for granted, like grammar, now attack the writer (*WC* 50). Increasingly in this book, grammar itself turns and attacks since its validity or place in the new language is in question. In fact, the whole poem is on one level a discussion of language and its powerlessness to embody the reality of intense emotion and thoughts adequately: so much writing is forced on the average person in school: reports and essays written on demand reveal the vacancy and absence in the words (*WC* 50). Finally, in a last attempt, the textual "I" asserts that poetic language speaks in the dialect of metaphor (*WC* 50).

Piling on metaphors in the manner of Allen Ginsberg constitutes an effective means of conveying the speed, pain, and intensity of rushing images. The ending of this poem, whose open form is reminiscent of Charles Olson's projective verse, articulates, however, a mission for the duration of her poetic career, a constant throughout her abiding will to change, which is to accomplish something "common" by herself (*WC* 50).

The word *common* used here has intentional connotations of *vulgar,* of the meaning the word *common* had for her when Rich was a child: it is the opposite of *nice* or *ladylike* or *genteel*; thus it clearly conveys the impetus of her mission to assist the oppressed and women through poetry.

At the end of *The Will to Change,* along with imagery, all outworn assumptions and literary allusions are jettisoned, even most punctuation and capitals. Nothing must interrupt the flow of truth. Rich is redefining her subject position as a person of integrity, and a poet with faith in change, stemming from a change in the national perspective on the role and position of women in America.

RIGOROUS HONESTY, LIES, AND "OUR WHOLE LIFE"

"Our Whole Life" (*WC* 37) articulates the new conviction that honesty and integrity are keys to women's wholeness and honor. Too often women of Rich's generation may have been taught to lie by mothers who merely wanted to keep peace in the family. Certainly this was the case throughout America in the pre–Kinsey Report era of the 1940s, the time when Rich was growing up in a respectable home in Baltimore—the sort of neighborhood where a man might insist that 2 + 2 = 5, and a woman would have to acquiesce to keep family harmony. Women had become accustomed to telling lies and keeping secrets when the heads of their families are domineering, illogical, and/or insensitive. "Our Whole Life" questions this morality: in the past "our" (here meaning *women's*) lives consisted entirely of a fabric of lies that society countenanced, yet at this point a bundle of lies is chewing through these binding ties or ropes to get undone (*WC* 37): women are liberated into trustworthiness and truth through arguments that cut through to the truth, cutting, honest words (*WC* 37) like those of poetry.

When in the early 1970s Robin Lakoff and others began examining women's language, they found that women did lie to help others around them, often men, or to save face. But in lying, of course, faith and women's real meanings are lost (*WC* 37). Hence "we" must rewrite virtually all books to ensure they contain the full truth.

The speaker in pain then observes that trying to change this might be cynically compared to attempting to describe how and where one hurts when one's whole body is on fire: one thinks of the "Algerian" seen in photos or on television, striding burning out of his village. All the while, since his entire body constitutes a mass of pain, nothing can express his pain's immensity except himself (*WC* 37). The body becomes the graphic sign of excruciating pain, the possibly fatal pain of rheumatoid arthritis.

In 1976 and after, Rich will address the topics of doctors for women, pain, and motherhood along with the ways women's bodies are co-opted in hospitals by male medical professionals, but at present the victim here is the man whose whole body has been burned, hence he might be mute when asked where it hurts. Similarly, concurrent with the publication of *The Will to Change,* Tillie Olsen, a contemporary, published her book *Silences,* dealing with the ways women had been silenced by the circumstances of their lives and by their families, the ways women artists and writers had frequently sacrificed their creativity in order to work to feed their children, for example, and how thus they had succumbed to silence. Like these silenced women writers, the Algerian walking mute and burning from his bombed village is a body and mind silenced by the oppressor.

In *The Will to Change* the speaker anticipates critics' objections to her championing the rights of the silenced to speak in another poem, "Shooting Script (11/69–7/70)": the reader might say she is making this up, being overdramatic to overwhelm her or him by shocking facts, subverting meaning through a colorful choice of words (*WC* 61). No, she counters, this is the proselike poetry of harsh reality: poetry's job is to feel all the pathos and burden of existence here and now and to chronicle reality, even in an unloved gritty back alley (*WC* 61).

Indeed this fierce, burning political poetry is "an instrument like a sword," and she had pledged herself to try any instrument that came her way and never to refuse out of a sense of incapacity (*WC* 66). The speaker refuses to accept that she might not be able to use instruments because she is a woman: in the penultimate poem in Part II of "Shooting Script," passionate, the lyric "I" imagines how the revolutionaries launch out sailing away into their new land, using the small vessel to get across the river to the other shore of women's—and the revolution's—potential (*WC* 66). The speaker has to teach herself and has to do it alone—this theme of the lonely heroic quest, a quest for the truth of history, returns in *Diving into the Wreck.* Her mastery of the revolutionary new poetry using her own adaptation of Dickinson's use of fracture, pause, and emphasis, and Olsen's projective verse in open form, has achieved the revolutionary urgency necessary at this point.

Before, darkness and water were thought of as forbidding, dangerous (*WC* 66). Her training or others' warnings had not prepared her well to venture out alone as a searching revolutionary, the champion of a new language and experimental filmic poetic forms. But "In spite of this, darkness and water helped me to arrive here." She achieves her goal anyway even though others such as Helen Vendler may have thought it could not be done. Still a pathos and an awareness of a roofwalker past may prevail: and she saw that each might have been her own light formerly (*WC* 66). Hence, this revolutionary does not think in terms of *either/or* but in terms of *both/and.*

The image of the light *indoors* she might have lit came before, of course, in "The Roofwalker." Yet here the poem does not condemn or reject the "old" ways of traditional womanhood, the woman indoors; she merely leaves traditional womanhood behind without regret, knowing that she herself might have lit those lights herself in the dim, distant past. Still, the lyrical "I" affirms it is her duty to put out to sea. Once she has acquired her hard won uncompromising honesty she must, like the Jews in their flight from Egypt, leave the old life behind: as in the Passover seder, you uproot yourself, eat your last hurried meal there before departure (*WC* 67). Then "you" start out on a quest like the ancient Jewish Exodus, as one might search for a way out of a lifetime of comfort and security (*WC* 65). The old protections no longer entice.

"Shooting Script" advances a series of pertinent axioms, the coda of Rich's newfound faith in womanhood and the capabilities of language to render it: her work as a feminist poet is to find the meaning searching for its language "like a hermit crab" (*WC* 53). Each poem is a reading awaiting the perfect listener (*WC* 53). The listener or audience is the open-minded reader, male or female, with the will to imagine change. In retrospect this book's title, *The Will to Change,* seems wholly appropriate; so is its dedication to her three sons, "David, Pablo and Jacob" (*Pablo* is Spanish for *Paul*).

DIVING INTO THE WRECK

As an advocate of change within the sphere of the poem along with progressive social change, even revolution, Rich proceeds in *Diving into the Wreck* to journey further than ever before into the unknown country of women's history; she goes down into the depths of the ocean, the other stretch of vast uncharted space one can and must fathom, if one is to know womanhood as it may have been before the existence of patriarchy. Nearly every poem in this book is a significant achievement, but here we chiefly focus on "Phenomenology of Anger" (*DW* 25–31), "Trying to Talk with a Man" (*DW* 3–4), and the title poem itself.

The poem "Diving into the Wreck" reflects a liberation from the constraints that hampered her earlier writing: it illustrates an attempt to go beneath gender and sex roles, into the lower depths of the psyche and women's history, and the unconscious, what W. B. Yeats called the *"foul rag and bone shop of the heart."*[9] If in these times, as she has said, poetry, love, and language all need to be re-visioned, so must women's very identities. The concepts of sex, gender, and all social norms must be regenerated and reconstituted. Consequently, the lyric "I" is now an androgynous diver, in whom the male and female halves of the psyche are integrated; the diver descends into the undersea realm, and the poem employs natural speech rhythms, the language of everyday life, to relate this journey of discovery. Visionary without being idealist or escapist, this poem explores diachronic historical geography, expressing the impetus of the feminist critics' search for and recovering of women's whole past—lost women astronomers, artists, musicians, and poets. Capturing spatial rather than temporal moments of that history, Rich wants to decolonize, reexplore, revise, and excavate a history that contains the drowned voices of all early women in particular and marginalized people generally. "We are, I am, you are" (*DW* 24) the ones who make the journey back. We travel not by "*cowardice or cunning*" as the cliché goes, but by cowardice or courage and collectively we are "the ones who find our way" through the depths of the past to the site of the wreckage (*DW* 24) to pick up the fragments gently and reassemble the pieces in order to discover the truth, as literary historians, anthropologists, and archaeologists do. Moving collectively, the seekers become "the one" who carry their essential equipment as well as "a book of myths" not containing the searchers' names (*DW* 24). If men wrote this book of myths, Rich conjectures that creative or powerful women's names were left out of it, similar to the way many women's characters go undeveloped in the Bible although scholarly history has proved certain women may have been among the apostles.[10]

Pharaohs, rich women, consorts, and politicians may have been remembered in history, but how many women artists, composers, or professionals were remembered before the first half of the eighteenth century? Precious few. By asking that question, Rich challenged scholars to start women's studies in earnest, and women's history in particular as well. The only appearance of women independent of early professional or public women before the modern era is in constellations, but there only mythological, not real, women (and men) appear. Rich, ever the emigrant and explorer, is not the sort of woman or writer to settle for anything less than the real and the true. Hence the treasure hunt aims to explore the wreckage of the female tradition in art, mythology, religion, literature, and history; it has evolved from this act of writing into the discipline we call women's studies.

The Will to Change is full of poems that are manifestoes declaring the new direction her poetry will take and new directions for the feminist revolution; *Diving into the Wreck,* also obsessed with the future, bids farewell to a man she has loved who has died, her husband, Alfred Hilton Conrad, but it also charts the trajectory of the long journey ahead for revolutionaries.

"From a Survivor" (*DW* 50) and "For the Dead" (*DW* 49) are poignant poems. The former begins with a reference to the pact the pair had made so optimistically in marrying one another, naive and ignorant of the difficulties they would encounter. The speaker now questions the validity or honesty of marriage itself: the poet and her husband had made the normal promise made in marriage then and that was the pact to live together in love forever. Apparently "we" thought our characters and our marriages kept us immune from failures of others (*DW* 50), the lyric "I" comments.

Surely "we" were naive because they were unaware an institution could fail so majestically and never suspected that they were going to partake of the failure (*DW* 50). At that innocent time, innocently, sadly, they thought they were immune from such tragedies. These assumptions and sentiments, possibly rehearsed here for benefit of their sons, have been echoed less eloquently down the decades in statements about marriage, divorce, and other institutions in the process of change, more recently in response to the cataclysm of 9/11/01. Lately, there has been an uproar over this and other similar failures and reverses (*DW* 50).

Recalling her marriage the lyric "I" remembers his body still, though it is not now the godlike body of anyone with power over her life (*DW* 50). The husband seems to recede into the distance of death: sadly, the couple no longer feel special. But isn't this the illusion of all couples getting married? Each married couple considers itself special.

The lyric "I" continues, musing that their marriage lasted nearly 20 years but "your" life is wasted now in death (*DW* 50). She assures him that he, too, could have taken the leap or step the couple discussed making—if only he had had the courage to make that leap (*DW* 50). It is a leap, a transcendent vaunt into a new country, a leap that enables the leaper to arrive in a world transformed by his or her mind; thus, the lyric "I" can envision it as only a small step (*DW* 50), each new step of consciousness, each new concept, effecting a transformation, making possible the next move until the new perspective is realized. This poem, along with "For the Dead," might be read as a final leave-taking of a loved, respected husband and partner, the father of her children. The emotion here is sincere, intense, and genuinely affectionate, but the poem itself leaps toward the future dialogically.

In the next poem, also written in 1972, the lyric "I" rings her husband in a dream, but he is ill and indisposed. She calls to tell him to be kinder to himself (*DW* 49), but as in life, he refuses to hear. The widow speaker likens the waste of human love to the last surge of passion as after a storm water rushing down a hill, running on (*DW* 49). Or she conjectures the waste is like abandoning a roaring fire you want to go to bed from but cannot, because it is burning down but not completely (*DW* 49). The speaker's love for the departed lasts like a fire long after his life has burnt out. Like someone not wanting to waste the love or fire, she sits on by it, watching the red coals flaring more dramatically and more curiously in their rhetoric of flashing and dying, more extreme than is comfortable while "you" linger long after midnight (*DW* 49). The flashing embers of passion do not subside because the speaker wishes they would and wants to withdraw from the spectacle. Grieving for a dead spouse cannot be extinguished at will but burns on absurdly, in the darkness of heart and soul. The passionate speaker may have some sort of rhetoric or argument going on inside and cannot help returning to the fire symbolizing their marriage even though nothing is left now but embers reminiscent of those late-night coals flickering in Edgar Allan Poe's tales.

This decent, subtle poem, devoid of self-pity, is a passionate tribute to the father of their sons, whom she later raised alone. Centered in the body, the poem is a poignant revisiting of and farewell to a lost partner.

Writing about a husband's death could finally free the poet, enabling her to emerge publicly as the person she has become, to come out as a feminist and lesbian. Many of her poems in this and in the previous book deal with lovemaking, but beginning with *The Will to Change,* her partner in love-making is a person whose sex is undisclosed. Her next step in her progression toward a new subject position is to announce herself as "the androgyne," a word Rachel Blau DuPlessis defines as "a new fused person."[11] In "The Stranger," whose title recalls Albert Camus's ambiguous existential novel by that name, the poet's double accounts for the speaker's gender identity thus: "if they ask me my identity" then the textual "I" can only proclaim it is *androgynous* (*DW* 19). A note in 1993 explains that this means "[*o*]*ne who has male and female characteristics physically or, as intended here, psychologically*" (*ARP* 53). Because her mind and abilities have both male and female characteristics, hers is the vibrant mind as yet undescribed by "you" in "your" expired language (*DW* 19). The lyrical "I" is comprised of fragments of her lost language, a lost substance and one verb extant (*DW* 19). Only an androgynous "I" can discern and interpret who I am and who I am becoming, says emerging womanhood.

The year 1972 was Rich's most important year so far for poetry writing. More first-rate poems were produced in this year of her life than in any previous year; yet none is more significant for the development of the new poetics than "Diving into the Wreck," in which the lone androgynous diver becomes the romantic hero/heroine of this venture into the lost female past, the buried world of the suppressed female tradition. Her work in this book "centers on a critique of the stories and meanings that have patterned a dominant perspective";[12] it is a critique of all the traditional myths and stories women may have learned, growing up. In "Diving into the Wreck," the androgynous/feminist subject has prepared conscientiously for the dive and investigation, having mastered existing mythology (*DW* 22). The diver has filled the camera, checked "the edge of the knife-blade." S/he dons the formidable rubber body suit, all black, and the "absurd" fins, and finally the absurdly grave and clumsy mask. This is all done without the help of a conscientious support staff like the late Cousteau's. The short declarative sentences of this poem underscore the essential simplicity of this quest, the vital nature of her mission, where each stage in the progression toward the revelation of the treasure is marked by a new stanza.

The second stanza begins by pointing out the ladder (*DW* 22). This is the only means of research into the buried female tradition, and the divers know what it is for since they have used it (*DW* 22). Certainly it is only for the brave and strong, and as in all life-and-death missions, the ladder should be used by researchers who have used it before: the textual "I" is exploring like a highly trained cosmonaut, except that s/he ventures under the sea instead of into space.

In the third stanza the action commences: "I go down" (*DW* 22). Gradually s/he is submerged in water; it is the oxygen that surrounds the "I" here. S/he describes the air first as blue, then bluer, then green, but finally the diver sees only black and blacks out. The diver's lyric "I" shows the way this investigation is deepening and becoming more dangerous just as the diver goes deeper into the ocean of prehistory until all around is finally black. According to DuPlessis:

> descent, detection, and exploration are metaphors for the acts of [literary and cultural] criticism. The poet, as an undersea diver, takes a journey down to an individual and collective past, where some mysterious, challenging "wreck" occurred that no prior research or instruction can clarify. We discover that the wreck is the personal and cultural foundering of the relations between the sexes.[13]

Seen in this light, "Diving into the Wreck" 's affinities with the two foregoing poems become clear since the poetics of the power struggle between the poet and her father, the poet and her husband, and between women and men—this sexual politics—has been a concern through all her poetry. She presents women and men together frequently in lovemaking but deplores the "foundering of the relations between the sexes" in the power plays of heterosexuality and the violence executed in the name of love. In the early 1970s, women were more often the victims than the aggressors in battles between the sexes. Rich's poetry is the first to speak out stridently against men's subordination of women. The poetry shows both how women resist this domination and how society and particularly women in America are undergoing revolutionary change.

Consequently a preoccupation with searching for something essential dominates *Leaflets* and animates the 1967 poem "The Key," which tells of a search where something glittering is found: something bright and shiny entices the eye, falters, then glitters and gleams again (*L* 34). What unlocks new doors in consciousness; what frees the spirit? That key is transmogrified into the wreck of "Diving into the Wreck." While in the earlier poem she had mused on her spirit and a sense of its being temporarily stunned, in "Diving" the lyrical "I" is an androgynous professional diver, concerned with the descent, discovery, and exploration; s/he moves relentlessly toward an apparently unmediated perception of the purpose of the mission, to reach the wreck itself and not the myth or story of it. What s/he finds is the debacle itself and not the made-up tale or myth (*DW* 23).

The intermediary filter of stories and myths, while culturally significant, is not what this speaker seeks since she "places her emphasis beyond the culturally validated frames of story and myth,"[14] on absolute clear perception. "The diver spends much of the poem in descent to arrive at dissent, moving deeper than the surface of meanings," clearly moving into the area where all is blackness, beyond the realm of history or recorded knowledge, beyond, in the words of DuPlessis, "atmospheres in which it is 'natural' to be the way we are."[15] Strength sustains the diver, along with the will and her/his mask. The sea, however, requires "another story," she puns. It is not a question of strength and one must master by oneself how to turn the body without power (*DW* 23). Moving through the sea is a skill one learns alone: undersea self-propulsion, like diving, is an individual skill, like the skills of investigative research, and one relearns all movement, how to "turn my body without force" at the bottom of the ocean, "in the deep element" (*DW* 23).

This last phrase, "in the deep element," echoes Lord Jim's order from Joseph Conrad's *Lord Jim: "in the dangerous element, immerse."* It is a directive to wade in and engage the difficult, dangerous "elements," as Rich's diver is definitely doing here. In life, philosophy, in all investigations—cultural, historical, scientific, or forensic—even in relationships, we move ahead by going deeper.

So much description has dominated the opening stanzas of the poem that there must now be a narrative transition and warning against getting off track: it's simple to lose sight of the goal. Gazing around, the diver is prompted to admire the brilliant flora and fauna of the deep, and besides, "you" respire in a new way here in the depths (*DW* 23).

The temptation Robert Frost alludes to in "Stopping by Woods on a Snowy Evening" is the same temptation the diver feels here. To wonder at and admire the beauty of this world without proceeding on to analysis is an attraction fatal to any researcher, whose strenuous work may take a toll on her or him physically and intellectually: if the oxygen runs out before the wreck is explored, the mission will end in failure.

This poem embodies a true epic quest, with hero, mission, myth, epic locale; what is new and original here is that the hero is a woman or androgyne: "I am she: I am he" (*DW* 24). This focus on androgyny was highly original when the poem was written in 1972, and it is still surprising and breathtaking. DuPlessis argues that Rich's diver goes "beyond the ending" (DuPlessis's term) of the implied story of a wreck to examine clues to alternative stories that—first unnoticed—would otherwise be doomed to be permanently muted."[16] The diver must remember his or her purpose since then those alternative stories would be lost for good; perhaps there will never be another chance to search this wreck or see the upturned drowned face of the figurehead (*DW* 23). This is the face that, in a jarring act of déjà vu, she later recognizes as her own: "I am she: I am he," the expired person who lies, eyes open, under the pressures of the depths (*DW* 24). The face is that of a ship's figurehead: she has been "drowned" and submerged for millennia, yet her breasts still bear the stress of the shipwreck, and she still "sleeps with open eyes" in the wreck.

As in all epic quests, *The Odyssey* for instance, this journey becomes both a spiritual quest and a recollection of alienated parts of the hero's—or rather heroine's—self, a reconciliation or restitution of what is lost. But here what has been lost is the heroic dimension of the female psyche, apparently killed in the wreckage. All woman's wealth of history lies on the bottom of the sea with her: "I am she: I am he" whose cargo of precious metals is hidden inside rotting barrels (*DW* 24). This declaration of identity with the drowned figure may or may not indicate the speaker's wealth and possible aristocratic status. Obviously the treasure has not yet been acknowledged or claimed by anyone. Women's heritage lies there largely unburied, ripe for the taking, but rotting now in barrels.

Leading the reader to recall the "Orion" image of the feminist poet—woman-shaped instrument—Rich speaks now in plural, collectively, insisting "we" are likened to "the fouled compass" (*DW* 24). Perhaps relationships between men and women are occasionally so intensely difficult because women have lost these very tools of reckoning and navigation, their "instruments" of reception of knowledge of themselves, their pre-culture, and their history. This omission may lead posterity to ask occasionally, What was she thinking? Women lack the equipment since it was abandoned here in the wreck, even though the log may be illegible now, as it is "water-eaten," soaked. Even worse, the compass is "fouled" so even if, collectively, women mustered the sense of purpose men generally have, they might not know which way to go without a working compass, with instruments "half-destroyed"; hence, modern women's confusion and the lack of unity in the women's movement.

Speaking collectively for all women—and implicating the reader in this conspiracy through the use of "you,"—the androgynous lyrical "I/we" announces "our" venture by reading "a book of myths" not containing "our names" (*DW* 24), so the genius of writing "the one who find our way" later in the poem is that this subject includes everyone interested in this discovery and/or any empathetic reader of the poem, following this unearthing of another dimension to female selfhood, original feminine identity.

What is carried down to the wreck appears to be an absurdly ineffective range of equipment for dealing with it: "a knife, a camera." Presumably, though, it is not impossible to salvage what is found either by retaining a photographic record or by cutting the treasure out of the barrels, reclaiming the log, the instruments, and fouled compass. All of these questions are beyond the scope of the poetic narrative; however, in ending with the three lines beginning "a book of myths," Rich places final emphasis on the fact that although "we" were there when myths were being created, the stories were incomplete, our names were left out; and ironically although only "we" went back to the wreck, our names do not appear in our "book of myths" (*DW* 24).

This revelation provides a poetic response to T. S. Eliot's quest in his epic *The Waste Land* where the speaker says, "These fragments I have shored against my ruin," since what is more like a wasteland than the site of the undersea wreck? This is Rich's answer to *The Waste Land,* itself a major work of cultural criticism. In 1971, Rich had written that the feminist critic sees contemporary men's work as revealing "a deep fatalistic pessimism" about the future or our potential for change; and I would agree with this. Women's poetry of that Vietnam War epoch, on the other hand, is new, revolutionary, and redemptive. It is as if the one threatens the other, she comments astutely, and "a new tide of phallocentric sadism and overt woman-hating" is manifesting itself, even as " 'Political' poetry by men remains stranded amid the struggles for power among male groups" (*ARP* 176). It puzzles me why Adrienne Rich is frequently underrated as a critic, because this seems a fair assessment of the state of American poetry in the early 1970s. In "Diving into the Wreck" Rich presents her own alternative to fatalistic male pessimism and the spiritual dead end.

The diver, who speaks more and more directly and openly to the audience as the poem "Diving into the Wreck" progresses, finds the wreck, is animated, even driven, finding "our" way back to the scene—the scene of the crime?—carrying the standard diver's equipment, now potentially either useful or useless depending on one's interpretation of the importance of the final painful fact that in the book their names are absent. Brilliantly, Rich leaves the question for the reader to solve since the future must ultimately resolve it anyway. Having awakened the culture's awareness of what has been lost, Rich leaves the long work of excavation to scholars since poets merely shine the light on what can be excavated.

Along with other critics, DuPlessis sees this poem as a major directive toward research into women's studies. It suggests the diver's finding "*the key to all the mythologies*"; what Casaubon was seeking in George Eliot's *Middlemarch* might truly be found by contemporary scholars. Further search down here will possibly turn up the other book of myths, the one in which "our names" do appear. Or exploring this wreck to gather those names, one could write the new book of myths. Although at this time Adrienne Rich was well aware of the research of Elizabeth Davis, Merlin Stone, and others on goddesses in women's prehistory and the ancient matriarchies throughout Africa, Europe, and the Middle East, still she deliberately does not make this a spiritual or religious quest. The wreck appears to be vastly more important as a historical and cultural record, a find of incalculable riches and wealth, than a spiritual quest. Independently at this time, Rich was likely intrigued intellectually by witchcraft, both as it figured in women's history and women's studies, fields Rich helped originate, and for herself spiritually, but no hint of this enters "Diving into the Wreck." Instead the poetic focus is on women's art, architecture, history, and archaeology—their lost treasure—and on questioning how much and what kinds of power women had in ancient civilizations. Alice Templeton clarifies the feminism in this volume of poetry, "The feminism at work in *Diving into the Wreck* is a sex/gender antagonism that is 'epic,' not just 'lyric,' in scope. Rich attempts to authorize the lyric self, and to legitimate a feminist hermeneutics, by positing that gender difference constitutes personal and social relationships as well as political power systems."[17] In her process-oriented poetics, the search is an imperative for women's intellectual survival—not simply recommended but mandatory for a future that may redeem "the ruinous state of modern civilization . . . [and] the damaged sexuality of the self."[18] What's more, as Alice Templeton declares,

> The necessity of survival, not the nostalgia for a lost cohesion, accounts for the epic desire in *Diving into the Wreck*. . . . In Rich's work the aspiration to legitimate the struggle of the poet/protagonist beyond merely subjective significance; it is the search for a communal context that can challenge the circularity of poetic self-reflexivity.[19]

"Diving into the Wreck" is Rich's public entreaty to the world for a change in the way we see everything—art, sex and gender, hermeneutics, society, history, and culture—while "The Phenomenology of Anger," also written in 1972, vents white-hot anger originating from female oppression. Wendy Martin explains this phenomenology of anger: "Exploring the effects of individual and social rage, this poem traces out the texture and tonality of anger—the feeling and course of the emotion."[20] This is powerful anger that could lead to madness, that might lead the madman or madwoman to delight in playing with and smearing unmentionables over the walls of a whole room (*DW* 27). If the poet expresses a sense of the injustice done to the oppressed, if an awareness of being alienated, her husband's suicide, and the madness of what she saw as the mindless slaughter of thousands of soldiers in Vietnam did not actually drive her mad, at least she had moments when she was able to visit and explore that state in poetry. The opening of the poem points out that this freedom cannot be a physical freedom to reverse one's course while walking in a city (*DW* 27). But this real madness could feel perhaps like a luxury to the compromised, those still hanging onto reality by their fingernails (*DW* 27).

Having real responsibilities as a mother, professor, and poet keeps one hanging onto one's values and integrity. The poem details the phenomenology of the very real anger the speaker must cope with daily. The poem deals with the question of the ways out of life: all involve termination of life. The lyric "I" inquires if self-annihilation is the only way out (*DW* 28). The slaughter of so many innocent civilians at My Lai in 1968, the defoliation of the fields, and the many other acts of atrocity associated with the Vietnam War, going on as she wrote, are all instigators to madness. What thinking person, the speaker asks boldly, could live through this war and time of change without feeling an anger that could drive an intelligent, sensitive person mad?

Diving into the Wreck is often cited as a book that marks a crisis in and culmination of her poetic career, and "Diving into the Wreck" and "The Phenomenology of Anger" are two of the most important poems in that book. DuPlessis explains the central significance of the Vietnam War as pivotal in Rich's poetry, as well as in the poetry of Denise Levertov and Muriel Rukeyser:

> The same concern to investigate, to criticize, to protest against the commonplaces of perception and behavior that animates their poems about women leads the poets to examine political forces and power relations that inform individual consciousness. The Vietnam War becomes a focal issue, since, in a historical sense, it is the concrete political reality in which they feel implicated, and, in a symbolic sense, it epitomizes the destructive values and acts that the old consciousness can produce. The Vietnam War also demystified the colonial-imperial relation. This swift delegitimation of a national mission made the process of critique especially sharp, a development that had, in turn, two intellectual effects on the generations to which these poets belonged: continual attention to the critical analysis of ideology on one hand, and on the other, the spiritual hope for an ungridded area of human activity without ideology—giving access to an epiphanal or purely experiential truth.[21]

Even though these two effects "are of course, contradictory," they were equally compelling to the poets and forceful in motivating and creating epiphanous woman-identified poetry with both traits—ideological analysis and dreams of what Rich came to call a common language. These elements figure in all her poetry written after this era.

In the second section of "The Phenomenology of Anger," Rich constructs an image of impossible futility, the image of attempting to kindle a log that has been water-soaked for a very long time. Acting effectively in the national political climate of protest, which was stirred by a mixture of rage and the sense of futility prevailing at the end of the Vietnam War, was as difficult as lighting a damp log. Even as the unnecessary slaughter continues in Vietnam, astronauts come back from the moon and firemen from fires (*DW* 27–28). It was a tasteless indecisive time (*DW* 28). Yet, without American citizens' knowing it, President Nixon was making many decisions for the whole country, decisions that would cost him his presidency.

Next, in the fourth section, her nightmare vision sees a combustion in the room since it fills with a blinding radiance, and her hands are sticky with her own blood: in internal monologue, the speaker wonders if the judges will attempt to explain which blood was whose (*DW* 28). Women's and men's blood are commingling in this violent, frustrating time of war, dissent, violation, violence. And in the fifth section, the persona reviews the means of escape from life either by going insane, killing oneself, or getting killed. The problem in the contemporary America of the Vietnam era, however, was that the enemy was nearby, maybe even next door, yet elusive, close by but invisible. He is a shadow warrior, busy at My Lai shooting the innocent and then disappearing when challenged (*DW* 28).

Like the dreaded Vietcong themselves, this enemy disappears before he can be confronted and beaten. The dreaded body counts figured in each nightly newscast from 1965–73: the lyric "I" conjures up a Satanic image of him as Lucifer or the Prince of Darkness adding up the body counts (*DW* 28), and in this image, the Vietcong, embodying the principle of evil, chief instigator of a war that seemed at that time as if it would never end, merge as the demons of this place and time. This poem swings on a dialectical axis between images of fighting and racial confrontations (she notes Cleaver gazing at a window display of knives, punning): on the one hand, and the lyric "I"'s private registering of the fear and anger these events evoke on the other. In section six, the radical "I" imagines harsh suffering and dreams of wreaking white acetylene vengeance on the enemy, setting his lie on fire as she abandons him in a new universe, a radically transformed man (*DW* 29). Yet the seventh section of "The Phenomenology of Anger," integrating the two themes, clarifies the rebel feminist speaker's relationship with those fighting in Vietnam: in a flash she recognizes that the world is just not working. American soldiers are out there incinerating the crops with a sublimate, yet upon waking today you got out of our bed to go to disseminate death and impotence everywhere (*DW* 29). Those who burn civilians' crops and towns are the true enemy, the poem asserts; those renegade soldiers are the real enemies of civilization and decency. It is their need to destroy out of impotence, a need that sometimes masks itself as hateful male chauvinism or militarism: she despises the masks they assume and the way they assume and pretend a wisdom or depth they lack (*DW* 29).

The human need to dominate and kill others is the real enemy. The poem continues in an intimate dialogue between the renegade soldier and his lover/rebel feminist, the speaker: she recounts how the evening before, here, crying she had demanded to know his feelings. She asks if he feels anything at all when he defoliates the ordinary citizens' fields, the fields that provide their food. He remains silent, and she understands his answer (*DW* 29).

If the poem's locus is Vietnam in the seventh section, the speaker is back in an urban environment—probably New York City—in the final two sections, where the tone is intensely angry, the anger transforming itself into consciousness as she writes.

The speaker confesses that she has only ever really loved women and children (*DW* 30). The tone of honesty continues as she states that all the other emotions she perceived as love were lust and pity along with hatred of self or despair. The last line operates like a signature from medieval times: she states that this is a female confession (*DW* 30). Having heard it, the reader is asked to revisit and consider the faces of Botticelli's Venus and Kali (*DW* 30) and other goddesses again. Presumably here the reader will observe divine female beauty and the love of the painter or sculptor for his female subject animating these creative works. Look again, she asks the reader, at art, history, love: as a founder of the discipline of women's studies, she sees the need for a visceral reexamination of all Western culture, its products, values, music, art, and of course, its literature.

In another image likening anger and fire at the beginning of section ten, she relates how "we" are consuming and wasting our lives. The poem reveals a woman traveling while dead tired, leaning over, sleeping or sedated, on the subway. Next to this woman, who is in a compromised position, is the quotation from a sign, in Spanish, warning subway travelers that the New York subway is dangerous, yet a lot of passengers doze the entire trip while others sit upright burning holes in the air with their stares until flames appear (*DW* 31). While each evening some plot revolutions, the lyric "I," imprisoned but alert, experiences a coming to consciousness thus: her incendiary mind consumes the mattress like a fire, and cell bursts into flame (*DW* 31). This prompts the poet to recall an image of Thoreau both drawn to and repulsed by the forest on fire when his campfire set it alight.

The poem ends with the gnomic declaration, a partly self-mocking epiphany: each imaginative leap toward greater consciousness—interjecting an assertion that the book in front of her says sardonically, parodying the learned pose of the overeducated—is contrary to nature (*DW* 31). Clearly historical consciousness demands a leap beyond merely natural observation into a synthesis, a recognition of the meaning of what one has seen; just as in "Diving" the diver could not merely look and wonder at the beauty down there but had to remember the purpose of the mission, so here the lyric "I" sets down a series of discrete images that affect that leap of consciousness and dissociation from the military mindset, from violence and victimization.

Earlier in this poem she had written that the world is no longer functional (*DW* 29). A new world is being born, as it was for the soldier facing death, and all her traditional convictions and familiar assumptions have gone up in smoke, burned through by purifying rage. As in "Diving into the Wreck," here in "The Phenomenology of Anger," the poem's words are maps and purposes (*DW* 23). Having written these purposeful poetic words, she sees she has reached a point of no return personally and could never return to the simple, ordinary heterosexual existence she once lived. There is no going back to traditional feminine roles. From now on, her commitment to the community of women and to feminist/lesbian causes is complete. Her poetry insists on it, even as it insists on retaining its visionary/political edge, following in the transcendentalist tradition of Walt Whitman. Helen Vendler writes in *Soul Says* that Rich's "most visible American" predecessor as a democratic visionary poet is Walt Whitman, but "her work goes back in English poetry at least to Langland's *Piers Plowman,* with its sociological personifications and stratified social analysis."[22] Always aware that her work has taken a political turn, Vendler must allude to it whenever she now comments on Rich's radical about-face.

Undetected by Vendler, Adrienne Rich also writes in the female tradition of Emily Dickinson, the tradition of the self-realized woman speaking in her own undervoice in poetry, perhaps living in continuity of women corresponding through letters and literature with other women, animated by vibrant discussions of poetry and ideas, exactly the kinds of discussion Rich was having with other intellectual activists and poets, like Muriel Rukeyser. Poetry full of anger, love, and the desire to make sense of the seemingly incomprehensible will remain Rich's chief instrument of social transformation in the groundbreaking books that follow this radical departure.

This is the pinnacle of her anti-war activism and her period of dissent: along with "When We Dead Awaken," *Diving into the Wreck* placed Rich and feminist poetry at the very center of the feminist movement in the United States. For Rich, at least, the early 1970s also represented "a high point of intraracial solidarity among women."[23] She affirms this sense of their common collective cause "in the name of all women" in the statement she read at the National Book Awards. In the two years following that award ceremony four anthologies of women's poetry were published. "For the first time women poets began to speak and write for a specifically female audience."[24]

> Like Helene Cixous, Luce Irigaray, Julia Kristeva, and other French feminist theorists, who sought to respond to the phallic emphasis of Freudian and Lacanian constructions of human nature by positing a two-lipped and essentially female body out of which women speak, write and name themselves, Rich began to move...toward an increasingly essentialist, maternal, and transhistorical construction of women, women writers and women's history.[25]

Adrienne Rich, along with other poets like Audre Lorde, June Jordan, Marge Piercy, Judy Grahn, Alta, and Susan Griffin, began to call forth and name the field of female subjectivity, charting the future course of the feminist movement, women's studies, and women's poetry.

Chapter 6

To Be an American Woman

A sense of solidarity and security emanates from the poetry Adrienne Rich writes after she has mourned her husband's death decently and come out as a lesbian and defender of women against social and physical violence waged against them. By 1973 or 1974, she is finally free to live independently, her sons finishing their teenage years. Professionally, her career is in ascendance: she has won the National Book Award, ensuring her reputation as a poet, good appointments, and an avid readership nationally. Her greater national recognition and the sheer volume of her output keep her in the running for many other poetry prizes and awards. These follow steadily, gradually building in importance and levels of honor.

SPEAKING AS AN AMERICAN WOMAN

Her poems in *Poems: Selected and New, 1950–1974*—"From an Old House in America" and others—exude a sense of peace even as they reflect her need to be rooted in one place and time, and identity, now that the age is ridding itself of the social evils she decried in the previous book. In "From an Old House in America," she declares that she is an American woman, and she sifts through all the meanings of that statement; she turns the fact over as one presses a twig in a book (*PS* 238). In this poem, her poetic double—an American pre-feminist—is a nameless transhistorical American woman. On her behalf Rich sends out an epic message, speaking of the American woman's life. She writes poems full of trenchant, original insights, and a rawer compassion for others silenced in America, beseeching, chastening, scolding. For the first time, she literally puts the whole woman into the body of the poem, inscribing her into the text. This poetry embodies, discusses, and addresses the totality of women's lives directly, employing the feminine pronouns "she" and "her" generically without evasion, jettisoning the androgynous "s/he": ultimately, Rich deems androgyny more liberating for men than for women and refuses to utter the word again. Her poetry expresses a consciousness of and conviction of solidarity with other women, and a shared identity with other women, not exclusively American women.

Since the 1950s, she has been translating poetry from various languages, including a large body of poems from Dutch, nine of which appeared in *Necessities of Life,* and then in the late 1960s, "White Night" and other poems by the Yiddish poet Kadia Molodovsky, whose poetry she read frequently at readings. Through watching how other women rendered in language the experience of being female, she was gradually expanding her own abilities to inscribe womanhood, identifying with the common woman.[1]

Her act of accepting the National Book Award in 1974 not for herself alone but on behalf of all the women nominated for it that year (Alice Walker and Audre Lorde as well) opened a new era in the critical reception of her work. Predictably from what we have observed in the two previous chapters, several powerful critics were not amused by this act of blatant feminism, this show of multicultural solidarity among women. She was now subjected to harsher reviews of her successive books of poetry and to no reviews in journals that previously reviewed her work.

Charlotte Templin in *Feminism and the Politics of Literary Reputation* calls it the shock and "dismay of the conservative reviewers" who were amazed at the effrontery of some contemporary women's poetry. She explains that "the 'club' ethic that dictates honorable treatment of males does not extend to women."[2] Originally made a member of this exclusive club when she won the Yale Younger Poets Award in 1951, in the 1970s Rich is expelled because she has espoused the lesbian/feminist liberation movement and has had the courage to insist on sharing her award with Black feminist poets in a major national competition. Now that both Eliot and Auden are dead, and Modernism has yielded to Postmodernism, a different ethos prevails in the domain of literary criticism. Templin explains that the feminist movement became the target of many angst-ridden young male critics hoping to win readers and approbation by ridiculing what they saw as women's folly:

> [the feminist movement] became an ideological lightning rod—the focus for a multitude of fears about changes in the status quo in a time of great social upheaval. It is an extraordinary thing that for well over a hundred years fears about social change in a rapidly developing industrial society have been focused

on women, and the women's movement has been blamed for the myriad social changes that characterized this period[.][3]

While American women poets were getting public attention by affirming they were feminists or lesbians, in the United Kingdom and in the eastern United States, the literary and academic worlds were still formal, conservative, patriarchal, and largely adverse to feminism. Publicly and privately, men and women of letters, academics especially, were surprised at the extremes to which Rich was going in her poetry.

In late 1976, in her ludicrously premature "Requiem for the Women's Movement," a member of the new group of women who won praise for criticizing radical women, the closet misogynist Veronica Geng, divided the movement into two camps: "the reformers, daughters of [Betty] Friedan [author of *The Feminine Mystique*] and the radicals, daughters of [Simone] de Beauvoir [author of *The Second Sex*]." Rich was associated with the second camp and it is a commonplace that she uses de Beauvoir's work, critiquing her concepts and theories effectively. As a radical daughter of the movement, she is interested in rebellion, giving voice to current horrors that keep her up sleepless far into the night.

Never an ameliorist, Adrienne Rich tells the truth bluntly, delighted to shock or scandalize the bourgeoisie, in the tradition of Charles Baudelaire, Edgar Allan Poe, Walt Whitman, and Emily Dickinson, with what Muriel Rukeyser called "her unappeasable thirst for fame."[4] Like Rich, these original poets wrote the truth as they perceived it, speaking their minds, well aware that their words would scandalize the conventional middle classes. Baudelaire even enjoyed provoking the ire of the bourgeoisie. For them, expressing their visions took precedence over life itself, and not to express the truth as they saw it was not to be a writer or poet or even fully human. They are what Rich called "beginners" in her essay by the same name in 1993, by which she meant originals or pioneers. They "aren't starters-out on a path others have traveled. They are openers of new paths, those who take the first steps, who therefore can seem strange and 'dreadful' to their place and time."[5] The poet-provocateur was hardly a fixture in American poetry at this time, so she initiated the guerrilla poetry of later decades.

Woman, formerly categorized as *l'autre,* "the Other," in critical theory, in Rich's poetry is now plainly emerging from her literary status as object of men's gaze—muse, goddess, whore, or witch—and becoming a radiating, creating subject, insisting on speaking for herself in her own voice. Rich, alongside her older contemporary Muriel Rukeyser, claims this right and privilege for the woman poet—that of the "beginner": "The woman choosing her inner life and language over inconvenient domestic, social and literary claims"[6]—these lines describe both Emily Dickinson and Muriel Rukeyser, but the words seem to apply equally well to herself and her own poetry. In all women poets she admires the qualities of originality, courage, and bravery not sanctioned or encouraged in women by American culture. Her current books and translations explore the lives and successes of these innovative female motivating spirits.

POEMS: SELECTED AND NEW, 1950–1974

Rich's *Poems: Selected and New, 1950–1974,* presents new themes and even freer poetic modes than those she experimented with in *Diving into the Wreck.* There she publishes one of her love poems for a woman, "For Judith, Taking Leave" (*FD* 191) and another kind of love poem, one for a woman she had left behind when they were girls, "For L. G.: Unseen for Twenty Years" (*PS* 232). Several of the poems take up themes found in "For a Sister" (*DW* 48), which opens ominously by saying that the lyric "I" trusts no one. It is addressed to the Russian poet Natalya Gorbanevskaya, who was for "two decades incarcerated in a Soviet penal mental asylum for her political activism"; in Soviet prisons those imprisoned do not trust their captors, but they learn to manipulate them. The concept of employing whatever is useful to the revolution becomes a central focus in this effort to reconstitute the world so that it is woman-friendly, not hostile to women. What better heroine and role model for the women's movement than a Russian woman poet imprisoned in a psychiatric hospital because of her activism? Women's international nationhood is forming, and around this time International Women's Day is established as March 8.

The poem "For a Sister" ends in a transcendent arresting image of a woman's being searched for anything illegal; police are making their notes. The poet warns that to look intelligent might mean "you" would be in jail for two decades. Instead, when arrested it's advisable to trace circles on a surface or to pretend to smile vacantly ahead like an imbecile. Elsewhere, a common flower burns and comes to belong to "you," who will come home after the years in jail to settle herself in her home again and begin writing. Now she ("you," the woman writer) has escaped at last, will tell her story. What a brilliant image of the writing life of the poet's sister-subversive who, by expressing her message, validates all the suffering that resistance and revolution have brought upon her! Since hers is a poetics of process and change, revolutionaries will always begin again, and so will the revolution. The last words, "Your story" indicate none too subtly that this political act of standing up to persecution, outlasting it, and defiantly writing again after imprisonment is "your" own story, telling your truth.

Even as Rich turns her attention and efforts to rescuing the prisoners of conscience in the Soviet Union, she also writes of the quiet heroism of women who may be American nurses in the Vietnam War. In "Dien Bien Phu" (*FD* 200–201), the speaker observes a solitary hand reaching out from the barbed wire fence toward the nurse and wonders whether, if she reaches out to it, will it once again cut her wrists with a razor (*FD* 201). The focus is on protection for women who confront danger as nurses, for instance, or international health aides, and it enters empathetically into their consciousness: although one realizes a poem cannot save them all, only address and possibly move poetically in the direction of change; it may alert some to potential dangers. Here Rich alludes to the bravery of professional health workers and nurses, or ordinary working women who quietly go on doing their jobs despite war, blood, national cataclysms, and the domestic violence confronting many women in the revolution throughout the world. These she embraces as her sisters.

The seeds of her new, blunter poetry are sown in the poem "Holding Out" written in 1965. Here the speaker is an embattled guerrilla fighter, a Che Guevara of women's liberation, holding out against those who would force women to comply. What is actually salvaged for women's new life is a place of refuge where they can rest inside. Having dwelt for a while in a similar refuge, in the late 1970s and early 1980s, the women's movement is now able to emerge, built on the foundations of a viable, fully articulated feminist theory and ideology. "Essential Resources" (*PS* 221) bears mentioning here, too, since it also shows the ways women artists recover and return to the essentials; correspondingly, Helene Cixous, Luce Irigaray, and others have returned to restructure feminist theory, reveal women's unique beauty, intelligence, and power independent of the "beauty myth" or our culturally imposed notions of femininity. Here in "Essential Resources" (*PS* 221), the aesthetic critic/lyric "I" speaks to another woman of a film they might make together in realistic style, their faces sweaty, lips dry, one with a spot of blood near her mouth (*PS* 221). Might women be shown as they really look without make-up, their true faces revealed? That is the look she wants to create, so that this could never be used to keep them weak and powerless. For that reason, she writes (*PS* 221).

Writing so late at night she loses track of time. But she transcribes her poetry with a small blunt pencil. One might imagine her writing on a soiled, torn envelope in a hasty scrawl, as Lincoln is said to have written the Gettysburg address on an envelope on the train from Washington D. C. to Pennsylvania. Fittingly, the poem concludes with her wondering what year it is, since she doesn't know, and reflecting on the films they have made but will not show, "films of the mind unfolding" (*PS* 222). The poem resolves itself in an image of potentiality, youth, when she sees herself and the other woman or women, as if in a dream: their youthful faces are perspiring with desire, eyes awake with a precocious lucidity.

In "The Wave" (*PS* 223), written for a friend, "J," she recalls the past, its hopes, and dwells more darkly on the lives they attempted to create for themselves. She thinks of their big hair, making them look protected as the middle and upper classes are protected from poverty or need, of their radiant gliding figures, safe from all turmoil. She thinks of them and how stunningly unsuccessful they were (*PS* 223). This last image brilliantly turns the entire meaning of the poem upside down and inside out, forcing readers to reevaluate all their measures of success. The poem asks, what is success and what is failure? In self-deprecating fashion, the lyric "I" attests to their personal failure, indicating that an entire class or generation has failed. In what ways might the poet be assessing failure here? As in the ironically titled "For a Survivor" for her husband, the speaker comments on how painfully their "pact" had been broken, here Rich notes with surprise how little all their protective gear helped, how they failed to live the lives they tried to live. Why? Here her personal pain coincides with the pain of a cross section of American women who have faced divorce or the death of spouses and had to relearn how to live without a man at a time when sex roles and gender expectations were being redefined and single women were stigmatized.

Poems here like "Reforming the Crystal" (*PS* 227)—re-envisioning sexuality—answer many of these profound questions by implying that desire is the answer to many of these larger questions. Does sexuality take precedence over ideological issues? Desire can awaken in a flash, as though the body were healing from the flu; there is a realization of the body erotic and of sexual feelings (*PS* 227). The poem ends with a cryptic prose poem, with Freudian images of the rites of a priestess/hierophant or the Goddess (*PS* 228).

So too, in a religious ritual of love and worship, Rich privately inscribes the name of the one she has chosen, her secret lover, on the ribs of the book. This act undoes the Biblical stealing of Adam's rib to create Eve since here she, the chieftainess/poet, Rich's poetic double, writes a beloved name in sacred characters on the rib in a cave. If once most scribes were men, now women rewrite history, sacred and arcane.[7]

In "For L. G.: Unseen for Twenty Years" (*PS* 232), Rich writes a poem for a "lost" friend, also a cripple, a girlfriend in youth who may have been an unacknowledged lesbian. As one does at reunions, Rich describes what her life has been like—describing it as acting her parts, cherished daughter, innocent child bride, token woman, and inspiration who heard what was being said occasionally, and recalls an inebriated poet mumble into her hair that he cannot make love to women he admires intellectually (*PS* 234). In each of these roles, of course, the poet has not played her real self, but just scenes. And, she implies in the next line, the "drunken" male poets are playing roles, too: they explain their lack of interest in intelligent women at parties by somehow making it seem the woman's fault (*PS* 234). Then she speculates about L. G.'s life in the intervening 20 years: she hopes that over the years she has fought through to a committed union, partnership, or marriage, since any two people living together through this moment of historical change and change of consciousness may have settled into an odd arrangement (*PS* 234).

This is as close as Rich has come up to this point of commenting on a homosexual relationship. What is intriguing is that she is now speaking, as it were, offstage, no longer interested in conventions or roles. She speaks naturally as friend to friend: in 1952, they, like all cripples, were fearful of being in a world where everyone else seemed physically flawless (*PS* 234). There may have been a moment when the two had a romantic relationship then, perhaps out of fear of never finding anyone to love because they were cripples. Then as if to justify herself for having left L. G. before L. G. was temporarily lost to her, she says she believes that then they would have left one another at the first gesture of a possible male suitor. Addressing her, she tells L. G. to be honest and to admit that at the first sign of any man interested in her, she would have left her, too, in quest of a man's love. A note of regret attends this revelation. Again, her sense of failure prevails in these poems, which culminate in "From an Old House in America" (*PS* 235–45), a poem seemingly written from the perspective of a female wanderer who began sleeping here in a place where a vacuum cleaner sucks up the dust of the past. This poem has no punctuation except the dash, and in this is reminiscent of Dickinson; as in poems from *The Dream of a Common Language,* she discovers what it is to be settled somewhere, to live there permanently; it describes a kind of coming together with a place and a union with the spirit of all women in a spiritual and psychic homeland, a coming home to female selfhood.

Just as in a number of the foregoing poems, Rich, in a new female subject position, makes amends to those whom she has left or possibly hurt, those whom she may feel she has failed in some way; here she first establishes herself in poetry in "The Old House in America," a place where American women have lived, given birth, loved others and their families, a place they have cleaned and kept. So in the second section she muses that others have lived out their lives in this place, mostly inarticulate lives that left no written record, but whose planting and scrawls occasionally tell an archaeological story in observing the modest persistence of objects (*PS* 235).

She came to the house, found it furnished, rummaged round in the drawers, and found a complete deck of cards, still usable, and in the basement looms a cistern full of dank rainwater (*PS* 236). So she searches for signs of the quiet lives lived there and supposes there may have been a child living here because she finds a small red truck, wheels still rolling (*PS* 236). And she discovers evidence of artistic creativity while sifting through a drawer and discovers, along with rusty screws and an empty flask, a box of watercolors, now too dried out ever to use (*PS* 236). Still, it had been used before.

The fourth section starts with a line from Emily Brontë, "*Oft rebuked, yet always back returning,*" which may refer here to a need to engage or locate those who once lived here, especially the lost women: one woman has planted her signature in a swath of narcissus. Presciently, she muses that these families may have had to live together for months, snowed in (*PS* 236). It is as if the lyric "I" could touch the invisible handprint of the former woman inhabitants on the doorsill (*PS* 236). In the quiet persistence of certain things remaining for ages (*PS* 236), daylilies that catch in the door, and narcissus, old postcards, she finds—all bear mute witness to the fact that a woman—or women—in a family lived here. She wants to touch and speak to and for those women.

Maybe the wife and husband fought. The speaker suddenly sees a married couple who fought for years a long time ago when the ink on the letters was still undried (*PS* 237). Although their love may have been alive when they moved here, it has dried like the dim ink. Throughout Rich resists abstractions, choosing instead to describe and link through telling images.

The fifth section begins defensively, addressing someone who knows her, stating that if "they" call her *man-hater,* "you" would know it was untrue (*PS* 237). But the "you," possibly her husband, addressed here has died. He can no longer stand up for her. She affirms in lyrical, rhythmic lines that some ethereal connection—she is unwilling to go so far as to call it a spiritual connection—something stays suspended between them, between couples, in this fiercely fathered and unmothered place (*PS* 237). What *does* lie in the next world where nonbeing speaks monotonously (*PS* 238)? In these chilling conjectures, she ventures to reach out into the realm of that other world, much as W. B. Yeats did in his later Tower poems, invoking friends who have died. Here Rich may veil her spiritual quest in the guise of curiosity, but this evening the lyric "I" throws herself into trying to understand a phenomenon more exceptional than resurrection from the dead (*PS* 238). Since established religions are unworkable for her now, privately she follows a singular spiritual path.

The quest to transform her poetry, discover new female subject positions, and a new identity beyond mother or widow, continues in the bold, longer seventh sequence of this poem where she reasserts the fact of her being an American woman, meditating on what that may mean. She both inscribes this identity into the poem and then finds herself in her creation. An inward voyage in the imagination revives her connnectedness with other women poets when she sees herself as an alter ego of Anne Bradstreet,[8] the first American woman to publish a book of poetry in the New World, leaping out of the Arabella to commit suicide (*PS* 238). Or, earlier, the American woman's voice is that of the Native American women dragging their feet across the Bering Strait (*PS* 238). Another of these forebears is the pregnant slave manacled to the dead body next to her, as so many slaves were during the ocean voyages across the Atlantic. So chained, this woman, brought here to have babies, goes into labor (*PS* 238).

Women are still needed, Rich indicates in haunting lines, by men chiefly for reproduction, their bodies the vehicles for populating the wilderness, bearing sons who will leave their mothers. The maternal reproductive body is transformed through metaphor into a hollow ship that bears unwilling cargo into "the wilderness" of the New World. She asks, How different actually is the white Jewish woman from the African slave who literally gives birth next to a corpse? The (once thought expendable) early women who first came to America were either strung up for witchcraft or purchased for breeding, thus her sisters leave her (*PS* 239). The speaker, too, is stranded on this shore, punning on the term "washed up." In colonial and revolutionary times American men's writing was full of images of wheat fields and virgin forests, but woman is neither a field nor a virgin forest: in other words, the speaker says, don't force me to be your symbol of abundance and nurturing.[9] Certainly she never had a choice of where she would be born and grow up; and, significantly, the entire process kept women isolated, hence exploited: mostly, "in my sex, I was alone" (*PS* 239).

This often-quoted axiom subsumes her sense of American woman's identity before the women's liberation movement in the late 1960s and 1970s. Consciously or not, the dominant American culture has divided women from one another. As she expresses it later in "Hunger," dedicated to Audre Lorde, in *The Dream of a Common Language,* which title echoes Judy Grahn's title for her book of poetry, *The Work of a Common Woman: "They can rule the world while they can persuade us / our pain belongs in some other order."*

Grahn affirms the strength of the common woman in her long poem in seven parts called "The Common Woman": *"the common woman is as common as the best of bread / and will rise."*[10] Rich writes a perceptive foreword to this book, which was published in 1978, the year Judy Chicago's *The Dinner Party* opened in San Francisco, a year of widespread debate about what it meant to be a woman and a lesbian in the United States and in the West generally.

"FROM AN OLD HOUSE IN AMERICA"

In "From an Old House in America," Rich shows that if women were often the child-bearers and the slaves of the new continent, they were also exceedingly brave, powerful within their sphere, and not afraid of blood: they were familiar with blood because they had to kill animals to survive (*PS* 239). She speaks as voice for all those who left no written record: the self-aware pioneer woman was aware that her power was not far-reaching; still, she possessed her own strength (*PS* 239). The lyric "I"'s power is to name and catalog the reality and strength of these stoic and uncomplaining women. Now that they have set off free and confident (*PS* 242) toward a different future for women, they will use whatever is usable (*PS* 242). If research into the history of women can unlock the reality beyond the myths and legends about women, it can help discern the truth of former women's lives. But myths and superstitions may also be the keys to revealing the actual lives of earlier women of the frontier, those who left no written record; when analyzed, superstitions can tell us much about society's attitudes about women in any given period. Look, for instance, Rich suggests, at their superstition that the mother could blind the child with her look (*PS* 243) or traditional medical practices involving the burial of the placenta (*PS* 243). Early superstitions claimed that the look of the mother could blind her children; hence in the days of slavery mothers were sometimes kept away from their children cruelly. The thirteenth sequence deals obliquely with the ways fear of and lust for women have perpetuated their oppression and even created the patriarchal exclusion of women from positions of leadership in the major organized religions. It makes sense just after this treatment of fear and lust to revisit another domain of women's oppression, marriage. There follows in the fourteenth sequence a dialogue between a woman who constantly inquires what he might be ready to do, and a man whose reply is, I am not responsible for all the sins of all men on earth and, Is there such a thing as collective guilt? Obviously, she is still thinking over these questions since her final request is simply to share a long gaze with him. That is the last we hear from the man in this poem.

The next stage on the mythological quest toward clarification of woman's identity, the next-to-last section, is the appearance of the Erinyes, the Furies who avenge the blood of Agamemnon and Clytemnestra, the murdered mother in Aeschylus's *Oresteia.* They come partially to judge, partially to bring calm and peace (*PS* 244). But the last renders the verdict, so on the wall one writes the judgment (*PS* 244). The poem inscribes in the writing on the wall, the vision of the way society should progress in future if it is to progress equitably.

Anyone is potentially guilty, she asserts, if she or he does not acknowledge how women have been hurt historically; men who will not admit that there has been some abuse of women in the past, or those who deny that women have been hurt, these people have not realized the extent of the injustice enacted, faced the fundamental truth of women's exploitation, or perceived how women's self-perceptions affect their views of other women. Last, the poet writes threateningly, be warned that if "you" have not faced up to the immensity of women's subjugation, if you are still avoiding that, then the Goddess is still anticipating your arrival. If you have come to terms with all these, the divine in feminine form, the ancient supplanted Goddess, who is the female counterpart to the Judeo-Christian God, patiently waits.

In the final sequence, Rich cites an anonymous early opinion expressed about Mary Wollstonecraft, a standard traditional response to the articulate, rebellious woman who stands up for her rights: these women were feared and ostracized as possible revolutionaries (*PS* 244). There is an awareness of woman's danger to herself now that she has reached this crossroads, this moment when she can at last be taken seriously. In a compelling image, Rich connects the dangerous jimson weed, datura, a poisonous, hallucinogenic weed that is also called deadly nightshade. The poison grows right next to the American woman's "old house" still, so she can endanger herself by ingesting the weed. This is sinister wisdom, available for the most part, to the woman researcher (*PS* 244).

Knitting all the strands of the poem together in a final image that subsumes the themes of rebellion, death, isolation, and the efforts and skills of the first women on the American continent, she sees a pioneer woman about to shoot a rifle along the fence surrounding their land (*PS* 245) and that we are proud of that woman. But pride is itself like the deadly nightshade, combustible, deadly if one consumes it (*PS* 245). Still, this woman commands our pride when we regard her in her incarnation as riflewoman, the strong forager for her household and children. This is an antiromantic image of the frontierswoman, one never before advanced. And hence we celebrate her and mourn for her. After all, she saw her life force disappearing into the void where massacred settlers and dead babies are thrown (*PS* 239). Reiterating John Donne's lines, *"any man's death diminishes me"*—or *"the Continent,"* as he calls it—Rich turns it around to write that any woman's death diminishes us all (*PS* 245). True to the spirit of the first frontierswomen, the person who only occupies space in her absence, an absence which Rich is quick to point out is not silence, she honors the stoic, suffering women who were our silenced great-great-grandmothers, great-grandmothers yet who constitute one of the reasons America has survived as a nation. Although plain and declarative in parts, this is a probing investigation into the history of American women, a tacit affirmation of women's historical connectedness to the old house, which is this continent.[11]

In the important poem "Natural Resources" in *The Dream of a Common Language: Poems 1974–1977*, Rich explores this sense of place in the poems, a rootedness and a love of the specificity that becomes a mainstay in her poetry during the late 1970s. She endorses womankind as one of America's most valuable natural resources. She has been, as she says in the opening lines of "Power," sifting through the many sedimentary layers of women's history, and this has emerged (*DC* 3). Significantly, the culminating section of the book is called "Not Somewhere Else but Here" as the present moment now is given first priority. This probing of the meaning of a particular local place becomes an obsession in her later work, since as she defines who she is after each of her successive transformations, she in fact defines who she is in this place and at this particular time. The style is now more jagged, fragmented, but more honest from a woman's perspective, more personal and direct. Now the reader is addressed as an intimate friend, sharing another individual's love and anguish.

"NATURAL RESOURCES"

"Natural Resources," itself almost a gloss on or extension of "From an Old House in America," catalogs those qualities, sites, and objects that women value. As her later poems become more anti-literary, anti-mythological, correspondingly Adrienne Rich chooses real heroines and even this working-class miner, a "real" miner, as more appropriate subjects, more fully realized subjectivities, for her new poems. The woman miner is truly human, subject to the laws of history, gravity, and biology: she enters a cage with the other miners, and then she is flung down into the shaft and down there she must change (*DC* 60). Despite her unfeminine occupation, the passive voice of the verb *is flung* and the coerciveness of the verb *must change* emphasize her helplessness as an object of environmental and physical forces, a person determined by all the conditions of her employment.

The speaker returns in the fourth verse sequence, the lines record an interview in which she was asked if she could imagine a world comprised only of women or one without women; she answered sadly that of course she could imagine the latter (*DC* 61). Thinking what a world without women would be like becomes a central focus of this poem; and its weary, rueful tone forces us to see the poem's negative image and wonder why such a world should be of interest to the interviewer—or to the audience.

Next, she muses on the universal female fantasy of an understanding man: like Orpheus, he would be the kindred spirit, brother, or twin from whom she was separated at birth, and he is the one each one marries (*DC* 62). Is this man a figment of all women's imaginations? Perhaps Rich has never truly known him, but each woman falling in love thinks she has found that man. For him, each woman betrays and leaves her family and enters marriage.

Last, the lyric "I" wonders if women have perhaps invented the man who wants to know us. Here, she takes "know" in both the standard sense and in the biblical sense; the lines may suggest that this man may have been willed, invented, conjured out of the fear that perhaps no one would deign or dare to know women, who in Judaism are thought to be the inferiors of men. Why? It wasn't sexuality alone we were after; the speaker asserts that women simply want a kindred spirit and a peer (*DC* 62). Women seek partnership, companionship, and friendship in their relationships with men.

In the next sequence, in lines that conjure up W. B. Yeats's "*rough beast slouching toward Bethlehem to be born,*" she states that another alien being, a bloodthirsty creature, a man who is inseparable from his gun and from blood, is hiding in the guise of the man women think of as their soulmate. This man finds his way into women's bedrooms and convinces them that they want to fulfill his desires when that was *not* their desire, she implies. It has lain on women's breasts: vampirelike, it needs to feed on their blood (*DC* 63). The woman-devouring vampire that "we" are thrilled by in the films is a representation of a type of romantic lover, the romantic lover who cannot live without appropriating women's breasts or blood.

This poetry is, more than ever before, both visionary and political, full of shockingly vivid imagery, yet critic Cary Nelson calls it "her most flatly didactic poetry," a style he thinks she later "outgrows." Other critics, however, counter that it incandescent in tone, white-hot in its desire to convey transformative states of consciousness.

In the following section, she says that since desperate-to-marry women crave gentleness in a man, they frequently mistake passivity for gentleness (*DC* 63); and the passive man is only another form of mutant being, another deception. Real gentleness, on the other hand, has a strong component of courage, perseverance, and much patience and consistency (*DC* 64). Real male gentleness masks real masculine strength, is uncowed, and is resolute against all enemies (*DC* 64). This is raw unselfconscious courage, the opposite of faintheartedness, a quality women have been forced to dissemble for centuries. The speaker is frustrated to see so many women of character and intelligence bend over backward to accommodate men's egos: in a neoclassical couplet, she rhymes bending to half their "height" with mining the choice vein and bringing it "to light" (*DC* 64). Here, the neat rhyme signals the equivalent of a Shakespearean end of an act at the same time that it revisits the mining image of the first lines: the mines force women to bend to half their height, even as American civilization in the 1970s forces women to act "feminine," to be gentle, fainthearted, and if not stupid, then not too bright, certainly not pushy. She is frustrated by the waste of the products of women's labor (*DC* 64). Is this the waste of our children and the waste of women's own natural resources and abilities?

Next, the textual "I" pensively watches a spider rebuild her web methodically, persistently, just as Robert the Bruce, a medieval king of Scotland, had watched a spider rebuild a web centuries earlier and in so doing gained the courage to rise up again in battle against the English—and win. So, too, the liberated female "I" realizes that she notes the similarity between her impatience and the speaker's own, but she also discerns the spider/creator's joy in creating and remaking. She will go on doing this in the face of chaos, never submit to the customary or expected (*DC* 64).

For all there is still wonder and joy in ordinary things: she perceives the wonder in the ordinary china saucers set on a table in a barn, with shoehorns and a fine book. These are valuable in a place like a homestead where women are endlessly starting all over again since these are the objects women have saved, and in some instances, it is all that is left of them and those they loved (*DC* 65). What are they, these albums full of old letters, photos, stuck in over the years (*DC* 65)? What do they symbolize here? Echoing T. S. Eliot's "*These fragments I have shored against my ruin,*" and perhaps Robert Frost's "Directive," her discussion of the fragments of their lives are now all that remains of them, fragments that may fall into strangers' hands, too: these cast-off fragments of cloth pieced together are a metaphor for this writing, this very poem. There are also dolls' dresses, white cloths to soak up blood, and an ancient bridal handkerchief, ironically ancient things of no value to anyone but a woman, and symbols of women's hope and innocence. Here in the barn it is possible to imagine their modest, decent lives.

The scholar almost seems to be saying that there is no memory of the woman's life—most women's lives—without things, hidden and saved. Without them, there is no memory, no loyalty to one's own or sense of purpose for days to come, and the past has no dignity. Such is the fabric of women's history, "a universe of humble things" (*DC* 66).

Because so much has been lost that belonged to women, so many lives were lived in obscurity, she writes that now there are meaningless abstractions that she could no longer utter like *humanism* or *androgyny* because by their abstraction and generality these words would affront our raging stoic grandmothers and dishonor their names and legacy; they do not show proper respect to working women whose lives were begun and ended in obscurity, whose belongings make up a world of ordinary possessions.

Considering her rejection of these concepts, Cary Nelson advances the theory that *humanism* and *androgyny* "do not embody [or encompass] the history of anguish, repression, and self-control that precedes them";[12] hence these words are cruel abstractions that avoid the realities they purport to name. *Humanism* and *androgyny* are words that have been used to exclude women in the past, and Rich will not use them now since they are evasions of feminist issues that Rich, in the name of all the women who were our unknown forebears, stands for and confronts (*DC* 66). Contemporary poetry by women must be accountable to the truth of history and to the silent early women who endured much and lost much before our century.

As Rich wrote of bisexuality in "Compulsory Heterosexuality and Lesbian Existence": "such a notion blurs and sentimentalizes the actualities within which women have experienced sexuality; it is the old liberal leap across the tasks and struggles of here and now" (*ARP* 216). Likewise the term *androgyny* simply does not go far enough in the direction of affirming the values of feminism and lesbian feminism, each in its own right. She contends that now feminist theory cannot afford merely to "voice a toleration of 'lesbianism' as an 'alternative life style' or make token allusion to lesbians" (*ARP* 206). Instead of heterocentricity, Rich advocates not essentialism, as critics have charged, but a lesbian feminism the allows women to counter their current state of compulsory heterosexuality while experiencing their own transforming identities and confronting "political repression, economic insecurity" (*ARP* 204), with strategies for enabling women to live peaceably, sometimes separately, establishing their own political and social order when necessary. Although she is not a separatist, she wants society to accord women the right and the "potential of loving and being loved by women in mutuality and integrity" (*ARP* 210).

The poem resumes the metaphor of mining, comparing the early proponents of women's liberation to miners, saying that these first miners in the cause have expired. Certainly one of these is Virginia Woolf, another is Muriel Rukeyser, whose retellings of myth like the Oedipus myth embodied her own revisioning of womanhood and discovery of the buried female—in part, though not solely, lesbian feminist—tradition that Rich explores here and in "Diving into the Wreck." Now, the poet urges, is the time for women to mine and investigate women's history and prehistory, to pursue a feminist archaeology (*DC* 67). All that can be brought to light awaits discovery and the gift of women's mining or what we now call feminist research. This image subsumes all the foregoing images of finding humble things and finding the as-yet-undiscovered, unknown, or unexplored truths that precede the final revelation. Here the multiple subject positions Rich has adopted so far in her poetry mingle in the common quest.

Then the poem ends in a statement of heartfelt, loyal commitment: she is passionate about these disappeared women and moved by everything here that she cannot redeem or resurrect (*DC* 67). She speaks in wonderment at all that has been damaged and lost, that one can only dedicate oneself to rebuilding and "reconstituting" their worlds. Hence she affirms solidarity with those ordinary women who transgressively and steadily repair and reassemble this lost world and the lives and spirit of the lost first American women (*DC* 67). Women of intellect and heart can all be miners, she implies, since women need to rebuild the world along what Alice Walker calls more "womanist" lines. It takes no special talent or genius to start rebuilding what has been ruined that women valued; any woman with a desire to join in can apply herself to it. This commitment is not just the natural evolution of this poem. It signals the final stage of her progression in *The Dream of a Common Language,* where she begins to see the poem itself as a transformative instrument at work in the poet and the reader both. She imagines a moment in which the readers' and poet's eyes meet: in that gaze, each is joined and made clear to the other simultaneously, hence each fully comprehends and understands the other (*DC* 19).

If at the will of the poet the poem might stare at the reader unblinkingly, forcing him or her to look back (*DC* 19), then direct visceral and spiritual communication could be established between poet and reader and true understanding could be reached.

THE DREAM OF A COMMON LANGUAGE

Consequently, *The Dream of a Common Language,* a radical progression from *Diving into the Wreck,* is the dream that all might communicate directly in this way, sharing in and speaking a common language of caring and concern for one another. All can speak this language to one another, but how can the poet reach out intimately to all? One way is to address the divine feminine in all women. Ntozake Shange writes in *For Colored Girls Who Have Considered Suicide When the Rainbow Is Enuf: A Choreopoem:*

I found god in myself
and I loved her
loved her fiercely[13]

The feminist movement gave Rich and many other women writers and artists a means of educating themselves—and all other people—through their art and literature, when they tapped into a communal reservoir of shared female experience formerly silenced, left in secret, or repressed. As Rich herself testified to the movement's influence on her life in an early interview:

> [T]he women's movement connected me with the conflicts and concerns I'd been feeling..., as well as with the intense rapid politicization of the 1960's New Left. It opened up possibilities, freed me from taboos and silence...; without a feminist movement I don't see how I could have gone on growing as a writer.[14]

That she would speak so openly, candidly, and passionately of this bears witness to the movement's formative impact on her as a writer and as a feminist, as a poet and as a lesbian. Becoming a feminist has transformed Rich's personal philosophy, transformed her critical theory and subject positionings, and forced her to rethink her political ideology: it has led her to a radically new vision of reality. From a literary perspective, her work is transformed since she must shine the light of truth into spaces that were previously lies, evasions, secrets, silences. Her pioneering poetry and politics are realized in relationship with her sisters—for lesbians, feminists, other women—and I have traced throughout the course of this chapter the ways she celebrates pioneer women and female heroes as realizations of her ideal of the motivating female spirit, embodiments in and "miners" in the female tradition.

"TWENTY-ONE LOVE POEMS"

A private dimension of the tradition is sexual love between woman and woman, between lesbians. Appropriately now in *The Dream of a Common Language,* her book whose desire is intimate emotional communication between women, she sets her "Twenty-One Love Poems" (*DC* 25–36). This beautiful sequence of poems addressed to her lover records the progress of a loving relationship in 21 poems ranging between 12 and 18 lines in length. The ways the lovers match is established early on, and the poems delineate all their points of rapport and connection, their hands the same size, and their capacity for trust impeccable (VI, *DC* 27–28). Silence between them only shows what has yet to be discovered in their relationship: inside her lover's silence live what is submerged and drowned, and the speaker wants to bring them out into the light, yet others' faces dwell under the water, within her (IX, *DC* 29). There is so much to communicate on both a verbal and a nonverbal level, and they have less time to experience everything, weeks substitute for years (III, *DC* 26). Certainly she feels buoyant and young, the speaker walks with her heart radiating pure joy. Asking another question, she continues, wonders if ever before she bent over the city on a balcony, awaiting a call in the same way she does today (*DC* 26). Knowing that formerly we expected to have all the time in the world at our disposal but now, in middle age, what their time together might be is a mystery the speaker wants to resolve (III, *DC* 26). The love poem embodies a tenderness hitherto unvisited in her poetry: they touch aware that they are not young, but that each will be there for the other throughout life, until death (III, *DC* 26). This is an eternal bond.

Adrienne Rich truly in love is a pure, lyrical love poet, a person unabashedly full of joy. She can even achieve a measure of self-deprecation here, aware of a certain wonder at the fact that she finds it necessary to record this love and this strong passion: Is rendering a life into words the goal of any creature (VII, *DC* 28)? Only a poet would do so, of course. Clearly this atonement is an "at-one-ment" with the youthful questing, exuberant part of herself that was always suppressed when she was a student and "child wife" as she herself described it (*DC* 28).

Echoes of earlier love poems abound, and here the image is of a far more compatible couple: our bodies both similar and dissimilar to one another. Now our history and race rushing through our blood are endowed with different cultural and linguistic backgrounds, ontologies foreign to each other (XII, *DC* 30–31). In the poem, the unnamed lover is wholly different from her in language, body, race, class, and background, yet paradoxically this very difference becomes a love that transcends all the differences. The poem declares her right to announce their love publicly through all shared media: certainly it might be inscribed with new meaning—that they were in love (XII, *DC* 31). It is this and the fact that they were women of the same generation and gender (XII, *DC* 31). The multiple meanings of the word "*generation*" resound at the end of this poem and evoke the multiple meanings of nation, female nationhood.

Resonating with all the emotions of strong, passionate love, this sequence of poems is reminiscent of Elizabeth Barrett Browning's *Sonnets from the Portuguese.* In their beauty and freshness, they are original, unforgettable; these are, certainly. In "(The Floating Poem, Unnumbered)" she writes of their present and future beautifully: whether or not their love endures forever, her beloved's body will remain with her, ever in consciousness, the experience of love "like the half-curled frond" of "the fiddlehead fern in forests," freshly washed by rain and sun ("[The Floating Poem, Unnumbered]," *DC* 32). Using alliteration and delicate similes for lovemaking, Rich envisions the body like a young fiddlehead frond unfurling in stippled light. This image is memorable and fixes the poem forever in the mind.

The speaker addresses her: it is as though the lyric "I" had been awaiting her firm, protective, searching touch over many years, possibly not realizing what she had been waiting for (*DC* 242). In these lines, the erotic impetus pushes on beyond the bounds of the line each time, concluding that this reality exists; whatever happens, this ecstatic experience has transcended time and space (*DC* 242). As if for the first time, these poems give a locus and a voice to new desire, fulfillment, and a new dimension to the female tradition in her poetry.

Thinking of woman-centered texts like this, Rich comments critically, "Any theory or cultural/political creation that treats lesbian experience as a marginal or less 'natural' phenomenon, as mere 'sexual preference' or as the mirror image of either heterosexual or male homosexual relations is profoundly weakened thereby" (*ARP1* 206). She seeks to create and support true lesbian/feminist texts, not only for their pure literary originality but also as reflecting a sexuality and passion previously as ignored, erased, or buried as the female tradition itself.

Shadows pass across the love affair in the final two poems of the series since in sequence XX she writes: the woman she loved is now submerged in secrets and choked with fear like hair wrapped round her neck (XX, *DC* 35). Secrets are largely what divide women, secrets and fear that dare not explore or express themselves. Her refusal to communicate ends the relationship: she longs for the beloved, whose expressive head she sees drowning, averting her eyes in pain and not listening to the poet, but the words the lyric "I" has uttered were not spoken in vain since "soon I shall know I was talking to my own soul" (XX, *DC* 35). The final poem XXI appears to be about framing the love, drawing a line, fixing a final boundary. She renders moonrise beautifully, tracing dark doorways, blue and foreign stones, and moonlight emanating from below, with the true rhymes of "night" and "light" affording a perfection to the scene (XXI, *DC* 36).

The subsequent image is both haunting and ideal for the ending of a sonnet sequence celebrating the great love of her life: she has triumphantly entered the great light of a lifelong love and chooses to walk in that life though she is sometimes partly eclipsed in shadow, still greeting the moon as a woman (XXI, *DC* 36). The speaker who has chosen to participate in these experiences and experiments in love continues, asserting forcefully that she elects to inhabit this space and draw this circle (XXI, *DC* 36). In the triple roles of woman, lover, and poet, the speaker and lesbian sexuality have been embodied and inscribed here; she is the poet's double moving across that space, the color of stone, saluting the moon. If the moon symbolizes both Diana and the Goddess along with the feminine principle here, in and through this experience she has partaken of the divine feminine power and now moves through it, inspired and animated by it.

"PHANTASIA FOR ELVIRA SHATAYEV"

A different yet related experience and memorial are consecrated to Elvira Shatayev, a brilliant woman pioneer, a person Rich would likely consider a forerunner or "miner." The moving, transcendent poem "Phantasia for Elvira Shatayev," whom Rich described in a note, "*Leader of a women's climbing team, all of whom died in a storm on Lenin Peak, August 1974*" (*ARP* 174), reveals the strategy Rich has for reaching through the membrane of the poem to touch and teach the reader how a woman of courage on the very edge of her powers behaves and thinks. Since as poet she, too, experiences pushing herself to the limits of human potentiality in her quest to rediscover a female tradition and psychic and spiritual bonds between women, Rich identifies with Elvira Shatayev and writes the "Phantasia" in her voice, but it is her impersonal immortal voice, the voice of one already dead, of course, since she is a kind of Soviet Christa MacAuliffe: even though I may be sleeping as "I" speak, "I" speak with a universal, collective voice, the voice of the whole team of valiant women (*DC* 4). The speaker adds parenthetically that she wants to say with the help of their words and voices (*DC* 4)—not *in* voices.

Having trained for a lifetime for her assault on this mountain, Elvira Shatayev's voice vouches for the entire team who died in that storm: unaccountably each one of us has been moved to say *yes*, that *yes* emerging from inside her, gradually growing as she gazed out from windows (*DC* 4).

Each one had felt a powerful sense of affirmation in saying *yes* to the commitment that would necessitate each woman's risking and ultimately losing her life: they were about to discover what their teamwork meant up on the mountain, and they prepared while the *yes* collected itself, its energies fused, in the nick of time (*DC* 4). The courage of affirmation is death-defying and a courage long in the making, a product of their learning how it feels to be a community of women climbers in the mountains—a sisterhood of brave spirits and strong women.

As though writing to all women, the poet describes Elvira Shatayev inscribing these words in her diary while the tents are being ripped apart in the wind. What she writes is a testament to all the courageous women, miners who push the limits of their physical, mental, emotional, and spiritual resources to excel: the poem asks and debates the meaning of "love and survival themselves" and how important could "our" physical survival be when "*we*" are linked eternally by our common quest and purpose, a blue fire bond connects us, each to the other (*DC* 6). They are linked forever in a chain of interconnected love, passion, and dedication. United women, Rich imagines, communicate from the heart, from the depths of their common experience today. For her *common* no longer connotes *vulgar* as it did in the 1950s and before. Now it describes those very links that join woman to woman, as in the *common* bonds of womanhood. The adventurous voice of Elvira Shatayev speaks symbolically of those bonds as a *cable* in the last lines of the poem, reenvisioning the imagery of transformative burning which figures in "Song" (*DW* 9), in "Burning Paper instead of Children," and now here: ice-burnt and freezing in the snow collectively, they shall not live to be content with less since all their hopes and dreams are invested in this transcendence or conquest (*DC* 6). This dreamlike tragic and romantic vision of women determined to risk their lives, linked together as one, united in a common purpose, interdependent in life and death inspires her "dream of a common language," the language of feminist heroines, pioneers—the language of the feminist movement. Burning is always a symbol of transformation in Rich, so here their burning together means a transforming together. The climber/speaker's ultimate desire and choice are just this once to give all for love and to love intelligently (*DC* 11). She wants to unite her love and intelligence as well as all the practical knowledge she has gained, and then to expend herself in a labor of love that parallels the work of the women's liberation movement. Their ascent of the mountain symbolizes women's coming out on top and ultimately realizing their dreams of female nationhood in the realm of poetry even though those dreams may have been unattained in real life.

ON LIES, SECRETS, AND SILENCE

Adrienne Rich's powerful intellect keeps her questing, ahead of the times on issues of equity for women; thus, perceiving a massive social and psychological anomaly like the problem of women's collective and individual lies, secrets, and silences, she is impelled to speak out, as a spokesperson for all women. Women are relegating themselves to subordinate positions and lower standards when they keep secrets, tell lies, and observe silence when they should speak the truth. Certainly *A Wild Patience Has Taken Me This Far* (its very title is a oxymoron—how can patience be "wild"?) contains some of her more polemical and ideological poetry: likely it is because during this period she was reexamining her entire ideological structure, articulating her theories and perceptions as a feminist critic, writing many articles, and, in association with others, launching the field of women's studies.

In *On Lies, Secrets, and Silence,* the reader can witness Rich's transformation from a Modernist to a feminist thinker (and critic) in a series of scholarly, thought-provoking essays on women writers, women in university education, lesbianism, and other relevant women's issues. Thoreau acknowledged that America's greatest heroes are her poets and revolutionaries. Rich is true to that heroic tradition in this and later books of poetry—indeed, she has been a heroine and revolutionary since *Diving into the Wreck.* To read *A Wild Patience* and *On Lies, Secrets, and Silence* together is to witness a dialogue between prose and poetry on the same subjects—questions of women's place in a changing world, women's higher education, gender issues, lesbian issues, and the wider field of women's studies. Here we see Adrienne Rich working as a brilliant critic and in the process becoming a foremother of women's studies. Her inquiry into the accepted literary canon and its justification in English departments throughout American and other English-speaking universities and colleges prompted a reexamination of what is taught in many English courses throughout the English-speaking world. Hence the importance of her volume of essays *On Lies, Secrets, and Silence* (and later *Of Woman Born*) should not be underestimated since these essays and those in the next volume *Blood, Bread, and Poetry* helped change the literary canon. Then, in protest, Harold Bloom expelled Adrienne Rich from the Western canon in a counterrevolutionary move.

In analyses of important or unknown, but definitely underrated, women's literature, she displays her agility in feminist literary analysis, for example, "Vesuvius at Home: The Power of Emily Dickinson" (1975), "Jane Eyre: The Temptations of a Motherless Woman" (1973), and "Woman Observing, Preserving, Conspiring, Surviving: The Poems of Eleanor Ross Taylor" (1972). In "Toward a Women-Centered University," she imagines a more feminist university than any hitherto existing, one where women's studies exist as a focus of accredited study. Considering a university like this was revolutionary in 1973–1974. Formerly, before the 1970s, she had been intellectually restricted by "the limitations of a point of view which took masculine history and literature as its center . . . and which tried from that perspective to view a women's life and work" (*LS* 21).

Following on in this vein is "Taking Women Students Seriously" (1978), whose title suggests that women students seldom were taken very seriously before the 1970s. Even in the best women's colleges, women were often patronized and treated arrogantly by male professors; they were sometimes made to feel they were lesser intellects. In this essay, Rich contrasts the ways that in "an all-girls' school" in the 1940s she was pushed to do her best by women teachers and their true dedication to their students, where the head and the majority of the faculty were independent unmarried women; one or two held doctorates (*LS* 237). Of the experience she had at her "Seven Sisters" college, she writes:

From that school, I went on to Radcliffe, congratulating myself that now I would have great men as my teachers. From 1947 to 1951, when I graduated, I never saw a single woman on a lecture platform, or in front of a class...The "great men" talked of other "great men," of the nature of Man, the history of Mankind, the future of Man; and never again was I to experience, from a teacher, the kind of prodding, the insistence that my best could be even better, that I had known in high school. (*LS* 238)

Clearly she was not treated as an equal by the male students or by her male professors:

Women students were simply not taken very seriously. Harvard's message to women was an elite mystification: we were, of course, part of Mankind; we were special, achieving women, or we would not have been there; but of course our real goal was to marry—if possible, a Harvard graduate. (*LS* 238)

As she writes in "Women and Honor: Some Notes on Lying," "Women have been driven mad,...for centuries by the refutation of our experience and our instincts in a culture which validates only male experience. The truth of our bodies and our minds has been mystified to us. We therefore have a primary obligation to each other: not to undermine each others' sense of reality for the sake of expediency" (*LS* 190). This sabotaging of women by other women continued during the decade of the 1940s, when some were unsure Western civilization could survive, and the strife between women continued well into the 1980s, the 1990s, when women competed for places in the professions. Far more painful to Adrienne Rich than the issue of education is the issue of how women remain divided from one another by lying. In *On Lies, Secrets, and Silence,* Rich publishes for the mass audience an essay she had previously published privately, a collection of epigrams and statements about lying. A selection follows:

Lying is done with words, and also with silence. The woman who tells lies in her personal relationship may or may not plan to....She may not even think of what she is doing in a calculated way. (*LS* 186–87)

Some women lie and sadly are not even aware they lie; they do not fathom the nature or depth of their deception. "The liar often suffers from amnesia. Amnesia is the silence of the unconscious" (LS 187). Worse, the liar "leads an existence of great loneliness" (LS 187). The worst part of this is that, "In lying to others we end up lying to ourselves. We deny the importance of an event, or a person, and thus deprive ourselves of a part of our lives. Thus we lose faith even with our own lives" (LS 188). Women lose faith in themselves.

The positive side of elimination of lying and women's cultivation of honor is the ensuing trust that grows in the community that forms the foundation of a healthy women's movement. In 1976, at the University of Pittsburgh, Rich made this clear in the following statement:

> The work that I want to do in my maturity could not be done without the existence of the growing women's culture, or without the support of a women's movement.... We need courage, and we draw on each other for courage, but we have to remember that there have been women who did not have the kind of networks, the kind of culture, the kind of politics surrounding them, that we have. And this in itself is an immense step forward, and it's something we have to protect, we have to further, we have to defend, in order for all of us to do the kind of work we want to do, and that the world needs us to do.

For Rich, building trust, eschewing lying, and transparent honesty are the most important values for women to espouse. The challenge of the women's liberation movement engages the "question of women's honor," the need for women to be truthful to one another and to themselves. Women's acculturation is often an education in tacitly if not openly lying:

> We have been required to tell different lies at different times, depending on what the men of the time needed to hear. The Victorian wife or the white southern lady, who were expected to have no sensuality, to "lie still"; the twentieth-century "free" woman who is expected to fake orgasms. (*LS* 188)

Regrettably today the lie persists as a fact of female experience across the world and across centuries. Because of social inequality and injustice, women have been forced by men to lie, Rich insists; and therefore, since patriarchy assumes no one can ever trust a woman, "Women have always lied to each other...Women have always been divided against each other." Traditional "women have always been in secret collusion" (*LS* 189), as she describes the phenomenon. Her challenge to the muted group was formulated as a question: "Women have been forced to lie, for survival...How to unlearn this among other women?" In my experience, by the 1960s and 1970s, women of integrity were beginning to "unlearn" lying. But in more recent decades, a backlash against the women's movement forced women to relearn lying. It has sometimes seemed as though the feminist revolution never occurred or that it had been turned back. Rich foresaw this, too: "There is a danger run by all powerless people that we forget we are lying, or that lying becomes a weapon we carry over into relationships with people who do not have power over us" (*LS* 189).

Women's love of other women has up until this point been an absence and silence in American women's writing, and Rich sees this absence as another lie. "Women's life for women has been represented almost entirely through silence and lies. The institution of heterosexuality has forced the lesbian to dissemble, or to be labeled a pervert, a criminal, a sick or dangerous woman . . ." (*LS* 190). Hence she asks:

> Does a life 'in the closet'—lying, perhaps of necessity, about ourselves to bosses, . . . clients, colleagues, family, . . . does this, can it, spread into private life, so that lying (described as discretion), becomes an easy way to avoid conflict or complication: can it become a strategy so ingrained that it is used even with close friends and lovers? (*LS* 190)

It can and had become such a strategy. Still, great numbers of women are afraid to declare themselves as lesbians. Yet their lies and silence condemn them to lives of unutterable fear and loneliness: "The liar in her terror wants to fill up the void, with anything. Her lies are a denial of her fear; a way of maintaining control" (*LS* 191). Ultimately, what is important between individuals in any relationship is "[T]hat I feel strong enough to hear your tentative groping words. That we both know we are trying, all the time, to extend the possibilities of truth between us" (*LS* 194). These prophetic words, Rich insists, still need to be heard and acted upon by all women today.

If, as she wrote in 1975, women are in bondage because of their fears, fear of one another, fear of what would happen if they told the truth, naturally motherhood is in bondage, too, since until recently women have often not had a choice of whether or not they will become mothers, and the politics of motherhood are under male domination and association with a male. In "Motherhood in Bondage" (1976), she calls for an analysis of motherhood as a political institution, and in *Of Women Born,* Rich gives us exactly this full-scale analysis. The short essay "Motherhood in Bondage" from *On Lies, Secrets, and Silence,* ably sums up the central issues:

> Motherhood is admirable, however, only so long as mother and child are attached to a legal father: Mothers out of wedlock, or under the welfare system, or lesbian motherhood, are harassed, humiliated, or neglected. (*LS* 196)

Indeed, when a woman seeks to have power over her own body, to control her own reproduction independent of a father or husband, it seems revolutionary, even in the twenty-first century.

Adrienne Rich bears the distinction of being among the first to signal this as a major issue of the last decades of the twentieth century. In the well-documented, well-reasoned book *Of Women Born* (1974), drawing on the anthropology of motherhood, "on the medicine, psychology, literature and history" of motherhood, and on her own experience as the mother of three sons, "personal testimony mingled with research," she analyzes the politics of motherhood and offers an articulate feminist perspective on the way motherhood has been used to manipulate and disempower women.

About this time, she was also writing "'It Is the Lesbian in Us'" (1976) and beginning life together with Michelle Cliff, her life partner; in 1978, she published "Disloyal to Civilization: Feminism, Racism, and Gynephobia" (1978). Both essays are important to the later evolution of her conceptual thought and feminist theory in *Blood, Bread, and Poetry,* which is the focus of the next chapter.

A WILD PATIENCE HAS TAKEN ME THIS FAR: POEMS 1978–1981

The abiding focus on women's lives, sexuality, and situation in American society persists in *A Wild Patience Has Taken Me This Far: Poems 1978–1981,* where Rich again dedicates some poems to the feminist cause and to the reconsideration of old words like *trust* and *fidelity:* since as yet we lack anything to replace them ("For Memory," *WP* 21). The feminist speaker asserts that too many women, stung by the wrongdoing of other women, are still experiencing dishonor and betrayal and telling one another: the lyric "I" hears another's voice across the telephone lines, stinging the wires. "For Memory" is a poignant call for honesty: self-revelation is crucial since neither woman can know the other until each is open, honest, and clear since our understandings have gaps and abysses in them (*WP* 21). Our fault, the poem implies, is that women seldom mention their differences to one another, possibly because they have been taught that that is impolite, unfeminine, or petty. This enrages the speaker: she screams that they unite in a common fury of direction, seemingly unaware of their dissimilarities (*WP* 21), yet "we" are different and the onus is upon "us" to speak it out since we must construct creative syntheses, understandings, and transformations of consciousness, whole star-fraught heavenly domes from all that has been lost in women's history, the lost collection (*WP* 22).

Here she reinvokes the sense of investigative research and leaps in consciousness that women moving toward the future must tirelessly engage in—the kind of investigation she described in "Diving into the Wreck." This research into the roots of honesty in ourselves and in community is necessary for women to do since each and every one is inventing herself anew through the revolution in consciousness.

In "Transcendental Etude" (*DC* 72), addressed to her lover Michelle Cliff, Rich touches on the same need for women's self-creation: we were not informed that the imperative was that we study our lives, as though we were studying natural history or music (*DC* 73). In *The Dream and the Dialogue,* Alice Templeton asserts:

> ...this poem fuses the lucidity of "Natural Resources" and "Toward the Solstice" with a visionary lyricism that the volume as a whole works to cultivate...she laments that "a lifetime is too narrow/to understand it all"...for...we are not trained in the art of living as "we" are taught music.[15]

Now women have to start afresh: no one told them they ought to start simply and progress to harder exercises, practicing until strength and accuracy joined their courage to take the ultimate leap, risk everything. Only through patient practice can women ever achieve the skill necessary to attempt the changes they must accomplish now, changes almost no woman in recent history has attempted. As Templeton puts it, "With no lessons or guides, the poet and her companion only approximate what they use and grope for it."[16] They—the "we" of the poems—turn themselves over to silence or a more austere listening until they are purified of the sentimental detritus—the choruses, laments, formulas, orations, and status—that have been crowding the wires, filling up the airwaves.

Templeton interprets these poems as divested of "cultural myths, methods, and false guides,"[17] all of which had previously kept women from hearing and creating mutual recognizable meaning or a common culture for themselves. Rich conceives thus of what women will say now that they are at last given liberty to speak: "This rootlessness and dismemberment are real constants for Rich, but 'knowing it makes all the difference.'"[18] Women's new language, her new parole, bursts through the imprisoning formulas and codes, which kept women passive. True women seek to "re-member" womanhood, formerly rootless, dismembered (*DC* 76), despite the fact that, growing up, they were told that women's love and homesickness for women is "for ourselves," is unnatural (*DC* 267). The result of these efforts is a "Vision" which appears in a woman's life (*DC* 76) as though she softly leaves the jargon in a room and goes to sit in the kitchen and starts piecing together scraps, bits of yarn, calico, and velvet, arranging them on the counter (*DC* 76). In creating anything at all, she affirms her oneness with the creativity in the universe and exercises her artist's responsibility to participate in an original act of creation. She creates order out of chaos in defiance of the argument and jargon in the room of contemporary life and debate over the women's movement.

The argument the woman walks away from is the typical argument of modern culture, one aspect of which is the American drive to compete in business or politics, raise money, or win at all costs versus the peace, community, the nurturing of native creativity in everyone, particularly the traditionally female arts and crafts; one can choose to opt out of the twentieth- and twenty-first-century evolutions of the American Dream and their jargon, should one wish to devote one's life to art or poetry or learning. The woman's creation in the poem is a metaphor for native creativity and native cultures assembled from scraps and bits of what has been saved or salvaged.

The woman's work of art as creating is not pompously transcendental as the poem's title might imply; it is assembling a universe of humble things. It has no interest in eternity or ambition; it is experiencing the joy of intelligence, the creativity of the mind in union with the body (*DC* 77).

The female creator is a sensitive artist who creates noncompetitively, unself-consciously, gently, sensuously, displaying no desire for mastery, only concern for the ceaseless, many-lived ways in which she discovers herself (*DC* 77). This is the new feminist artist who creates harmoniously, assembling out of pieces and fragments a unified field.

Like Alice Walker, who has celebrated the humble, yet useful, art of quilt making as a precious treasure handed down by accomplished, if anonymous quilters from earlier centuries, or the quiet creators of the subversive stitch, here Rich celebrates the woman working first of all to please herself with her aesthetic creation: she creates out of rare and exotic or discrete elements a product which is unique and intrinsically beautiful, using natural resources, local milkweed, silk, "the finest findings"—petunia petals of deep blue (*DC* 76). Here, through alliteration, Rich consciously stresses a poetic unity through the musicality of her language. She links the fragments together as a whole product through meshing the sounds of words both in image and music. Perhaps especially because this quilt could probably never really hold together, the genius here is in the telling, in the linking through language of dark brown lacy seaweed and a feline whisker, or a spiral of wasp nest nestled next to a yellow finch's feather (*DC* 76). Poetry creates a unity perhaps impossible in real space or collages.

What are these weavings but items the small boys mentioned in the poem might bring to their mother to rejoice in? These are what mothers traditionally have lost when their children grow up and leave, but the beauty of this poem inheres in the fact that none of these small expendable gifts, none of women's devalued talents need ever be lost now women have their own valued arts, crafts, and an awareness of the constant tradition of women's arts and the female tradition in literature.

To whom is this pivotal poem addressed? Some critics have assumed that it is addressed to all women, but its dedication indicates that it is initially addressed to one woman, Michelle Cliff. Still, it seems to expand outward to include all women in its scope.

In "Turning the Wheel" in *A Wild Patience,* Rich presents another image for women's art: she begins, tellingly, that of Colcha embroidery, she finds that "women use raveled yarn from old wool blankets" to draw scenes on homespun woolen sacks (*WP* 52); this is a manifestation, an example of women's ancestral skill of creating something beautiful out of what others considered expendable (*WP* 52).

A vision of the Goddess comes in the sixth section of this poem: the focus is on how "Unborn sisters" will see those who, like Rich, carve out the new female tradition: the poem envisions her appearing with rings the lyric "I" has seen only in dreams on her hands, jasper, sardonyx, and agate gleam (*WP* 57). One might conjecture whether or not she wears shawls made of blood and fire or shawls of natural fiber, untouched by tints (*WP* 57). Even if she appears dead, all must still respect and acknowledge her, even if she is wrist-deep in mud or utterly unknown to you, the reader is instructed to be brave enough to look her in the eye and not to think you have seen her cheekbones before (*WP* 57). One must not assume one knows her *yes*, either, or her bushy hair (*WP* 57). She can be recognized without being feared in that she is the ancient Goddess, the Great Earth Mother. Even the girls not yet born should be told how to recognize her if they see her in visions, because her divine essence, Rich implies, indwells in every woman.

Other poems are dedicated both to public figures (for her they are heroines) like Ethel Rosenberg, tried and executed for espionage in 1953, and to her private heroines, her own grandmothers; each one is dedicated to a woman who has been "erased," who because of our culture was unable to make any lasting contribution or make her mark in a positive way. All the heroine poems are grounded in her roots in foremothers, in women of power whose stories animate her imagination and inspire her own life; they are her sources as a poet and as a lesbian feminist. But Helen Vendler argues that Rich is less a

> "social" or purely political poet; she is more often a personal poet, psychological rather than social.... Rich's is a poetry of conversion. Like many writers who have undergone a conversion, she wants the process she has felt to be repeated in others.
>
> What we call, from the outside, a "conversion" is often seen by the person experiencing it, not as a change from an old self to a new one, but as the discovery of the authentic self that had been there all along, but had been forced into hiding by pressure from familial or social structure, structures experienced as intolerably powerful, even annihilating. Hence the subsequent quest of the converted for power, enough power to destroy, in turn, those structures which had proved so inhuman.[19]

While Vendler's forebodings about revolution have not been borne out in recent history, Rich is a psychological, political, and personal poet, reclaiming the spiritual and poetic dimensions of her legacy in the female tradition, as defined by critics Sandra Gilbert and Susan Gubar.[20]

Vendler's theory of conversion explains Rich's radicalization from *Necessities of Life* onward, her urge to destroy, her need to convert and embrace other women, whom she had hitherto been taught to view as inferior. Vendler continues:

> It could be argued, against Rich, that the structures she found repressive might not have been so for others. Could any social structures invented by an unoriginal heterosexual tribally grouped majority ever have been nurturing ones for a child half-Jewish, half-Christian, destined to be an original writer, on the one hand, and a lesbian, on the other?
>
> Rich is only one of thousands of "outsiders" or "outlaws"...who find the expectations of the herd impossible for themselves. The herd is of course...cruel

to outsiders. Those among the "marginal" who become writers often unleash an entirely realistic anger against "the system," variously conceived as the established church, ... or the class structure, or the warmongers. For Rich the oppressive rule is the rule of "compulsory heterosexuality," by which she means that most women have to buy economic survival by marriage.[21]

Clearly Vendler has little sympathy with reforming zeal or political causes when the social issues seem to take precedence over the poetry. Writing about six years after the Kent State University killing of protesting students and having taught at Boston University (Martin Luther King's alma mater), Vendler might have taken the women's movement and contemporary social and political unrest into account, but she refuses to take the cultural revolution seriously. Likely, Rich would tell her that she is simply unaware of the social change quietly transpiring around her and feels no need to be reconciled with the face in the mirror. Still Vendler acknowledges that Rich's anger is entirely "realistic," and her point about a certain repetitiveness in Rich's poetry bears noting. Vendler finds it ironic that "[R]eformers imagine that once the offending structures have been removed, people will be free."[22] She reasons, following Freud, that Rich's very rebellion is condemned to perpetuate the repression she deplores:

> The activist view of a better reality struggling toward rebirth is profoundly opposed to the more pessimistic Freudian view in which no perfect originating structure can be imagined by the psyche, which is always wounded by its psychologically dependent status in childhood. Its repressions and Oedipal reenactments ensure the perpetuation of social conventionality and tribal hostilities. Hence the strain in Rich between two poetries. One is introspective and psychologically framed poetry, which retells, many times, the story of her own rebellion and struggle for self-liberation.[23]

As she is an important, intelligent critic, we must take note of Vendler's Freudian perspective, but readers of Rich's poetry enjoy and celebrate her prophetic or messianic strains since she alone of contemporary poets seems to intuit the events of 9/11/01 in her poetry of the early 1990s.

IN-LAWS AND OUTLAWS: "MOTHER-IN-LAW" AND "THE IMAGES"

If Rich encounters professional literary critics externally, she has critics within the family as well. The fact that there is in *A Wild Patience Has Taken Me This Far: Poems 1978–1981* a humorous, self-mocking sketch of her mother-in-law, who remains her mother-in-law despite the fact that her husband has now been dead ten years, shows that Rich does have a sense of humor. In fact, she herself must apparently suffer—is it the mute fate of many wives?—her mother-in-law's criticisms about what she is doing, answer questions she has tried to answer in exasperation hundreds of times before. Of course, she must submit to unreasonable tirades, yet her mother-in-law has apparently acquiesced to the subordinate treatment others accord her: because I'm considered weak they refrain from telling me the whole truth: this is something she acquiesced to long ago (*WP* 32). The mother-in-law's disjointed rampage continues, pathetically, searchingly imploring her daughter-in-law, "strange" as she was, to discuss something real and true, tell her anything at all (*WP* 32), revealing the mother-in-law's desire for a simple connection with another human being.

This poem recounts Rich's daughter-in-law's truth, updated nearly 20 years after "Snapshots of a Daughter-in-Law," asking if perhaps they should try again, one more time, to get along. Even though they are worlds apart as women they may find some common ground. The speaker continues asking what mothers ask their own daughters all over the world; but she appears not to know, inquiring if there is a real question in all this (*WP* 32).

Is the poet suggesting that family life, communication between generations of women in a family, must be reinvented now? What might previously warring or vastly dissimilar mothers- and daughters-in-law say to one another when at last they are free to speak uncensored? Someone has to start by asking the other a simple question.

Like "Mother-in-Law," other poems in this book are addressed to her political and personal foremothers—"For Julia in Nebraska," "For Ethel Rosenberg," who, as Rich states in the epigraph, was "[c]onvicted with her husband of 'conspiracy to commit espionage'; killed in the electric chair June 19, 1953"; and who, later evidence has revealed, may not have been entirely innocent or entirely guilty. For the poet, she represents a wife and mother innocent yet persecuted at least in part because she was a Jew: the thought of that saddened her more deeply than she could register, and the recollection of her as wife and mother haunts her still (*WP* 26). Rosenberg resembles many women who have lived and died before, women whom life only rewarded with their offspring and with nothing else (*WP* 26). Like the raging stoic grandmothers, Rosenberg is a terminally silenced woman whose talents never came into true fruition; hence she, too, embodies an aspect of Rich's wreckage of drowned feminine creativity—her own and, of course, largely others'.

In this book her last, best poems are "Heroines" and "Grandmothers," written for her own much-loved grandmothers. In these two, she is quite consciously and overtly claiming these women as her own, much as she claimed the humble, anonymous common women in *The Dream of a Common Language*. "Heroines" begins with the attention-grabbing adjectives *exceptional* and *deviant*. The poem tells of women who were forbidden to vote and forbidden to speak in public, yet, it is implied, they resisted the sanctions, rules, and laws designed to keep them in their places. Troubling the poet and possibly the reader is the fact that, until recent decades, throughout the United States women were considered the chattels of their husbands after marriage: a woman became legally dead when she married hence she couldn't leave her property to anyone except her own children or male relatives (*WP* 34). Did you know, the speaker continues, that if she were to run away, the wife could be hunted down and forced to return home like a slave (*WP* 34)?

Strangely, in the South, Rich says, white women of the upper classes formerly could inherit slaves although they were powerless to liberate them (*WP* 33): in earlier centuries, a woman's position may have been closer to that of a slave's than we realize. But as if to keep the southern woman from uniting in common cause with African Americans, the *she* was brainwashed into thinking that light arrived in Africa "with white power": in other words, there was no civilization or religion in Africa before the whites came, she was taught, and Indians live in barbarous conditions and engage in pagan animal worship (*WP* 34).

Addressing the southern woman, this poem's subject, Rich compares her mind with a raging fire, so if she starts to protest, a great gust of freedom will flow with her words (*WP* 35). The irregular, split lines—a new pattern in her poetry—emphasize the newness of their speech, taking up the transformative image of fire as agent of change, showing how "a great gust of freedom" affects the lines metrically, rhythmically, and conceptually, as it has affected the poet and these heroines.

The heroines' words are not purely or perfectly enunciated: they still express themselves in the broken language of an incomplete vision (*WP* 35). Are these lines a tacit apology to anyone who may be offended by anything that might seem rude or uncouth? Perhaps. Still she reveres these early feminists: how to resist falling in love with their passionate lucidity, she asks, and how might a poet render a suitable offering to them and draw courage from their example (*WP* 35)?

Finally, *A Wild Patience Has Taken Me This Far: Poems 1978–1981* continues her explorations of the fertile ground of the love poem. "The Images" speaks of a woman returning home hungry for images to tell you that her hunger is so ancient, so elemental that all the disappeared, crumbled, smashed, burned, shattered, painted over, or defaced faces in history should arise so as to re-collect and re-member themselves as she pulls herself back together in their presence (*WP* 5).

Here and throughout the book in more proselike poetry, she is reexperiencing "The Spirit of Place," her lyric "I" in this locus, fathoming the meaning and uses of power, and in "Culture and Anarchy" (whose title comes from Matthew Arnold's work of criticism by that name), the strongest reasons for women's suffrage shows: the most compelling argument for allowing women to avail themselves of any and all professions in order to entitle them to develop all their forces of body and mind is the unique individual responsibility of their own lives and solitude (*WP* 14).

Women's personal sources, resources, and origins are at issue in contemporary cultural paroxysms, and these are the foci in a later book of poetry, *Sources* (1983), where Rich explores her own sense of a personal destiny even as she pursues new dialogues with formative figures in her development, her father and her husband. Next, she reaffirms the spiritual core of her work: "and here I write the words, in their fullness: *powerful; womanly*" (*SO* 35). These two words, *powerful* and *womanly,* have seldom been linked together in the English language, but they will be riveted together from now on.

Similar concerns and strategies structure and inform the prose collection *Your Native Land, Your Life* (1986), reclaiming her native land, America, reexamining the concept of nationhood; here Rich traverses the poetic field or nation of her life and homeland. This and other contemporary works exposing her views on nationhood are fully assessed in their relation to other earlier and later works in the Rich canon in the next chapter.

Chapter 7

A New Relationship to the Universe

The Fact of a Doorframe, another compilation of Adrienne Rich's poetry, largely repeats *Poems: Selected and New, 1950–1974,* with a few additions such as selections from *The Dream of a Common Language, A Wild Patience Has Taken Me This Far,* and six poems from 1982–1983. The pivotal, title poem, "The Fact of a Doorframe," (one that appears earlier in *Poems: Selected and New, 1950–1974*), returns to the door imagery introduced earlier in "Prospective Immigrants Please Note," where passage from one nation to another is explored. Significantly, Rich has so named this new edition of her collected poems *The Fact of a Doorframe* because it is a step into a new stage in her poetry. Her poetry will now exist in the new nation, one where women and their sexuality are free and equal. "The Fact of a Doorframe" also chronicles a central rite of passage for Rich: it symbolizes her entry into the new life she has dreamed of for so long, what she calls in *Of Woman Born* "a new relationship to the universe" (*OWB* 286). It represents something concrete and material to the one who crosses over the threshold: that the doorframe exists means one has a sure grip on reality when one ventures outside convention or tradition. The speaker in the poem is silently pressing or banging her forehead against the doorframe, like a Jew at the Wailing Wall: this motion is one of the oldest motions of suffering (*FD* iv), and it denotes liberated women's pain at choosing the road less followed, evoking the classic suffering of women from time immemorial.

Such suffering, also poignantly embodied in Miriam Makeba's courage-song for warriors, is the subject of the first stanza of "The Fact of a Doorframe," which concludes with the observation that music simply amplifies suffering (*FD* iv)—and as Rich shows, poetry is a purer form of suffering, too. Indeed, this raw new vision of what poetry could be, a cry that might make a difference in the universe, might ease real suffering or end it. The subtext here is that this poem, too, may heal and/or inspire its readers with passion and courage, as Makeba's warrior-songs do. Like a doorway, it marks a transition, an opportunity to move forward. Rich conveys a compelling vision in her work of nonfiction on the male appropriation and control of motherhood in *Of Woman Born:*

> We need to imagine a world in which every woman is the presiding genius of her own body. In such a world women will truly create new life, bring forth not only children (if and as we choose) but the visions, and the thinking, necessary to sustain, console, and alter human existence—a new relationship to the universe. Sexuality, politics, intelligence, power, motherhood, work, community, intimacy will develop new meanings; thinking itself will be transformed. (*OWB* 285–86)

She defines her mission in radiant prose that articulates the foundation of the field of women's studies. As such, *Of Woman Born* carves out for itself a far larger domain than could be covered here: it examines the reverence for and fear of women in ancient matriarchies and the history of relationships between the sexes as it affects or pertains to the institution of motherhood today.

In the second stanza of "The Fact of a Doorframe," Rich engages the Grimms' dark and perplexing tale "The Goose Girl," where in the fairy tale the head of a girl's favorite mare utters to her, "*If she could see thee now, thy mother's heart would break*" (*FD* iv). Seen one way, this is merely an admonition to the girl. Seen another way, these lines might be the poet's way of giving voice to a criticism from the past, possibly a criticism of the lesbian lifestyle or the strident protests against the Vietnam War. Her own mother would likely never acknowledge the socially radical, unacceptable aspects of her nature. Anger or passion directed at anyone may have been impermissible in her family because of the rules of decorum, but "Reforming the Crystal" laments that the woman the lyric "I" "needed" to call her mother had been "silenced" as a girl; thus, she had not been able to develop a normal mother-daughter relationship with her mother because she had been taught that the husband fully controlled a woman's activities, and she existed to please him first (*FD* 205).

Another of Rich's contributions to research and knowledge has been the field of women's studies, a field that explores the "unity and resonance of our physicality, the corporeal ground of our intelligence." Rich's position as breaker of conventions and silences necessitates that she put meaning, action, and all female subjects where the silences were.

While in "The Fact of a Doorframe" painful recrimination and guilt prevail, in crossing that doorframe the goose girl is made aware that she has transgressed, violated a moral law, passed a point of no return, as evidenced by the words of Falada, the dead mare of the tale. In fact the daughterly "I" feels sorry for herself at the same time that she resents the fact of her mother's silencing. This is one of the only poems where Rich mentions a mother intimately.

Now that her poetry is expressing so much that was hidden before, the textual "I" addresses the subject of her mother, breaking with convention, crossing through the doorways to express her truths. Just as her mother constituted an absence or erasure for the daughter, the poet, many other women of her generation, and later ones, have felt motherless. Even though her mother was in the home, Rich likely spent her girlhood being groomed by her father to live up to his dreams for the son he never had. Looking back, she may have realized there was a blank where her mother should have been: she has been writing on that absence ever since.[1] These poems are acts of liberation from all that constrained her in her natal home and final breaks with convention.

Rich's vitality and tone of intimacy return in the final stanza of "The Fact of a Doorframe" (*FD* 1), when she advocates a new order of poetry that is violent, arcane, and common because it meets primal needs and addresses basic instincts.

Marking a new departure from the old poetry that turns to painting and music for its aesthetic models, this new poetry of raw, naked power is carved of the commonest living material or substance—wood—because it signifies the passage from one nation to the other, a passage from the patriarchy to feminist nationhood where men and women are equal. Of course, it is itself a doorway that the lyric "I" grasps to sustain her physically, emotionally, politically, and spiritually as the poet enters new terrain. It appears that others have come through before since the doorframe's splinters are bloodstained. Still, it has "a certain old, unrelenting dignity, burning out from the grain." William Carlos Williams's famous directive on writing is called *In the American Grain,* and the "burning out from the grain" is a radical theoretical play on the concepts in "In the American Grain" because it makes a subtle claim for Rich's inclusion in the main line of American poetry, and it is burning, hence, transforming and transgressive. A doorframe that burns out from the grain during an earthquake is one that opens onto an upheaval both in the private life and in collective consciousness. As in 1972, in "Burning Oneself Out," this poetry inscribes a burning that devours all in its path until everything in life has nourished that fire (*DW* 47). She vows to tell the truth about the experience of women's lives and communities—their nationhood. In the searingly angry poem "Translations" from *Diving,* Rich says compellingly that woman's every grief is a grief she holds in common with other women, unnecessary at the same time as it is political (*DW* 41).

SOURCES

If *A Wild Patience Has Taken Me This Far* was a search for heroines and forebears, an exploration of a new place akin to that she inhabits in "From an Old House in America," a search for rootedness or grounding in American soil—physical and poetic—permeates the book *Your Native Land, Your Life,* published in 1986. The important poem "Sources," first published separately in 1983, is full of a private examination of the meanings of integrity and a poet's integrity in the world. A more private voice speaks in "Sources." A long poem dedicated to an old friend, Helen Smelser, "Sources" is imbued with a courageous spirit of steely calm, of refusal to compromise, evoked in "Turning the Wheel" where she begs future feminist sisters, the women of the twenty-first century, to regard feminist trailblazers with pity and mercy, noting where they failed themselves and to see them three-dimensionally, as part of the past: almost like a corrective lens, she suggests they should use the first generation of the late twentieth-century women's movement for guidance (*FD* 307–8). This inspirational tone breathes through the second section of "Sources": the speaker affirms that whatever has helped her in transitions, sharp corners, or hard decisions in the past already resided inside her and had been part of her character and mind from the beginning.

What we need we need not seek outside since the divine lies "stored" within us. In her heart, "[o]ld things, diffuse, unnamed, lie strong" (*YNL* 4). Intensifying this point, she repeats in bald intensity that this is the source of her strength, even when her strength seems to desert her or when it reverses itself and attacks her (*YNL* 4).

At one level, "Sources" is a search for the origins of her poetic strength and personal character—her poetic origins as well as the origin of her conviction of feminist nationhood. In imagination she returns both to Maryland where she was raised and to the New England of her college and early married years, with the steadfast, Bible-believing residents of the stingiest space in America (*YNL* 11). The New England forebears attract her attention in this spiritual, ontological quest for identity and roots. The transhistorical American lyric "I" is drawn to speak of the supplanting of the native peoples, too, as an evil consequence of the arrival of her ancestors—and those of so many other immigrants to America.

"Sources" is an intriguing dialogue between various female speakers, between the wise woman and the intellectual inquirer, representing a return to places she has inhabited, either in life or in imagination—to Vermont where she was 16 years earlier and, later in the poem, to her homeland, Maryland. The third section begins with a questing inquiry from this inner voice where her sources are (*YNL* 5). In the reply to its question of *where,* the speaker introduces a concept important to Rich, the fact of her being split at the root, that she will struggle with for several years (*YNL* 5):

the lyric "I" feels hypocritical since she is split at the root as a southern Jewish lesbian, one closer to the traditions of the South, although no less Jewish.

Anger rouses against her parents, especially her father, for raising her outside the synagogue, but in the fantasy world of stories and books, in a princess's isolation. Like the African Americans fired on in 1968 in Irasburg (*YNL* 102), her family was isolated from other Jews since her father had virtually denied his Jewish ancestry. (Later in this book, in "Yom Kippur 1984," she asks whether one could define a Jew in solitude [*YNL* 79].)

"Sources" is the poet/daughter's passage through her anger at a father into a connectedness to national identity, whether it be identity in a feminist, Marxist, lesbian community or in a freer, more ethical America where injustices are redressed and all are equal. She expresses her anger at her father for raising a daughter who was self-divided or split at the root, unable to feel native anywhere. The essay "Split at the Root," published in *Blood, Bread, and Poetry* (1986), testifies to all the ways her upbringing made her feel an impostor, a "white-skinned social christian," a Jew who passed for a Christian, "Neither Jew nor gentile." Hence, her lack of spiritual roots in traditional organized religion and her sense of living perpetually in what Paul Claudel called *"the shadow that is formed in the absence of God."*[2]

Articulating the crucial questions that determine one's selection of female identity and unique female subjectivity, section 4 begins by the speaker's asking who "your" (her) lot is cast with and what is the source of her strength, essential questions anyone on the road to individuality must answer. This exploration of sources has as its purpose the search of one's own identity, past and present, not to show how she was victimized, but to help the lyric "I" and each of us take responsibility for our own identities so that we can use our citizenship, lives, and our solitude most constructively.

Most important, candidly and lucidly, she now refers to the fact that she must answer the question of where her strength comes from to establish where she is coming from and where she is going, confiding that all her poetry treats this issue of her sources (*YNL* 6). This formidable statement appears printed on the cover of *Your Native Land, Your Life,* as a statement of purpose. The book's impetus is both her own exploration of her native land and the reader's as well: it is an attempt to ask readers to consider their affiliations—ethnic, religious, sexual—seriously:

> In these poems I have been trying to speak from, and of, and to, my country. To speak a different claim from those staked by the patriots of the sword; to speak of the land itself, the cities, and of the imaginations that have dwelt here, at risk, unfree, assaulted, erased. I believe more than ever that the search for justice and compassion is the great wellspring for poetry in our time, throughout the world, though the theme of despair has been canonized in this century. I draw strength

from the traditions of all those who, with every reason to despair, have refused to do so.[3]

She inquires of each reader, essentially, Who are your family and friends?, as if to prompt awareness that America is in a time of transition, and all may be forced to choose between an old and new order. One must also identify the sources of one's own strength, so as to own it. But beware of blurring the questions, Who are your kindred? and What are the sources of your strength?, she directs the reader, since they are discrete questions. One concerns itself with *"a whom"* and the other with *"a where,"* but one cannot trust that the where has substance since the young grab whatever they can hold onto to go up and become themselves (*YNL* 6). At first, as individuals establishing our maturity we find those with whom we believe our lot is cast—as she found other southern aristocrats, then other Jews, married and embraced Jewish and New England intellectual traditions. Finding sources of strength from within is the transition each of us makes at maturity, when we come to know our own integrity. Rich speaks in her clearest and most open lyric "I" yet as a poet witnessing to the development of a true integrity, a selfhood transcending sex, gender, and ethnic origins, although it is rooted in all three.

Here she reclaims the sense of poetic mission that directed her poetic vocation: the fact that she had not starved to death in Europe in the Holocaust meant she had a particular purpose for her life, she thought (*YNL* 6). Later, the survivor "I" writes that the Jews she has felt kinship with are those who were incinerated, like Anne Frank and her family, those who died in the concentration camps of World War II; the lyric "I" claims blood ties and commonality with those killed in the gas chambers. It is impossible to say whether or not Rich claimed this affinity or identity with them in defiance of her father, who said they were not her kindred and she should be a citizen of the world.

He had abandoned his faith and people and thought she should, too, so he raised his daughters to be rootless "social christians." But it was not in her nature to live a lie nor could she perpetuate the masquerade after the Holocaust. Of course, she believed she was a chosen person, even though today such a belief is antiquated belief, maybe even preposterous, to have a conviction of one's destiny (*YNL* 7). Believing this may be a characteristic of those born to rank, wealth, or privilege (*YNL* 7), but what drives the speaker *her* on is her faith in the oppressed, abused, and marginalized, faith that their lives were not in vain, not merely a series of injustices, hurts, and harms (*YNL* 17). They have faith that they can transcend all their obstacles, the immigrant's faith in the future, faith that animated all who came to America seeking a better future for their children. This return to roots, this return both to her family home and ethos, resolves itself in a final, after-death spiritual confrontation with her father, a sort of exorcism of his domination of her upbringing and youth. The speaker now is an arrogant, silent, inwardly frantic little girl who has been cornered by an adult "I" in punishment but whose pride demands she will not cry; the child is ambushed and frightened, angry yet stubborn, unyielding. This child knew she was different from others, brighter, born to a different future than that her father may have envisaged for her.

Now she conceives of herself as the firstborn daughter picked by her father to be raised as a son, and who later came to believe she must supplant her father, must "take what he taught her and use it against him" (*YNL* 9). The angry lines in section 7 flow into prose as they express intensity of feeling:

> After your death I met you again as the face of patriarchy, could name at last precisely the principle you embodied...identify the suffering you caused, hate you righteously as part of a system, the kingdom of the fathers. I saw the power and arrogance of the male as your true watermark; I did not see beneath it the suffering of the Jew, the alien stamp you bore. (*YNL* 9)

For Rich and her family, his convictions, manner, and dictatorial style had caused undue suffering, and the growing poet watched her father construct his own castle in air, for himself alone, and what she called his "rootless ideology" (*YNL* 8).

Isolated from his forebears and family, the reclusive Arnold Rich might have seemed to her in retrospect both poignant and pathetic, yet looking back on that time later, she read his suffering and, through accepting it, stopped denying her own (*YNL* 9).

Growing up, she may have had less sympathy for what she conceived of as his dishonesty and may have failed to see how alien and alone he must have felt, hiding it from her deliberately. Only in decoding his suffering can she deny none of her own (*YNL* 9). To maintain his sense of dignity and authority in his household he never let his daughters see his softer side: like many self-made men of his generation, he wanted only to be viewed as successful while those around him may have desired a more personal relationship. Yet not only did her father's selfhood seem false—perhaps a purloined identity—the very land her neighbors' homesteads and farms are built on is, she claims in section 10. Guilt and anxiety stem from these perceptions (Who is to blame? Is she?), and she tries to imagine the lives and perspectives of those who are not her kin: instead they are Yankee Puritans or Quebec Catholics (*YNL* 13). These lines imply that these farmers to whom the speaker is unrelated are the ones responsible; and she must imagine a lust to take others' land, stemming from their needing to dwell on land and other periodic occurrences. Their passion was ferocious and unconditional, leaving the Native Americans no quarter, and the fact that the growing season is shorter there than elsewhere is not an excuse to take others' land (*YNL* 13). The speaker describes their greedy passion for the land and farms, a desire she calls, in section 10, white with death and righteousness (*YNL* 12). Here the word *white* connotes the white WASP usurpers, fields white with harvest, and passionate white-hot anger of the lyric "I." This intense white-hot imagery also resonates with an integrity central to her poetic credo and sense of a national identity that reflects both lives of the dispossessed and her own sense of being split at the root.

In section 13, the narrator goes back and scrutinizes the family home, most hazardous to one's emotional health (*YNL* 15). Here, because the speaker may have been persecuted and verbally abused here, she finds articulation in speech wrested from the walls like dog whips, and once again she feels like the arrogant child being punished who thinks she will never betray herself, her fear, and panic (*YNL* 15).

Still, ironically, this poem "Sources" is an effort to let the father know how much she revered and owed him, albeit posthumously, and how she transformed herself in opposition to him to live according to her own premises, as Emily Dickinson had. As the lyric "I" says in section 10, those who know best how to torture are those who have been tortured, so if now she appears to persecute him, she is complicit in the blame and the cycle of persecution. In that acknowledgment, she is doing what Vendler said she could not do—share a personal connection with the victim who later victimizes others. This speaker is convinced that if her father is guilty, so is she; this poem reveals it.

In section 14, she asks, if my anger transforms itself into a bomb that blows up the home, is that actually betrayal (*YNL* 16)? Is it her right to slice off a side of the house that was always closed to prying eyes during her childhood there, so that visible from the street outside are their stairs, just as anyone might have seen houses bombed open and staircases torn away in photographs of World War II. Through this bombing, she again expresses her kinship with the incinerated Jews. She will expose her house, however, so that the closets, once full of clothes, now stand naked in the poem. She conjures up where the old grandmother had been sleeping in full view of the street. Equally visible is the library where the stern father paces, strictly demanding repeatedly that the child apply herself to her studies (*YNL* 16). It would seem that the lyric "I" herself is that child who worked more zealously than anyone ever has. The problem is that once the speaker began to see homes sliced open like this, she perceives them like that everywhere. Blasting through walls to reveal the family's inner secrets, she can only see into the hidden heart of the family, seeing its secret coercions and parental domination and manipulations. The speaker witnesses a family knot or trap like the one she writes of in "In the Wake of Home" where whoever is attempting to get out of this household has to fire on the field and reduce the premises down, she says, playing on the double meaning of *premises*, as assumptions and values, and as places (*YNL* 56).

This is clearly what the lyric "I" must do to rid herself violently of the domination of her father and of the past. In section 7, she had begun, by asserting that she had quarreled with him for years and with his mixed love and brutality, his premises and theories (*YNL* 9). This long poem is not just a complaint or a rant: it is a coming-to-terms with a rigid, loved, respected father, whom she left for a husband who, in his way, ironically may have been very like her father (*YNL* 19).

Metaphorically speaking, Rich may have married her husband because she felt liberated and empowered against her father, possibly even exhilaratingly rebellious, when she chose "the other Jew. The one you [her father] most feared, the one from the *shtetl,*... from the wrong part of history, the wrong accent, the wrong class, who explained you to me for years, who could not explain himself" (*YNL* 19). However she later discovered that her husband could not explain himself any more than her father could. She may have been rebelling against her father and his airy castle built to hold her captive, his daughter, his perfect creation, the brilliant poet; breaking away, she may have thought at first that she was reclaiming her lost roots and identity; but she was marrying a man more like her father than she realized, one who explained him to her for years. Her father had redeeming qualities certainly: he had recognized her talent and driven her genius, forced her to work, polishing her intellectual talents as one would polish a diamond. But in his own words, he had made her a citizen of the world.

In this poem she explores and explodes the myth that she was acting independently in marrying. She had not wanted to write this poem because, as she says to him in the next prose section of "Sources," section 22, she had wanted to let her father abide in death in others' minds in their own way (*YNL* 25). She chose not to project her own feelings upon him in death the way other writers still alive, possibly like Robert Lowell, for instance, do in their poetry (*YNL* 25). For 12 or 13 years, she had bravely refrained from writing about her husband, protecting her family's memories of him, wishing not to indulge in maudlin public grief at the family's expense. But now she returns to these former homes of her heart and articulates the connection to exorcise the ghosts, the influences, of the two men who helped shape the first half of her life.

In section 20, she had admitted she was puzzled about her sense of mission here—how it happened to fall on her shoulders, nor can anyone explain how former boundaries of perfection ignite, leaving her cheekbone smoking (*YNL* 23). Escaped from the war zone of the family, the speaker can only relate her epic tale. It is significant, though, that her cheekbones are gray, both with smoke and with grim dedication to life's purpose. How she got it is unknown—divine fiat?—but her dedication, devotion to it, and hard work are beyond question. All the enigmatic lyric "I" can do is explain her sources prosaically, explaining that she was raised in a literary home where utopias were discussed (*YNL* 23). Later, a "desert absolute" grabs her that fuels her sense of mission. This absolute impels her, and her will's roots force her into another area of choices (*YNL* 23). Danger imbues this entire sequence, and the challenge is to fulfill the mission by telling the truth about her father and their life.

In *Of Woman Born,* she meditates on the impetus to begin building a more harmonious, woman-friendly world:

> Radical feminism is about transforming all relationships and about the creation of a human society in which human needs are met, and in which there is no exploitation of one group of human beings by another, beginning with women. (*OWB* 229)

This might serve as a definition of the feminism Rich espoused at this time, along with the following:

> [F]eminism—woman's consciousness—ultimately has to break down that dichotomy [between masculine power and feminine powerlessness]. Once you stop splitting inner and outer, you have to stop splitting all these other dichotomies,... Yourself—other, head-body, psyche-politics, them—us. The good society would be one in which those divisions would be broken down, and there was much more flow back and forth. (*ARP1* 119)

Power would be shared more equally, effortlessly. Power need not be a male hegemony. Because women's power has been supplanted and partially "silenced" in modern times, women today:

> have a mission to survive... and to be whole people. I believe that this can save the world, but I don't think that women have a mission to clean up after men's messes. I think we have to save the world by doing it for ourselves—for all women—I don't mean some narrow, restricted notion of who women are, only white women or only middle-class women and only Western women. (*OWB* 232)

It is her mission to ensure that women's communities and a woman-friendly world benefit all people (not just women) of every race, class, ideology, religion, and nation and that every woman can be a citizen of the world. But since to build this utopia she must leave behind, physically and psychologically, the old world, she writes this poem to bid farewell to two men who controlled her early world, her father and husband. In seeing how alike they are, she also sees reasons to pity and love each of them. The lyric "I" speaks words of consolation to her dead husband, telling him he need not have felt so alone. Refusing to feel guilt about his suicide, she speaks to his aloneness at death. Alluding to nineteenth-century women writers like the Brontës who sewed their novels or small packets of poems together with thread, she writes of this effort at communication with the dead: here is the daughter's last present for the father, an odd parcel threaded with rage and love (*YNL* 25).

Ironically, she believes he died because he could not envision a purer, better world in which he had a place, yet in a final prose section she conjectures that no one becoming accountable as an independent person needs to be as alone as he was; there must have been others with whom he might have sat down and wept and still be deemed a warrior (*YNL* 25). In his generation, it was not masculine to weep, although the Jews wept by the rivers of Babylon, and in ancient Greece men wept. Still, she assures him, referring again to her mission, heroes and heroines who want to alter history and achieve suffering's demise shall have to create a place for ourselves in the future.

Returning after 16 years of pain to this homeland, she writes the poem that will release her from the past and ultimately enable her to leave Maryland behind. The last section opens with her recalling reading Gilbert White's *Natural History* and knowing she shall never be as familiar with this land as he was with his part of England. Her bookish upbringing almost precluded such close and detailed knowledge since he chose to learn and know another dimension of life. She grew up sensing her split because paradoxically, *he* was faithful despite his lack of *a faith.* All the stark paradoxes of her life are subsumed or implied here.

Counterbalancing the old existence in an airy kingdom is the lyric "I" 's new solidly established life purpose as a lesbian/feminist poet. Rhythmically echoing Walt Whitman in a return to the peace and the placid existence of the animals in his lines, "*I wish I could go and live awhile with the animals / They are so peaceful and serene,*" here Rich imagines a similar pastoral world after the pressures and anger of her growing up in the final prose section:

> I have wished I could rest among the beautiful and common weeds I can name: both here and in other tracts of the globe. But there is no finite knowing, no such rest. Innocent birds, deserts, morning-glories point to choices.... When I speak of the end of suffering I don't mean anesthesia. I mean knowing the world, and my place in it, not in order to stare with bitterness or detachment, but as a powerful and womanly series of choices: and here I write the words, in their fullness: powerful; womanly. (*YNL* 27)

Releasing the past, the speaker is able to find a stasis, if not rest, in the knowledge that places, things, and people can be known and out of these she can reconstitute her world. This is an alternative to the castle in air, an independent world of and for those who seek an end to suffering and desire to change the laws of history (*YNL* 25). In a utopian quest lacking a Messiah, a heroic quest lacking a hero, she envisions a world where war did not mar every century, where upper classes do not keep lower classes in bondage, and where everyone has equal access to power. The keywords are "powerful" and "womanly" since previously these words have never before been integrally linked.

In this world, former injustices would be rectified, and no one need live in fear, poverty, or disease. Each woman would have power over her own body, mind, and spirit. At this point Adrienne Rich and a few others are the virtual voice of women's studies, at the vanguard of the women's movement. Within the decade, the Equal Rights Amendment will make its rounds for ratification, and a woman will run for vice president. In the heady climate of optimism motivating women everywhere to achieve higher personal and professional goals, Rich speaks up, the spokeswoman of the women's movement; this is the one role Rich chooses to play in American political and cultural life.

HER NATIVE LAND

A tone of defensiveness can occasionally permeate these poems in open form, poems that are part prose and part poetry, full of references to her North American native land. Just as "Sources" examined her place of origin and the part of her that is native and responsible for what happens in America, in *Your Native Land, Your Life,* she equates her native land with her life and her mission. She is more polemical and driven here, perhaps because she realizes that it is imperative to convey the news that poetry conveys; there is a clarity that traditional or Modernist critics find off-putting, deeming the poems too prosaic and allegorical.[4] Yet what she is about is capturing the American language, articulating the American subject on American premises: like Dickinson, she prefers to have it out on her own premises and state her claim as an American poet. In "A Communal Poetry" she quotes Native America writer Leslie Marmon Silko's "vision of an American poetic diction" as expressed in her letter to the American poet James Wright:

> When I say "American" language I mean it in the widest sense—with the expansiveness of spirit which the great land and many peoples allow. No need ever to have limited it to so few sensibilities, so few visions of what there might be in the world. (*WF* 179–80)

Henceforth, Rich's poetic diction will also embrace this expanded notion of American poetic diction just as the body of her new poems will inscribe the body of America. Yet she is not alone in this enterprise; women's dawning feminist consciousness engendered a new movement in poetry, amounting to a collective revolution in diction, form, style, message, and content:

> It was in the women's poetry and publishing movement that I—and, I think, many others—began to perceive something about the language we were writing in.... For the first time I understood that my poetic language wasn't "English,"... it was

> American, though I had no full sense of what that might mean except that my voice belonged here. (*WF* 179)

She adopts the real language actually spoken in America, constructs more neologisms, and uses slang and profanity or merely quotes others' words to invite their actual lines into her poetry.

In the 1980s, Adrienne Rich receives even more national recognition as a popular poet who speaks to the mass consciousness, drawing huge (sometimes exclusively female) audiences, but she is less celebrated by former admirers who gave her access to the elite inner circle of "the best" American poets. She is no longer a poet's poet. "In my case," she wrote, when I

> published... a book of poems which was informed by any conscious sexual politics, I was told, in print, that this work was "bitter," "personal," that I had sacrificed the sweetly flowing measures of my earlier books for a ragged line and a coarsened voice. It took a long time not to hear those voices internally whenever I picked up my pen.[5]

From this moment on, Rich is valued instead for her expression of political consciousness in poetry as much as she is for her competence as a poet.

She wishes to speak to and for the American people. Hence, her tone of direct address in the new poetry: from now on, her work, though not oversimplified, is less imagistically complex; she speaks urgently to all readers of American poetry, all open-minded people worldwide. It is as though Rich writes from a deeper, stronger conviction that poetry keeps us all alive, that poems matter. In 1986, she publishes *What Is Found There,* a book deriving its title from its epigraph:

> *It is difficult*
> *to get the news from poems*
> *yet men [and women] die miserably every day*
> *for lack*
> *of what is found there.*[6]

These lines by William Carlos Williams are like a talisman embodying her personal mission from this time forward: however difficult it is to glean the news—what's applicable to one's own life—from poems, readers must try hard since the lives they save may be their own.

What strikes one in this book, *Your Native Land, Your Life,* is the way Rich employs imagery to explore her own emerging identity as an American poet rooted in the land. Some imagery derives naturally from creatures in the wild: the fox imagery has persisted down the years throughout her poetry, an image of instinctual wild female self-preservation. In "For an Occupant," for instance, the speaker's first question is, if the fox spoke to the occupant (*YNL* 63).

And in "Sources," the fox reappears near the start, as if to greet her again upon her return to Vermont. Although the fox of 16 years earlier is certainly now dead, still this fox is more akin to the totem animal of Native American and other traditions, a kind of spirit guide to accompany her on her vision quest.

Giving authority to her work are the images of the unity of women and images for the process of making poetry, as in "Blue Rock" and "Poetry I," "Poetry II," and "Poetry III"; from various perspectives Rich traces her own developmental process as a poet ("Education of a Novelist"). She is concerned with the nature and aesthetics of poetry here and now, as explored, for instance, in "North American Time." Finally, in this book there is more direct address to the reader, as if Rich wants to lift the living words right off the page and send them as news to the reader. The identity of the reader has rapport with her own identity and provokes a need to contact the reader, make her think, feel, bring her to awareness: it as if an older sister were speaking to a younger sister. Together, both form a "we," a free, no-fire zone where intimacies can be shared.

Along with Rich's conviction that poetry has bearing on history and is political comes an intense desire to make the poetry reflect her life and its premises more and more faithfully. The poet frees herself to be more open in poetry. She moves to a freer town, a California beach town, choosing the more ecologically aware west coast of America: she moves from her home on the east coast to Santa Cruz, where she has lived with the Caribbean poet, novelist, and essayist Michelle Cliff since 1984.

Whether she aimed to or not, Rich became a role model and exemplar to a great many common women, as well as an unofficial spokeswoman for alternative political causes affecting the place of poetry in America, lesbian/feminist and gay rights along with new ventures in publishing. Her activities increase on behalf of women's publishing collectives and other women poets who have not yet enjoyed the success she has. Still, privately she is drawn to ask in the poetry, *Who am I?* In *Voices and Visions,* Helen Vendler argues:

> It is true, as Stephen Gould Axelrod has argued, that [Robert] Lowell in a sense had fulfilled a prophecy of Emerson's that the poet in America would come to value authentic seeing over "skill of experience and command of language," would "[traverse] the whole scale of experience" and "tell us how it was with him," and that this was an affirmation in art of democratic individualism, each man's experience being all men.[7]

Vendler comments similarly on what Rich is doing in her late poetry—transforming Emerson's dictum into the feminine mode: Adrienne Rich is now fulfilling Emerson's prophecy and mission for the American poet, telling us how it is with *her,* telling us who the American woman is, giving herself in a local habitation with a name. She affirms and relates in her poetry to the whole scale of woman's experience, making *woman* as universal a term as the generic *man*. Indeed, she herself had excluded her in the early poems. She does value "authentic seeing" over " 'skill or experience.' " Most important, if Robert Lowell fulfills that prophecy in his generation, speaking largely for all men, Rich fulfills it for all women for the 1980s, 1990s, and later, knowing it is time a poet spoke to and for women and men alike.

As in "Sources," many poems in *Your Native Land, Your Life* are ontological in thrust. In their attempt to tell the reader how it is with her, she searches through her background as an American—Jewish, upper-class southern, eastern intellectual, with its emphasis on work as the American means of salvation—to find the meaning of her life and her mission in poetry. Democratically, in her Whitmanlike cataloging of female selves, subject positions, she traverses a cross section of American female experience, developing a sense of the American woman's and her particular brand of integrity, owning female subjectivity in life and in poetry.

Resisting the tyranny of reason and logic in poetry, she occasionally employs the French surrealist technique of stating a proposition or fact and its contradiction, one right after the other (in the manner of avant garde filmmakers of the 1960s like Godard or Buñuel). For example, at the end of the first section in "In the Wake of Home," she concludes, after advancing an idyllic vision of a child's being watched at night by adoring parents, both that this occurs nightly and next that it never occurs (*YNL* 56). This contradiction partakes of mysteries of childhood: we can never fathom when we are older what actually happened in our earliest years. Were our parents adoring or not? Dreams take us in either direction and contradict themselves.

Her mother exists now only as a disembodied voice in memory: her mother's voice, formerly summoning her home, has now merged with the wind and has swirled down new streets (*YNL* 57). This is hardly a consoling image of nurturing motherhood: the poet follows this image of void, abandonment, and loss with conjectures about what happened to that voice, cataloging how many people have been left unparented for a wide range of reasons as a result of war (*YNL* 57).

In this work about the homelessness of lost children, the children who live without real homes, she creates the possibility that there may be a place, a small intimate place, where the mother's and children's language is the only language (*YNL* 59), where women and children can take shelter and can speak the mother tongue without fear of reprisal. In this small, heavenly oasis whoever they were promised would be there are there, the family lives its life there (*YNL* 59). Since this is the image of the idyllic, old-fashioned family, it is tempting to think this is how it was for everyone (*YNL* 59). But this isn't true. The next section may shock the reader into awareness that modern America is the continent of homelessness and child labor or slavery, a country she perceives as too uncaring about its homeless, hungry children: It is a continent of children seized, forced by adults and sometimes murdered by their own mothers to keep them from being taken (*YNL* 59–60), anticipating Toni Morrison's *Beloved*. Here, too, Rich alludes to the old Apache practice of killing children who might otherwise have been captured and raised white. "Yours," she insists, speaking to Americans, is a land of racial mixes and ethnic melding, undocumented workers, refugees from diasporas: it is a continent that invented underground railroads and trails of tears (*YNL* 60). Linking the Cherokee trail of tears, Jewish diasporas, and the African-American underground railroad and Mexican-American undocumented refugees, the lyric "I" forges an identification among the dispossessed, lost, and homeless, all those whom many have despaired of saving when the list of those endangered is already long. The ending addresses the plight of everyone who feels alienated from his or her family of origin: the lyric "I" asks what you might say if she told you that the family albums misrepresent family life. Each of us may feel we are different because our families may not have been idyllic, but we need not believe the propaganda. And if I tell you that, the speaker continues, if that comforts you, why (*YNL* 60)? Does it absolve a guilty conscience or any sense of being different?

The questions ending the eleventh section sum up the meaning of the poem, How might children in sorrow and loss console themselves (*YNL* 60)? The rest of the book probes similar challenging philosophical questions she continues to answer in poetry.

Championing these voiceless women and children moves her—and has moved a number of readers—to pity and terror. Another poem speaking to the related problem, one of incest and sexual molestation of children, is "Virginia 1906" (*YNL* 41–43), where the refrain, uttered by the girl molested before the age of five and continually repeated, is that for years she has been numb (*YNL* 42).

The epigraph for "Dreams Before Waking" translates from the Spanish of Nancy Morejón, "*Hasta tu país cambió. Lo has cambiado tú mismo.*" [Even your country has changed. You yourself have changed it. (That is, You have changed your country yourself by changing yourself.)] (*YNL* 44), a line that expresses the element of personal change necessary in a revolutionary time, the need for change within each individual corresponding to the national change without. Her difficult line used as an epigraph implies that because our country is in the midst of an all-pervading cultural, social, even perhaps political revolution, each individual must change so as to enable the revolution to occur; and, by extension, ultimately for the individual to change, with change in the individual, the country must and will change. What is needed across cultures transnationally, to take another of her titles, is the intrinsic spiritual will to change.

Another epigraph from Eli Wiesel advances the notion that "*Despair is the question*"—a question that demands an answer. Despair—and its opposite, hope—motivate Rich's move from East to West, to a milder climate suitable to her health. This poem, like several others in this collection, exists in the philosophical realm of the unconscious, between waking and sleeping, the place where literally anything is possible. At this moment, the speaker assesses herself and where she wants to live, allowing the reader a private insight into her self-appraisal. If she stays here, she can still just afford the rent and tell herself it's the old neighborhood. But that is an illusion: in truth it isn't (*YNL* 45); and where she lives now, despite being the same space, is transformed into somewhere unlike itself as it lacks a view of the sunset. Like any other person considering whether or not to make a major move from coast to coast, the lyric "I" addresses the fear felt by women generally: on her door in New York are four locks, and she has her pride, savings, respectability, but also a "strangely querulous body, suffering" and some mysterious unknown urban illnesses (*YNL* 45–46). Having reached this doubtful eminence in the poem, the lyric "I" asserts, you think if you refuse to dwell on despair you will get through to death as though it were a matter of willpower (*YNL* 45–46). This sounds like a morale-boosting pep talk anyone tied to an apartment and facing old age in New York might give oneself, almost by way of avoiding self-pity, despair, and the other temptations of loneliness and old age. Her arthritic body she refers to chivalrously as being *querulous* and *suffering* since a chronic condition has rendered her disabled with a crippled foot and rheumatoid arthritis. But living courageously and intelligently despite the temptation to despair seems wiser, more mature, and more imaginative at 54, so the textual "I" considers the benefits of moving to a place where people were more optimistic about the human capacity for change than those in the American Northeast. Any number of factors may have participated in the decision. What might it be like to live in a sunnier, more idealistic place (*YNL* 46)?

These lines reminiscent of Nancy Morejón's epigraph were written during the Reagan and first Bush administrations, in a time when the gap between rich and poor was widening and some individual rights of Americans (like their First Amendment rights) were being eroded; it is a time when many liberals were tempted to despair. Still, as Rich says in *What is Found There, "Despair . . . is, like war, the failure of imagination"* (*WF* 17). There is never an excuse to give up. The final lines afford the lyric "I" courage and a dynamic sense of potential, asking what anyone might ask oneself, *How would it feel to start all over again at midlife in a new place* (*YNL* 46)?

Personal growth toward hope is a dominant concern in these midlife poems where she adopts a more mature subject position and is making crucial decisions for the second half of her life, the unmapped and strange future. Rich explores within her life and in the domain of the poem whether it is possible to live into old age free of despair; but her emphasis is not on the therapeutic dimension of self-expression (she deplores the confessional poem that tells all, vapidly venting feelings), but the fact that a poem can inscribe, bear witness to, and motivate change. This poem can be transformative for both the poet and the reader—and for women in general.

If this outlook abides in many poems, a more negative, fugitive consciousness dwells in others. In "North American Time," one of the best poems in the book, she writes candidly and pessimistically about the dangers of being a writer who publishes self-revelatory poetry: she warns that whatever we write can be used against the poet or against the poet's loved ones because poetry stands inside history (*YNL* 33). Poetry cannot stand outside history but must resonate with it. Poetry joins revolutions as yet unborn when it is written down: its spirit anticipates them. In a 1994 interview with Matthew Rothschild, Rich said more positively of the power of poetry:

> When you think about almost any other country, any other culture, it's been taken for granted that poets would take part in the government, that their being poets was part of why they would be sent... as ambassadors by the State proudly, that their being poets was part of why they were considered valuable citizens—Yeats in Ireland, Neruda in Chile, St.-John Perse in France. At the same time, poets like Hikmet in Turkey, Mandelstam in the Soviet Union, Ritsos in Greece, hundreds of others, have been severely penalized for a single poem. But here it's the censorship of "who wants to listen to you, anyway?" (*B* 32)

Of course this censorship is outrageous to Rich. And seeing it, she may feel impelled to protest.

But since Rich's dual mission, as declared in "Sources," is both to find "an end to suffering" (perhaps prompted by Nadine Gordimer's thought that no one knows where the end of suffering may begin) and "to change the laws of history," the way her words may be twisted cannot stop her from speaking them loud and clear since of course poems are liberated once published. She pursues this line of thought in "North American Time": even though we move on past the place we were when the poem was created, our words are fixed in time and come to mean more than intended (*YNL* 33). In an interview with Bill Moyers in *The Language of Life*, she relates telling her students to let go of every poem they publish. In addition, any poet must have faith that the poem is one's best, most truthful, creation and will survive, not in "a totally mutilated form either."[8]

Although 20 years before, in "Snapshots," she had written archly of time's masculinity, here time is the dynamic continuum of present moments of consciousness. As she says in section 3, it is impossible to pretend your time is unimportant and our thoughts merely wander (*YNL* 34). No one lacks purpose, nor is the imagination given us for no reason, she contends: we are all accountable both for the life of our tribes, for our country, and the global breath (*YNL* 34)—the earth's ecosystems, the atmosphere and all that human life impacts. Hence, Rich is a patriot out of integrity and responsibility rather than for any sentimental or for any more conventional reason.

Because one is a poet, one has to have knowledge of many topics, a host of disparate things, about the earth and one's country (*YNL* 34–35). This is:

> [b]ecause I think that the truth of art allows us to take a microcosm, a tiny thing like one woman braiding another woman's hair, and let it stand for so much else. But the artist needs to know a great deal more than she or he is necessarily going to put into the work of art. The artist needs to have reflected on things that may not go into that poem. There's a work of constant reflection on one's own consciousness and on the conditions of life that surround the words and images that go on the page.[9]

In section 6, she addresses a sister poet and tells those who have been persecuted and assassinated for political reasons that words "stand in a time of their own" (*YNL* 35).

The end of *Your Native Land, Your Life* is devoted to "Contradictions: Tracking Poems," where she tracks her own inner dialogue and growth in consciousness as she did in "Sources." First establishing that we live within a mass of paradoxes, the textual "I" shows how contradictory yet necessary it is to identify our bodies and our native lands, the life they share: our task must be to connect our own personal pain with the world's serenely, since others want to obliterate the body's world (*YNL* 100). She affirms her existence, her pain as a disabled poet suffering, an aging Jewish lesbian split at the root, and says that a muse is not what she has wanted, only an understanding reader (*YNL* 102). Intimately the lyric "I" addresses an unknown "you," possibly the understanding readers, urging them to remember the difference between the body's and the world's pain. The ultimate aim of this poem is to inspire the reader "by whom I could not be mistaken" to observe the "edges that blur" (*YNL* 111) since "I was talking about trying to connect, as I said in those days, 'the war in Viet Nam and the lovers' bed.' "[10] E. M. Forster said, "*Only connect*"; although Rich states that the body's pain and the streets' pain are different, one can learn from "the edges that blur": there may be some overlap between an individual's pain and urban pain, homelessness, and the suffering of the poor. Blurred edges, like abridged principles, tell a story, show us where to watch what's happening. "You"—her reader (s) and audience—must discern where they blur and create meaning for your own life, where you can create change yourself (*YNL* 111).

In this book, she writes more candidly as a private person able to connect the pain of her own body and that of the "body's world,"—or the world's body?—the larger worlds of the women's movement, and the exciting world of feminist poetry in the Bay Area. One of the few good contemporary poets who are well-known, even famous, Rich attends women's poetry readings both to encourage young writers to develop a voice and to connect with them as well as to stay in touch. This book tracks a strong development in her dialogue between that ideal reader and the lyric "I" as wise woman, mentor, or teacher.

TIME'S POWER: "LOVE'S NOT TIME'S FOOL"

Time's Power, published in 1989, bears witness to the power of time and love. The title comes from William Shakespeare's Sonnet 116 about the eternal nature of love, the sonnet beginning *"Let me not to the marriage of true minds admit impediments."* This sonnet plays with the eternal nature of love in that it doesn't bow to "Time's Power," and the subject of this book is eternal love, *"the marriage of true minds."*

Four kinds of love are abiding focuses in *Time's Power*—first, the love of family, specifically, her love for her mother and sons; second, the love of what is sacred; third, Rich's love for anonymous silent women worldwide ("One Life," *T* 43)—for common women who may have no access to education or freedom from predestined grueling work, her love of the women's causes she has espoused and her commitment to a mission transcending the span of her own life; and fourth, her love of her own generation and peers, members of her class at Radcliffe and others, so much challenged by being born at a crossroads in history, some now passing away. She asks provocatively what it means to know you are part of a generation that must die (*T* 29). Because many of her poetry-writing peers are old, have died, or are terminally ill—most of her feminist peers are dead—Rich may feel alone among poets of this generation in her prescient consciousness of mortality, a consciousness many more were to come to share after 9/11/01.

Here the lines are split, as they have been since certain poems in *The Dream of a Common Language*, with a pause reminiscent of Dickinson's dash. They are even more fractured—sometimes each broken into three segments, splitting each line in successively lower thirds: to represent the fracturing of reality itself, the poet breaks the laws of form in order to change the world. The breathless lines seem to suggest she is speaking before it is too late, and time's sinister power prevails.

Since the mother is the first woman in her daughter's life, the girl/mother relationship is the basis for future female-to-female relationships. A girl's mother is often her revered model for womanhood, but revolutionary daughters may also hate their mothers or grandmothers, whom they think have not measured up as women. Rich's relationship with her mother was not close, perhaps because her mother had been "socialized into the norms of patriarchal society," hence as was common in the 1930s and 1940s, she assumed "responsibility... for socializing her daughter into these norms, male-definitions, superseding the primary female connection of the pre-Oedipal bond, causing a disruption of female continuity."[11] In memory, the mother is hated virulently as a laborer in the fields of the enemy. It is thus ironic that we hear of Rich's mother first classically as "a woman mourned by daughters," an image of Niobe of ancient Greece.

Her mother partially shaped her character as much through her weakness as through force of character: she became the martinet charged with teaching her daughter manners and proper behavior. The mother collaborated with her father in this rigid socialization; hence both were figures of mistrust. Since any personal anger must be transformed before it can enter Rich's poetry, her mother appears as a presence against whom she rebels genteelly in "Solfeggietto" (*T* 3–5). According to the note, this word means a *"little study"* and is *"a term used by composers as the title of a keyboard piece" (ARP* 131). The poem is addressed to her mother, yet her mother's name or initials do not appear in it. What had been "[y]our windfall at fifteen," her Steinway grand piano—this line reminiscent rhythmically of Diderot's comment in "Snapshots," "You all die at fifteen"—became her daughter's birthright, and *curse,* since this mother and daughter battled over the music lessons taught by the mother throughout the daughter's childhood (*T* 3–5). Rich was forced to do hours of practice while she had no talent or love for the piano, which became their fateful exhaustion and common "mystery" (*T* 4). Here the use of the word *mystery* instead of the more predictable *misery* opens a perspective on their relationship's mystery.

Because her mother's early life had been devoted to music and she had been a composer manqué, her daughter's very small hands were placed on the keys, wired to the keys in hopes that she would succeed as a pianist, too. The child was propped up on a large book to encounter this world of black and white keys, already knowing she would be given no choice in the matter of whether she would have music lessons. The reader can only sympathize with the child coerced beyond the limits of normal discipline, as many girls were in this epoch.

Obviously, the mother who loved music did this to inspire discipline and dedication in her offspring; but as children who are forced often do, Rich came to hate what she was made to practice. It is clear from the poem that she delighted in hearing her mother play, and some of these scenes of evening music enjoyed by all the family evoke Joyce's descriptions of music on Dublin evenings or Lawrence's poem "Piano," where he describes watching his mother play and feeling close to her as a child. He speaks of the irretrievability of the past: the adult speaker now desires to re-enter the past—a Freudian might say, to re-enter the womb. But neither Joyce nor Lawrence describes having been forced to play. The source of the conflict here is a *common mystery,* Rich writes; playing on the double meanings of *common,* the daughter struggles with the strange notations (*T* 4). In these conflicted split lines, the splitting of the relationship is rendered in the poetry. Their being together at the piano is hardly joyous because her wrists and her mother's voice are strained (*T* 4) The slow line, full of pauses where the pain breaks through, displays the hardships of a failure to teach because the mother could not teach her daughter the magic of music (*T* 4), but this is the story of a mother's forcing the child to go against her own grain, to play against her will.

Why, the poet now wonders, *Why?* The dramatic interior monologue, sometimes hesitating, sometimes moving swiftly, like a varied piano composition, ends by asking the questions the mother answered, the probing rational questions the young child couldn't ask if she thought she would be a virtuoso. More important, Why did we need to fight? Did she think I had musical talent (*T* 5)? The girl's experience in this poem reflects a common experience of children forced senselessly to endure long hours of practice without any explanation. Is this child abuse? No one would have thought it in those days, and it was a common practice through the 1940s, 1950s, and 1960s—and even today.

Some parents seek too hard to mold their children into their image of perfection. As the hiatuses and pauses illustrate mother's unconscious tyranny here, stressed in many broken lines, so the poem bears witness to her poetic double's sense of failure as a pianist herself. A mother who had taught at a girls' school and been complimented by the great musicians of the day might have made a successful career in music rather than retiring upon marrying to raise her children as the genteel custom dictated for middle- and upper-class wives. No hint of blame suffuses these lines, only a sense of the futility of all this. All that endures is the child's questions and trials with the strange notations, the disappointment at not being allowed to love music her own way, learn it her own way "by ear and heart." Poetry was the language to which she was so much better adapted naturally.

This frustrating experience, inducing some self-doubt, remains with the daughter speaker (*T* 5). This resonates a brave note of the confessional mixed with irony—that the poet could not "speak" her own mother's "mother tongue" explains much about how patriarchal culture separates woman from woman. It also explains much about the poet herself. This poem is unique in its courage in revealing her own areas of vulnerability. You may think me extraordinarily accomplished and more learned than you will ever be, she is saying to the reader, but truly music is a language I can't read, despite my mother's efforts (*T* 5). A poet who has translated poetry from more than eight languages here admits defeat before another's native language; her humility is disarming and surprising, yet it is also a natural refreshing humility of grown daughter before her mother.

Cosmopolitan and well read, Rich can never be pretentious or vague. The fact that this five-part poem took four years to write testifies to the depth of emotions it plumbs without sentimentality. "Solfeggietto" is an original poem in the female tradition since it concentrates purely on the interaction between two generations of women, thus illuminating a subject near to many women's experience not yet depicted in literature.

A more common love, anticipated but not often encountered directly in her poetry, is one's love for one's children. Some of the personae may have been taught as children, as girls of her generation often were, that one should not say anything at all if one cannot say something polite. Publicly Rich has not been known for having a nurturing, motherly presence with children: she is a poet addressing herself for the most part to grown women. But in this book the poem "Living Memory" addresses the way an author can unite her love of the things of this world and her love of stories with her love of her children and friends by mingling everything together in a story. In other words, her love of tales and old roads empowers her love of family because she combines both loves in the reading of the story: the mother opens a book of fairy tales she knew "by heart" and finds the sentences slightly transformed from what she remembers (*T* 46). The poet illustrates subtly that her memory was not perfect, even though she thought she knew the stories by heart before opening the book.

Like the poems of *Diving into the Wreck,* this poem casts a glance into the diachronic world of the past, history redolent with tales. Equating traveling old roads into memories with reading and remembering well-loved tales, the speaker explores how one sometimes remembers the paragraphs, phrasings, and words of a story accurately just as the traveler does or does not remember places accurately. In a poem seeking to distance readers from material reality and draw them into the story, myth, or a tale, she manipulates the imagery successfully.

"Living Memory" is reminiscent of Frost's "Directive," whose speaker returns to a world in the past to reclaim a chalice, an image of the Holy Grail. Half-humorously, Frost leads the reader back to this place of regeneration and refreshment, where the adventurer finds the Holy Grail. Here in the Rich poem, on the other hand, the focus is more on the wholehearted joy of telling stories of childhood or of familiar places, less on the development of a controlling lyric "I" who may be simply playing with the reader or leading her or him astray. Rich is in earnest about the joy of relating memories as the activity becomes storytelling at its best. Now that the past is purged of its haunting presences, she can enjoy it, "Chapter and verse" (*T* 46). Rarely has Rich written warm lines suffused with love for the children's trust in entering into the past like entering stories just as one would enter and move into a home.

In "Living Memory," certainly the horrors still exist in real life: the immigrants having come as others did, Puritans, Catholics, Scots Irish, Quebeçois, they came, Jews following Yankees. They believe all the myths, but mostly the myth that land saves us and that nature frees us, even though they were neither pioneering nor ingenious (*T* 47). The American Dream was a delusion from the start, this poem implies. These American myths that attracted the pioneers to their lives in our native land are false since the true pioneers are those who first took possession of the land and planted crops here, doing backbreaking work. She would like to write the stories and memories of those now gone, who first cultivated the land, the first pioneers, actually able and resourceful (*T* 47).

Their stories are still untold since their lives were too full of hard work to write. Even worse, there are the local tragedies marring the Danville area: one woman's clavicle was smashed, presumably by a family member, inside her tidy "white clapboard house with an apple tree"—this old place is hardly idyllic. The poem tells of another woman escaping barefooted over the stubble. Those of all races have hoped to found their families in America's farmlands and find freedom, but America has not saved many, Gentile and Jew. In fact, the country has burst many hearts (*T* 47). Clearly Rich's vision of the American Dream is anti-romantic, anti-ideological, yet it seeks to render actual life in a small town. The poem culminates in a beautiful mythic tale, coincidentally about a mother and her three sons who become human again when their mother says their names (*T* 48). Ending by stressing there is no one single legend, the poet suggests that each of us is free to choose a life legend from all the legends, and that legend can become one's individual "story" but stories cannot be dictated. Recollecting the legend means re-gathering together, as in "Diving into the Wreck," what has been lost, restoring parts of our souls, minds, history, and psyches, and reconstituting the world. We must constantly keep reinterpreting, reinventing the legends and definitions as we grow and learn more over the course of our lives: no one legend speaks to every age. The past exists in an eternal mythic present we navigate daily, yearly, seeing new turns in the road.

Throughout Rich illustrates the link between the past in multiple dimensions and the present. The last stanza of this aptly named rhythmical poem, "Living Memory," begins with a vision of the eternal in the ordinary, in what is present before our eyes every day: the view is of a picture of her taken just after her birth, and one can see there the same road where she saw meteors one August as a girl or young woman, the road looking rougher and ironically older than it does now (*T* 50). What we take for granted as always being there, a local road where we might go to see the Perseid meteors in August, can be viewed as eternal, somehow both different and the same, when seen through the lens of a camera the year you were born and compared with its smoother gentle plane of maturity.

In the final lines of "Dreamwood" she comes to a similar spiritual conclusion. A woman who should be typing a late report but instead goes into a dream contemplating the landscape: the dreaming woman wants to join the material world and the dream worlds (*T* 35). This is the place where the edges blur and we see into imaginative truth, apart from observed reality.

The dream and the material can and should join since we realize that poetry, while different from revolution, makes us aware of it and affords us knowledge of why it must come (*T* 35). Poetry shows us why revolution must come. And like the poet's typing stand, poetry is useful, durable, being here now. Hence, poetry is a material necessity, not a luxury. In this time when violence attracts too many, and the young can be prejudiced against poetry, Rich has something compelling to say about a revolution in the way we as a culture see women, revolution, and poetry.

Since Rich sees herself as one who represents or speaks for the silenced or those whose work has forced them into a silence, she writes in "The Desert as Garden of Paradise" about silenced common women: she describes the ways the Spanish padres envisioned building a garden of paradise for Christ in what one, Padre Miguel Venegas, privately called "*a land the most unfortunate / ungrateful and miserable of this world*" (*T* 28–29). Rich imagines the similarity between unlikely survivors, some women, and drought-resistant plants: "both have had to get accustomed to thirst and lack of nourishment or water; each would prefer not to be so well acquainted with deprivation" (*T* 27).

Each has had to get along with less and less in an arid spiritual climate. She writes ruefully to and for all survivors of oppression and conscious neglect, wondering how it would feel, what it would mean, to think one could not remedy or throw off the slavery one was born into, effectively evoking the situation of the slaves before the Civil War (*T* 29–30). Common sense and the tone of the poem may lead to the assumption that that the lyric "I" was not born to such circumstances, nor was anyone in her neighborhood who was white and middle class, but even white, middle-class women did grow up with an ideology of lack of entitlement in the 1940s, 1950s, and 1960s; and not all women were the apples of their father's eyes. Some of every race, class, and gender grew up fatherless and unconsciously neglected, if not actively oppressed; despite being born into the richest country on earth, they grew up believing they were of little value in their families or towns. Those condemned to slavish existences in Third World countries, in child labor or forced labor in America, Asia, or Europe, and throughout the world, are born into the despair of endless oppression. The knee jerk assumption is to conclude the poet is talking about those of the brown, black, and red races, but here Rich's native elegance and discretion saves the poem from directly implying that as many similar poems by her contemporaries and successors would. Her compassionate embrace of those who cannot speak for themselves stems from a perception of the sacred qualities in the suffering of the poor, hence this book defines the sacred: the sacred is named, moves in an eyeflash, holds still in a circle of a valley that was once fertile and blooming. What's sacred, the divine or sacred, inhabits twigbark or thorn and is "a green ghost" or life force "inhabiting" all nature. It is the principle of life; what Dylan Thomas before had called *"The force that through the green fuse drives the flower"* is the same divine force that *"drives my green age."*[12] As the next stanza continues, what's sacred is singular (*T* 31). The fact about the sacred is that it makes an effort once again, constantly, eternally, ineluctably. It is the perpetual divine force that moves forever throughout the universe—the power of God.

Like the name of God or Yahweh, what's sacred cannot be named, moves instantaneously, cannot be pinned down or may not translate directly into words, as life springs forth unheralded and unexpected from apparently lifeless sticks.

A contemplation of the sacred enters into the poetry in an important way that has significance for her oeuvre. She states that a poet's job is "to examine the wreck of perspective," distortions in our own perspective, and see how what's sacred "tries itself" (playing on the double meanings of, first, making an attempt for itself and second, trying *itself*) once more (*T* 31). Earlier in "The Desert" the spiritual "I" confesses she does not pray frequently but occasionally prays to music or a sunset (*T* 26). This revelation discloses her private spiritual connection with the sacred in nature and to God, who to her mind is neither male nor female.

In "6/21," the "I" invokes the summer solstice's ancient pagan meaning as a time of increase in the life force for primitive peoples, a time when they awaken spiritually to the light within as the outer light will gradually abate and the days will get shorter from here on. The "I" enjoins the reader to appreciate the longest day as this is the best day and sunniest of the year and for us (*T* 33). This light has found an alphabet, a way of writing only for us and a mouth to talk to us. Spirituality and a groping toward God will come to take on a greater and greater role in her later poetry, and we shall return to it in successive chapters.

WOMEN FIGHTING WARS

Time's Power engages intriguing question about love and work as love made visible—seeing the ways different cultures have tried to create a paradise in the desert. The life force is there in the desert (read: wasteland of modern American culture), Rich says, even though the land may look dead and desolate; there is no reason to despair. "Letters in the Family" is a poem seemingly addressed to the unspoken question, Why do we never hear of women heroes in wartime? Each letter—one from the Spanish Civil War, one from Yugoslavia during World War II, and a final one from South Africa in 1986—tells the firsthand story of a courageous women living her principles in a fight for justice; in each a young woman writes home to tell of her life on the front. "Rochelle," involved in the Spanish

Civil War in 1936, writes poignantly to her parents; another is an unmarried traveler with bad grades in Spanish (*T* 22). Ironically, despite this fact, she is the one who travels in the poem to Latin America to become a revolutionary. This rebel daughter may be the poet's poetic alter ego: she, too, was the unblessed daughter and is now a poet/warrior fighting for justice and equal treatment of all humanity.

The last and saddest letter is from a woman fighting for freedom in South Africa, addressed to her children, whom she cannot tell about her activities, for their own safety. These women whose stories are rarely told in history books, victims of the "wreck of perspective," are the women who matter in history; theirs are names of the lost, Rich implies. But in "Turning," a major poem in the book, she affirms that the persistence of the common woman's everyday efforts will effect a change and achieve the "slow turn of consciousness" (*T* 53). The ordinary woman's goal is to abandon her own superstitions, then to help others do so, and then to experience her own authenticity (*T* 53).

The struggle contains all work you may not live to complete, but work you cannot pass up. Here the metaphor of swimming against the current invokes the salmon struggling upstream to mate—symbolic of the necessity of keeping active to perpetuate the movement. In the next part, she explains the joy of perceiving her lover sitting across the room attending to a public meeting. They hear a speaker address the subject of Semites, Israel, displacement, deracination (*T* 54); but what the speaker is describing on a political level comes to have private ramifications on a personal level for the poet: shame, coercion, women trying to talk with other women, their minds gradually changing. The subject is changing, however slowly it happens; minds do change and a "mutual recognition" surprises everyone involved (*T* 54).

Enduring love is built on this "mutual recognition." This allusion to women's causes and communication reveals a quiet revolution in women's lives going on in this era, springs from a love of all women that the poet cannot directly express in words, only in untiring action. They are swimming against the current (here she echoes a phrase from Virginia Woolf's journals, "*writing against the current*"), since theirs is a subversive, underground movement whose members are not safe from pursuit, persecution, or ridicule.

In the final part of "Turning" the speaker addresses what throughout the book is called "the sacred." Addressing the sacred, what has been tracking us for so long, the lyric "I" merely thought that "you" did not judge "us," not that you were "on our side." "You" may be God here, or what Alice Walker calls "*Spirit*" or the spiritual dimension of life, experienced as a cell might hallucinate God under a microscope (*T* 54), so she regards "you" who may be mindfulness, beyond all barriers or green lines (*T* 54).

The nonjudgmental cosmic eye of God observing us spiritually is "Unnameable by choice" as is the case in Judaism; God's name cannot be spoken or even known. And if God is "Unnameable" the spiritual "I" asks, Why, then, do I try to read "your" name in open space, "illegible" sky (*T* 54)?

Now a fully realized roofwalker, a prophet of women's surprising changes and global change, the female subject feels the breath of change in the air; she even feels a desire to name God and write God's name in the air.

Adrienne Rich's role as a poet has been evolving from the depiction of an individual subject position to a more collective, spiritual one: a unique spiritual search now informs her poetry. Her characters are embodiments of activists who have fought for political or personal freedom, all people of good will, all who have stood up for others in mutual recognition, and all who have tried to read the name of the "Unnameable by choice." Drawing on the energy and support of women's collectives, she enjoys an intimate sense both of who she is and who her readers are, an even stronger motif in the next book. Having crossed the doorframe, inhabited the old house in America, and claimed her identity as a common American woman, she is now rooted more securely in the changing national consciousness and speaks to and for all Americans: as early as 1958, when asked by *The New Yorker,* Rich declined the offer of a "'first reading' arrangement [because she] desire[s]...not only to write a new kind of poetry, but also to reach a different audience." By now her audience and poetry are radically transformed. The composite of selves and subject positions informs her concepts of spirituality and community, sharing the common language of American mass culture (*T* 36). Communicating with an intimate hearer, she ends the book with the haunting question, Why am I trying to read God's name in "illegible air" (*T* 54)?

Chapter 8

Here Is a Map of Our Country

What is most important for a poet/revolutionary? A guidebook for the revolution and for correct social change, of course. That is what Rich supplies in *An Atlas of the Difficult World,* a survey of its terrain. The subject positions here are more neutral and cosmic, more aloof, yet paradoxically she speaks in direct address to the reader, who is challenged, given an identity, and discussed. An atlas embraces the spiritual contiguity of states of the American continent and shows the reader where those countries that dominate our dreams and nightmares are. If *Your Native Land, Your Life* and *Time's Power* explained and explored the dimensions of the sacred, a personal sacred geography of her native land, in *Atlas* and *Dark Fields of the Republic,* Rich further defines the responsibilities of American citizens. *Dark Fields* examines the varieties of patriotism possible to the American facing the future even as she defines the great universal constants in human life—love, community, history, and solitude versus loneliness.

AN ATLAS OF THE DIFFICULT WORLD

This is an atlas composed of pieces of our lives (*A* 57), a metaphor for pieces of land, instead of maps of countries, starting with Soledad, the poet's second favorite place, moral solitude; or, as it is defined in the first line of section X, "*Soledad* = f. *Solitude, loneliness, homesickness; lonely retreat*" (*A* 20), and Soledad also became the epithet of George Jackson; hence it evokes George Jackson, Soledad brother.

Loneliness addresses the reader at the beginning of the book "on this earth, in this life, as I read your story, you're lonely." "You" are alone in a bar, or fishing with your best friend, and his wife, and your wife (*A* 19). Plainly *Atlas* is address to a male at least as much as a female audience.

If Americans have sometimes been a violent people, they have also been a lonely people. "I wonder if this is a white man's madness," the lyric "I" asks. Is loneliness woven into the fabric of North American culture because of the white man's vision of Manifest Destiny and its dominance in the settling of North America? Are Americans lonely because they were mad enough to usurp land belonging to the Native Americans illegally? She counters this in lines echoing Whitman, addressing either the white man or the victim of his madness: "*I honor your truth and refuse to leave it at that*" (*A* 19). But this is not entirely so. This atlas is a kind of underground manual, composed of quotations from George Jackson, the Soledad Brother, brief mysterious references to the lives of pioneer women, some well-known and some obscure. Here she personifies *La Nuestra Senora de la Soledad* as the enigmatic essential spirit of the North American continent, "the difficult world" under white man's domination, and investigates how to navigate this difficult world if one is neither white, nor male. "*La Nuestra Senora de la Soledad*" presents a perfect image for Catholicism's domination of the Indians: the fathers' gravestones weigh down the Native American craftsmen (*A* 20).

The lyric "I" speaks for America, now nearly wholly abandoned by those who see. The poem is addressed to those who are aware that America must re-find a national direction, a nationhood, and guide the country forward. The oracular poet, writing in the tradition of Emerson, has a mission to show the nation its direction in difficult times when minority voices and dissenters are simply not given the credence they deserve.

Yet she is under no illusion that her guidance will be either read or heeded. The crone speaker here is crippled, sixty. She drives the great grades of North America from "sea level to high desert" and feels "a century" slipping off her shoulders—one hundred years younger in an instant (*A* 41). Still, wisdom or "knowledge" has invaded her connective tissue and ground her cartilage into sea sand (*A* 41). The visionary speaker cannot sleep, however, since each midnight she is awake seeing youth, not wandering outside in moonlight; the lyric "I" sees them in her mind's eye searching "armed streets" for peace and an end to "degradation" (*A* 41).

This female speaker's search for the end of humiliation can be found in "An Atlas of the Difficult World," a visit to "the Difficult World," places where a page of history may be ripped out of conventional history books. The poem traces a long ruminative progress of the transhistorical American soul through the Rockies and California deserts, with a quick detour in Section VI to Ireland of the potato famine and the IRA, then to the New York subways, and the Grand Canyon; all are parts of this difficult, sometimes alien world Americans inhabit at the end of the twentieth century. This is a world where women and men have suffered and died hopelessly, a world that is in places homophobic, misogynist; hence her style is reminiscent of the long oracular lines of Whitman and Ginsberg. The lyric "I" is mournful, personal, or bitter, even more private, more anguished, and guarded in direct address. A potato exploding in the oven triggers the memory of the Irish Potato Famine, as well as poets who survived ironically, and the starving passengers on ships to America, one of whom was Annie Sullivan, soon to be a great teacher, with her hoard of poetry, half-blind in the workhouse, enthralling fellow children on the ship (*A* 15).

Here Rich treats both the starving Irish feeling the potato famine and Annie Sullivan, the genius who saves the life of the blind, mute, deaf American heroine Helen Keller, teaching her speech and writing; Sullivan was as a child an inmate in a workhouse before she was educated and came to teach Helen. She had been kept alive on poetry, nursed on "lore" or poetry brought by her father, who dreamed his gift for verse might make him rich and famous in America (*A* 15). For the most part, though the poetic Irish starved to death in huge numbers, and few of the British were aware of this, shed tears, or sent food until it was almost too late.

Of course, the Irish have always united poetry and politics. Yet American poets today neither starve nor have the courage to challenge the American status quo. Section II begins with a map of America's salt-covered "Sea of Indifference" (is the salt evocative of idealists' tears?). In another declarative sentence, Rich presents the "haunted river" whose water is undrinkable (*A* 6). Its style reminiscent of William Blake, the map includes every major feature of the United States: clearly allegorical, a kind of Pilgrim's Progress across America, the political lyric "I" spies missile sites in desert cornrows along with the "cemetery of democracy where those impoverished persons who died for democracy lie, and nearby the suburbs of acquiescence, whence silence is rising in fumes" (*A* 6). The long declarative lines, also reminiscent of *Howl,* invoke the prophetic authority of Ginsberg. But, as she indicates to an interlocutor and fellow seeker for America, this is really neither an atlas nor a map but a mural, signifying and portraying the levels of the poet's and citizens' patriotic responsibility. This slippage from cartography to public art betrays the fact that Rich's map of America is a map of its history of silent pain and dishonor: in question here is our perspective, where we see from. The "I" wants to reveal a map, but the reader protests that it's a "mural." So it is, the political "I" concedes (*A* 6). Demanding that the reader take into account where we see it from, Rich challenges the reader to be aware of his or her perspective on democracy and on the republic. This book implies that it's best to see America from a revisionary historical perspective, a map of pain shows the sites of anguished loss, the burials of unwritten dreams.

Speaking in a 1994 interview with Matthew Rothschild about it, Rich describes her political and spiritual purpose in *An Atlas of the Difficult*

World and the ways the book shows where we are—or should be?—socially and politically positioned:

> To a certain extent in *Atlas,* I was trying to talk about the location, the privileges, the complexity of loving my country and hating the ways our national interest is being defined for us. In... *What is Found There,* I've been coming out as a poet, a poet who is a citizen, a citizen who is a poet. How do those two identities come together in a country with the particular traditions and attitudes regarding poetry that ours has? (*B* 15)

Both books show her coming out as an American poet and responsible citizen; they reveal her "refusal to separate love from action and her understanding of power deeply influence[s] her poetic practice,"[1] and here as elsewhere in her poetry, action can be defined as poetic action since for her the pen has always been a powerful instrument of change. She refuses to participate in degradation—to use people or sell ideas as commodities—repudiating commercialism. Instead love stirs her into dynamic poetic action, which may in turn move readers into action since poetry must reverberate to the movements of history. This poet has fully internalized the message of Marie Curie's life, expressed in "Power," noting that her power created her fatal sores, the wounds she ultimately died of (*DC* 3), hence she is a scientific martyr.

Three motifs in imagery figure in *Atlas*: first, the spiritual solitude of the reformer in a difficult world; second, sacred places and objects, including a "Tattered Kaddish"; and third, her revolutionary patriotism—or *matriotism?*—the investigation of "the location, the privileges, the complexity of loving my country and hating the ways our national interest is being defined for us."[2] Together with the development of these themes and images is a bolder use of the address to her readership, her inclusion of "you," her audience, in the body of the poem: for example, the poem is for the reader skimming a poem late at night when she is meant to be traveling home (*A* 25). Is this reader an urban professional or simply an office worker? The point of this line from "(Dedications)" is her intuitive spiritual connection with the envisioned reader to whom she writes, the intimate Other, her "*semblable, soeur,*" a silent, perhaps lonely listener, another inhabitant of the planet.

The poem's litany of lines all start identically, psalmicly; "*I know you are reading this poem... because*" (*A* 25); it addresses a range of potential readers, from a mother reading while holding a baby to those more desperate, possibly in prison: "*I know you are reading this poem because there is nothing left to read,*" there where you are stranded, stripped (*A* 26). The "you" enters most of the poems here, the lines are far longer, not split, the style reminiscent of Allen Ginsberg's in "Kaddish" and "Howl." They trumpet forth a visionary directive to all America and make the reader complicit in the work of the country's conscious redemption: though the poetry is somewhat abstract, clearly the message is restoration of America to a freer nationhood where the lost out and marginalized poor might be re-enfranchised.

Loneliness is integral to the American psyche—both for the individual American, the poet, and many individual readers of poetry. Of course, here the word "Soledad" also incorporates a reference to George Jackson, "Soledad Brother," whose *Prison Letters* served as an inspiration to the Black Panthers. The title poem, "An Atlas of the Difficult World," includes 13 sections, and 37 notes in the second Norton Critical Edition (*ARP* 142–58). In section 10, the Soledad Brother takes center stage: this section shows his origins and growth as political thinker; it is about political and private acts of oppression and antidotes to oppression. Interspersed between passages from his letters are poem sequences on his self-education in prison: a young man schools himself, argues debates, trains, lectures to himself, and masters English, Swahili, and Spanish. He also reads and writes letters home and to fellow revolutionaries. He finds that in a "college" of force he has to struggle with bitterness, of course, as well as all forms of hatred and sexual anger. In a line beautifully resonant with S alliteration, the lyric he/I states that he serves "Seven of these years in solitary. Soledad" (*A* 21). Of course irony and serendipity inhere in the fact that *Soledad* means *solitary* in Spanish, hence his is appropriate behavior for the lonely place.

The poem lionizes Jackson and reverses the occasionally stereotypical thinking of unreflective middle class Americans—reversing the supposition that Black militants are always ignorant and violent. It also challenges the assumptions that a man's killing or beating his wife in rage is just something men do or that poor children should have to go to school without food. In the first section, a teacher of elementary-school children is aware that some of her charges have come to school with no breakfast, and she recalls the Black Panthers "spooning cereal" into small mouths (*A* 4).

One reason a reflective, philosophical poet may feel lonely in America is the fact that the divisions between people and divisions of labor in this segregated republic may be widening, not narrowing. America needs citizens who could "repair the rifts," but those who could unite others in a more democratic society and regenerate the country are at a premium now; they are in danger in this segregated republic because they are frequently thrown into prison; hence they often cannot persuade people or weigh arguments even though they are urgently needed for the work of perception and the work of the poet. The speaker and thinker "who also listens," a rare person, this eternal, as yet unbegun work of repair cannot be completed without them, yet the speaker wonders, "Where are they now?" (*A* 11). Is Rich commenting here on the defection of protesters, the absence of those who were hippies two decades ago, but who have vanished now?

Naturally the female lyric "I" is lonely, saddened because she does not think there will be enough workers to reform American society. In the next section, section V, of "Atlas" she exhorts the reader rhythmically and uncharacteristically enthusiastically to catch if you can your country's moment (*A* 12). Start at the point Appomattox or Wounded Knee, Los Alamos, Selma, the last airlift from Saigon, anywhere grave injustices have been perpetrated (*A* 12). At what moment did democracy die? When was our country's moment?, the lyric "I" inquires. The revisionist "I" prefers rewriting the future to telling the past, though.

To get the country back on track, find the moments the country is ashamed of and try to "catch" and free America, this unbound land, and save these (formerly rebel?) states "without a cause" (*A* 12). Catch the moments of dishonor where the country's ideals have been compromised. Rectify those.

America, with its agribusiness empires and multiculturalism has been called "THE SALAD BOWL OF THE WORLD" (*A* 3): the mixture of races here is likened to the host of ingredients in a varied salad bowl. Because they are composed of so many different backgrounds, ethnic, racial, and religious, not even all speaking the same language, Americans can have a hard time communicating with each other. Alluding to Chinese immigrants in San Francisco, she writes that when the light swirls off Angel Island or Alcatraz and the bays leap in the light, when at the moment of sunset over the San Francisco bridges, pay attention because still there "old ghosts crouch hoarsely whispering" under "Gold Mountain" (*A* 13), the Chinese term for America. In other words, *gold* here connotes both money and the shade of light at sunset, so Rich is writing not just in admiration of San Francisco, one of the most beautiful cities in the world, but also to comment on the American Dream as it has influenced the Chinese.

The lure of the golden sunset reflected on Golden Gate Bridge in San Francisco creates the stunning gold imagery in these lines. "Gold Mountain" embodies the dreams of wealth in America of immigrant Chinese in the nineteenth century; even with the beauty of the bays leaping into golden life, "old ghosts" still crouch "hoarsely whispering" that the land was not in fact all the Chinese immigrants had dreamed of. Throughout, Rich stresses ways immigrants from every nation who came expecting to find freedom, gold, and justice were unfulfilled. True revolutionary Americans of both genders could change that now, reversing the disappointment so many faced in earlier centuries.

But the Chinese are not the only ethnic group to have lost out in the "Gold Rush" for American plenty. In section VI, a potato explodes in the oven, prompting a section on the dashed hopes of the Irish. In three lines she succinctly summarizes every turning point and motivation of the Irish toward America: formerly starved out, "rack-rented," dull from unending labor in fields rotted by potato blight in 1847. The "I" reviews the myths immigrants tell one another about America—that she is the country of the free and the meat-fed (*A* 15). So they, immigrants from all over the world, aim for the land of freedom.

The dark irony of heavily stressed, terse lines, the sprung rhythm enlivening them, is not lost on readers familiar with her dialogic protest poems. In this exquisite sequence, she is concerned about the interweaving of poetry, love of talk—their love of the rhetoric of Catholicism, IRA, dreams spoken of in kitchens by scorned tongues in cities drowning in jargon (*A* 15). Just as the beautiful English spoken by the Irish captured by John Millington Synge in his plays and Yeats in his poetry rots into mere jargon after 50 years in cities where the Irish are devalued, so their dreams fester, too. This is the potential fate of all who cross the doorframe.

Not comprehending how he or she has reached this sense of hopelessness, the immigrant lyric "I" grieves in homesickness, asking, if this is a white man's madness (*A* 19). Addressing the reader, the speaker declares, "*I honor your truth and refuse to leave it at that.*" Yet retuning to the theme of the book, loneliness and solitude, the speaker asks provocatively what we have learned from tales of chases and hunts about heart-starved, tenderness-starved men in gangs (*A* 19). What Rich suggests she has learned is that men join gangs out of loneliness, so perhaps the problem of violence in America can be attributed to its existential loneliness.

Rich transcends Ginsberg's or Whitman's wide-ranging, encyclopedic embrace of America here in the title poem; this is not just one lonely American suffering, but all suffer privately, loving and suffering in solitude, since Americans are mostly recent immigrants or children of former immigrants.

Still, she conjectures, maybe the first male European frontiersman was happy to be alone: she conjures up a lonely man riding across the Mohave Desert (*A* 19) at the same time as she envisions another walking the Grand Canyon (*A* 19). The speaker thought all those solitary explorers were as happy as they could ever be (*A* 19). Probably that is true. But maybe, the poem implies, they are not.

The next woman traveler she mentions is one who died in Twentynine Palms in California in 1903, and whose mother went to mining camps by herself as a cook (*A* 19). These are hardly tales of a free or happy exploration of the West, instead Rich's atlas is a call to redeem or reconstitute America along freer, more democratic lines.

In the second-to-last section of this long dialogic diatribe against the mission of every American citizen now, the lyric "I" declares firmly that "a *patriot* is not a gun." Instead, she would define *patriot* as "one who wrestles for" the "soul of her country" as "she wrestles for her own being" (*A* 23); this patriot alternates from gender to gender and gazes through the great circle at Window Rock onto the "sheen" of the Vietnam Wall. Patriots are citizens trying to rouse and extricate themselves from the loss of the American dream of innocence, a dream now transformed into a nightmare (*A* 23).

Playing linguistically on the fact that the word *patriot* has come to connote *weapon* in modern parlance—and even Patriot Act, Adrienne Rich insists that the patriot is a person whose vision of America's ideals remains clear even though America, the nation as a whole, may lack clear vision or ethical focus. The true patriot is the one who—like the poet—is prepared to die for her country even though she may be too old and crippled to be called to fight as a soldier, one who like Cassandra is unafraid to speak out and criticize or prophesy. Perhaps an unlikely patriot, especially in the eyes of critics of her poetry, Rich argues that the visionary, the woman who still envisions the ideals America was founded on, is someone who deserves a hearing, whose passionate words should, according to Rich, be translated into passionate action, as subsequent events may have indicated.

Americans mistake legitimate dissent—blessing—for hate speech or cursing, not realizing that blessing and cursing are born as twins and separated at birth, who expect to meet again in mourning (*A* 23). This "internal emigrant" is the most homesick of all men or women (*A* 23), and this emigrant perceives every flag as a burst of pain. So the speaker inquires, Where are we moored? and also asks, Where are the bindings? Equally, What behooves us (*A* 23)? These are hard questions, asked prophetically of the nation by one of the only American poets who seemed to anticipate the events of 9/11/01. Who else was asking in the mid-1990s: Where are our moorings and our bindings? What behooves us? Who was resisting the tide of capitalist consumer culture in the buoyant late 1980s and early 90s?

What might behoove us, the speaker suggests, is to reconnect with original American ideals, civil liberties, and with freedom, the poet speaks in these repetitive, homoeomerical lines. Clearly what behooves us is to recognize that we as Americans must acknowledge the living conditions of the rest of the world—Arab states as well as all the countries of Africa, the Middle East, and Asia. We might begin to see ourselves as part of the world, not simply as the most privileged country in the world.

In lines echoing Ginsberg's and Whitman's attempts to capture and speak from and to the soul of America, she expresses the conviction that this moment in history is a time when the lyric "I" thinks about what it means to love her country while flags bloom everywhere in deserts without other flowers or vegetation (*A* 22).

Remembering one's homeland and suffering lands prompts remembering what behooves us and knowing why every flag that flies today is a cry of pain. Contemporary politics often evokes cries of pain in Rich, as well. Real patriots, like the original patriots of the Revolutionary War, should take the time to get the news from poems.

In the last section of *An Atlas of the Difficult World* there are " (Dedications)": readers may be surprised to find that the poem is dedicated to themselves. In her signature homoeomerical prosody, she addresses those who read "this poem" just before leaving your office late (*A* 25). Continuing in this intimate vein, she speaks to the working mother, affirming she knows who she is, heating milk for a crying baby, "you" stand reading quickly since the mother, too, is thirsty for the news and nourishment poetry can give, and we haven't much time. Having been a mother solely responsible for her own three sons, Rich experienced the maternal depletion, the sense that although you spend all your time nourishing your young, you yourself are intellectually hungry; thus, she assumes her reader is reading poems not even in her own language, guessing at words (*A* 25–26). Still, as the poet and the writer of these words, she would like the poor mother's evaluation and asks to know which words confuse her audience. Now the lyric "I" addresses the reader intimately, saying she realizes that "you" read this poem, waiting to glean some truth applicable to your life, reading in the night in a foreign language torn between bitterness and hope (*A* 25–26).

While the young Adrienne Rich almost never addressed her audience, here she is reaching out to the national soul or to a universal "you," a reader by whom she would not be misunderstood. Her voice here is far more direct and egalitarian, her style more forceful, political, yet visionary.

When 35 years before, Allen Ginsberg wrote in "Howl:" "*I saw the best minds of my generation destroyed by madness, staring hysterical naked,*"[3] he first struck the note of spontaneous visionary desperation and used the contemporary American diction Rich uses—a judicious mingling of abstract and concrete language. When at the end of "America" he sends out a half-comic "queer" challenge, "*America I'm putting my queer shoulder to the wheel,*" he sets the precedent for Rich's *Atlas* and her American lesbian subject position. Her readership and San Francisco audience for her readings overlap with some of the poetry lovers who read Allen Ginsberg and identify as "queers" and/or Jews.

Her "Tattered Kaddish" is reminiscent of Ginsberg's famous 1961 poem "Kaddish," dedicated to his beloved mother Naomi, whom he mourns. His is a poem about the meaning of life and suffering. In "Tattered Kaddish," she intones words of mourning and praise for her late husband, vindicating his suicide (*A* 45). The bereaved lyric "I" then addresses this beloved suicide, giving praise to life although its windows sometimes slammed shut and choked the breath of loved ones, and praise "to life" even though it may have tightened around the beloved's neck like a hangman's noose, and around the hearts of those who betrayed us (*A* 45).

All through this book, the personal pronouns dominate the poetry since here Rich becomes, for the space of this poem at least, a savior of the lost and marginalized in America, and the "you" becomes literally self-reflective, a smoky mirror, while lifting a smoky mirror; "I" plant myself here at the center of "your poem" unsatisfied (*A* 44). The haunting words of a protester-within-the-poem end "Eastern War Time," where the earlier order is reversed: and "I" and not "you" are in the poem now, so it has become "your poem," not the poet's. And in "Tattered Kaddish," at last it is no longer "you" or "I" (as it had been in her marriage poems) but at last "we" who embrace, mourn, love, praise, and remember those unfortunate dead, the suicides. The embrace of this new collective subject position transcends individuality and speaks to and for the emerging America. Rich sees her fight as a battle for the nation's soul: offering thanks to life, giving room and reason to ones we knew and loved who felt unpraiseworthy (*A* 45).

The lyric "I", now speaking for the collective "we," the nation's suicides, accords justice to the departed husband who felt *unpraisable,* or may have felt unloved unreasonably, though he was loved; so after the catharsis generated by the poem he need no longer stand unsatisfied lifting a smoky mirror reflecting how we live.

Later in *Atlas,* "For a Friend in Travail," following a poem about near-death, has as its refrain, *What are you going through, there on the other edge?* (*A* 51). Dominated by two rhapsodic poems, "An Atlas" in Part I and in Part II "Eastern War Time" (*A* 35–44) about a 60-year-old woman who remembers growing up during World War II, the book ends in prophetic utterances and cryptic questions, "Final Notations" (*A* 57). Recalling the rhythms of the Kaddish, "Final Notations" is about realizing what "behooves" us as a nation, is an interweaving of the two refrains, *it will not be simple* and the repetition of sentences beginning *"it will take all your heart... breath"*; although it is short, it won't be simple (*A* 57). "[I]t" is the political accomplishments of the American citizens'—and the poet's—mission, their commitment to social and political change and resolve now ripening since they have mastered the atlas. Of course, *Atlas* was also the person of fortitude who held up the world in classical mythology. Similarly, a poet creates a space here where a book of poems upholds a new America.

DARK FIELDS OF THE REPUBLIC

Dark Fields of the Republic begins provocatively and proceeds in couplets; while the living and the dead populate this place, the lyric "I" has never been alone here (*D* 19). Yet as a prescient, awakened poet/prophet, she wears her "triple eye" for spiritual vision on the road, discovering "past, present, future" all are at her side. I am a weather-beaten, strong-winged voyager, but nothing I buried will die (*D* 19). No one the poet has lost and nothing buried can die because she can immortalize in poetry.

If in *Your Native Land, Your Life* and *Time's Power* Rich explored the sacred, the spiritual dimension of the American nation, in *An Atlas of the Difficult World,* and *Dark Fields of the Republic,* Rich defines and embodies the new American citizenry, ruefully establishing a conscious contact with the open-hearted—if lonely—reader. In *Dark Fields of the Republic,* she imagines viewing the American republic through her mystical "triple eye," seeing past, present, and future simultaneously spiritually. She walks with spirits of the dead, but because the dead and living spirits intermingle here (*D* 19). The epigraph for "Then and Now" seems to address her readers and critics alike: Is it necessary for me to write obliquely about the situation (*D* 19)? Apparently she believes it is, but still she asks the reader, What would you have me do (*D* 19)? The reader is again forced back upon his or her own mental resources to think and determine what strategies are the most successful for a poet to accomplish social and cultural change and which might behoove a nation.

In communing with the divine and with the living and the dead, she is unafraid, powerful, speaking the news to the "dark fields of the republic," America in a time of mental and spiritual darkness. As a child Rich had loved singing Julia Ward Howe's "The Battle Hymn of the Republic" at home in the evenings while her mother played the piano: "*We shall die to make men free.*"

Dark Fields examines the varieties of patriotism and preparation for the future possible in the last decade of the twentieth century. The excellent long poem, "Calle Vision," considers the sort of vision possible in that dark time of fin de siècle angst. There are also tender love poems—"Sending Love" and "Late Ghazal"—where she practices a complex form she is attempting to master (the form is as elusive and hard to render as love itself). Last comes her search for meanings: in "Inscriptions," Rich challenges the meanings of words that have been used to convey community, political quest, and to express one's rootedness in something more meaningful than one's individual life—*history, movement, origins,* and *voices.* Exploring the nature of her own and others' urge to form movements, to discover the intellectual and personal origins of a drive toward freedom, to develop their own ideas and voices, and to become part of history, she comes to terms with her own place in the nation, having established both a national identity and female subject position through her speakers in poetry and her feminist essays, thereby establishing her own and other women's places in history.

Certain constants remain throughout the duration of her impressive poetic career: ironically, two were noted by early critics of her work. She retains her commitment to "personal lyrics,... [she] stretches all human activities on the frame of social and political consciousness."[4] Her rigorous testing of experience and insistence on inscribing the real American nation into her poetry stretches all significant experience on the frame of social, ethical, and political consciousness. The transformations that have fueled her poetry have led Rich to her current convictions that the political still derives from each American's mind and body. Poetry today must be reconciled with the new language, rhythms, and forms of American life. In *Dark Fields,* the cataloging poems full of witnesses to atrocities disappear; instead the voice here is of one sole woman, almost ghostlike, visiting and revisiting visionary sites. In *Women and Honor: Some Notes on Lying,* there is a telling line of prose Rich wrote in 1977, "When a woman tells the truth she is creating the possibility for more truth around her" (*WH* 6).

> When someone tells me a piece of truth which has been withheld from me, and which I needed in order to see my life more clearly, it may bring acute pain, but it can also flood me with a cold, sea-sharp wash of relief.
>
> Often such truths come by accident, or from strangers. It means that... we both know we are trying, all the time, to extend the possibilities of truth between us. The possibility of life between us. (*WH* 9)

Adrienne Rich addresses other women since it was her original premise that women are brought up to believe that as long as they are sexually faithful, they do not need to be honest within the sphere of their everyday conversation and in relationships with men, other women, or children. A host of women poets of her generation ran aground on this lack of faith, betrayal, honesty, or trust, ending their lives in suicide or alcoholism or other addictions. Others may have lacked the courage and energetic support that later came to Rich from other women.

If in F. Scott Fitzgerald's *The Great Gatsby,* from which the phrase "*dark fields of the republic*" comes, the dead Gatsby is viewed as having all his life yearned toward a goal which he thought was up ahead of him but which was in fact back behind him in "the dark fields of the republic," back in his youth where he lost innocence, ideals, and courage, Rich's mission in this book is to explore those fields, scrupulously scouring them for the truths America as a nation has overlooked and died for want of. In "Sunset, December, 1993" (*D* 29), she poses the question, "Is it dangerous not to think" about how the earth still was in places when the chimneys shuddered with the first "dischargements"? So much emphasis on this last word evokes an association with the chimneys releasing the smoke from the Nazi concentration camps. The poem began pointing out it is dangerous of course to draw such "parallels" and it becomes more and more difficult to write, unprotected now, as though one could steer a steady course, as if "poems, ideas," glided "suspended in midair, innocent" (*D* 29). Clearly no poet has been protected for decades, yet only Rich, of all poets writing in America in the 1990s, seems to anticipate how very vulnerable we honestly were as the nation approached 9/11/01.

As if anticipating that dark day in New York, *Dark Fields of the Republic* states that poetry cannot be protected or separated from the world around it any more than politics can be separated from real life or citizens can be protected from their nations. As she pointed out in *Blood, Bread, and Poetry,* Rich is openly quite concerned about aestheticizing into irrelevance what we might loosely call the real world—gilding over people's legitimate life-and-death concerns and problems:

> A burgeoning women's movement in the 1970s and early 1980's incited and provided the occasion for [her essays on feminism and the revolution in women's place and power in the world]... But, as I suggested in "Notes toward a Politics of Location," my thinking was unable to fulfill itself within feminism alone. (*B* 23)

Thus, in later years she has moved away somewhat from feminism in the direction of Marxism.

The poem asserts that it is imperative that citizens and poet-citizens think: it is dangerous not to (*D* 29). The stanza starting "poems, ideas, gliding" suggests that ideas can be like planes gliding through midair, innocent (though possibly about to crash). Just as it is dangerous to presume a plane cannot be shot down or crash, so too it is dangerous to write as though there were a steady course toward one's destination, one political or personal perspective, and as though our poems are "protected" (*D* 29)—if this is a covert political struggle, no one is protected. Arguably, though, it is also dangerous *not* to write. In "And Now," she espouses what is close to a poetic credo, addressed to her understanding reader: "you" are warned that these poems don't amount to real arguments and do not "construct a scenery"—build a political platform. Realize that she has attempted to listen and respond to the public voice of our time and attempted to survey republic and public space, remaining true to the details (*D* 31). Her prophetic "I"/eye tries to show exactly how the air moves (*D* 31). The lyric "I" records the truth of this age—how it feels to be alive and American, and in this resides Rich's genius.

Only by trying to listen hard to what the nation says in its public voice, thus, only by surveying our public space, can one become a good poet, giving the public the news, reporting the public voice. The work is urgent since someone must observe "where the clocks' hands stood," who created the received *definitions* Americans live by; poets must be aware of the time when *compassion* became *guilt* (*D* 31). Definitions of what is liberal and what is conservative keep changing in America, where opportunities and personal liberties appear to be dwindling. As she wrote in *The Los Angeles Times Book Review* of August 3, 1997, declining the National Medal for the Arts and protesting the end of the National Endowment for the Arts:

> Art can never be totally legislated by any system...; nor can it, in our specifically compromised system, be really free...it needs breathing space, cultivation...to fulfill itself. Just as people do. New artists... need education in their art,...chances to study,...get the criticism and encouragement of mentors, learn they are not alone. As the social compact withers, fewer and fewer people will be told, yes, you can do this, this also belongs to you.[5]

Far from being elitist or supportive of a certain clique of insider poets, Rich reads and recommends others read a cross section of new, undiscovered American artists and writers, concerned that they get the education, tools, encouragement, and support they deserve. America today, she argues, is too dominated by centrifugal competitive forces that pull communities—and artists—apart and by an urge to pigeonhole and categorize all experience, by "quantification and abstraction":

> It is precisely where fear and hatred of art join the pull toward quantification and abstraction, where the human face is mechanically deleted, that human dignity disappears from the social equation. Because it is to those "complex equations of human nature and experience" that art addresses itself.[6]

In place of dignity, we have electronic media and the Internet; we have entertainment systems and surround sound instead of art.

> In a society tyrannized by its own false gods of concentration of wealth,...recognized artists have, perhaps, a new opportunity to work out our connnectedness as artists, with other people who are beleaguered, suffering, disenfranchised—precariously employed workers, trashed elders, throwaway youth, and the art they too are nonetheless making and seeking.[7]

Rich hopes that these alienated groups can unite, form common cause.

The last of the "Six Narratives" (*D* 47–52) in *Dark Fields of the Republic* augurs differently; perhaps five years later, Rich is even less optimistic: "the ship of hope shuddered" on an iceberg at the same time that intimate bonds of affection sway and stagger (*D* 52). The ship of hope designates the republic, swaying and staggering against its nemesis, the iceberg: in dramatic, frightening lines, the poem describes how "we" are "racked apart" in a republic only just gliding on, with parted lips (*D* 52). In retrospect, this seems prescient of events a decade later, events that changed our sense of America and what it is to be an American forever.

But certainly this concept of developing bonds, private affections, between disparate groups in communities is in part what she is exploring in "Inscriptions" (*D* 59–73), the long poem sequence concluding *Dark Fields.* In "One: comrade" the lyric "I" imagines "the other" with whom faith and trust could be sustained (*D* 59), even if that other is not currently in contact with the poet or is known to the poet. Later in the same poem, the speaker links security in a sense of community with the development of a probing, prophetic voice, necessary to the (unheard?) prophet of the republic, stating that a singing voice can be heard as dangerous and when it learns to listen it can be heard as desperate (*D* 59). Likewise, the voice of a poet opposing the Gulf War in a time when patriotism was the order of the day could be seen as both "dangerous" and "desperate": for that reason Laura Bush, the First Lady, cancelled a White House poetry reading in the spring of 2003, just before America attacked Iraq.

Certainly the first poems in *Dark Fields*, "What Kind of Times Are These" (*D* 3) and "In Those Years" (*D* 4), are poems Rich has read frequently at the start of poetry readings to rivet her audience, to let them know how it is with her politically and what she thinks of the times we live in, echoing Bertholt Brecht's ironic complaint that his were difficult times "*When it's almost a crime to talk about trees*" (*D* 75).

In "What Kind of Times Are These," the poet abruptly plunges into the center of the matter: our nation, moving closer "to its own truth and dread," has found ways to make some persons vanish (*D* 3). Audiences hearing this poem often applaud enthusiastically: they feel saddened and honestly understand her cynicism—or realism.

"In Those Years" completes the conceptual and spiritual development begun in the first poem and constitutes an appropriate point of stasis for this argument and the rhythm of thought since it captures most succinctly her sense that we need to rediscover the communal "we" and "us," and Americans' sense of national solidarity: it will be reported that in those years historians will say we lost track of the meaning of the words *we* and *you* (*D* 4). Many members of the American middle class—Rich would likely see them as spoiled—utter only the subjective "I" in the language and culture of the last two decades of the twentieth century. She mocks those who are trying to live a personal life as if that were the only life we could bear witness to (*D* 4). Referring to the hedonism, rampant commercialism, and extreme waste and narcissism of the late 1980s and 1990s, she castigates those trying to live a purely selfish personal life and the insular view of existence and the selfishness of contemporary American individualism. Leading life only for ourselves alone, she asserts, is self-indulgent folly, "ironic, terrible" (*D* 4); it is the way to remain in the dark fields of the republic, a sure way to lose the American Dream in the aftermath of Gulf Wars I and II.

The sybaritic life of self-indulgent narcissism was the only life "we" could testify to until on 9/11/01 "the great dark birds of history screamed and plunged" from the skies "into our personal weather," into New York, the Pentagon, and a Pennsylvania field where we stood selfishly, "saying I" (*D* 4), ignoring the rest of the world. The poem implies that the American empire will fall if we continue merely to stand, saying "I."

Correspondingly, the poem "One: comrade" speaks movingly of the strength that comes from communicating together as "we," as a community. In unsentimental lines, dedicated to a Marxist "comrade," she writes, that s/he deserves an ethical flower (*D* 59) and the lyric would reach it to her comrade through landmines. One reaches them across the city's *whyless sleeplight,* reaching over "bacterial" waters with determination (*D* 59). Writing before 9/11/01, her mission in speaking to America about the need for change seems difficult, even impossible, or futile. Now, more people are beginning *to think globally, act locally.*

It is hard to keep the ideal of beauty alive when the drinking water may be polluted, but the poet has no choice but to tell the truth as she sees it. Rich observes and names both the beauty and the horror of America's future, lovingly, positively. This is her vocation. The subject position here is that of a prophet to the new listening radical America, an intimate voice speaking to those with wisdom and insight to understand something about the state of the republic in the wake of the Gulf War.

WHAT IS FOUND THERE

Although she focuses on his limitations in *What is Found There,* T. S. Eliot, one of Rich's early mentors, said that the poet should be "constantly amalgamating disparate experience," and this is what her poetry does here. Her poems of the 1990s combine poetry, prose passages from journals, nonfiction prison narratives, bits of memoirs and history, incidents in ordinary lives and in history of the country's oppressed, even slogans, quotations (*A* 6)—a mural or graphic composite of disparate materials.

What is Found There (1993) is composed of Rich's re-visioning of her past so as to find how she became a revolutionary: she defines the revolutionary poem there as one that:

> will not tell you...how to theorize. It reminds you (for you have known, somehow, all along, maybe lost track) where and when and how you are living and might live—it is a wick of desire. (*WF* 241)

Only a graphic mural assembling all the scattered media from which we form our consciousness and ideas now, only this kind of poem renders the depth and breadth of reality at this precise historical moment. A true revolutionary poem asks that challenging question, *What if?* This is the first revolutionary question, the question the dying forces don't know how to ask (*WF* 241–42). This question precedes all change. In a final summation she crystallizes the definition:

> A revolutionary poem is written out of one individual's confrontation with her/his own longings (including all that s/he is expected to deny) in the belief that

its readers or hearers...deserve an art as complex, [and] as open to contradiction as themselves. (*WF* 241)

Rich has mastered the politically provocative lines, lines that seem to have been crafted for their dramatic effect: the revolutionary "I" doesn't care how the murderer tracked the women who were his prey across the Appalachian Trail, or hid near their tent, pitched in a safe place (*A* 14). The "I" does not want to know how horribly he killed one while another woman crawled to town afterward (*A* 14). Recounting incidents like this both reveal and withhold historical truth: they reveal the sad truth of misogyny but refrain from divulging all the facts. The poet's restraint keeps the genre lyrical, not historical. Consequently, she publishes *What is Found There,* a book of essays on her development as a poet, in 1993, just after the Los Angeles riots, in an attempt to express a vision for revolutionary America more clearly and to articulate her resentment about the erosion of individual rights.

Committed to what might be called the poetry of the interrogation room, poetry addressed to those devoted to achieving social change, and seeing its place in the continuum of American history, the book contains essays on her sense of her own place in the world, her identity, and community. In "Not how to write poetry, but wherefore," she writes of William Carlos Williams, praising his poetic grasp of American reality:

William Carlos Williams wrote from the landscape of ordinary urban, contemporary America, of ordinary poor and working people, in a diction of everyday speech, plainspoken yet astonishingly musical and flexible...later I would work with his phrasing and ways of breaking a line as a means of shedding formal metrics. (*WF* 195)

Rich uses William Carlos Williams's phrasing and three-part broken line in *The Desert Music* (1954) and *A Journey to Love* (1955) in her latest books of poetry. A phrase from his poem "Asphodel, That Greeney Flower," cited above, is the source of this book's title. What Williams did to convey a sense of persons in a place, the character of a place, in the poetry of *Paterson* and in prose writings like *In the American Grain,* Rich does for the Northern Pacific Coast of California and the Bay Area, where she has settled. Assuming the subject position of true American prophet and visionary, she energetically endorses and inscribes the place, the role and responsibilities of the national poet today. In spirit, if not in fact, she speaks as America's Unofficial Poet Laureate (although she would likely decline the honor, if offered it), assuming moral direction for a country she may see as having lost its way. Virtually alone now in the last decade of the millennium Rich tries to record the public voice of the country in her poetry, show "where the clocks' hands stood," who was issuing orders and enforcing crucial political definitions, noting when compassion turned into guilt (*D* 31).

Here in *What is Found There,* Rich examines her own reasons for writing poetry, discusses poetics and her favorite poets, speaks to those who read American poetry so as to learn how to deal with possible changes in our future, what Rich anticipates could be a revolution in consciousness. Official America today is caught, she avers (as if foreseeing the Monica Lewinsky/Clinton scandal, Whitewater, or Bush's grounds for going to war with Iraq), in a "[m]isprision of power," witnessing wide scale military "misconduct or neglect of duty" (*WF* 107): she was writing particularly about the Gulf War when she penned these phrases but they are relevant to the War on Iraq as well as all wars thereafter. Rich's conviction here is that authentic American poets must change, evolve, and begin "renaming" the earth, becoming its voice and the voice of the American citizen.

Rich starts by reexamining the relationship between poetry and politics: to find a common ground, a "re-marriage" between science, poetry, and politics is another aim of Rich's poetic mission. In a time when science dominates and overshadows poetry, she speaks up for poetry as the most important part of the triad. All three, poetry, politics, and science, are informed by original insights into the world around us. But poets can forge new correspondences and links between poetry, politics, and science:

> And poetry, too, begins this way: the crossing of trajectories of two... elements that might not otherwise have known simultaneity. When this happens, a piece of the universe is revealed. (*WF* 8)

In some sense, this book is about tracing poetic and political correspondences between her various female subject positions and Rich's evolving concepts of community, making poetic connections political or political ones poetic, largely those correspondences she herself considers valuable and important naturally. One of her goals here is to prove that poetry has a crucial part to play in the lives of all on the planet. Trotsky alludes to the need to integrate art and life: he endorses "*The effort to set art free from life, to declare it a craft sufficient unto itself, devitalizes and kills art.*" (*WF* 45). She has smashed the verbal icon that she created in her first poems; now she could not conceive of a poetry not intermingled with the raw material of real life, danger, sweat, and politics.

SPEAKING OF AND TO FORMER MENTORS, NOW DEAD OR OUTGROWN

Reading through Wallace Stevens in Twentynine Palms, California, Rich voices the same thought, expressed by Stevens. "Of Modern Poetry" affirms poetry must be "living" and know the "speech of the place." While it has to meet the men and women of the place, "It has to think about war" and "it has to find what will suffice." She says in response to these lines:

I took this quite literally. It was he who said to me, "Ourselves in poetry must take their place," who told me that poetry must change, our ideas of order, of the romantic, of language itself must change. The last line in the *Collected Poems* is *"A new knowledge of reality."* (*WF* 101)

Stevens expresses what all poets seek—to take their own places in poetry—and to convey in their poems *"a new knowledge of reality."* Poetry, mathematics, and physics are equally important fields of original research. And, as she explains to "Arturo" in the chapter "Dearest Arturo," "poetry and politics aren't mutually exclusive" (*WF* 22), even though "we're unable to write love, as we so much wish to do, without writing politics" (*A* 23).

Much of the book is devoted to conveying the vitality of politically aware poetry and excitement of women's publishing networks, the nationwide community of women poets—feminist/lesbian/gay or not, or "border" poets, who write some of the most stimulating and original poetry around. Consequently, this is an informative book on the state of good American poetry from a poet whose whole life is poetry and who gives and attends readings regularly. She discusses many poets in sufficient depth for poetry lovers to discover some they may want to read.

Muriel Rukeyser is a poet revered and frequently discussed in Rich's essays. Rich's meditations on women's poetry in *What is Found There* show she acknowledges indebtedness to Muriel Rukeyser for her ideas on the need to integrate the whole of one's life into poetry in order to keep one's poetry real and vibrant. Muriel Rukeyser insisted perceptively, *"It isn't that one brings life together—it's that one will not allow it to be torn apart"* (*WF* 158). Poetry challenges the forces that seek to fragment and polarize modern life and destroy bonds between family members, especially mother and child; the true woman "refuses to hide her sexuality, abnegate her maternity, silence her hungers and angers in her poetry" (*WF* 158). And when the lesbian/feminist poet does this, coming raw to the poem, she "creates—as Rukeyser did, as Audre Lorde has, as Pratt and Olds are doing—a force field of extraordinary energy" (*WF* 158).

In celebrating the power and ideas of so many good women poets confronting the negative forces of history and restoring poetry to its full power and originality, Rich displays her powers as a critic of subtle integrative intelligence and a figure of capable imagination. She interweaves her own criticism with pertinent reflections on other contemporary poets. For instance, the poet Dave Mura's question echoes through the entirety of the book:

What does it mean when poets surrender vast realms of experience to journalists, to political scientists, economists? What does it mean when we allow the "objectivity" of these disciplines to be the sole voice which speaks on events and topics of relevance to us all? (*WF* 121)

These questions present one of the foci of this book—to show how even though politics enters contemporary poetry, form in poetry can be "if not utterly lyrical, generically lyrical."[8] In addition to asking and giving answers to the questions above, the book introduces its reader to all the poets that Octavio Paz, Helen Vendler, Ira Sadoff, or other prominent literary figures appear to be either unaware or disapproving of.

Rich asserts that there is better poetry being written and enjoyed lately; unfortunately, much of this poetry does not receive sufficient public recognition, so she publishes it in her anthology of *The Best American Poets*. There the selection ranges from Yiddish to African-American poets to lesbian poets like Minnie Bruce Pratt to "border" poets like Irene Klepfisz and the Chicana poet Gloria Anzaldua, who complains of being in "*a constant state of* mental *nepantilism, an Aztec word meaning 'torn between ways'* " (*WF* 139), because she is a citizen of both Mexico and America and feels *doublehearted,* torn between the two cultures.

All these American poets sensitive to the nation's pulse and heartbeat experience a sense of loss when cut off from their native roots. Indeed, Rich thinks Americans have been cut off from truth for five hundred years because the land was usurped:

From the first invasion, the first arrogant claiming, it became a tragic land. In all the explicit destructions, all the particular locations of the tragedy, this is the fatal contradiction, the knowledge Whitman couldn't bear or utter...—the great rip in the imaginative fabric of the country-to-be: the extraordinary cruelty, greed, and willful obliteration on which the land of the free was founded. (*WF* 122)

To wrest a "vast, fertile, generous, dangerous" land, "filling the needs of many forms of life" (*WF* 121) away from its original owners was to build a republic, constitute a democracy, on an outrage. Only a radical or revolutionary poetics (*AR* 122) confronts these problems; and it is to this revolutionary tradition, the tradition of Walt Whitman, William Carlos Williams, Allen Ginsberg, and Muriel Rukeyser, she consciously pledges her allegiance. The poetic lines of *Dark Fields,* elaborately split into three and four parts, may be taken from William Carlos Williams, and the litanies, psalmic in their rhythmic repetitions, tone and style, recall Ginsberg and Whitman. Clearly she believes that only poets with a sense of the irony implicit in the national fallibility of the United States can speak truthfully and cogently to America about this usurpation and its discontents—about what she calls "the rupture of imagination" in America.

One problem that Muriel Rukeyser, Allen Ginsberg, and Rich address in this volume is that we have been staggering under the weight of a national fantasy that the history of the conquest of the Americas, "the westward movement," was different—was a history of bravery, enlightenment, righteous claiming, service to religious values and civilizing spirit. (*AR* 122)

Any poet writing in America now must find a way of meeting the challenge to deal with falsehoods, liberate the national imagination and conscience from brutalities and injustices buried in its past, and to help the nation navigate through its perilous future.

Rich eloquently articulates the purpose of the poetic enterprise, the mission of poets, in America in the twenty-first century:

in a history of spiritual rupture, a social compact built on fantasy and collective secrets, poetry becomes more necessary than ever: it keeps the underground aquafiers flowing; it is the liquid voice that can wear through stone. (*AR* 122)

Chapter 9

Poetry's Inadmissible Untimely Messenger

"Hungry man, reach for the book, it is a weapon"

—Bertolt Brecht

Although it has been misunderstood, not surprisingly Adrienne Rich's book of poetry *Midnight Salvage* presents yet another transformation in her poetry. My purpose in this chapter is to clarify this new transfiguration, as it relates to the rest of her oeuvre. In *Midnight Salvage,* her stated purposes are far simpler, more basic than ever before: here she declares herself to be poetry's "inadmissible" and "untimely messenger" (*MS* 24), one who wanted to show the lives of common men and women as beauty and terror (*MS* 67)—in this way she keeps faith with the elusive "you," her readers (*MS* 18). Her work in poetry is gathering the "full dissident story" and to ensure those less fortunate are receiving what she calls "*full human rights*" (*MS* 55) even while the nation sends its gaze, weapons, and troops elsewhere. The subject position is again that of the radical dissident prophet who haunts the nation and whose work also reflects the ghosting of love, "the apparitional lesbian,"[1] demanding a hearing; she is the messenger America may need but does not always want to hear.

In passages from *What is Found There,* Adrienne Rich speaks of Americans' need to transform ourselves through the exercise of personal creative energies in order to transform a tradition that "was never meant for us in the first place." She says, in effect, *Vive la Difference!* Capitalize on the difference between the old tradition and the new. Use it to effect a complete political, cultural, and social transformation.

Issuer of clarion calls to mobilize, Rich "haunts" the American nation with poetry that is "complex, polished and subtly kinetic."[2] This poetry seems to be spoken to and for ghosts—for the spirits of those who perished at Auschwitz; for the poet Rene Char, dead in the French Resistance; and for the revolutionary Mexican photographer, Tina Modotti. She bears witness to an alternative sexuality and radical female subject positions, "haunting" the language with this book, directly addressed to what she would never call the soul of the American people and the American republic, appropriately named *Midnight Salvage.*

Critics have disputed its worth and criticized her for writing proselike ideological poetry. Although she is speaking of an earlier Rich critic, Margaret Dickie correctly delineated Rich's problem with her critics:

> Clearly in all these cases and others like them, critics find it more important to cite Rich's poem than to read it carefully because, curiously, the sequence has a larger and more ghostly life as political statement than as poetry. The poem that announces that Adrienne Rich, a major figure even in establishment poetry, has come out has itself [,] not come out of the shadow of its own notoriety.... The denial of visibility, the ghosting of women's passion for women, has one meaning in the cultural criticism of Rich's prose; it has almost the opposite meaning in her poetry where ghosting is a way of possession, a new understanding of what it means to possess.[3]

Besides having been criticized for these reasons, Rich has also been charged with trying to manipulate the critical reception of her work and twist public opinion through the vehicle of her prose. This may have some truth in it, but it in no way detracts from the value of her poetry.

The emotionally freighted prose with which some writers describe her poetry strikes some as intrusively political—or merely tired. Here is a sampling from one review:

> *Midnight Salvage* uses all the sad properties of Rich's recent work: the fragmentary sentences of a decrepit Pound: the reckless phrasing ("my art's pouch /crammed with your bristling juices"); the clumsy typographical invention, by Cummings out of Chrysler; lines vain with vanity ("wanted for the crime of being ourselves"), or stiff with cant...[4]

While one or two poems in *Midnight Salvage* may contain "reckless phrasing," other poems are some of her best work. Does this critic totally miss the point? As a New York poet more interested in language than in revolution, he clearly fails to comprehend the failure of imagination she seeks to rekindle in America today. He mocks her effort to speak to the soul of the nation. Certainly he is unaware of the premises, impetus, and purpose of celebrating and articulating a variety of subversive subject positions so as to give voice to a radical feminist American poetics. Perhaps Logan believes, with Auden, that "*Poetry makes nothing happen.*" Does Rich's poetry have bearing on a realm of experience beyond the scope of this heterosexual male critic? Is that an unfair critique of the critic? Or is it fair to say her moral and political stance outstrips her control of the poetry?

CAN POETRY MAKE ANYTHING HAPPEN?

What can poetry accomplish? This is the question the poet who is dedicated to social activism asks legitimately and intimately here although the mood is not always sanguine: Rich admits she never expected hope to flourish in her lifetime (*MS* 10). *Midnight Salvage* is, as its name implies, her bold effort to salvage America and to save the country at the midnight hour. She investigates and finds what can be redeemed by poetry. Rich takes this title from a local salvage yard: one poem in the book notes that there is a yard "called" Midnight Salvage near where the old craftsman was run over (*MS* 13).

Intellectually challenging Auden's Modernist assertion that *"Poetry makes nothing happen,"* Rich approaches this question from various angles. Prophetically envisioning the American nation as a site of conflict involving the committed activist in a life-and-death struggle as a resistance-worker, hence evoking the 9/11/01 vision of America before the fact, Rich captures vivid images powered by her driving will to both arrest and to frame: these lines anticipate the ruthless, rushed search to capture the perpetrators of the bombing of the World Trade Center. Beyond this, here Rich is also an interlocutor in dialogue either with the American psyche or with an apparitional listener. Throughout, she addresses a "you" who may be the reader but is never identified. This mystery, along with her style, themes, and sometimes esoteric, sometimes limpid, subject give the book a haunting beauty and terror.

But if the "you" or the audience is obscure, metaphors for the creative social activist who lives on the fringes of society, a revolutionary like Marx or Brecht, populate and propel the book. In one poem, "Modotti," the focus is on the photographer, both a seer but also a miner of truths that may help the people: the speaker assures her that she does not follow her to frighten or "to arrest you" (*MS* 19). The line's meaning hinges on the triple meanings of the word "arrest": on the one hand, the photographer "arrests" the image in the flash of her lens, and on the other hand, she arrests time, and third, a policeman would follow her to arrest a dissident. The lyric "I" keeps insisting, however, that she is not here to "arrest" the photographer, hinting at her revolutionary activities. Verbal play this complex may have escaped some readers who choose to attack her politics rather than read the poems.

Addressing the reader/listener, the poet can imagine "your" exposure of manifestos and is compelled to explain—almost apologize for—her dogged pursuit of Modotti, each stanza ending with an almost traditional refrain: *"then this is where I'll find you"* or *"of course this is how I'll find you"*

(*MS* 19–20). The refrain conjures up her presence and their encounter while the poet's double justifies her pursuit. The tone is a mixture of fear, love, and admiration for a person hunted down for her engagement in what she understood to be ethical exposure.

In another poem, "Char," addressing the French Resistance worker/ poet Rene Char, she asserts, that he was never a poet who was paralyzed by war. Instead, Char ("you") made terrible, delicate life-and-death decisions (*MS* 18). Living in a time of war, every decision he made had to be weighed in the balance of its repercussions in history: he lived poised on the edge of the abyss in the French Resistance, yet retained a strong sense of discipline and personal integrity. Praising solitary witnesses, keeping her wits about her, Rich speaks here as one alone seeing the desire for courage which looks steadily at the truth. Here is the poem dedicated to Char, like a natural herbal thyme, but thyme seized from a burning meadow (*MS* 18).

Here is an act of *salvage*: the poet rescues what is in imminent danger of being destroyed or lost. And Rich's lines evoke Eliot's theme from "The Waste Land:" "*These fragments I have shored against my ruin.*"[5] The difference is that Eliot utters that statement in guarded despair while she is courageously affirming the act of rescue as a necessary fact of life, the duty of each citizen of the endangered American republic in the decade between the Gulf War and the War on Iraq.

Further on in "Char," poetry is alluded to as a mimosa twig from still "unravaged country." The poet's double saves both past and present beauty for the nation, and in so doing saves the future; she imagines the as yet "unravaged country" of the future (and perhaps the wilderness, for as Thoreau said, "*in wildness is the preservation of the world,*") or does future here connote the innocence of children and unborn generations? The poet's role is that of heroic observer or recorder. Truly effective revolutionary activists or poets are able to retain a realistic sense of perspective where others fail: they keep their wits and senses about them and keep the faith. Her prophetic gaze is trustworthy and sees the truth of the republic steadily and whole.

The poet keeps vigil over the (darkest) fields of the republic but here it is also to save what can be saved at the midnight hour, to do the thankless, laborious work of midnight salvaging. Addressed, like "Char," to a poet, "Letters to a Young Poet" has a striking resonance with the eponymous work by Rainer Maria Rilke. As in William Carlos Williams's poetics, the poet's job is to get the news to the common person; the reader needs to have the real news (*MS* 25). A real poet, the speaker suggests, will not get free of this: his or her fate is ineluctable; real poets are doomed to write (*MS* 25). The poet's vocation arises from pure will and ineluctable dedication for this reason (*MS* 26). If poetry is not a force for evil, it can be a catalyst for change. Might it even stop the woman from flinging herself any day from the fourteenth floor? A book of poetry transformed Rich's life when she herself was at a low ebb of maternal fatigue, even exhaustion, so she believes that the poetic word really can save its reader, "you."

In the last line in section 4 of the poem, she offers a symbolic hand to the poets, who may be close to despair themselves (*MS* 27). The lines reflect a sense of a poem's passivity or ineffectiveness in the face of the movement of contemporary American culture in the light of a national misunderstanding and/or devaluation and passivity of the poet's role: after having stressed in previous lines that the prefix "*Be*" is the "infernal" prefix of the actionless (*MS* 28).

The raw lyric "I" is reminiscent of the miner of *Dark Fields of the Republic:* her head wrapped in a scarf, a lanterned helmet, she is a miner for truth in a time of public dishonesty. The speaker's lips are caked with silt; but they can still clearly pronounce greetings, appropriately saluting a new poet as the gladiator saluted his emperor (*MS* 28).

The haunted narrator returns belligerently asking who wants to know who she is: the poet's surrealistic, amusing self-description shows the ludicrousness of pursuing her with her "drag queen's vocal chords" and "bitter beat" (*MS* 28). The jocular self-portrait is enticing and amusing, yet hardly the womanly ideal: this is more like Shakespeare's "*My mistress's eyes are nothing like the Sun.*" Is this self-disparagement designed to disarm fledgling poets in pursuit of her, to put them at ease? If this poet with a *bitter beat,* whose every new book is a publishing event, (she implies through self-deprecation that such an imperfect human being as herself) can have the effect she's had, the young poet can succeed, too. This is the sort of encouragement to poets that has never before graced Rich's work. The poetry reflects a keener sense of humor and balance in her later years; making fun of her "drag queen's" voice, for instance, reveals more humility than it has displayed before (*MS* 29), but characteristically the subject position is mysteriously anonymous, occluded, and intimate; the national poet speaks from underground and seems to see and address everyone and everything in America.

While she does not disclose either her own identity or that of "you,"—the reader?—and she is edgy about who is there watching or reading, in the final line of the poem she concludes poignantly, giving it a whimsical, vatic twist, expressing a desire to go somewhere the mind had never been before and go feeling some companionship.

The lines appear to spring both from loneliness and a desire to reach out to the young poet, who may be able to continue this work of salvage and will when the lyric "I" may be unable to.

Coming after "Midnight Salvage," "Char," "Modotti," the grisly visual poem "Shattered Head," and the revelatory "Letters to a Young Poet," the poem "Camino Real" in the middle of this book is named for the Spanish Franciscan Friars' Road of the Kings, the road traveled by the friars up and down California as they established missions. It concerns scenes of torture and poignant testimony of the tortured (*MS* 31). Quoting Tiresius, the man whose voice emanates from the life after death in Eliot's *The Waste Land,* Rich intersperses images of sexual intimacy with images of torture, evoking the frequent theme in Rich's earlier poetry, sexual exploitation and violence against women. As the word "arrest" became pivotal in "Modotti," "happiness"—the lack of or pursuit thereof—dominates "Camino Real." The lyric "I" is on a dream journey south down "Camino Real," driving to the home of her son, passing graffiti-defaced walls proclaiming a wanter is wanted for wanting, a wanter who is "armed in love" and dangerous (*MS* 30).

Signs of love, danger, and weapons are encoded throughout her entire poetic mission on Camino Real. An image of torture follows: she recounts the horror of a torture, saying that to make clear assessments of the cruel mouth-bit or the fire-ravaged skull found at a mission is beyond the lyric "I"'s ability. One is led to question historians who coolly report violent deeds perpetrated against Native Americans, enacted methodically and repeatedly at these houses of God. Rich's sense of responsibility will not let her travel the royal road of the mission founders without acknowledging that many of them, too, were torturers and murderers although no mission museum is likely to dwell on this. One is reminded, too, here of the Nazi historians who documented unblinkingly each atrocious act of torture and mutilation.

Since at that time California's history was just being properly gathered and written down, so the lyric "I" reimagines the ways the landowners and friars whipped and tortured Indians: these horrific acts speak of seemingly universal human cruelty. She resolves to rely on her memory alone but to return to the place in clothes that the original inhabitants might have been surprised to see, with a notebook, and find out the truth. The researcher's purpose is to prove that then barbarous masters invented a reason to torture the helpless—and this happened throughout the South, too, up to and after the Civil War (*MS* 31). Memory is always fallible, and only the most accurate reporting will preserve the truth for the future. Perhaps in the lines above, she has in mind the preservation of historical truth in poetry; but on the other hand, it would seem she is discussing the tasks of the historian of women's and Native American studies. The records that a group like Amnesty International keeps to register and preserve the facts about the torture of prisoners of conscience, Rich may consider true and reliable.

Yet having documented for a lifetime the horrors of racism and sexual exploitation, the psyche yearns for release into happiness; and after having faced and integrated into a national poetry resolutions to these challenges, the lyric "I" says in mutual compassion for the tortured that she experiences their pain, in a moving citation: "*I was the one, I suffered, I was there*" (*MS* 31).

An arresting problem the researching "I" encounters in contemporary history is that these deeds occurred and were never exposed, exonerated, or forgiven. Scholars may know what happened, but these facts do not enter "santabarbara's barbarous," if beautifully landscaped, mind, nor the minds of other (barbarous?) Californians. In a transport evocative of Wallace Stevens's lyrics, she argues first, then, reveling in the light, the speaker exclaims on the beauty of the light on the ocean's rough surface, like light on raw silk; and she quotes Charles Olson asking " *'Can you afford not to make/the magical study'* " of " *'happiness...?'* " No, one cannot afford not to find one's own happiness, which for her might be a physically freer life, one without pain. And the poem ends in the hope that this might perform the work of alchemy or transformation for someone (*MS* 32).

George Oppen himself says in the book's epigraph about happiness, "*there is no other issue,...one has a right to think about for other people, to think about politically....*"[6] As a visionary, oracular poet, Adrienne Rich is alert to the problems of trying to write a politically responsible revolutionary poetry while keeping in sight the Americans' headlong pursuit of happiness.

In "Camino Real" she claims happiness as a primary end of life, aligning with Charles Olson and Karl Marx, she ends the poem when a day of the greatest imaginable happiness is over, she is moved by love merely to sign this with her first name, to just "*Adrienne*" (*MS* 33), endorsing this illumination that love is intrinsic to a happy life. Affixing her name to the end of this poem, as a child might sign, announces that she is adopting a more intimate, open relationship with the public. Cynthia Hogue comments that a "letter-poem" like this one "puts readers in a position very much like John Stuart Mill's definition of the lyric as utterance 'overheard'—albeit in Rich's poem, it is a letter read over the recipient's metaphoric shoulder."[7] This letter-poem becomes a pledge or promise of hope to the reader that one day, they too would be moved by love to act. If "Camino Real" contains images of violence and oppression visited on the individual in California history, "The Night Has a Thousand Eyes" is a love poem to the city of New York, homage to its matchless glamour, the beauty of its lights at night, mirrored on the lordly Hudson River.

A DIALECTIC OF POLARITIES REACHING FOR RESOLUTION

Juggling two contrasting points of view—the belief that poetry is useful, can save America, and the belief that poetry, indeed life itself, is about experiencing beauty and happiness—not surprisingly, Rich's poetry explores a terrain new to feminist dialogue about the poet's role as transformer of the nation. Hortense Spillers best discusses the relationship between feminist discourse and symbolic power thus in the essay "Interstices":

> Symbolist power, like the genetic parent, begets power, takes pleasure in proliferating itself. Feminist discourse, to extend the figure, keeps on talking or reproducing itself, tending to do so in its own image, on the basis of initiating symbolic gestures, against which it might struggle.[8]

Feminist discourse reproduces itself, "initiating symbolic gestures, against which it might struggle." In other words, dissent among feminist critics may be inevitable and should be expected. Exploring the complex ways poetry constructs and deconstructs symbolism, seeing that our lives are potentially structured by it, Rich's imagery, themes, and syntax in *Midnight Salvage* reproduce themselves, evolving resonantly throughout the book, examining the ways poetry inhabits shifting political, strategic, or ontological positions on the question of happiness, Marx's question for the masses.

A central poem in the book brings us to that time of welling resistance in the war zone in Belgium or the Netherlands in "1941." Pain for Rich is a constant of the human condition; her work is a spiritual seismic graph of dimensions of pain, a register of the kinds of human pain we have yet to atone for, the injuries no one may have the right to forgive, and the inevitable pain of illness. The body of the poem is inscribed with the imagery of pain. Jagged poetic form evokes the unpredictability of bouts of pain one may endure experiencing a chronic illness. The conjunction "if" operates as the first word in many stanzas, organizing the poem, weaving a psalmic litany: "if" there were once atrocities and fear in this place, today it is not evil but had essential amenities like water and signs of habitation (*MS* 23). The "I" imagines how one would feel if she were asked (*MS* 23) those questions the Nazi interrogator may have asked her own relatives who may have been sent to die in concentration camps: "*How did you get here anyway?*" Then, "*Are you poetry's inadmissible, already too late messenger?*" and "*By what right? In whose name?*" do you come to speak (*MS* 24)? This unsolicited voice must describe the truth of the present moment in its clarity and danger, must judge the historical moment, the moral implications of the past for the future.

By plunging the reader into the consciousness of the Holocaust victim being arrested, the poet confronts the problem of human evil again: the place was not evil in itself; the officers who persecuted the Jews, following Hitler's commands, were evil. Victims' lives were lost, but the pain and the evil itself appear as part of the eternal human condition, according to Rich. Survivor guilt may be a motivator in the poetry here, since as she has written elsewhere, had she been in Europe during World War II, her ethnic ancestry would have qualified her for the gas chambers.

On the other hand, the worldwide epidemic of AIDs threatens large portions of the Third World and challenges all nations today. With a constant, conscious awareness of the moral vision of historical events, Rich awakens her readers to America's need to think beyond merely the present or local to the global or universal dimensions of our experience. "Char" may be read as her epitaph for the twentieth century since in it, the corn is ground by a windmill to make bread for a peasant century against its dread of starvation (*MS* 23). If the twentieth was a peasant century, her sense of noblesse oblige leads her to awaken her readers to the plight of all those in need of bread in the twenty-first, even the bread of poetry.

Elsewhere in the book Rich touches on another level of salvaging, the saving of memories, permitting herself some rollicking self-mockery and metaphysical bouts of imagery in "Seven Skins," perhaps the most free and best poem in the book. She had just eaten lobster, out on a date at the finest place at Harvard with Vic Greenberg, a paraplegic she may have dated while in college, yet here the dating ritual is ironically likened to devouring one's date—to cannibalism. He orders her a delicious meal, then attempts to rip her open like a lobster.

His talk is an exhilarating speech, and he too has a keen sense of humor, born of—even reveling in—his sense of his own ridiculousness as a brilliant cripple (*MS* 38). Though lapsing here and there comically into bombast or exaggeration for effect, this second part of the poem generates a litany of nostalgic images for her immaturity, even provinciality as a nubile, young Radcliffe student in that lonely decade the 1940s (*MS* 38). The sequence beginning "What a girl" provides other surrealist images around this naive college girl, whom Stephen Burt has called "her best character" in the book of poetry.[9] In a surrealist sequence she likens herself to a provincial hamlet, a beach of roaring shoals, a thundercloud at sea, one aware she was poised at a crossroad in her life (*MS* 41). The imagery evokes Eliot's lines in *The Waste Land*—"*I should have been a pair of ragged claws scuttling along the floor of silent seas.*"[10] It dwells graphically on that one moment of feminine power when the young women of that lonely decade were able to choose their husbands, and it focuses girlhood's potential fertility: looking back, the nubile "I" notes she was a walking sac of eggs, full of eagerness and desire (*MS* 41). Ultimately, the young man initiates a sexual union while the woman seeks a security, which may "disembody" or devour her. His goal appears to be merely the satisfaction of his erotic desires, whereas she is conscious that her decisions on this night could disembody or undermine her whole future.

Surrounded by false smiles, they inhabit a milieu of hypocrisy in which they discovered they were stuck (*MS* 38). The sexual repression of this era combined with the rigidity of traditional sex roles forces everyone to run aground on the postwar rock while an odd assortment of students keep company in an eager rush to find a marriage partner (*MS* 38).

In his dorm room, the talk is sophisticated (*MS* 39). They listen to Billie Holiday, discuss literature and questions of the future of American civilization (*MS* 39). These recollections foreground the next lines, explaining that this is only memory; this is how memory works (*MS* 39). Aware of the reconstructive process of memory, the poem takes a glance at the exciting time when she had many choices of possible futures and husbands. Yet this glance is unsentimental, simply a visit to that time of possibilities and assumptions, a restrained examination of the ironies overlooked then. There is no hint of the road not taken in this poem: ultimately it is an affectionate, relieved good-bye to all that.

Of course, the essay "Compulsory Heterosexuality" had covered this terrain before, although it takes from the perspective of the social pressure on everyone to form heterosexual unions in youth. But viewed in the light of her previous essay, this poem shows the irony of ridiculous extravagance that university men shower on the women they find attractive. Like "Snapshots of a Daughter-in-Law," it is a poignant look inside the girl's consciousness of how such a date feels in a society where men are seen as having all the power and all the money while women have all the beauty and taste. It captures the exhilaration of dating, plus its awkward moments, naturally made more awkward here by the fact of Vic's being a paraplegic and Rich's ambivalence. Hence their imagined union can be seen as a gentle, regretful memory encompassing both all that was good and all that was bad, the unconscious humor and all the ignorance of the (bad) good old days.

This was a time when America was rebuilding herself after the deprivations of World War II, a time of hope and, ironically, also later a time of Cold War, a time when intellectuals could debate aloofly whether or not there *was* a uniquely American civilization. Rich's memories of her youth contain zesty, hilarious bouts of self-parody and eerie insights into sexual politics of her college and post-college years. This visit to the past is part of what Rich has called "gathering the full dissident story" (*MS* 10). Social pressures on those deemed different—on the physically challenged, those she calls the "handicapped," for example—create strong psychological pressures to conform even more brilliantly to the social norms. Using sexual repression, the limitations of physical handicap—until now a repressed subject in Rich's work—and humor in the salvaging of courtship, "Seven Skins" is a meditation on the skins or layers of assumptions about the limitations placed on a handicapped women, assumptions she had to shed; it achieves a harmonious balance through the surrealistic blending of opposites, a reconciliation of schizoid tensions. It both mocks and celebrates dating couples' awkwardness and yearning for love while it presents memorable images of harsh contrasts: the sharp contrast between what they discuss and the physical reality of the situation reveals the clash of emotions and dreams, and a subtext of helplessness, anxiety, and tension unsettles the evening's civilized entertainment. Because her persistent concern up to this point has been the sexual exploitation and consumption of nubile women in the sexual marketplace, this poem affords rare comic relief from the protests about the objectification of women. It peels away the layers of social assumptions about the role and place of a handicapped woman: then a limping woman was expected to marry a handicapped man and not seek to fulfill all the possible roles open to women. When they unite, handicapped and handicapped, a haunting question is raised, Which of my fears will wind itself around which of yours (*MS* 42)? The answers signal how each might have held the other back.

A favorite meditative poem in the collection is "The Night Has a Thousand Eyes," but even the title of this classic jazz tune evokes her suspicion of being watched. It celebrates her joy in a bitter-chocolate vein in New York streets and the city's mood. The words "can't afford" recur here, describing taxi drivers and their customers trying to pay fares. Despite its anonymity, New York is a kind of home for the poet, more so than California, with its gnarled history of land monopolies, police and ecclesiastical corruption, and racial exploitation. In New York there is nothing new for the lyric "I," nothing she hasn't thought or taught. She contemplates familiar New York, with its predictably acerbic atmosphere of bustle, crass commercialism, and ambition. But friends remembered actually take priority over the place: they are Paul Goodman, the influential writer, and Muriel Rukeyser, whose forceful, revolutionary poetry would likely have lent Rich courage in the early days of her poetic struggle for women's liberation. All the persons alluded to here are those who inspired her during prior turning points in her life. If, to Rich, writing is "re-naming," and "Poetry comes out of silence, seeking connection with unseen others," these are the persons with whom she dwells in silent, intimate communion when she imagines the city, and both are dead.

"The Night Has a Thousand Eyes" is the poem that the *Progressive* critic Rafael Campo calls the "book's crowning achievement"[11] because of the way it revisits the mining and retrieval metaphors of *Diving into the Wreck* and presents Marxist thought, the artist/poet visionary William Blake—note this direct quotation from Blake: *"energy : Eternal Delight"* (*MS* 53)—Hart Crane, and Julia de Burgos. It reflects on the poet Muriel Rukeyser, Rich's friend, whose energy before her stroke was phenomenal; she envisions Rukeyser after her stroke gazing at "The Lordly Hudson" with her mind stretching on the water (*MS* 47).

Rafael Campo sees this as a "vision of a world where art—pure product of the crafter's hands—takes ironic precedence over industry," and we literally "view industry through the filter of art or poetry." Thus "[t]he nearly vanishing nature of the poet's art is distilled to a name written in breath on a windowpane." He concludes, "always mindful of her difficult place in this imperfect world, yet courageous enough (as they were) to envision its eventual healing, Rich is the worthy successor to these poets. In honoring them, and in fashioning her own astonishing poems, she teaches us all humility."[12] This is heady praise.

Another critic, Adam Newley in the *New Statesman,* notes that while *Dark Fields of the Republic* moved "in vast landscapes," *Midnight Salvage* confines itself to "tighter more intimate spaces and urban snapshots: a New York subway, a Harvard Restaurant, the house of the photographer and revolutionary Tina Modotti"[13]—all of these are, as it were, caught on "film" in her poetry. But this is not entirely true, as "Camino Real" investigates both the beauty of the Pacific alongside Highway 1, ranging the entire length of the state, and it overlooks, too, the scenes of torture, which a perusal of California history conjures up. "Still, the tide of anger so evident in earlier work has abated here."[14]

Adam Newley focuses on her use of "incremental repetition, repetition-with-variation, anaphora, aposiopesis, direct address, and apostrophe, techniques that suggest (or trope) oral delivery, techniques that won't repel inexperienced readers." He comments on how Rich's "drive for democracy, for readerly access, alters and sometimes damages her style (especially her diction)."[15] Is this a valid criticism? Her democratic drive is born of a need to reach out to "unseen others" and an effort to make her language truly accessible to working-class Americans.

Newley focuses on her concern with "Happiness," that quality long absent from her work, and comments on her assertion here of poetry's ability to render the pull of love and fix the moment photographically, and emotionally in the medium of words (*MS* 33). Her vulnerability and candor are uncharacteristic, hence disarming: in a poem like this she shatters the logical contrarieties to produce a transcendent synthesis, a reconciliation of the opposites dividing the powerful from the oppressed, and of all intellectual dichotomies or opposing fields, revealing the deftness with which she embodies Marxism in this poem.

In the final poem, "A Long Conversation," she consciously articulates and resolves this need for community. No longer held fast in loneliness, having mourned good friends who have died, she still gets up and writes every day since at work she may find the intellectual connection she needs to remain actively writing (*MS* 67). She desires a sense of community and "wants desperately to see her poems as part of a conversation, as social actions, as *something,* anything more than solitary struggles with words." Her need to reach out to the audience and to convey affectionate perceptions requires a more intimate tone, a freer style, and more experimental form.

"A Long Conversation" again accesses the discursive to make political points, crossing the borders between prose and poetry to produce a more philosophical poem. Her love for the ideas and causes she has espoused and her love for humanity drive her desire to incorporate Marx (Coleridge's request to Wordsworth to write a poem encouraging those who have given up on "*the amelioration of mankind*"[*MS* 63]), teaching through the medium of the poem. And what follows the rhythmical quotation from Coleridge is in fact a strong poem sounding a familiar apologia—that the poetry is only just beginning to match the desire of "visionaries" and revolutionaries (*MS* 63). Here strong internal rhyme, alliteration, and thrilling imagery convey both great urgency and a strong sense of the periodic pull of the revolutionary cycle. Arguably this is reasonably difficult poetry for the person on the street who does not know the meaning of "abraded," for instance. Stephen Burt was right when he argued, in reviewing this book, that " (some of the people who say they dislike Rich's past few books haven't tried hard to read them)."[16] This is undeniably true. The "visionary!" Rich writes poems that are gnomic, memorable, and true to the future or the past, not necessarily the present, striving to link the right words with fragile images, subtle emotions, and revolutionary desires (*MS* 63).

A possible future American Poet Laureate, Rich speaks to the heart of the nation and the republic, dispelling a national mental fog that tends to creep in. The poem moves through links between the way people from different professions in society fall into the proletariat (*MS* 62) in the random way that words from every language or walk of life turn up in a poem (*MS* 60), and the connection between love for one's craft and love for a beloved. The poem winds on subtly and hopefully toward the affirmation that the speaker could think of a line that one day might end in *love* (*MS* 64). It might be a poem resembling the one written by the young revolutionary Che Guevara, who spoke of love in connection with revolution most eloquently and whose life, to Rich, embodies the ideal of an effective political activist. Imagining love or a harmonious socialist or Marxist community as a culmination of the revolution is an effective political strategy. Naturally, too, Karl Marx's ideas inform the political passions in this poem, as do Bertholt Brecht's.

Clearly Rich wants to share with her readers the political philosophies that have driven her recent quest to move beyond feminism into Marxism: the first revolution she effected was women's, and the next embraces the equality of men and women governing together. None of these thinkers are women, a fact soon noted by feminist critics. These poems afford the reader a glimpse of her other political passion, Marxist thought, an intellectual vein she has been mining of late as more conducive to social and political reform, now that the wave of the women's liberation has broken and slightly subsided, and traditional feminism may appear too white, academic, and elitist to accommodate the range of women still suffering injustice on earth. Having spoken the buzz words *love* and *happiness,* touchstone concept of Marxist thought, in the final poem, she mixes archaic language and rhetoric, some banal prose, some flashes of beauty in images; it is clear that the book is still imbued by the poet's need to discern whose image she sees "in the dark windowglass"—and to see truth clearly. Like the narrator trying to catch a glimpse of Heathcliffe's Catherine through the window in *Wuthering Heights,* she yearns to catch sight of a hazy face that may be her own and she asks the same of burnt out, cramped, all-too-human language, saluting it and inquiring if it is still "you" (*MS* 69)?

How can human language ever successfully give voice to the spirit of revolution? This is Rich's problem and challenge. Her great strength inheres in her ability to give voice to the spirits of both the Marxist and feminist revolutions, hoping to inspire readers to see more possibilities in history and in well-informed direct action. She has already reclaimed the feminine majority of America and now wants to involve and mobilize all men.

Chapter 10

A Revolutionary Textual Strategy Embodying the Materiality of Women's Experience

In poetry and prose, for Adrienne Rich, the self-defined passionate skeptic, as we have seen, self-creation and self-transformation through poetic practice is an integral part of her feminist thinking and consciousness. Her poetry shows how *"a revolutionary textual strategy connects with the materiality of women's oppression."*[1] To that end, it embodies an alternative feminist selfhood and subjectivity and contacts a transpersonal ideal democracy where all Americans are—or can be—politically, intellectually, and spiritually linked the way sections of the American continent are linked. Poetry is obviously more than a vocation for Rich: it is a mission. In her later poetry it is apparent that she yearns for limpid clarity through generating concrete images and engaging in a philosophical discourse with the reader. Without communication with her ideal, intimate, omniscient reader (and of course her real audience), she would not enjoy what traditionalists consider a complete life because it would not be a useful one. She sees lives lived apart from community as lacking in usefulness or meaning; lives lived selfishly are *"silly, ironic, terrible,"* echoing the same succession of descriptors in Tolstoy's *Death of Ivan Ilich,* where these adjectives describes Ilich's life. Her mission is—at least in part—to awaken America to a realization of how it has forgotten the meaning of "we," how to unite in community, and no longer have any interest in "you," so we are left with only "I." The events of 9/11/01 awoke the nation to a consciousness of the importance of defining "we"—the real intrinsic state of the union. As Rich puts it, "It is exhilarating to be alive in a time of awakening of consciousness; it can also be confusing, disorienting, and painful."[2]

Adrienne Rich may see Helen Vendler, Harold Bloom—and others who accuse her of making her poetry too political—as critics who misunderstand the interrelationship between poetry and real life, science, and the American national vision. Valuing a poem chiefly for the beauty of its rhythm, rhyme, style, or its musicality overlooks the importance—even the necessity—of forging common bonds of community and a common zeal to reform and *re-member* the American nation, so that everyone might develop a vision and have equal access to work, recreation, and natural resources. Those who formerly praised her may now occasionally criticize the lack of craftsmanship and musicality in her poetry. Rich publishes a retort to this criticism, quoting Vendler in *What Is Found There,* as one voice of opposition:

> In this time, a critic of poetry writes, *The question for an American poet, living in relative personal and national peace and plenty, is how to find the imaginative interest in life without invoking a false theatricality, how to be modest without being dull, how to be moving without being maudlin.* (*WF* 108)

Rich's reply is sharp and on-target; the lyric "I" points out the numbers of wars and killings going on at this very moment. Scornfully she comments that their difference in perspectives reveals a difference both in class, economic level, and ethics:

> Vendler's phrase "To find the imaginative interest in life" suggests the mission of a vigorous, comfortably retired middle-class citizen considering the choice of a hobby or volunteer work—hardly a poet. For most people, let alone most poets, the problem is not "finding an imaginative interest in life," but sustaining the blows of the material and imaginative challenges of our time. A growing, perhaps predominant, number of poets write—when and as they are able to—out of fields of stress that cannot be evaded, public crises of neglect and violence. (*WF* 108)

As Rich wrote in *Atlas,* in times of crisis we must face the most difficult challenges facing the country imaginatively and intelligently, seeing them in the light of history and of philosophical analysis. Only then, once we have a formulated a careful strategy, is it possible to discuss how important it is to examine the national obsession with violence in art as well as "theatricality and maudlinity."

Only then can we deal with the "problems of creating an art rooted in language"—and life (*WF* 115)—but which or whose American English is real?

Equally, Rich deplores the narcissistic sprawling American middle class addicted to "self-entertainment." How to teach them to say "we" and experience a sense of social compact or trusting community again? She wants to stop blinkered, narcissistic North Americans from endlessly, selfishly repeating "I" without awareness of the suffering in the rest of the world (*D* 4). She hopes that hers might be the persistent voice of water dripping on the stone of the national heart (*WF* 122), patiently wearing away smug, middle-class American complacency and greed.

Not only are these political motives for poetry important in themselves, they reveal her impetus to contact and renew the nation itself. The use of the word *fields* in the prose passage above—"fields of stress that cannot be avoided"—is significant since her next book is *Dark Fields of the Republic,* taking its title from Fitzgerald's phrase from *The Great Gatsby,* "the dark fields of the republic," flowing out westward from his home on the Atlantic. In those fields Gatsby had long ago left his innocence and faith.

In the same essay, she recounts how she had recently dreamed of being at a restaurant and had a waitress ask her if she would let a homeless woman finish the plate of pasta she was leaving. After assenting to this, she realizes that she is expected to sit with the woman while she finishes it, too. This dream vision literally brings home the real state of the poor and homeless in America now and their proximity to those well-enough-off to eat in restaurants. In "A clearing in the imagination" Rich asserts that the real problem for North American poets is to find a way of capturing the public's attention and "bearing witness to a reality" the public—and even the poet—may want to avoid (*WF* 115).

Just as the dreaming speaker may have wanted to leave the homeless woman with the food and go, so, too, average Americans wish someone else would take care of the problem of homelessness, so they might get on with life and not have to worry about the poor. This represents a central conflict in Rich's poetry: like all intelligent people facing the new millennium, she remains faithful though without a faith, ambivalent about the homeless; her integrity demands she sit with the homeless woman although her background as a southern Jew might make it difficult.

Two concepts of the purpose of poetry are also at war here: critics attack her, but Rich sees herself as one of those who truly understands the historical moment and is behaving responsibly. In the words of British critic Ann Curthoys, "We live in an obscurely apocalyptic moment."[3] Rich has a prophetic vision of how America should be changing, but is not. Her female subject positions and haunting questions force the reader to think about the American body politic as it actually is—or could be remembered—rather than as background or landscape for an intellectual foreground of concepts, thought, and feeling.

Adrienne Rich might concur with David Mura, chronicler of the Japanese-Americans' experience in the internment camps during World War II, who said, "If poetry gets too far towards the realm of the aesthetic, the formal, and the beautiful and doesn't acknowledge the other side of existence—the history that we live in, the changes and the darkness of history—then the life goes out of poetry, and it becomes an escape."[4] For those who would exclude a majority of the human race in order to bring imaginative interest to poetry, poems are an escape. But for those open to fresh ideas and the possibility of political, even poetic change, poetry is necessary for American citizens, so many of whom are apathetic and do not vote, in that it indicates directions for useful social change.

Opposing those who would cast her out of the Western canon are feminist and other critics like Margaret Dickie, Wendy Martin, Betsy Erkkila, Cynthia Hogue, and Paula Bennett, among others, who judge Rich by standards crafted from a wide variety of postmodern theoretical positions—French feminist theory, feminist theory, cultural studies or the New Modernism. Rich speaks mainly to them, their students, and her readers worldwide, not to the older generation of critics. At present Rich is less interested in literary criticism, than in rectifying more pressing moral and political concerns in contemporary America. Rich still speaks to the ideal American reader and the marginalized "common woman," who may either resemble the homeless woman or the one whom AnaLouise Keating imagines as

> not "white," but not "black" either; not "straight," but not quite "lesbian"—spends almost her entire life reading, searching for an explanation to account for her sense of difference, her feeling of not—ever—fitting in...she experiences...re (con)ceived otherness.[5]

I suggest this woman may be Rich's ideal audience. For all people crossing over into a new consciousness of the republic, of self, and American national potential, Rich is the prophet and visionary, the poet who offers some perspective, asking "us," *Where do we view it from?* (*A* 6), echoing Freud and Nietzsche. More than any other poet writing in and to America, she encourages her reader to think, indeed, *demands* that one review and reintegrate one's life with a view to contemporary history.

Marianne Moore wrote, "*As contagion of / sickness makes sickness / contagion of trust can make trust.*"[6] The older Adrienne Rich courageously assumes that Americans can be trusted and encouraged to think, share common perceptions, and develop more national cooperation, focusing together on a higher vision of the republic and citizens' responsibilities to it. She is most alive as a poet when exploring the ethical, spiritual, or political terrain and charting the atlas of this difficult land.

DECLINING THE NATIONAL MEDAL FOR THE ARTS

If she is so interested in America, then why did she decline the National Medal for the Arts in 1997? In comes the published statement of her belief in the poet's responsibility toward her community and her country:

> My "no" came directly out of my work as a poet and essayist and citizen drawn to the interfold of personal and public experience. I had recently been thinking and writing about the growing fragmentation of the social compact, of whatever it was

this country had ever meant when it called itself a democracy, the shredding of the vision of government of the people, by the people, for the people. "We the people—still an excellent phrase," said the prize-winning playwright Lorraine Hansberry in 1962...I had for years been feeling both personal and public grief, fear, hunger and the need to render this, my time, in the language of my art.[7]

Rich's goal is in part to wake America up to an increasing fragmentation of the social compact and of democracy, using the language of her art, where since the beginning of her awakening, she has felt both personal and public grief, fear, hunger, and the urge to make it public in print. Using Lorraine Hansberry's courageous words against government during the Cuban missile crisis, at a public meeting in New York to abolish the House Un-American Activities Committee, Rich claims Hansberry as a model of courage; and at the time Hansberry, as Rich points out, did not say "*My government is wrong.*'" Instead, she claimed and owned "her government as a citizen, African-American and female, and she challenged it." Characteristically, Rich is modest and unsentimental about this; instead she asks others to follow Hansberry's example and question governmental decisions:

In a similar spirit, many of us today might wish to hold government accountable, challenge the agendas of private power and wealth that have displaced historical tendencies toward genuinely representative government in the United States. We might still wish to claim our government, to say, This belongs to us—we, the people, as we are now.[8]

In fact, many are doing so today, and many are rereading these words with a new sense of urgency.

Seeing so many alienated and disenfranchised citizens and so much voter apathy in the United States today, she suggests that nonvoting citizens, angered by politicians' misuse and abuse of power, should reclaim their right to hold government accountable to the people, consequently changing the current state of injustice and inequity into truly democratic government. Because of such criticisms of the government, she refused the National Medal for the Arts. She asks:

What would it require for people to live and work together in conditions of radical equality?...And what about art? Mistrusted, adored, pietized, condemned, dismissed as entertainment,...It's also reborn hourly in prisons, women's shelters, small-town garages, community college workshops, halfway houses—wherever someone picks up a pencil,...this regeneration process, could help you save your life.[9]

Rich's courage of her convictions speaks loud and clear here, as do her antielitism, and her putting poetry, language, and government back into the hands of the common people, and her abiding desire is to write from what she calls in this essay the "interfold of personal and public experience." Not the lesbian separatist some critics have accused her of being, Adrienne Rich has emerged as fully realized lesbian-feminist-Marxist poet. She is still a visionary or oracular poet of the people in the tradition of Emerson, Thoreau, and Whitman more than ever before, but like Neruda and Aimé Cesaire, whose lines she quotes in her refusal of the National Medal for the Arts, her radical feminism now embraces Marxism, too, as well as a poetry of selfhood in which the poem rehearses the process of translating what society first called "Other" into the self; this process is, in Gayatri Spivak's resistant discourse, a common matter of mainstream feminist "selfing"; the self we see in the mirror is, herself, a sign of process, construction, erasure.[10]

If some have not comprehended her vision of the integration of poems, power, government, and life in all its current manifestations, *Arts of the Possible* is her political *ars poetica,* explaining what she writes.

ARTS OF THE POSSIBLE

Alice Templeton has analyzed what she calls Rich's "dialogic imagination" sensitively and perceptively, showing how it develops from *Diving into the Wreck* through *A Wild Patience Has Taken Me This Far*: she traces the way the poems engage in intellectual and imaginative dialogues on concerns of our times, responding to each other successively. I see the same progression in both Rich's later poetry and her prose, continuing on in *Time's Power, Your Native Land, Your Life,* the last books, and *Arts of the Possible.* The progression of her political philosophy culminates in these final works: these subsume all her most important ideas and clarify the dialectic of her thinking about politics, the interrelationship of poetry, life, and politics, existing at the border or joint where "personal and public experience"[11] connect, and expressing her desire to reach out to the intimate listening reader, who may feel alone in America.

Adrienne Rich is one of the most important American poets writing today. Always original and unique, her work demands a closer reading. Alicia Ostriker has commented:

> For nearly half a century the voice of Adrienne Rich has charted America's changing mental, emotional, and moral landscape in poetry in essays fueled by the twin motives of a thirst for justice and a quest to stretch the imagination.[12]

And Albert Gelpi analyzes her impact:

> Her poetry, always implicitly political and feminist, became overtly and radically so in the late 1960s and 1970s, and the large and remarkable body of work she has written since then has marked her as one of the defining poets of the second half

> of the [twentieth] century. Her work is read throughout the world and has altered our sense of the scope of poetry and its function in social and cultural change. (*ARP* 291)

Virtually transforming all our ideas about womanhood and woman's place in Western civilization, Rich has advanced political and cultural purposes through subtle, brilliantly evocative poetry, giving expression to the thoughts and feelings of many ordinary Americans—women and men alike. Many read her work even if they read no other poet, probably because, as Alice Templeton expresses it, "Rich's work confronts the romantic promise of liberation through aesthetic experience."[13] This book has explored the ways she integrates women's drive to integrity and full citizenship into material poetry and the ways she fashions the female subject and selfhood.

In her own words, in "Dearest Arturo," she writes, "in the act of writing, to feel our own 'questions' meeting the world's 'questions,' to recognize how we are in the world and the world in us" (*WF* 26), Rich explores all the large social and political questions haunting the new millennium in her poetry and assumes nearly every female subject position, exploring women's self-fashioning as self-creating in her poetry. The sense of being "Split at the Root" she has stuck with her from early on stimulates her to a greater compassion for those the world she was born into excluded—especially women, African Americans, and Jews.

Adrienne Rich is a Jewish Marxist feminist and lesbian; as such, she has been praised or castigated by many, honored at the highest levels, and is ignored by none who actually read and are open to poetry today.[14] She is recognized as one of the best poets and critics writing in America today. Her own powerful critical essays expounding feminist theory have greatly influenced our understanding and evaluation of her poetry; consciously or unconsciously, through her theoretical and critical writings, Rich, Sylvia Henneberg alleges, has even molded her own critical reception,[15] manipulating how her readership sees her work. But is this attributing Rich with more power than she actually has? Is it possible that a poet could control her own critical reception? Other critics, like Willard Spiegelman, insist that no critic has ever given her "the literary criticism she most deserves."[16] Certainly all critics and commentators have likely labored under the influence of her authorial authority as well as under what Michie has called "the enabling authority of experience."[17]

While on the one hand these objections pay a backhanded compliment to Rich's power as a critic and theorist and to her position as founder of women's studies and gender studies, I do not ultimately think she has controlled her critical reception, nor can any poet do that. I agree with Willard Spiegelman that she needs the literary criticism that would lead readers to confront the poetry for themselves so as to discern what sort of a poet Adrienne Rich is. Indeed, her critical triumph in *Arts of the Possible,* plainly an effort to trace the development of her political thought, has clarified the major premises of her oeuvre.

Although except in the classroom Rich seldom engages in explications of her own individual poems or publishes accounts of her poems' origin, over the past three decades she has published many essays, occasional pieces including journal-like writings, and reviews, that reflect on her process of poetic composition and her essential aesthetic and political philosophy. *Arts of the Possible* collects a number of essays on poetry and her politics of literature, her clarifications. Yet another aim of this book is to evaluate this original approach and to accord her poetry the depth of independent criticism it deserves.

Arts of the Possible may be seen as Rich's personal credo and testimony, her effort to make clear to her readership how America might change and re-envision herself with each citizen's help, morally, politically, and spiritually. "To read . . . [her] sharp, clear, and uncompromising essays on gender, art, and social responsibility is to enter a place where the light is brighter than in everyday life, where sound is crisper, and the line between right and wrong holds firm."[18] She has arranged these seminal essays in a sequence that clarifies her social and political philosophy and corrects any potential misapprehensions. Giving her declaration of faith in revolution in the essay "Blood, Bread, and Poetry," moving through the necessity of stamping out dishonesty in the body politic in *On Lies, Secrets, and Silence,* she shows the "trajectory of her thinking—from the now-classic 'When We Dead Awaken: Writing as Re-Vision,' through her engagements with issues of gender and sexuality, language and its corruptions, political systems and their possibilities—keenly arguing with herself and others, avidly reading other poetry from around the globe, and always asking how poetry can break free of its traps to further what is 'humanly possible' in our lives."[19] The book provides the necessary counterbalance to her poetry, articulating ideas hinted at in the poetry, expanding on allusions, rounding out the concepts she can only touch on in poems.

A POET OF OPPOSITIONAL AND DIALECTICAL IMAGINATION

Tellingly, Adrienne Rich has defined herself as "a poet of oppositional imagination" (*AR* 8). Although her roots are those of a fundamentally Jewish woman raised as a Christian, she is Other, a cultural, ethnic outsider, and her sense of being a member of a community of "oppositional" women is one point of departure. On the dual exclusion of Jewish women, she writes in "If Not with Others, How?":

We exist everywhere under laws we did not make; speaking a multitude of languages; excluded by law and custom from certain spaces... resources associated with power; often accused of wielding too much power, of wielding dark and devious powers. Like Black and other dark-skinned people, Jews and women have haunted white Western thought as Other, as fantasy, as projected obsession. (*B* 203)

At one point, she explains the tentative, exploratory nature of her quest more poetically than politically in *Arts of the Possible:*

For more than fifty years I have been writing, tearing up, revising poems, studying poets from every culture and century available to me. I have been a poet of the oppositional imagination, meaning that I don't think my only argument is with myself. (*AR* 8)

Rich's assertion is that we must make poetry out of the quarrels with ourselves and with others. Poetry of oppositional imagination or the exploration of conflicts of the imagination and intellect (in poetry) with our culture can bear witness to the real problems and suffering in the contemporary world or can testify to the realities of life after Auschwitz, after which Theodor Adorno declared no poetry was possible.

The title of *Arts of the Possible* has, as one would expect, double and triple entendres: politics is the art of the possible; therefore, the book accounts for her development as a poet exploring everything to confront the causes of suffering and end it—or at least to force its reader into an awareness of what is and what is humanly possible both in art and in what we call real life:

What is humanly possible if we require something beyond the horrible culture of production for profit? Human beings aren't merely determined by capitalist production—Marx never said that. These are conditions "not of our choosing" in which we can make history. What's humanly possible might be what we bring to the refusal to let our humanity be stolen from us.

It may seem aggrandizing to say that poetry can have a hand in this, but I believe it can, in its own way and on its own terms. (*AR* 145)

Actually, Rich believes fervently in the redeeming role poetry may play in national revolution. She believes art must

grow organically out of the social compost nourishing to everyone, a literate citizenry, a free, universal, public education complex with art as an integral element, a society honoring both human individuality and the search for a decent, sustainable common life. In such conditions, art would still be a voice of hunger, desire, discontent, passion, reminding us that the democratic project is never-ending. (*AR* 146)

And, she immediately after inquires in another context, "For that to happen, what else would have to change?" (*AR* 105). Clearly, "you," the reader, she and I—everyone alive—must change. Elsewhere she writes, "If you are tying to transform a brutalized society into one where people can live in dignity and hope, you begin with the empowering of the most powerless. You build from the ground up."[20]

In shifting the final responsibility back onto the "you," the reader, she is well aware that in other ages and cultures or countries, poets have been honored and respected as civic and political leaders. Witness Vaclav Havel, former president of the Czech Republic and poet. In Latin America, too, writers like Gabriel García Márquez, the Peruvian novelist Mario Vargas Losa, and many other poets and writers have earned the right to give political counsel and be listened to by ordinary citizens of their countries. In other countries people look to poets to help them make political decisions and for leadership in time of war. But in America today, Rich attests, poetry is frequently mocked, trivialized as irrelevant, devalued, or ignored. But clearly Rich sees it as a time when, more than ever, citizens of conscience should be speaking out. She perceives herself as writing in a tradition of activist poets committed to social and political change, beginning with Muriel Rukeyser, Denise Levertov, and June Jordan, and culminating in a number of contemporary poets like Mahmoud Darwish (*AR* 159), some revolutionary, who articulate the reality of the interfold between poetry and politics for the individual of conscience in times of war, over-incarceration, and slavery.

Clearly here in *Arts of the Possible,* the poetry provokes serious thought and a radical postmodern reevaluation of the premises of Western culture globally; these are not only explicit themes but also dynamic life-transforming conduits to moral action, soul directives. She avers, "I have thought recently that my poetry exposes that scarring of the human psyche under the conditions of a runaway, racist capitalism. But that's because my psyche is also scarred by these conditions" (*AR* 145). Poetry's work is to expose and heal all scarrings of the psyche to the extent that is humanly possible. My task has been to assess Rich's strategies for aesthetic and literary liberation critically in the evolution of her philosophical and spiritual effort to advance a reawakening to a new American identity and democracy and building community through poetry. The question of how to fight oppression and injustice is still uppermost in her mind, and as long as she lives, she will probably never stop speaking out and criticizing politicians.

WOMEN'S STUDIES

Adrienne Rich's work has been the creative impetus for the new academic field of women's studies; her conceptual essays have prompted a reexamination of literature, language, history, and every field from women's perspective. In the 1930s, in "Men and Women," Virginia Woolf posed the problem intellectual women have always faced, a situation that Krista Ratcliffe calls "Bathsheba's dilemma": "'I have the feelings of a woman,' says Bathsheba in *Far from the Madding Crowd* [a novel by Thomas Hardy], 'but I have only the language of men.'"[21] How women might develop their own language and rhetoric, their own structures of thought, their own studies, revisioning all study so as to restore the female voice history had silenced—these are the tasks of women's studies. Not surprisingly most references to Adrienne Rich on the internet at present—and there are more than one hundred thousand—are from quotations in women's studies syllabi. Her essays on the subject constitute a central source for readings in women's studies. From the prophetically titled "When We Dead Awaken" on through "Toward a More Feminist Criticism" in *Blood, Bread, and Poetry,* to all the essays in *What is Found There,* Rich has pulled together the central premises, theory, and questions in women's studies. Ratcliffe states, "Adrienne Rich explores Bathsheba's [or "the daughter-in-law's"] dilemma in both her poetry and her prose, articulating the dilemma,"[22] citing Rich's observation of the absence of writing women in classical literature as her motive for problematic resistance and revision.

Rich was one of the first to point out that any real woman is absent from the text, hence this creates a woman's sense of herself as Other, as different from the implied reader, and this is nullifying, puzzling to the female reader. An image of woman exists in men's literature, but it is not that of the woman who writes, gropes for words, is sometimes inspired and sometimes not (*ARP* 170–71).

Rich herself confesses that she was barely aware of other women poets at the start of her career. Those she read did not particularly impress her, nor were they her poetic models. Of her youthful first efforts at poetry, she has acknowledged that her style was first formed by male poets. In order to restore the balance, over the past 30 years she has written a poetry of transgressive female selfhood and of feminist subject positions for *all* readers. Since her feminist awakening she has modeled female self-fashioning.

As she says to the entire postmodern reading community, everyone must reenvision what has influenced our intellectual and philosophical development so "we" can learn to criticize it and alter its influence over us, revising our assumptions. It is important to know what has been written before, not to pass on a tradition, but to be able to be aware of and resist its hold on "us" (*ARP* 168). Consequently, the past 50 years have seen an explosion of a war against sexism worldwide and a readjustment of the sex roles. And in "Toward a More Feminist Criticism," Adrienne Rich says to her postmodern critical audience, but at that moment, particularly to women, "we need to support each other in rejecting the limitations of a tradition—a manner of reading, of speaking, of writing, of criticizing—which was never really designed to include us at all" (*ARP* 168). By deconstructing the racist or sexist assumptions in our canon, we can test each literary masterpiece to assess its value and authenticity for the present.

It would be practically impossible to teach women's studies, feminist theory, or feminist criticism anywhere in the world without reference to Adrienne Rich's prose and poetry. Contemplating women's studies without Adrienne Rich is like contemplating psychoanalysis without Freud and Jung. In her critical essays and since "Diving into the Wreck," she has shown feminist scholars—women and men alike—how to search the traditional canon of literature: "*I came to see the damage that was done*" and "*the treasures that prevail*" (*DW* 23). Rich is fully aware of men's contributions to culture and civilization: she merely wants women's contributions acknowledged equally and for women to be given the credit justly due them, as she said in "Resisting Amnesia" (*B* 154–55).

The exhilaration and sense of adventure the lyrical "I" felt exploring the treasures of a whole new field still imbue her essays; and the impetus toward truth and exploration, what is humanly possible, remains the same: "*there is the challenge and promise of a whole new psychic geography to be explored*" (*ARP* 168).

Despite her pioneering efforts in women's studies, however, she sees herself first and foremost as a poet. Poetry can undo some of the damage the industrial and technological revolutions may have done to the human imagination. It repairs the fragmentation and compartmentalization of modern life, of private and public, restoring a sense of community and the social compact: poetry can heal divisions between different groups and help create "happiness, collectivity, community," and bring about "a loss of isolation" (*WF* 239). Of her future, Rich writes, "I intend to go on trying to be part of what I think of as an underground stream—of voices resisting the voices that tell us we are nothing" (*WF* 241).

A REVOLUTIONARY POETRY, A LIFE OF SERVICE

For Rich, poetry reflects hope and performs a work of service. In some circles, "Service" may be considered a beautiful word fallen upon hard times. Matthew Arnold, other Victorians—and indeed some Romantics—had a conception of the usefulness of poetry and the need for poets to be of service to mankind. In nineteenth century America, Walt Whitman saw the poet's vocation of service as the salvation and unification of the nation. Today very few poets think of poetry as a service to humanity.

Adrienne Rich sees America as torn by divisions, its revolutionary spirit occasionally quelled by despair. Claire Keyes shows the purpose of her poetry's lived connection with the contemporary:

An awareness of these [political and cultural] influences can tell us as much about our institutions as about the poet. In effect, Adrienne Rich's poetry constitutes an indictment of the times, specifically those power structures that limit and dehumanize us all.[23]

In Rich's more recent essays she indicates that the best poetry by women *or men* **can** heal and mend those divisions, give us all the courage we need to keep working for constructive social change.

The epigraph to Rich's anthology *The Best American Poetry 1996* comes from John Berger's "The Hour of Poetry" and testifies to poetry's healing abilities:

Every authentic poem contributes to the labour of poetry... to bring together what life has separated or violence has torn apart.... Poetry can repair no loss, but it defies the space which separates. And it does this by continual labour of reassembling what has been scattered.[24]

True poetry heals what has been separated or torn apart—the scars in the psyche. Making original connections, reknitting the bones in the body of the American imagination and national vision—that is the calling of poetry, Adrienne Rich's calling, one she shares with Muriel Rukeyser. Of Rukeyser's metaphor of knitting, she writes in *Arts of the Possible:* "The opening of 'Poem out of Childhood' points to her lifelong project of knitting together personal experience with politics." "Knitting together" does not apply to Rukeyser's poetry; according to Rich, "in her words, she simply did not allow them to be torn apart" (*AR* 122). Typically, Rich plays with an image and then reverses its meaning to make an important point: American citizens must never allow politics to be sundered or separated from their personal philosophies and convictions.

As one of the first feminist poets to have the courage to write directly as a woman and defy the ordeals Aunt Jennifer, her first feminine hero, was mastered by, Adrienne Rich imparts an ever-transforming courage through her poetry and prose. She forces us to reexamine rigorously or restructure social and political institutions and female subject positions that objectify women and drive them apart. On another level, her work expresses the strength born of an honestly examined, fulfilled literary life, one where the creative intellect and life collaborate to produce an integrated whole at the interfold of the personal and the political.

Rich's poetry imparts a regenerative strength as an antidote to despair, even as it gives voice to much pain. Surprisingly, over a century after Matthew Arnold, Rich quietly reclaims the Victorian redemptive function of poetry as a powerful force for good, an imperative to social action. She has always seen this vocation as a challenge and never expected poetry to be easy. Hers is the uncompromising rebel voice of "oppositional imagination." Hence she continues to take the path of *most* resistance.

In *Blood, Bread, and Poetry,* she defines her position as a revolutionary woman poet, constantly in the state of transformation as the American body politic itself transforms. She voices her sense of being compelled to fashion the female subject:

> [t]o write directly and overtly as a woman, out of a woman's body and experience, to take women's existence seriously as theme and source for art, was something I had been hungering to do, needing to do, all my writing life....
>
> Women have understood that we needed an art of our own: to remind us of our history and what we might be; to show us our true faces—all of them, including the unacceptable; to speak of what has been muffled in code or silence; to make concrete the values our movement was bringing forth....
>
> ...As a lesbian-feminist poet and writer, I need to understand how this location affects me, along with the realities of blood and bread within this nation. (*B* 182–83)

Her politics of location has stirred up much debate in that it crystallizes and names what had previously been undefined: unless politics and poetry mutually inform and interweave emotionally and conceptually with one another, Rich asserts, there can be no authentic poetry. On the other hand, extending this premise logically, is nationhood or multiculturalism impossible if everyone is writing from his or her own separate location? How might understanding be achieved between diverse groups?

Better at provoking questions than answering them, Rich's poetry continues its successive radical transformations, registering poetically how current intellectual currents and political and military realities affect us all.

CHANGING THE (FEMALE) SUBJECT: WOMEN'S POETRY REVISITED

Throughout this book we have seen how her subject positions and self-fashioning have operated as a seismograph for the American woman's self-knowledge in her quest for a fuller identity and new selfhood. In the essay "The Hermit's Scream," she has accounted for the incendiary component in her poetic process, valuing poetry's "incendiary power to reconnect her with others"—with other men and women and "unseen others"—as well as with the body and all that is outside it, making external the inner text of her poetic career:

> The relationship among so many feelings remains unclear. But these thoughts and feelings, suppressed and stored up and whispered, have an incendiary component. You cannot tell where or how they will connect, spreading underground from rootlet to rootlet till every grassblade is afire from every other. Poetry, in its

own way, is a carrier of the sparks, because it too comes out of silence, seeking connection with unseen others.[25]

Early on, she viewed herself as *an instrument in the shape of a woman* translating electrical impulses into meaning, as in "Orion." Like the light-beams of stars, her poetry "comes out of silence," the crucible of psychic and cultural transformation; it is "a carrier of the sparks... seeking connection with unseen others."[26] We have traced the first 50 years of her evolution as a poet, and in its course, sparks have flown out to millions of unseen others who have been touched and ignited by them. Her poetry shows that one poetic vision can illuminate our ordinary world so that we see it in a new light, and as a result American poetry is changed forever. Eventually we may come to learn from her to read a common language that is both *womanly* and *powerful.*

CODA

Of course Adrienne Rich's current poetry and prose is ostensibly for and about the poor and oppressed, to whom Rich wants to bring the news that is only found in poems. Both as a critic and a poet she espouses "feminist reading" as a "liberating intellectual act" and argues

> A radical critique of literature, feminist in its impulse, would take the work first of all as a clue to how we live, how we have been living, how we have been led to imagine ourselves, how our language has trapped as well as liberated us, how the very act of naming has been till now a male prerogative and how we can begin to see and name—and therefore live—afresh. (*ARP1* 232)

Marianne Moore spoke of poems as being imaginary gardens with real toads in them: Rich would likely say poems should have real women in them.

Wallace Stevens said, "Ourselves in poetry must take their place"; similarly, citizens must take their part in America's future. All people may benefit from engaging in the creative self-integration achieved by poetry by opening the door of the poem onto the real world. Poetically, in the tradition of the oracular poets Dickinson, Emerson, and Whitman, poets following her advice must take part in the continuum of regenerative visionary poets. Rich's criticism and poetry express the spirit of the Gospel of Thomas, which says: "*When you bring forth what is in you, what you have will save you. That which you do not have in you will kill you if you do not know it within you.*"[27] Salvation can only come when the creative meets the spiritual, and both develop synergistically.

Significantly, Rich's most impressive venture outside of poetry, theory, and criticism, *Of Woman Born,* a book researching attitudes toward women in maternity aimed at redeeming maternity through a reconsideration of women's bodies and health, advances her conviction that

> female biology...has far more radical implications than we have yet come to appreciate. Patriarchal thought has limited female biology to its own narrow specifications. The feminist vision has recoiled from female biology for these reasons; it will, I believe, come to view our physicality as a resource rather than a destiny. In order to live a fully human life, we require not only control of our bodies...we must touch the unity and resonance of our physicality, the corporeal background of our intelligence. (*OWB* 62)

This mandate to "touch...the corporeal" ground "of our intelligence" seems to foresee the fact that subsequent feminism has become progressively more focused on the female body and the way culture has overwritten and inscribed the female body. Professor Leslie Calman, director of the Center for Research on Women at Barnard College, has claimed that "[academic] women's studies...has focused increasingly on symbols of the body and less on social action and social change." Professionally and intellectually, she affirms their right to speak out even though she continues to articulate "the patterns of history [and oppression] shared by women everywhere." While many writers of Rich's generation focused on symbols of the body, a younger generation of women writers wants to see the female body and female sexuality as dynamic conceptual resources in the formulation of feminist theory and to touch the "unity and resonance of our physicality, the corporeal ground of our intelligence."

In her movement toward her own theoretical approach, Rich seeks, as Jane Marcus expresses it in "Still Practice, A/Wrested Alphabet: Toward a Feminist Aesthetic," to "read the body of the text of the oppressed and silenced...a frustrating and selfless activity that must include...a recognition of one's own complicity in the silencing of the subject."[28] Adrienne Rich might resist the acceptance of her complicity, but she will never be silenced: her poetry and essays bear witness to her grappling with the problem of how to find *"a revolutionary textual strategy [that] connects with the materiality of women's oppression."* Rich seeks the social and political equivalent—to create a literary revolution through poetry and political action to end all human oppression. Considering the success she has enjoyed in helping to initiate social change and rethink gender, helping transform the concept of what it is to be female over the last part of the twentieth century and the first decade of the twenty-first, perhaps this dream is not as strange. Adrienne Rich will go down in history as a woman who did the most to change Western civilization's perception of women and impel the rise in women's status and standing worldwide. Along with founding the disciplines of women's studies and feminist criticism, she was the first to insist that not only were women equal, they were entitled to receive equal recognition for their intellectual, artistic, and professional creativity. Condoleeza Rice on one end of the political spectrum and bell hooks on the other, would not have been possible without Rich's and other feminists' courageous work on behalf of American women. Rich's efforts and those of all the supporters of women's liberation gave women what the Declaration of Independence originally failed to offer them—true citizenship, entitlement, and equality as thinkers, poets, voters, soldiers, legislators, and professionals. Two hundred years ago, the French woman novelist and poet George Sand imagined the New Woman that Adrienne Rich has worked to bring to life in her poetry—perhaps Rich herself?: "*The older woman I shall become will be quite different from the woman I am now. Another is beginning and so far I have not had to complain of her.*"[29]

Chapter 11

Fox: Postmodern Adrienne Rich

"I am a transparent eyeball."

—Emerson

Discussing the lyrical "I" in the poetry of an American poet writing and publishing in the twenty-first century is problematical at best. In this time after the death of the author, the lyrical "I" may be essentially what Adrienne Rich might deem old-fashioned. But in her latest book, *Fox: Poems 1998–2000,* containing more of the dark, prophetic millennial poems for which she become known in *An Atlas of the Difficult World* and *Midnight Salvage,* she declares that although mentally into the new century, our body parts are "still there" in the old.

Defining the dimensions of her postmodern lyrical "I" will be my focus in this chapter. I shall analyze the range of *"I"*s she employs and the range of *"you"*s she addresses, teasing out her poetic purposes in the light of these intimate relationships, illustrating her sense of mission to America at this moment.

Seen in Native American terms, some poems for the book *Fox* can be read as a paean to her totem animal, the fox, the original female wildness that has been bred out of civilized contemporary women. Her inner fox is a savage, free female: she is the female spirit whom Rich aspires to embody in her poetry—a vixen, utterly rebellious and antithetical to contemporary bourgeois American culture. Her fox has been a lifelong listener in the forest since at least the 1960s and in earlier fox poems the lyric "I" strongly identifies with the wild vixen; like the Native American, she is forever hunted by and ever fleeing "civilized" man and woman. Hence to understand the book *Fox,* one needs to understand that she is addressing parts of herself along with "you," her mysterious audience, composed in part of Michelle Cliff, all those who consistently read her poetry, including academic friends like Barbara Charlesworth Gelpi and Albert Gelpi, along with Rich's former husband Alfred H. Conrad, dead in 1970, and fellow poets, former students, her Santa Cruz poetry community, and feminist poetry lovers worldwide.

The book *Fox* is addressed to the vixen since she is one of the lyrical "I"s of the native, original, free Adrienne Rich. If two decades ago she wrote she was split at the root, the fox represents a current personal integration of formerly conflicting parts of *herpsyche* and selfhood. Her first chosen spirit guide, the fox, is a natural observer here, an animal few of us see very frequently in the wild, a reclusive, private perceiver, possibly critical of contemporary American civilization, as Rich herself may be.

Rich's lyrical "I"/Eye in *Fox* and her two prior books of poetry, as with many contemporary American women poets, is ever-changing, shifting, forever transforming itself from book to book, and is subtly influenced by her current readership, current events, perceptions, recognitions, and theory she is encountering at the moment of writing. She began a few books ago to address her imaginary reader directly, positively, politically, yet intimately, as if concerned to save her, and the simplest way of imagining this endangered species that she was addressing was perhaps to envision a fox.

It was her luck, as Rich puts it, to have been the mother of boys only, yet as a lesbian, feminist Jew, coming from the South, educated in the Northeast, she has a perennial need to identify with females of all species, too. Even though her own children were all male, boys whom she has loved dearly, protected fiercely, and who have given her grandchildren who delight her in her old age, she is also a mentor to the questing, intelligent twenty-first-century-female, her ideal reader; in many of the poems over the past decade she has addressed her in the first person (poems like "Victory"). The "you" here is the "fox" whom she encounters only in sacred sites, up sheer mountains or in the country around isolated cabins like the one where her husband died in Vermont.

Because Rich finds so much of contemporary American politics corrupt, reprehensible, or dishonest and unjust, it suits her, perhaps in the way Ted Hughes employed the *crow* as his totem animal, to adopt a fox as her ideal listener in the wilds, since along with Thoreau, she seems to believe that only in nature in wildness and in freedom, wild creatures have the capacity to save the world.

Much as she may hate to admit it, Rich came to fame first as the select, token female poet praised by the Modernist W. H. Auden, who published her first book as part of the prestigious Yale Younger Poets series. She and W. S. Merwin emerged into the same rarified poetic atmosphere of postwar Modernism; both were radicalized in the 1960s and 1970s. But unlike

Merwin, whose current poetry is not markedly different stylistically from what he was writing in the 1970s and 1980s, Rich's poetry transforms itself with each new book, and her poetic trajectory since 1970 has been through and out the other side of feminism to the point where she is disgusted with her following of faithful feminists and, like a vixen, tries to escape them. Among her other accomplishments, she is the celebrated founder of women's studies and the feminist movement, but in *Fox* and *Midnight Salvage* one would never suspect this. Her lyric "I" still addresses readers intimately and directly in lines that arrest their interest and envision them as alone reading at night, possibly heating milk for a baby, perhaps someone like her younger self—a young mother and developing poet, forced after the first years of marriage to raise her three boys by herself. So when she says in the first line of "Victory," "Something spreading underground won't speak to us," something moving in the forests won't declare its name (*F* 25), she is speaking of the fox who symbolizes the lost wildness and innocence in America, the part in each citizen that feels lonely and reaches out to poetry from time to time to discover *what is found there,* the part that is original and free. After all, "There's of course, poetry," she's just stated, yet her lyrical "I" here is informed by an awareness of the fissures and faults in the American psyche, national leadership, and American political system. For a number of years, she has been speaking to her fellow Americans as a voice crying in the wilderness, trying to awaken the poets and democratic ideals in our country. If, as many have said, poetry today is marginalized, considered trivial or inconsequential by mass America, she has been interested in bringing the country the vital, life-saving news that can be found in poems. The dark fields of the republic need illumination to Rich's mind, and the soul of America can only be saved by what is found on the shadow side of the closed postmodern American mind. Hence, in *An Atlas of the Difficult World,* she prepares an atlas of the North American continent; she travels across it while writing. For instance, she traverses "the fields of indifference" that may symbolize voter apathy, or American citizens' neglect of the old-fashioned civic virtues like honesty, integrity, self-reliance, and the habit of thinking for oneself. In *Dark Fields of the Republic,* the poetic gaze is more urban; she renounces feminist ties and cites Marx. The tone is more rebellious, antagonistic, in your face: "Shall I speak more simply of my life?" she asks in "History," entreating the reader not to ask how she began to love men or how she began to love women—like a vixen she defies any intruder who might nosily inquire into her personal life. In true postmodernist fashion, in the wake of the death of the author and the subject, she refuses to answer any question too personal or private, defensively, almost fearfully it would seem.

In this dialogue with Rich and her poetry, I hear her speaking quietly from *Dark Fields of the Republic* in "Sunset, December, 1993" about the dangers a writer faces: today, no one is protected or secure. Citizens and poets should not be deluded into imagining that "poems, ideas," glide "in mid-air innocent"—words have a political, almost physical impact. Freedom inheres in her poetry.

She defies anyone who may seek to interpret her poems in association with her life; but there is still a necessity to write, think, and publish because, as Jacque Vaught Brogan has argued, along with the African American women writers Audre Lorde, June Jordan, and Alice Walker, with whom she is personally most closely associated, Rich endorses the viability of an American spiritual/political community committed to social change, a group devoted to salvaging, to use one of her words, the goodness left in American republic in the twenty-first century, hence her collection of poems, 1995–1998, is called "midnight salvage"; it consists of salvaging what is left of what America stands for at this midnight hour.

In *Dark Fields of the Republic,* she speaks sardonically of Calle Vision, a street in Santa Cruz she visits clairvoyantly in the poem. The lyric "I" is a prophet "Being lodged in the difficult hotel" of contemporary American culture, where all help is withheld from the poet or spiritual seeker. America is not a place to live but a place to die, not a hotel but a hospital. Over the last decade her poetry has had an insubstantial dreamlike clarity. In true postmodernist mode, she dispenses with narrative and presents a series of images that record her observations on her thoughts on what is found here.

"To the Days" affirms that the love of life and poetry is immortal, and in "Miracle Ice Cream" the poet relishes and appreciates natural beauty, believing the beauty of women is part of what is given. The textual "I" is deeply displeased with what she sees now in contemporary American politics, and she does not enjoy being the ignored bearer of bad tidings in despairing poems like "In Those Years" (*D* 4–6).

"In a dark time," said Theodore Roethke, *"the eye begins to see."* And so does the poet: the eye/"I" begins to see, and who better to prophesy to America than Rich, whose "I" includes you, the reader, in its purview, whose "I" has now become a collective American "we?"

In *Fox, Midnight Salvage,* and *Dark Fields,* her prophetic books responding to the state of the American soul and psyche, Rich traces the landscape of desire and loss, writing both of erotic love and the possibilities still inherent in life and poetry. Her transparent "I"/eyeball must record all the joy and beauty of life as well as America's doom because the role of the poet as seer is to bear witness to her times. Invoking the fierce biblical prophet, the lyric claims, *"And the fire shall try every man's work:* Calle Vision": and she adds ruefully "and every woman's."

If you took the road less traveled, Calle Vision or Vision Road, and have led an authentic life, the experience here at Calle Vision is your "revelation" and your "source." Having crossed the terrain of our collective

American failures in the two painful books before *Fox,* she is now writing more openly of the disenfranchised parts of the American self and of her self and psyche, addressing first ostensibly her spirit guide the fox, and later in the book, the mysterious "you" to whom she is always speaking, you who may be American, alive now, reading and listening to this poetry.

Together the lyrical "I" and "you" journey in the poem "Terza Rima" where, like Dante,[1] she assesses her life up until this midpoint at the turning of the millennium, starting, like him, with a descent into the inferno of contemporary America, what W. B. Yeats called the *"foul rag-and-bone shop of the heart."*[2] Forced by circumstances to become a leader of the Women's Liberation Movement in the 1970s and early 1980s, Rich issues here a kind of apologia for her willed absence from the ranks of leadership in feminism of late. The lyric "I" is no longer the voice of *The Dream of a Common Language* speaking, but an "I" defined negatively in relationship with her reader. The emphasis is on her selfhood and subject position as the unknowable Other: "If you have a sister I am not she" nor "your mother nor you my daughter" nor "are we lovers any kind." We see her commenting here on her lyric "I," as elder-stateswoman and prophet, a person who has lived her entire life here, never thinking of going into exile as many other successful American poets of her generation have. Spiritually, then, the point of departure in *Fox* is similar to that in *The Pianist* by Roman Polanski, a film Rich might enjoy, in that it traverses the postmodern wasteland she surveys in an effort like that of Abraham in reclaiming ten good men or, more pertinently, some beauty, truth, and courage in today's world. The speaker is a traveler, of course, who descends into the inferno of contemporary American culture, and she says of herself that she became a "derailed memory-raided" and limping mentor and teacher she never had (*F* 41), hence her leading was a form of following, too. She leads by default because there is no one else to lead and the group chose her as its leader without an election or a vote—by acclamation actually rather than by default.

Section 1 of "Terza Rima" announces her sense of her own failure as a political or cultural leader (*F* 41). In the next section, her personal default merges into an earthquake fault in the next line: the speaker leads through meadows, up the hills where, while the earth trembles, we re-experience the video of the earthquake, the story of California's seismic past (*F* 42).

"This will never happen again"—what happened here will never happen again proclaims the poem of the century just past and earthquakes past. The turn of the millennium is a kind of watershed in history: at the end of the road, the pilgrims on this quest are sold free rather than *set* free, "tickets for the celebration" of the death of history (*F* 43), and they expect the apocalypse to come at midnight on the last day of the millennium, the last page of the calendar going up in flames (*F* 43). This problematizes history along with the origins and history of consciousness. What does it mean for the poem itself?

The speaker is plainly a guide whom circumstances appointed rather than a guide by choice. The voice is that of the unknown neutral "I" of "Diving into the Wreck," and the same issue is revisited and reexamined after 30 years, what might be loosely termed her involvement in the women's movement, women's studies, and feminism. In section 4 of "Terza Rima" she confesses that she was not the leader she had hoped to be: playing on the double meaning of "fault" she confesses she has lost "our way" and "the fault is mine" or, in the next line, "ours" (*F* 44). The fault belongs to "us": although it was she who became the guide, I "should have defaulted" and should have remained the novice since she was a guide who failed. One whose gifts were those of a poet took on the role of leader and failed: even though other women thought of her as a leader; inside she "trembled" and feels she ought to have been stronger, held us all together (*F* 44). The "us" are feminists and those in the Movement with her. Does she blame herself for the schisms in the women's movement and the violent verbal clashes between radical, liberal, academic, and working-class feminists, or between various ethnic groups, inviting the inevitable backlash of the 1980s? Could she think that if she had been a stronger or better leader she might have kept the American feminist movement unified?

"Terza Rima" says the public has put her on a pedestal as leader of the women's movement and looked to her to supply their needs for love, spirituality, or money. Her sentiments here are reminiscent of those in the song "It Ain't Me, Babe" in that Adrienne Rich sees herself primarily as a poet, *not* primarily a political leader, just a poet who wants to change the world, but who also desires privacy, calm, and happiness in her later years. In section 8, she visits an inferno in a film, Almodovar's *All about My Mother,* a "theater of love" which she imagines is the ninth circle of Dante's Hell (*F* 48), the lowest circle of the inferno of contemporary culture. There transvestite prostitutes ply their wares as two of the film's most sympathetic characters search for the father of a baby among the ladies of the night. The section ends in a desperate series of fearful questions, one of which is a query about whether or not "you" understand "you" could get your face slashed down here, where people are preyed on and are preying on others sexually.

Emerging from the inferno both in the film's and the speaker's own psyche, the lyric "I" suddenly turns on the reader, asking with humorous vehemence if s/he thinks this is a film (*F* 48). In closing, speaking directly as her integral historic "I", she reports that she gave her name and it was stolen, so she no longer has it. She also pledged her word but it was broken, so her words are learning now to walk through traffic on crutches (*F* 49). Self-mockingly she continues, referring to her vixenlike embrace of pure privacy, her rejection of being categorized, commercialized, or coopted, her refusal to let others use her name since she is the Other: her name is jailed and refuses "to name names" (*F* 49), she quips. It was singled out because "I dared mix beauty with courage" and because "they were my lovers," beauty and courage were tortured together (*F* 49). Rich deplores having been misunderstood, having her beauty and courage misinterpreted in poetry, criticism, history, and even women's studies.

In the poem's climactic section 10, she inquires into the meaning and purpose of her later life, her life after feminist leadership, and she finds a personal truth in some lines that Pier Paolo Pasolini wrote for her hero Gramsci: *"Vivo nel non volere / deltramontato dopoguerra: // amando / il mondo che odio..."* meaning, *"I have lived in the failed will of the post-war time: / loving the world I hate"* (*F* 64): this could be Rich's self-reflection as well as Pasolini's. In *Fox,* Adrienne Rich, the lyric "I"/eye, seems to have lived her life in what might be called the failed epoch and culture of post–World War II America, simultaneously loving and hating her nation. As a self-described failed reformer, here she is self-critical, but to her credit she is honest, unsparing of herself in this global midlife evaluation.

In the penultimate section, she vents her wrath on those who would attribute to her a "woman's vision," making her an essentialist, or taking her as a representative of all women poets; this concept of writing as a woman conjures up for her visions of coffeepots, coziness, and curtains (*F* 52). The lyric "I" declares she has hated speaking as a woman for sheer continuity and union when what is broken is what she saw, how she hates being limited by the perceptions of others and having to fit herself into their understanding of womanhood. How much better it is for her to remain free of interpretation or connections! Instead she has depicted "a grain of hope" in her poetry like some bitter chocolate awaking the senses so as to live her life wholly (*F* 51). Staying in close touch with the senses enables the "I" to avoid despair.

She addresses the reader once more in the concluding section 13, describing their relationship as that between a novice and a guide on a long journey through ice and snow, expressing the awkwardness of journeying "difficultly," stumbling across this rough terrain, journeying "with you" while she both leads and follows as their shadows loom "reindeer-huge" and slip onto the map of chance and purpose (*F* 53). First, their shadows loom large, and then in a kind of foreshortening of the subjects, a cinematic panning out, they are seen in historical perspective, slipping onto the map of public record, together making history, and reacting to chance and purpose. The reader and speaker walking together, chatting, and eating, have effectively changed places and continue to change places at the end of the poem. The former antagonistic tone alternates in *Fox* between the mysteriousness of the unknown Other and a fuller rapport with her readership, as at the end of "Terza Rima." These lines ring of equality, not strife, and here no consciousness of gender or race exists.

In their poetic journey together, the speaker has re-knit the parts of her split self in her poetic walk with the reader. Does this imply she will continue on for the rest of the journey—the rest of her life—walking side by side with "you," her reader, who may or may not be a friend or lover, or who may be unknown to her, or reading across the world? She'll be relating, woman to reader, her vision of the dark fields of the republic, her thoughtful, engaged insights into postmodern America.

According to Adrienne Rich, logically we all need to wake up our finer sensitivities to what is happening at exactly this moment in history. And if we don't write poetry, we should try to read it, since the poet's work is to keep an accurate record of how she sees the change transpiring and to say, at any given time, "where the clocks' hands stood" (*D* 31)—in other words, what exactly is happening in this moment in history—since "this is not somewhere else but here" (*D* 3). Hence, it is our own responsibility to stayed tuned and attuned to the currents of history and politics and be accountable. Shelley wrote that "Poets are the unacknowledged legislators of the world,"[3] because sometimes only poets, prophets, and those standing outside politics and government can see clearly into the inner workings of government and power and can best discern corruption, greed, abuse of the law, and/or heroism. Consequently, poetry is particularly necessary reading in a dark chaotic time, in war time, and our communal survival depends in some part on what is found there in poetry, since, ultimately, "The moment of change is the only poem" (*WC* 49).

Notes

CHAPTER 1: INTRODUCTION: A WOMAN SWORN TO LUCIDITY

1. *Dark Fields of the Republic,* 31. Each of Rich's works has been accorded an abbreviation: for example, *Dark Fields of the Republic* is *D.* The list of abbreviations appears at the beginning of the book.

2. Fred Moramarco, "Stevens, Rich, and Merrill," *Wallace Stevens Journal* 25.1 (2001): 3. See also "A Whole New Poetry Beginning Here," a chapter on feminist poetry featuring that of Adrienne Rich, in *Containing Multitudes: Poetry in the United States since 1950* (New York: Twayne, 1998).

3. Camille Roman, e-mail letter to author, 17 December 2000.

4. Patricia Roth Schwartz, "A Feast for the Intellect," *Lambda Book Report* 9.10 (May 2001): 22.

5. For a full elaboration of this argument, see Peter Erickson's, "Singing America: From Walt Whitman to Adrienne Rich," *Kenyon Review* 17.1 (Winter 1995): 103–20.

6. Nadine Gordimer's quote on the back cover of *Dark Fields of the Republic:* "In her vision of warning and her celebration of life, Adrienne Rich is the Blake of American letters."

7. Wendy Martin, *An American Triptych. Anne Bradstreet, Emily Dickinson, Adrienne Rich* (Chapel Hill, N.C.: The University of North Carolina Press, 1984), 171.

CHAPTER 2: BEGINNINGS: DELIBERATE DETACHMENT AND CONSCIOUS CRAFT

1. See Stephanie Coontz's excellent sociological studies *The Way We Never Were: American Families and the Nostalgia Trap* (New York: Basic Books, 2000) and

The Way We Really Are: Coming to Terms with America's Changing Families (New York: Basic Books, 1998).

2. In this, she resembles Virginia Woolf, who got her education from her brilliant father's (Leslie Stephens) library.

3. Sabine Sielke, *Fashioning the Female Subject: The Intertextual Networking of Dickinson, Moore, and Rich* (Ann Arbor: University of Michigan Press, 1997), 219.

4. Ibid., 17.

5. Adrienne Rich, "An Interview with Adrienne Rich," interview by Elly Bulkin, *Conditions One* 1 (April 1977): 50–65.

6. Albert Gelpi, "The Poetics of Recovery: A Reading of Adrienne Rich's *Sources*," in *Adrienne Rich's Poetry and Prose: Poems, Prose, Reviews and Criticism*, Norton Critical Edition, 2nd ed., ed. Barbara Charlesworth Gelpi and Albert Gelpi (New York: W. W. Norton, 1993), 297.

7. Adrienne Rich, "Beyond the Heirlooms of Tradition," review of *Found Objects* by Louis Zukovsky, *Poetry* 105.2 (November 1964): 128.

8. Maggie Humm, *The Dictionary of Feminist Theory* (Columbus: Ohio State University Press, 1995), 192.

9. Ibid., 192.

10. Ibid.

11. Later, however, after the publication of Paula Bennett's *My Life—A Loaded Gun*, she renounces this position as feminist leader and discourages from then on any personal or biographical interpretation of her poetry, guarding her privacy and that of her family.

12. Rich, interview, 52.

13. Jeri Johnston, "Undoing the Folded Lie," *TLS* (8 July 1994): 9.

14. Quoted in Johnson, "Undoing the Folded Lie," 9.

15. Rich, interview, 52.

16. Ibid.

17. Elaine Showalter, "Dancing through the Minefield," in *Writing and Sexual Difference*, ed. Elizabeth Abel (Chicago: University of Chicago Press, 1982), 29.

18. Ibid.

19. Claire Keyes, *The Aesthetics of Power: The Poetry of Adrienne Rich* (Athens, Ga.: The University of Georgia Press, 1986), 15.

20. Rich, review of *Found Objects*, 128.

21. Wendy Martin, *An American Triptych: Anne Bradstreet, Emily Dickinson, Adrienne Rich* (Chapel Hill: The University of North Carolina Press, 1984).

22. Alan Filreis, *Wallace Stevens and the Actual World* (Princeton, N.J.: Princeton University Press, 1991), 34, quoted in Fred Moramarco, "A Whole New Poetry Beginning Here," *Women's Studies* 27.4 (June 1998): 3–4.

23. Rich, review of *Found Objects*, 128.

24. See Katharine Graham, *Personal History* (New York: Random House, 1998).

25. Luce Irigaray, *I Love You: Sketch of a Possible Felicity in History*, trans. Alison Martin (New York: Routledge, 1996), 100.

26. Walter Jackson Bate, ed., *Criticism: The Major Texts* (New York: Harcourt, Brace, Jovanovich, 1970), 135.

27. Keyes, *The Aesthetics of Power*, 32.

28. Carmen Birkle, *Women's Stories of the Looking Glass. Autobiographical Reflections and Self-Representations in the Poetry of Sylvia Plath, Adrienne Rich, and Audre*

Lorde, American Studies, A Monograph Series, Vol. 72 (Munich: Wilhelm Fink, 1996), 118.

29. C.f. "When This Clangor in the Brain" (*DI* 108).

30. Birkle, *Women's Stories of the Looking Glass,* 119.

31. Karl Malkoff, *Crowell's Handbook of Contemporary American Poetry* (New York: Thomas Y. Crowell, 1973), 255.

32. Jacqueline Vaught Brogan, "'I Can't Be Still': Adrienne Rich and the Refusal to Gild the Fields of Guilt," *Women's Studies* 27.4 (1998): 313.

CHAPTER 3: ERUPTIONS OF THE FEMALE PSYCHE

1. Donald Hall, *Life Work* (Boston: Beacon, 1993), 72–73.

2. Carmen Birkle, *Women's Stories of the Looking Glass. Autobiographical Reflections and Self-Representations in the Poetry of Sylvia Plath, Adrienne Rich, and Audre Lorde,* American Studies, A Monograph Series, Vol. 72 (Munich: Wilhelm Fink, 1996), 125.

3. Betsy Erkkila, *The Wicked Sisters. Women Poets, Literary History, and Discord* (New York: Oxford University Press, 1992), 157.

4. See Erkkila, *The Wicked Sisters,* 22–23, 47–49, 58–60, 62–62; and Paula Bennett, *My Life—A Loaded Gun* (Boston: Beacon, 1986), 67–83.

5. Craig Werner, *Adrienne Rich. The Poet and Her Critics* (Chicago: American Library Association, 1988), 2.

6. T. S. Eliot, "The Hollow Men," 1936, in *Collected Poems* (New York: Harcourt Brace & Company, 1963), 129.

7. Rachel Blau DuPlessis, *Writing Beyond the Ending* (Bloomington: Indiana University Press, 1986), 125.

8. Werner, *Adrienne Rich,* 51–54.

9. See the reviews of *Snapshots of a Daughter-in-Law* in Jane Roberta Cooper's *Reading Adrienne Rich: Reviews and Re-Visions, 1951–81* (Ann Arbor: The University of Michigan Press, 1984).

10. DuPlessis, *Writing beyond the Ending,* 125.

11. Ibid.

12. Ibid.

13. Ibid.

14. "Power and Danger" in *On Lies, Secrets and Silence,* 248. Here Rich is praising Judy Grahn's poetry.

CHAPTER 4: NEW POETRY ENTERS THE WORLD

1. Quoted in Roland Barthes, *Mythologies* (New York: Macmillan, 1959), 331.

2. Alicia Ostriker, *Stealing the Language: The Emergence of Women's Poetry in America* (London: The Women's Press, 1986), 194.

3. Sylvia Henneberg, "The 'Slow Turn of Conciousness': Adrienne Rich's Family Plot," *Women's Studies* 27.4 (June 1998): 357.

4. Ostriker, *Stealing the Language,* 195–96.

5. Kevin Stein, *Private Poets, Worldly Acts: Public and Private History in Contemporary American Poetry* (Athens: Ohio University Press, 1996), 42.

6. Philip Booth, "Rethinking the World," reprinted in *Reading Adrienne Rich: Reviews and Re-Visions, 1951–1981,* ed. Jane Roberta Cooper (Ann Arbor: The University of Michigan Press, 1984), 216. First published in *Christian Science Monitor,* January 3, 1963.

7. W. B. Yeats, *Collected Poems of W. B. Yeats,* Definitive ed. (New York: Macmillan, 1968), 336.

8. John Ashbery, "Tradition and Talent," reprinted in *Reading Adrienne Rich: Reviews and Re-Visions, 1951–1981,* ed. Jane Roberta Cooper (Ann Arbor: The University of Michigan Press, 1984), 216. First published in *New York Herald Tribune Book Week,* 4 September 1966.

9. Ibid., 218.

10. Adrienne Rich, "Voices in the Wilderness: Review of *Monster* by Robin Morgan," *Washington Post Book World,* 31 December 1972, 3.

11. Ibid.

12. Ibid.

13. Wendy Martin, *An American Triptych: Anne Bradstreet, Emily Dickinson, Adrienne Rich* (Chapel Hill: The University of North Carolina Press, 1984), 140.

14. Rich uses Virginia Woolf's phrase in *OWB* 27.

15. Martin, *An American Triptych,* 140.

16. Ibid., 179.

17. Ibid., 183.

18. This is a theme Rich returns to later when she makes her controversial "It Is the Lesbian in Us . . ." speech before the Modern Language Association in 1976 (*LS* 199–202). For a fuller discussion of this controversial speech and lesbianism, see Paula Bennett, *My Life—a Loaded Gun: Female Creativity and Feminist Poetics* (Boston: Beacon, 1986).

19. Betsy Erkkila, *The Wicked Sisters. Women Poets, Literary History, and Discord* (New York: Oxford University Press, 1992), 166.

20. Ibid.

21. Ibid., 172.

22. Ibid., 174.

23. Ibid., 164.

24. The words in italics are taken from Dickinson's letters to Higginson.

25. Erkkila, *The Wicked Sisters,* 166.

26. Ibid.

27. Ibid., 164.

28. David Kalstone, *Five Temperaments* (New York: Oxford University Press, 1977), 138.

29. Erkkila, *The Wicked Sisters,* 164.

30. Ibid., 166.

31. Ostriker, *Stealing the Language,* 194.

32. Helen Vendler, *Soul Says. On Recent Poetry* (Cambridge, Mass.: Belknap Press of Harvard University Press, 1995), 214.

33. Ibid.

34. Robert Peters does this later in *The Great American Poetry Bake Off* (New York: Rowman and Littlefield, 1979).

35. Margaret Cooter, et al., *Reviewing the Reviews: A Woman's Place on the Book Page,* written and edited by Women in Publishing (London: Journeyman, 1987), 199.

36. See Harold Bloom, ed., *The Best of the Best American Poetry, 1988–1997* (New York: Scribner Poetry, 1998), "Introduction."
37. Vendler, *Soul Says,* 214.
38. Ibid.
39. Ibid., 215.
40. Ibid.
41. Suzanne Juhasz, *Naked and Fiery Forms. Modern Poetry by Women: A New Tradition* (New York: Harper & Row, 1976), 194.
42. Erkkila, *The Wicked Sisters,* 166.

CHAPTER 5: SEEING IS CHANGING, WRITING IS RENAMING

1. Betsy Erkkila, *The Wicked Sisters. Women Poets, Literary History, and Discord* (New York: Oxford University Press, 1992), 166.
2. Ibid., 167.
3. Suzanne Juhasz, *Naked and Fiery Forms. Modern Poetry by Women: A New Tradition* (New York: Harper & Row, 1976), 196.
4. Ibid., 195.
5. Ibid.
6. Antonin Artaud, a French surrealist, demanded the overthrow of all present social structures in an aesthetic and political movement toward a new age of freedom around the time of World War I.
7. Helen Vendler, *Part of Nature, Part of Us. Modern American Poets* (Cambridge, Mass.: Harvard University Press, 1980), 257–58.
8. Ibid., 258.
9. W. B. Yeats, *Collected Poems of W. B. Yeats,* Definitive ed. (New York: Macmillan, 1968), 336.
10. See the books and articles by Mary June Nestler and other biblical scholars of the last decade.
11. Rachel Blau DuPlessis, *Writing beyond the Ending* (Bloomington: Indiana University Press, 1986), 232.
12. Ibid., 131.
13. Ibid., 131–32.
14. Ibid., 132.
15. Ibid.
16. Ibid.
17. Alice Templeton, *The Dream and the Dialogue: Adrienne Rich's Feminist Poetics* (Knoxville: The University of Tennessee Press, 1994), 34.
18. Ibid., 44.
19. Ibid., 37.
20. Wendy Martin, *An American Triptych. Anne Bradstreet, Emily Dickinson, Adrienne Rich* (Chapel Hill, N.C.: The University of North Carolina Press, 1984), 192–93.
21. DuPlessis, *Writing Beyond the Ending,* 127–28.
22. Helen Vendler, *Soul Says. On Recent Poetry* (Cambridge, Mass.: Belknap Press of Harvard University Press, 1995), 215.
23. Erkkila, *The Wicked Sisters,* 169.
24. Ibid, 170.
25. Ibid.

CHAPTER 6: TO BE AN AMERICAN WOMAN

1. To this end, throughout her life she has translated poetry from, and has been translated, into many languages—French, German, Spanish, Swedish, Dutch, Hebrew, Greek, Italian, and Japanese.

2. Charlotte Templin, *Feminism and the Politics of Literary Reputation. The Example of Erica Jong* (Lawrence: University Press of Kansas, 1995), 33.

3. Ibid., 30–31.

4. Muriel Rukeyser, *The Life of Poetry* (New York: A. A. Wyn, 1949), 93.

5. Adrienne Rich, "Beginners," In *How Shall We Tell Each Other of the Poet,* ed. Anne F. Herzog and Janet E. Kaufman, 62–69 (New York: St. Martin's Press, 1999), 62.

6. Ibid., 65–66.

7. Compare this with Muriel Rukeyser's poem "Myth," in *Breaking Open* (New York: Random House, 1973), 20.

8. See Rich's foreword to *The Works of Anne Bradstreet,* Jeannette Hensley, ed. (Cambridge and London: Belknap Press, 1967), ix–xxi.

9. The classic book on the equation of womanhood and nature is Susan Griffin's *Woman and Nature: The Roaring Inside Her* (San Francisco: Sierra Club Books, 2000).

10. Judy Grahn, *The Work of a Common Woman* (New York: St. Martin's, 1980), 73.

11. It would be interesting to explore the connection between the ways Rich deals with these themes and how Toni Morrison traverses the same territory in *Beloved.*

12. Cary Nelson, *Our Last First Poets* (Urbana: University of Illinois Press, 1981), 146.

13. Ntozake Shange, *for colored girls who have considered suicide when the rainbow is enuf: a choreopoem* (New York: Simon & Schuster, 1997), 12.

14. Adrienne Rich, "An Interview with Adrienne Rich," interview by Elly Bulkin, *Conditions One* 1 (April 1977): 51.

15. Alice Templeton, *The Dream and the Dialogue: Adrienne Rich's Feminist Poetics* (Knoxville, TN: University of Tennessee Press, 1994), 84.

16. Ibid.

17. Ibid.

18. Ibid.

19. Helen Vendler, *The Music of What Happens* (Cambridge: Harvard University Press, 1988), 370.

20. Sandra M. Gilbert and Susan Gubar, *The Madwoman in the Attic* (New Haven and London: Yale University Press, 1979), 99. See also 3–104.

21. Vendler, *The Music of What Happens,* 370–71.

22. Ibid., 371.

23. Ibid.

CHAPTER 7: A NEW RELATIONSHIP TO THE UNIVERSE

1. Perhaps confounding poignant analysis with self-pity, Vendler criticizes Rich for frequently casting herself as a complaining daughter or an innocent victim: "Join me in condemning the reprobates and grieving for the victims, she seems to say.... This suggests that Rich still imagines herself in the position of the

helpless child rather than that of the adult. She presents herself less as a champion or leader than as a co-sufferer, pitying herself (indirectly) in others" (Helen Vendler, *Soul Says: On Recent Poetry* [Cambridge, Mass.: Belknap Press of Harvard University Press, 1995], 217). Vendler criticizes Rich's failure to work through the social ills she observes or to implement constructive social change and sees that as a weakness in her work. Ever the "co-suffering" radical, in Vendler's eyes, she seems to be the weak complaining victim. Vendler sees her as the female counterpart to the eternal youth—*puella aeterna,* the eternal girl, who whines overmuch. Is this unfair?

2. Paul Claudel, "Les Muses," in *Cinq Grands Odes, Oeuvres Completes,* vol. 1 (Paris: Editions Gallimard, 1950), 88.

3. Comment on the dust jacket of *Your Native Land, Your Life.*

4. See Cary Nelson, *Our Last First Poets* (Urbana: University of Illinois Press, 1981), 140–51; Walter B Kalaidjian, *Languages of Liberation: The Social Text in Contemporary American Poetry* (New York: Columbia University Press, 1989), 242–46; Jonathan Holden, *The Fate of American Poetry* (Athens, Gra: University of Georgia Press, 1991), 46–49; and Betsy Erkkila astutely deconstructs the "limits of sisterhood" in *The Wicked Sisters* (Oxford: Oxford University Press, 1992), 152–84.

5. Quoted in "Adrienne Rich," in *The Hand of the Poet, Poems and Papers in Manuscript,* ed. Rodney Phillips (New York: The New York Public Library, 1997), 292.

6. William Carlos Williams, *Collected Poems of William Carlos Williams 1939–1962,* vol. 2 (New York: New Directions, 1988), 284.

7. Helen Vendler, *Voices and Visions* (New York: Random House, 1987), 428.

8. Bill D. Moyers, *The Language of Life: A Festival of Poets* (New York: Doubleday, 1995), 349.

9. Quoted in Moyers, *The Language of Life,* 349.

10. Ibid.

11. Karen Horney, *Collected Works* (New York: Routledge & Kegan Paul, 1979), 323–24.

12. Dylan Thomas, *The Poems of Dylan Thomas* (New York: New Directions, 1971), 222.

CHAPTER 8: HERE IS A MAP OF OUR COUNTRY

1. Alice Templeton, *The Dream and the Dialogue, Adrienne Rich's Feminist Poems* (Knoxville: The University of Tennessee Press, 1994), 86. Here she is speaking of the poem "Transcendental Etude."

2. Ibid.

3. Alan Ginsberg, "Howl," in *Howl and Other Poems* (New York: Grove Press, 1990), 131.

4. Helena Michie, *Sororophobia: Differences among Women in Literature and Culture* (New York: Oxford University Press, 1992), 129.

5. Adrienne Rich, "Why I Refused the National Medal for the Arts," *Los Angeles Times Book Review,* 3 August 1997, 3.

6. Ibid., 3.

7. Ibid., 3.

8. Cynthia Hogue, "The 'Possible Poet': Pain, Form, and the Embodied Poetics of Adrienne Rich in Wallace Stevens' Wake," *Wallace Stevens Journal* 25.1 (Spring 2001): 43.

CHAPTER 9: POETRY'S INADMISSIBLE UNTIMELY MESSENGER

1. See Terry Castle, *The Apparitional Lesbian* (New York: Columbia University Press, 1993), passim.

2. Margaret Dickie, *Lyric Contingencies* (Philadelphia: University of Pennsylvania Press, 1991), 154.

3. Ibid., 154–55.

4. William Logan, "Criterion," review of *Midnight Salvage,* by Adrienne Rich, *Vanity Fair,* June 1999, 60.

5. T. S. Eliot, *Collected Poems: 1909–1962* (New York: Harcourt Brace & Company, 1963), 238.

6. "Letter to June Oppen Degnan," June 5, 1970, in *Midnight Salvage: Poems 1995–1998* by Adrienne Rich (New York: W. W. Norton, 1990), 1.

7. Cynthia Hogue, "The 'Possible Poet': Pain, Form, and the Embodied Poetics of Adrienne Rich in Wallace Stevens's Wake," *Wallace Stevens Journal* 25.1 (spring 2001): 43.

8. Hortense J. Spillers, *Black, White, and in Color: Essays on American Literature and Culture* (Chicago: University of Chicago Press, 2003), 45.

9. Stephen Burt, "Charles Baxter, August Kleinzahler, Adrienne Rich: Contemporary Stevensians and the Problem of 'Other Lives,' " *Wallace Stevens Journal* 24.2 (2000): 116.

10. T. S. Eliot, *Collected Poems,* 230.

11. Rafael Campo, Review of *Midnight Salvage, The Progressive* 63.7 (July 1999): 43.

12. Ibid.

13. Adam Newley, Review of *Midnight Salvage: Poems 1995–1998, New Statesman,* 25 March 1999, 58.

14. Ibid.

15. Ibid.

16. Burt, "Charles Baxter, August Kleinzahler, Adrienne Rich," 116.

CHAPTER 10: A REVOLUTIONARY TEXTUAL STRATEGY EMBODYING THE MATERIALITY OF WOMEN'S EXPERIENCE

1. Mary Loeffelholz, "Etruscan Invitations," 19, quoted in Cynthia Hogue, "Adrienne Rich's Political Ecstatic Subject," *Women's Studies* 27.4 (1998): 425.

2. Adrienne Rich, quoted in "Adrienne Rich Station," http://www.adriennerich.hpg.ig.com.br/resources.htm (accessed 12 February 2004).

3. Ann Curthoys, "Adventures of Feminism," *Feminist Review* 64 (spring 2000): 3.

4. Quoted in Bill D. Moyers, *The Language of Life: A Festival of* Poets (New York: Doubleday, 1995), 300.

5. AnaLouise Keating, *Women Reading Women Writing: Self-Invention in Paula Gunn Allen, Gloria Anzaldua, and Audre Lorde* (Philadelphia: Temple University Press, 1996), 185.

6. Marianne Moore, *The Complete Poems of Marianne Moore* (New York: Macmillan, 1967), 136.

7. Adrienne Rich, "Why I Refused the National Medal for the Arts," *Los Angeles Times Book Review,* 3 August 1997, 3.

8. Ibid.

9. Ibid.

10. Helena Michie, *Sororophobia: Differences among Women in Literature and Culture* (New York: Oxford University Press, 1992), 4.

11. Rich, "Why I Refused," 3.

12. Blurb on dustjacket, *Arts of the Possible: Essays and Conversations* (New York: W. W. Norton, 2001).

13. Alice Templeton, *The Dream and the Dialogue: Adrienne Rich's Feminist Poetics* (Knoxville: The University of Tennessee Press, 1994), 16.

14. Marjorie Perloff (*The Dance of the Intellect: Studies in the Poetry of the Pound Tradition* [Cambridge: Cambridge University Press, 1985]) sees a contradiction between her prose and her poetry: while the prose advocates a free play of the imagination, Perloff argues that her poetry does not reflect freedom: she says that it is defensive and does not accord the same freedom to others as it arrogates to itself. While I maintain, along with Cynthia Hogue ("Adrienne Rich's Political Ecstatic Subject," *Women's Studies* 27.4 [June 1998]: 413–29), that Rich's poetry always stays within the realm of the lyric, Helen Vendler (*Soul Says: On Recent Poetry* [Cambridge, Mass.: Belknap Press of Harvard University Press, 1995]) has asserted that Rich's poetry from 1970 onward verges on prose, weighed down by what Vendler considers "excessive political content."

15. Sylvia Henneberg, "The 'Slow Turn of Consciousness': Adrienne Rich's Family Plot," *Women's Studies* 27.4 (June 1998): 348.

16. Willard Spiegelman, "Voice of the Survivor: The Poetry of Adrienne Rich," *Southwest Review* (Autumn 1975): 386.

17. Michie, *Sororophobia,* 79.

18. Donna Seaman, blurb on dustjacket, *Arts of the Possible: Essays and Conversations* (New York: W. W. Norton, 2001).

19. Henneberg, "The 'Slow Turn of Consciousness,'" 348.

20. Adrienne Rich, quoted in "Adrienne Rich Station," http://www.adriennerich.hpg.ig.com.br/resources.htm (accessed 12 February 2004).

21. Krista Ratcliffe, *Anglo-American Feminist Challenges to the Rhetorical Traditions* (Carbondale: Southern Illinois University Press, 1996), 4.

22. Ibid., 107.

23. Claire Keyes, *The Aesthetics of Power: The Poetry of Adrienne Rich* (Athens, Ga.: The University of Georgia Press, 1986), 14.

24. Adrienne Rich, ed., *The Best American Poetry, 1996* (New York: Scribner's, 1996), 15.

25. Adrienne Rich, "The Hermit's Scream," *PMLA* 108.5 (1993): 1158–59.

26. Ibid.

27. John Dart and Ray Riegert, eds., *The Gospel of Thomas, Unearthing the Lost Words of Jesus* (Berkeley, Calif.: Seastone, 2000), 70.

28. Jane Marcus, "Still Practice, A / Wrested Alphabet: Toward a Feminist Aesthetic," *Tulsa Studies in Women's Literature* 2.1–2 (1984): 80.

29. George Sand, "Isidora," in *Oeuvres Completes,* vol. 18 (Geneva: Slatkine, 1980), 26.

CHAPTER 11: *FOX:* POSTMODERN ADRIENNE RICH

1. Dante's *Divina Commedia* was written entirely in terza rima, and for this reason, she gives the poem this title since it depicts a quest, but hardly one on such a cosmic scale as Dante's.

2. W. B. Yeats, *Collected Poems of W. B. Yeats,* Definitive ed. (New York: Macmillan, 1968), 336.

3. Percy Bysshe Shelley, "A Defence of Poetry," in *The English Romantics: Major Poetry and Critical Theory,* ed. John L. Mahoney (Prospect Heights, Ill.: Waveland Press, 1997), 537.

Bibliography

PRIMARY SOURCES

Poetry

An Atlas of the Difficult World: Poems 1988–1991. New York: W. W. Norton, 1991.
A Change of World. New Haven: Yale University Press, 1952.
Collected Early Poems 1950–1970. New York: W. W. Norton, 1993.
Dark Fields of the Republic: Poems 1991–1995. New York: W.W. Norton, 1995.
The Diamond Cutters and Other Poems. New York: Harper & Brothers, 1955.
Diving into the Wreck: Poems 1971–1972. New York: W. W. Norton, 1973.
The Dream of a Common Language: Poems 1974–1977. New York: W. W. Norton, 1978.
The Fact of a Doorframe: Poems Selected and New, 1950–1984. New York: W. W. Norton, 1984.
The Fantasy Poets. No. 12. Oxford, U.K.: The Fantasy Press, 1952.
Fox: Poems 1998–2000. New York: W. W. Norton, 2001.
Leaflets: Poems 1965–68. New York: W. W. Norton, 1969; London: Chatto & Windus, 1972.
Midnight Salvage: Poems 1995–1998. New York and London: W. W. Norton, 1999.
Necessities of Life: Poems 1962–1965. New York: W. W. Norton, 1966.
Poems: Selected and New, 1950–1974. New York: W. W. Norton, 1975.
Snapshots of a Daughter-in-Law. New York: Harper & Row, 1963; New York: W. W. Norton, 1967; London: Chatto & Windus, 1970.
Sources. Woodside, Calif.: Heyeck Press, 1983.
Time's Power: Poems 1985–1988. New York: W. W. Norton, 1989.
Twenty-One Love Poems. Emeryville, Calif.: Effie's Press, 1976.
A Wild Patience Has Taken Me This Far: Poems 1978–1981. New York: W. W. Norton, 1981.

The Will to Change: Poems 1968–1972. New York: W.W. Norton, 1972.
Your Native Land, Your Life. New York: W.W. Norton, 1986.

Nonfiction

Arts of the Possible: Essays and Conversations. New York and London: W.W. Norton, 2001.
Blood, Bread, and Poetry: Selected Prose 1979–1985. New York: W.W. Norton, 1986.
Of Woman Born: Motherhood as Experience and Institution. 1976. 10th anniversary ed., with a new forward, New York: W.W. Norton, 1986.
On Lies, Secrets, and Silence: Selected Prose 1966–1978. London: Virago, 1979.
What Is Found There: Notebooks on Poetry and Politics. New York: W.W. Norton, 1993.
Women and Honor: Some Notes on Lying. Pittsburgh: Motherroot/Pittsburgh Women Writers, 1972.

Selected Critical Writings

"Beginners." In *How Shall We Tell Each Other of the Poet,* ed. Anne F. Herzog and Janet E. Kaufman, 62–69. New York: St. Martin's Press, 1999.
"Beyond the Heirlooms of Tradition." Review of *Found Objects* by Louis Zukovsky. *Poetry* 105.2 (November 1964): 128–29.
"Feminism and Fascism: An Exchange." By Adrienne Rich and Susan Sontag. *New York Review of Books* 22.4 (20 March 1974): 31–32.
"Foreword." In *The Best American Poetry 1996,* ed. Adrienne Rich, 15–17. New York: Scribner's, 1996.
"The Hermit's Scream." *PMLA* 108.5 (1993): 1157–64.
"Poetry, Personality and Wholeness: A Response to Galway Kinnell." *Field: Contemporary Poetry and Poetics* 7 (fall 1972): 11–18.
"Reflections on Lawrence: Review of *The Complete Poems of D.H. Lawrence.*" *Poetry* 106.3 (June 1965): 218–225.
"Review of *Women and Madness* by Phyllis Chesler." *New York Times Book Review,* 31 December 1972, 1, 20–21.
"Review of *Women and Nature* by Susan Griffin." *New Women's Times Feminist Review,* November 1978, 5.
"The Transformation of Silence into Language and Action." *Sinister Wisdom* 6 (1978): 17–25; *Washington Post Book World,* 1 November 1973, 2–3.
"Voices in the Wilderness: Review of *Monster* by Robin Morgan." *Washington Post Book World,* 31 December 1972, 3.
"What Does Separatism Mean?" *Sinister Wisdom* 18 (Fall 1981): 83–91.
"Why I Refused the National Medal for the Arts." *Los Angeles Times Book Review,* 3 August 1997, 3ff.
"Women's Studies—Renaissance or Revolution." *Women's Studies* 3 (1976): 121–26.

Edited Anthology

Adrienne Rich, ed. *The Best American Poetry 1996.* New York: Scribner, 1996.

Collaborative Translation

Poems by Ghalib. Trans. Aijaz Ahmad, with William Stafford and Adrienne Rich. New York: The Hudson Review, 1969.

Interviews

Lorde, Audre. "An Interview with Audre Lorde." Interview by Adrienne Rich. *Signs: Journal of Women in Culture and Society* 6 (summer 1981): 713–36.

Rich, Adrienne. "An Interview with Adrienne Rich." Interview by Elly Bulkin. *Conditions* 1 (April 1977): 50–65.

———. "Talking with Adrienne Rich." Interview by David Kalstone. *The Arts* 4.17 (22 April 1972): 29–46.

———. "Three Conversations with Adrienne Rich." Interview by Barbara Charlesworth Gelpi and Albert Gelpi. In *Adrienne Rich's Poetry,* ed. Barbara Charlesworth Gelpi and Albert Gelpi 105–22. New York: Norton, 1975.

Rich, Adrienne, and Robin Morgan. "Adrienne Rich and Robin Morgan Talk About Poetry and Women's Culture." In *The New Women's Survival Sourcebook,* edited by Susan Rennie and Kristen Grimstad, 106–11. New York: Knopf, 1975.

Anthologies and Compilations of Adrienne Rich's Works

Cooper, Jane Roberta, ed. *Reading Adrienne Rich: Reviews and Re-Visions, 1951–81.* Ann Arbor: The University of Michigan Press, 1984.

Gelpi, Barbara Charlesworth, and Albert Gelpi, eds. *Adrienne Rich's Poetry: Texts of the Poems, the Poet on Her Work, Reviews and Criticism.* Norton Critical Edition. New York: W. W. Norton, 1975.

———. *Adrienne Rich's Poetry and Prose: Poems, Prose, Reviews and Criticism.* Norton Critical Edition, 2d ed. New York: W. W. Norton, 1993.

SECONDARY SOURCES

Literary Criticisms and Critical Theory

Altieri, Charles. *Canons and Consequences: Reflections on the Ethical Force of Imaginative Ideals.* Chicago: Northwestern University Press, 1991.

———. *Self and Sensibility in Contemporary American Culture.* Cambridge: Cambridge University Press, 1984.

Axelrod, Steven Gould, Camille Roman, and Thomas Travisano, eds. *The New Anthology of American Poetry,* Vol. 1. New Brunswick, N.J.: Rutgers University Press, 2003.

Bennett, Paula. *My Life—A Loaded Gun: Female Creativity and Feministy Poetics.* Boston: Beacon, 1986.

Birkle, Carmen. *Women's Stories of the Looking Glass: Autobiographical Reflections and Self-Representations in the Poetry of Sylvia Plath, Adrienne Rich, and Audre*

Lorde. American Studies, A Monograph Series. Vol. 72. Munich: Wilhelm Fink, 1996.

Bloom, Harold, ed. *The Best of the Best American Poetry, 1988–1997.* New York: Scribner Poetry, 1998.

Brogan, Jacqueline Vaught. "I Can't Be Still" Adrienne Rich and the Refusal to Gild the Fields of Guilt." *Women's Studies* 27.4 (1998): 313.

Bundtzen, Lynda K. "Adrienne Rich's Identity Poetics: A Partly Common Language" *Women's Studies* 27.4 (June 1998): 331–46.

Bunkels, Suzanne L. and Cynthia Hall, eds. *Inscribing the Daily: Critical Essays on Women's Diaries.* Amherst: Univeristy of Massachusetts Press, 1996.

Burt, Stephen. "Charles Baxter, August Kleinzahler, Adrienne Rich: Contemporary Stevensians and the Problem of 'Other Lives.' " *Wallace Stevens Journal* 24.2 (2000): 115–34.

Butler, Judith. *Bodies that Matter: On the Discursive Limits of "Sex."* New York: Routledge, 1993.

———. *Excitable Speech: A Politics of the Performative.* New York: Routledge, 1997.

———. *Gender Trouble.* 10th anniversary ed. New York: Routledge, 1999.

———. *The Psychic Life of Power: Theories in Subjection.* Stanford, Calif.: Stanford University Press, 1997.

———, ed. *What's Left of Theory? New Work on the Politics of Literary Theory.* New York: Routledge, 2000.

Campo, Rafael. Review of *Midnight Salvage. The Progressive* 63.7 (July 1999): 43–44.

Castle, Terry. *The Apparitional Lesbian: Female Homosexuality and Modern Culture.* New York: Columbia University Press, 1993.

Caws, Mary Ann. "Rage Begins at Home," *Massachusetts Review* 34.1 (spring 1993): 65–76.

Clausen, Jan. *A Movement of Poets: Thoughts on Poetry and Feminism.* Brooklyn, N.Y.: Long Haul, 1982.

Coontz, Stephanie. *The Way We Never Were: American Families and the Nostalgia Trap.* New York: Basic Books, 2000.

———. *The Way We Really Are: Coming to Terms with America's Changing Families.* New York: Basic Books, 1998.

Cooter, Margaret, et al. *Reviewing the Reviews: A Woman's Place on the Book Page.* Written and edited by Women in Publishing. London: Journeyman, 1987.

Curthoys, Ann. "Adventures of Feminism." *Feminist Review* 64 (spring 2000): 3–9.

Dart, John, and Ray Riegert, eds., *The Gospel of Thomas: Unearthing the Lost Words of Jesus.* Berkeley, Calif.: Seastone, 2000.

Dennis, Helen. "Adrienne Rich: Consciousness Raising as Poetic Method." In *Contemporary Poetry Meets Modern Theory,* ed. Anthony Easthope. Toronto: University of Toronto Press, 1991.

Diaz-Diocaretz, Myriam. *The Transforming Power of Language: The Poetry of Adrienne Rich.* Utrecht: H. E. S. Publishers, 1984.

Di Bernard, Barbara. "Zami: A Portrait of an Artist as a Black Lesbian." *The Kenyon Review* 13.4 (1991): 195–213.

Dickie, Margaret. *Lyric Contingencies.* Philadelphia: University of Pennsylvania Press, 1991.

———. *Stein, Bishop and Rich: Lyrics of Love, War and Place.* Chapel Hill: University of North Carolina Press, 1997.

Dickie, Margaret, and Thomas Travisano, eds. *Gendered Modernisms: American Women Poets and Their Readers.* Philadelphia: University of Pennsylvania Press, 1996.

DuPlessis, Rachel Blau. *Writing Beyond the Ending.* Bloomington: Indiana University Press, 1986.

Eagleton, Mary. "Adrienne Rich, Location and the Body." *Journal of Gender Studies* 9.3 (November 2000): 299–312.

———, ed. *Feminist Literary Theory.* 2d ed. Cambridge, Mass.: Blackwell, 1996.

Eliot, T. S. *Collected Poems: 1909–1962.* New York: Harcourt Brace & Company, 1963.

Erickson, Peter. "Singing America: From Walt Whitman to Adrienne Rich." *Kenyon Review* 17.1 (winter 1995): 103–20.

Erkkila, Betsy. *The Wicked Sisters: Women Poets, Literary History, and Discord.* New York: Oxford University Press, 1992.

Faderman, Lillian. *Odd Girls and Twilight Lovers: A History of Lesbian Life in Twentieth-Century America.* New York: Columbia University Press, 1991.

———. *Surpassing the Love of Men: Romantic Friendship and Love between Women from the Renaissance to the Present.* New York: William Morrow, 1991.

Gelpi, Albert. "Afterword: The Transformation of the Body: Adrienne Rich's Vision." *Women's Studies* 27.4 (1998): 431-32.

———. *A Coherent Splendor: The American Poetic Renaissance, 1910–1950.* New York: Cambridge University Press, 1990.

———. Introduction. *"A Whole New Poetry Beginning Here": Adrienne Rich in the Eighties and Nineties*, ed. Albert Gelpi and Jacqueline Vaught Brogan. Special issue devoted exclusively to Adrienne Rich. *Women's Studies* 27.4 (June 1998): 309–310.

———. "The Poetics of Recovery: A Reading of Adrienne Rich's Sources." In *Adrienne Rich's Poetry: Texts of the Poems, The Poet on Her Work, Reviews and Criticism,* ed. Barbara Charlesworth Gelpi and Albert Gelpi. Norton Critical Edition. 2d ed. New York: W. W. Norton, 1973.

———. "The Transfiguration of the Body: Adrienne Rich's Witness." *Wallace Stevens Journal* 25.1 (spring 2001): 7–18.

Geng. Victoria. "Requiem for the Women's Movement." *Harper's* (November 1976) 49–56.

Gilbert, Sandra M., and Susan Gubar. *The Madwoman in the Attic: The Woman Writer and the Nineteenth Century Literary Imagination.* New Haven: Yale University Press, 1979.

———. *No Man's Land: The Place of the Woman Writer in the Twentieth Century.* Vol. 1, *The War of the Words.* New Haven: Yale University Press, 1988.

———. *Shakespeare's Sisters. Feminist Essays on Women Poets.* Bloomington: Indiana University Press, 1979.

———, eds. *The Norton Anthology of Literature by Women: The Traditions in English.* 2d ed. New York: W. W. Norton, 1996.

Ginsberg, Alan. "Howl." In *Howl and Other Poems.* New York: Grove Press, 1990.

Graham, Katharine. *Personal History,* New York: Random House, 1998.

Grahn, Judy. *The Work of a Common Woman.* New York: St. Martins, 1980.

Griffin, Susan. *Woman and Nature: The Roaring Inside Her.* San Francisco: Sierra Club Books, 2000.

Gubar, Susan. *Critical Condition: Feminism at the Turn of the Century.* New York: Columbia University Press, 2000.

Hall, Donald. *Life Work.* Boston: Beacon, 1993.

Halpern, Nick. *Everyday and Prophetic.* London and Madison, Wis.: University of Wisconsin Press, 2003.

Heilbrun, Carolyn G. *Writing a Woman's Life.* New York: Ballantine, 1988.

Henneberg, Sylvia. "Rich's 'Autumn Equinox.'" *Explicator* 55.3 (spring 1997): 169–27.

———. "The 'Slow Turn of Consciousness': Adrienne Rich's Family Plot." *Women's Studies* 27.4 (June 1998): 347–58.

Hensley, Jeannette, ed. *The Works of Anne Bradstreet.* Cambridge, Mass.: Belknap Press, 1967.

Herzog, Anne F., and Janet E. Kaufman, eds. *How Shall We Tell Each Other of the Poet?* New York: St Martin's, 1999.

Heyen, William, ed. *American Poets in 1976.* Indianapolis: Bobbs-Merrill, 1976.

Hogue, Cynthia. "Adrienne Rich's Political Ecstatic Subject." *Women's Studies* 27.4 (June 1998): 413–29.

———."The 'Possible Poet': Pain, Form, and the Embodied Poetics of Adrienne Rich in Wallace Stevens's Wake." *Wallace Stevens Journal* 25.1 (spring 2001): 43.

———. *Scheming Women: Poetry, Privilege, and the Politics of Subjectivity.* Albany: State University of New York Press, 1995.

Holden, Jonathan. *The Fate of American Poetry.* Athens, Ga.: The University of Georgia Press, 1991.

Hollenberg, Donna Krolik. "Holocaust Consciousness in the 1990s: Adrienne Rich's 'Then and Now.' " *Women's Studies* 27.4 (June 1998): 377–67.

Horney, Karen. *Collected Works.* New York: Routledge & Kegan Paul, 1979.

Howard, Richard. *Alone with America: Essays on the Art of Poetry in the United States to 1950.* Enlarged ed. New York: Atheneum, 1980.

Howe, Florence. *Tradition and the Talents of Women.* Urbana, Ill.: University of Illinois Press, 1991.

Humm, Maggie. *The Dictionary of Feminist Theory.* Columbus: Ohio State University Press, 1995.

Irigaray, Luce. *An Ethics of Sexual Difference.* Trans. Carolyn Burke and Gillian C. Gill. Ithaca, N.Y.: Cornell University Press, 1993.

———. *I Love to You: Sketch of a Possible Felicity in History.* Trans. Alison Martin. New York: Routledge, 1996.

———. *Je, Tu, Nous: Toward a Culture of Difference.* Trans. Alison Martin. New York: Routledge, 1993.

———. *Thinking the Difference: For a Peaceful Revolution.* Trans. Karin Montin. New York: Routledge, 1994.

Jacobus, Mary. *Reading Women: Essays in Feminist Criticism.* London: Methuen, 1986.

Jardine, Alice. *Gynesis: Configurations of Women and Modernity.* Ithaca, N.Y.: Cornell University Press, 1985.

Johnson, Jeri. "Undoing the Folded Lie." *TLS,* 8 July 1994, 9.

Juhasz, Suzanne. *Naked and Fiery Forms. Modern Poetry by Women: A New Tradition.* New York: Harper & Row, 1976.

Kalaidjian, Walter B. *Languages of Liberation: The Social Text in Contemporary American Poetry.* New York: Columbia University Press, 1989.

Kalstone, David. *Five Temperaments.* New York: Oxford University Press, 1977.

Keating, AnaLouise. *Women Reading Women Writing: Self-Invention in Paula Gunn Allen, Gloria Anzaldua, and Audre Lorde.* Philadelphia: Temple University Press, 1996.

Keyes, Claire. *The Aesthetics of Power: The Poetry of Adrienne Rich.* Athens: The University of Georgia Press, 1986.

Kostelanetz, Richard, ed. *American Writing Today.* Troy, N.Y.: Whitson, 1991.

Kristeva, Julia. *Revolution in Poetic Language.* Trans. Marguerite Waller. New York: Columbia University Press, 1984.

Loeffelholz, Mary. "The Burning Bed: 'Calle Vision.' " *Women's Studies* 27.4 (June 1998): 359–76.

Logan, William. "Criterion." Review of *Midnight Salvage* by Adrienne Rich. *Vanity Fair* (June 1999) 60.

Malkoff, Karl. *Crowell's Handbook of Contemporary American Poetry.* New York: Thomas Y. Crowell, 1973.

Marcus, Jane. "Still Practice, A/Wrested Alphabet: Toward a Feminist Aesthetic." *Tulsa Studies in Women's Literature* 2.1–2 (1984): 79–97.

Mark, Allison and Deryn Rees-Jones, eds. *Contemporary Women's Poetry: Reading, Writing, and Practice.* New York: St. Martin's 2000.

Martin, Wendy. "Adrienne Rich: The Evolution of a Poet." In *American Writing Today,* ed. Richard Kostelanetz, 334–42. Troy, N.Y.: Whitston, 1991.

———. *An American Triptych: Anne Bradstreet, Emily Dickinson, Adrienne Rich.* Chapel Hill: The University of North Carolina Press, 1984.

McDaniel, Judith. *Reconstituting the World: The Poetry and Vision of Adrienne Rich.* Argyle, N.Y.: Spinsters, 1978.

McGann, Jerome. "Contemporary Poetry, Alternate Routes." In *Politics and Poetic Value,* 253–76. Chicago: Chicago University Press, 1987.

———. *The Textual Condition.* Princeton, N.J.: Princeton University Press, 1991.

McQuaide, Molly, ed. *By Herself: Women Reclaim Poetry.* St. Paul, Minn.: Graywolf Press, 2000.

Michie, Helena. *Sororophobia: Differences among Women in Literature and Culture.* New York: Oxford University Press, 1992.

Moeurs, Ellen. "A Poet's Prose." Review of *On Lies, Secrets, and Silence. The New York Times Book Review,* 22 April 1979, 12.

Moi, Toril. *Sexual/Textual Politics: Feminist Literary Theory.* London: Methuen, 1985.

Moore, Marianne. *The Complete Poems of Marianne Moore.* New York: Macmillan, 1967.

Moramarco, Fred. "Stevens, Rich and Merrill." *Wallace Stevens Journal* 25.1 (2001): 3–6.

Moramarco, Fred, and William J. Sullivan. *Containing Multitudes: Poetry in the United States Since 1950.* New York: Twayne Publishers, 1998.

Morrison, Tony. *Beloved.* New York: Penguin, 1988.

Moyers, Bill D. *The Language of Life: A Festival of Poets.* New York: Doubleday, 1995.

Nelson, Cary. *Our Last First Poets.* Urbana: University of Illinois Press, 1981.

Newley, Adam. Review of *Midnight Salvage: Poems 1995–1998. New Statesman,* 26 March 1999, 57.

Osbourne, Peter. *The Politics of Time: Modernity and Avant-Garde.* London: Verso, 1995.

Ostriker, Alicia. *Stealing the Language: The Emergence of Women's Poetry in America.* London: The Women's Press, 1986.

Perloff, Marjorie. *The Dance of the Intellect: Studies in the Poetry of the Pound Tradition.* Cambridge: Cambridge University Press, 1985.

Peters, Robert. *The Great American Poetry Bake-Off.* New York: Rowman and Littlefield, 1979.

Phillips, Rodney. *The Hand of the Poet.* New York: Rizzoli, 1997.

Pizurie, Dian J. "The Emergence of Woman's Voice in the Poetry of Adrienne Rich." Ph.D. diss., University of California at Riverside, 1990.

Poulin Jr., A., and Michael Waters, eds. *Contemporary American Poetry.* 7th ed. Boston: Houghton Mifflin, 2001.

Ratcliffe, Krista. *Anglo-American Feminist Challenges to the Rhetorical Traditions.* Carbondale: Southern Illinois University Press, 1996.

Reichhardt, Ulfried. *Innenansichten der Postmoderne.* Wurzburg, Germany: Konigshausen & Neumann, 1991.

Rukeyser, Muriel. *Breaking Open.* New York: Random House, 1973.

———. *The Life of Poetry.* New York: A. A. Wyn, 1949.

Schwartz, Patricia Roth. "A Feast for the Intellect." *Lambda Book Report* 9.10 (May 2001): 22.

Shange, Ntozake. *for colored girls who have considered suicide when the rainbow is enuf: a choreopoem.* New York: Simon & Schuster, 1997.

Shelley, Percy Bysshe. "A Defence of Poetry." In *The English Romantics: Major Poetry and Critical Theory,* ed. John L. Mahoney, 535–50. Prospect Heights, Ill.: Waveland Press, 1997.

Showalter, Elaine. "Dancing through the Minefield." In *Writing and Sexual Difference,* ed. Elizabeth Abel. Chicago: University of Chicago Press, 1982.

———."Feminist Criticism in the Wilderness." In *Writing and Sexual Difference,* ed. Elizabeth Abel. Chicago: University of Chicago Press, 1982.

———. *A Literature of Their Own.* Princeton, N.J.: Princeton University Press, 1977.

Sielke, Sabine. *Fashioning the Female Subject: The Intertextual Networking of Dickinson, Moore, and Rich.* Ann Arbor: University of Michigan Press, 1997.

Spiegelman, Willard. "Voice of the Survivor: The Poetry of Adrienne Rich." *Southwest Review* (autumn 1975): 381–89.

Spillers, Hortense J. *Black, White, and in Color: Essays on American Literature and Culture.* Chicago: University of Chicago Press, 2003.

Stein, Kevin. *Private Poets, Worldly Acts: Public and Private History in Contemporary American Poetry.* Athens: Ohio University Press, 1996.

Stimpson, Catherine. "Adrienne Rich and Lesbian/Feminist Poetry." *Parnassus* 12/13 (1985): 249–68. Reprinted in *Where the Meanings Are: Feminism and Cultural Spaces,* 140–54. New York: Routledge, 1988.

Templeton, Alice. *The Dream and the Dialogue: Adrienne Rich's Feminist Poetics.* Knoxville: The University of Tennessee Press, 1994.

Templin, Charlotte. *Feminism and the Politics of Literary Reputation: The Example of Erica Jong.* Lawrence: University Press of Kansas, 1995.

Thomas, Dylan. *The Poems of Dylan Thomas.* New York: New Directions, 1971.

Vaught Brown, Jacqueline. " 'I Can't Be Still'; or Adrienne Rich and the Refusal to Gild the Fields of Guilt." *Women's Studies* 27.4 (June 1998): 311–31.

Vendler, Helen. *The Music of What Happens.* Cambridge, Mass.: Harvard University Press, 1988.

———. *Part of Nature, Part of Us: Modern American Poets.* Cambridge, Mass.: Harvard University Press, 1980.

———. *Soul Says: On Recent Poetry.* Cambridge, Mass.: Belknap Press of Harvard University Press, 1995.

———, ed. *Voices and Visions: The Poet in America.* New York: Random House, 1987.

Werner, Craig. *Adrienne Rich: The Poet and Her Critics.* Chicago: American Library Association, 1988.

Williams, William Carlos. *The Collected Poems of William Carlos Williams 1939–1962.* Vol. 2. Ed. A. Walton Litz and Christopher MacGowan. New York: New Directions, 1988.

Yeats, W. B. *The Collected Poems of W. B. Yeats.* Definitive ed. New York: Macmillan, 1968.

Yorke, Liz. *Impertinent Voices: Subversive Strategies in Contemporary Women's Poetry.* London: Routledge, 1991.

Index of Adrienne Rich's Works

BOOKS OF POETRY AND PROSE

INDIVIDUAL WORKS

General Index

About the Author

CHERI COLBY LANGDELL is Adjunct Professor of English at Azusa Pacific University.